TEACHINGS of the BUDDHA

Selected Mahāyāna Sūtras

Translated by Rulu

authorHOUSE®

AuthorHouse™
1663 Liberty Drive
Bloomington, IN 47403
www.authorhouse.com
Phone: 1-800-839-8640

Published by AuthorHouse 1/13/2012

ISBN: 978-1-4685-0904-5 (sc)
ISBN: 978-1-4685-0903-8 (e)

Library of Congress Control Number: 2011962055

To those who read and recite sūtras
pronounced by the Buddha

Contents

Preface xi

Translator's Note xiii

Translator's Introduction 1

PART I Sūtras from Six Sections in the Chinese Canon 37

From the Esoteric Teachings Section 39

Foreword to Sūtra 1 43

1 Sūtra of the Buddha-Crown Superb Victory Dhāraṇī 最勝佛頂陀羅尼淨除業障咒經 (T19n0970) 45

2 Buddha Pronounces the Sūtra of the Great Cundī Dhāraṇī 七俱胝佛母心大准提陀羅尼經 (T20n1077) 56

3 Sūtra of the Whole-Body Relic Treasure Chest Seal Dhāraṇī 一切如來心祕密全身舍利寶篋印陀羅尼經 (T19n1022B) 59

4 Buddha Pronounces the Mahāyāna Sūtra of the Dhāraṇī of Infinite-Life Resolute Radiance King Tathāgata 佛說大乘聖無量壽決定光明王如來陀羅尼經 (T19n0937) 66

From the Nirvāṇa Section 71

5 Buddha Pronounces the Sūtra of the Total Annihilation of the Dharma 佛說法滅盡經 (T12n0396) 72

From the Sūtra Collection Section 75

6 Buddha Pronounces the Sūtra of Maitreya Bodhisattva's Attainment of Buddhahood 佛說彌勒大成佛經 (T14n0456) 78

7 Buddha Pronounces the Sūtra of Neither Increase Nor Decrease 佛說不增不減經 (T16n0668) 97

8 Mahāyāna Sūtra of the Illuminating Everywhere Radiance-Store Wordless Dharma Door 大乘遍照光明藏無字法門經 (T17n0830) 103

9 Sūtra of Detecting Good or Evil Karma and Requital, fascicle 2 占察善惡業報經卷下 (T17n0839) 108

From the Prajñā Section 119
10 Sūtra of the Great Illumination Mantra of Mahā-Prajñā-Pāramitā 摩訶般若波羅蜜大明呪經 (T08n0250) 120
11 Sūtra of the Heart of Prajñā-Pāramitā 般若波羅蜜多心經 (T08n0251) 121
12 Sūtra of the All-Encompassing Knowledge Store, the Heart of Prajñā-Pāramitā 普遍智藏般若波羅蜜多心經 (T08n0252) 122

From the Treasure Pile Section 125
13 Mahāyāna Sūtra of Consciousness Revealed (in 2 fascicles) 大乘顯識經 (T12n0347) 126

From the Dharma Flower Section 151
14 Sūtra of the Great Dharma Drum (in 2 fascicles) 大法鼓經 (T09n0270) 154
15 Mahāyāna Vaipulya Sūtra of Total Retention 大乘方廣總持經 (T09n0275) 184
16 Sūtra of Immeasurable Meaning 無量義經 (T09n0276) 196

PART II Ancient Translators, Prayers, Mantras 213

Ancient Translators 215
Kumārajīva (344–413). Guṇabhadra (394–468). Dharmagatayaśas (5th–6th centuries). Bodhiruci (5th–6th centuries). Vinītaruci (?–594). Xuanzang (600– or 602–664). Divākara (613–687). Dharmacandra (653–743). Amoghavajra (705–774). Fatian (?–1001). 215

Prayers 222
Opening the Sūtra. Transferring Merit. Four Vast Vows. Universally Worthy Vow of the Ten Great Actions. Always Walking the Bodhisattva Way. Repenting of All Sins. Wishing to Be Reborn in the Pure Land. Supplicating to Be Reborn in the Pure Land. Ascending the Golden Steps. Praising Amitābha Buddha. 222

Mantras 226

How to Recite a Mantra 226

Introduction to the Eleven Mantras 227

The Eleven Mantras 229

1 Buddha-Crown Superb Victory Dhāraṇī 佛頂尊勝陀羅尼 229

2 Great Cundī Dhāraṇī 准提神咒 229

3 Whole-Body Relic Treasure Chest Seal Dhāraṇī 全身舍利寶篋印陀羅尼 229

4 Dhāraṇī of Infinite-Life Resolute Radiance King Tathāgata 聖無量壽決定光明王如來陀羅尼 230

5 Dhāraṇī for Rebirth in the Pure Land 往生咒 230

6 Root Dhāraṇī of Infinite Life Tathāgata 無量壽如來根本陀羅尼 230

7 Mantra of Medicine Master Tathāgata 藥師灌頂真言 230

8 Heart Mantra of the White Umbrella Dhāraṇī 楞嚴咒心 231

9 Samantabhadra Bodhisattva's Mantra 普賢菩薩所說咒 231

10 Great Compassion-Mind Dhāraṇī 大悲咒 231

11 Prajñā-Pāramitā Mantra 般若波羅蜜多咒 231

Appendix 233

Table A. The Sanskrit Alphabet 233

Table B. Pronunciation of the 13 Vowels 234

Table C. Pronunciation of the 33 Consonants 235

Glossary 237

Reference 269

Preface

Buddhists generally recognize that we are well into the latter days of the Buddha Dharma, as reflected in the agonizing events in the world, such as epidemics, terrorism, war, and financial crises, as well as ravages of earth, water, fire, and wind. One saving grace for the Buddha Dharma in this age is the advance in technology. Like a miracle, within the first decade of this twenty-first century, the Digital Sanskrit Buddhist Canon has been posted on the Internet by the University of the West, Rosemead, California. In addition, the Chinese Buddhist Electronic Text Association (CBETA) in Taiwan has digitized the Chinese Buddhist Canon and posted it on the Internet. Now, people worldwide have ready access to Sanskrit and Chinese texts to study Buddhist doctrine in the words of the Buddha. Those who read Chinese can, for the first time, read all the sūtras in the Chinese Canon. This would have been unthinkable in the ancient days when the literacy rate was low and precious copies of the voluminous Canon were guarded in China's Buddhist monasteries.

Since the Dharma came to the West in the twentieth century, some Westerners have shown interest in finding the truth about life and the universe through the teachings of the Buddha. As a result, all of the sūtras in the Pāli Canon have been translated into English and are available in print and on the Internet. However, less than one hundred sūtras in the Mahāyāna Canon have been translated into English. The daunting task of translating the Mahāyāna Canon from Sanskrit, Chinese, or Tibetan texts has not gathered any momentum.

Some time ago, after reviewing a few English translations of sūtras in books and on the Internet, I had thoughts of translating Mahāyāna sūtras into English, but these thoughts went by, as passing thoughts always do. Then, in December 2005, to my surprise, my translation project suddenly began after I received the Chinese Canon on a CD-ROM, 2002 version, distributed by CBETA. This digital Chinese Canon is based on the Taishō Tripiṭaka「大正新脩大藏經」© Daizo Shuppansha 大藏出版株式會社, vols. 1–55, 85. Without this CD-ROM, my translation work would not have been possible because I would never have considered buying the 100-volume Chinese Canon or spending my life leafing through these volumes in the reference department of a library.

Translators should follow three guidelines in their work: faithfulness, clarity, and elegance. I have done my best to keep these translations as faithful to the Chinese texts as possible. Although the meaning of Chinese texts may seem obscure even to Chinese readers, I have tried to translate them into plain English and avoid syntactic errors. How well I've achieved elegance lies in the perception of you, the reader.

This book is a fruit plucked from the tree of my website at http://www.sutrasmantras.info, which began on April 21, 2007 with only seven sūtras. I hope that this book, though but a drop in the Dharma ocean, can contribute to a massive pool of efforts to translate the Mahāyāna Buddhist Canon into English, for the benefit of Western readers. As the Buddha teaches with one tone, all sentient beings receive benefits according to their needs and preferences. Therefore, this book is for readers at any level, whether or not they regard themselves as Buddhists.

It has been an honor and a humbling learning experience for me to translate sūtras from Chinese into English. For the generous help I have received, I thank the following beneficent learned friends: Dharma Masters Shi Huiguan (釋慧觀), Shi Hongzheng (釋宏正), and Shi Yinhai (釋印海), who discussed with me some passages in the Chinese texts; Bruce Long and Linda Pheiffer Pauwels, who read the first draft of Sūtra 1; Alisa Kanouse, who edited six sūtras; Anne Moses, who edited all sixteen sūtras; Stephen Colley, who with great care edited the entire manuscript of this book; Kottegoda S. Warnasuriya, who helped correct errors in the texts of the mantras; Avinash Sathaye, who with infinite patience further edited the mantras; the Ch'an Meditation Center, Elmhurst, NY, which provided a picture of its Buddha statue for the cover of this book; visitors to my website, who appreciate the teachings of the Buddha; and earlier translators, who have benefited readers and inspired later translators.

I especially thank Rider Cheng (鄭勝一), who unwittingly dropped a seed into my mind on November 15, 2004. That morning, he had me recite with him three times the Chinese version of the Buddha-Crown Superb Victory Dhāraṇī, in honor of my late mother. This seed lay dormant for a year, then took more than a year to germinate into a website, and then into this book.

I also extend my belated gratitude to a Chinese lama who happened to ride the same slow train as I did in the summer of 1962, going from Jilong to Taipei. Seated not far from me, he, for unknown reasons, once in a while babbled an intriguing foreign word *anuttara-samyak-saṁbodhi*. Too shy or too arrogant to ask him about the meaning of this word, I just memorized it and never forgot it. That seed took many years to germinate.

Any flaws in my translations are my sole responsibility. May the merit of all contributors be transferred to all sentient beings for their rebirth in the Western Pure Land of Ultimate Bliss and for their ultimate enlightenment!

Rulu (如露)
December 21, 2009

Translator's Note

Organization of the Sūtras

Out of the vast body of the teachings of the Buddha, this book offers the English translations of sixteen Mahāyāna sūtras selected from six sections of the digital Chinese Buddhist Canon on a DVD-ROM, 2008 version, produced by the Chinese Buddhist Electronic Text Association (CBETA) in Taiwan. These six sections are not in their original order, but are arranged by sūtra numbers. Sūtras 1–4 belong in the Esoteric Teachings Section; Sūtra 5 belongs in the Nirvāṇa Section; Sūtras 6–9 belong in the Sūtra Collection Section; Sūtras 10–12 belong in the Prajñā Section; Sūtra 13 belongs in the Treasure Pile (ratnakūṭa) Section; and Sūtras 14–16 belong in the Dharma Flower Section. The Chinese name of each sūtra is followed by a volume number and a text number according to the CBETA system. For example, Sūtra 1 is translated from T19n0970, which means Taishō volume 19, text 970.

Sūtras 10–12 in this book are *Heart Sūtras* translated from three Chinese texts (T08n0250–52). There are quite a few English translations of the *Heart Sūtra* in print and online. For example, the two versions in *Buddhist Mahāyāna Texts* (Cowell et al. 1969, 147–54), translated from Sanskrit, are probably the earliest English translations. Sūtra 13, the *Mahāyāna Sūtra of Consciousness Revealed*, is translated from T12n0347. An earlier English translation of the same text is found in *A Treasury of Mahāyāna Sūtras* (Chang 1985, 223–40). That translation omits certain passages in the text. Sūtra 16, the *Sūtra of Immeasurable Meaning,* is translated from T09n0276. An earlier English translation of the same text is found in *The Threefold Lotus Sūtra* (Kato, Tamura, and Miyasaka 1975, 1–30). The rest of the sūtras in this book, to the best of my knowledge, have never before been published in book form.

Forms of Sanskrit Nouns

The English translations in this book include some transliterated (romanized) Sanskrit words. Consistent with words already admitted into the English vocabulary, such as Buddha, guru, karma, samādhi, sūtra, and nirvāṇa, which are not italicized, romanized Sanskrit words as foreign words are not italicized. However, they are italicized when they are used as words, not used functionally.

Unlike most English nouns, the plural of a Sanskrit noun is never formed by adding *s* or *es* to its singular. For example, the plural of *sūtra* is *sūtrāni*. However, to make life simpler, a hybrid plural is constructed by adding *s* to the stem of a Sanskrit noun, as is already done in English translations by scholars.

Although romanized Sanskrit words are never capitalized, all proper nouns are capitalized. For example, the Three-Thousand Large Thousandfold World is treated as the generic name of a galaxy, and specific heavens and hells are treated as countries. As the ten epithets of a Buddha are capitalized, so too are holy beings, such as Srotāpanna, Sakradāgāmin, Anāgāmin, Arhat,

Pratyekabuddha, and Bodhisattva, though novice Bodhisattvas are not yet holy beings.

Special Sanskrit Names

In the ancient past, a Buddhist term in a sūtra was translated from Sanskrit into Chinese either by sound or by meaning. If it had been translated by sound, the term is now restored if possible, or is constructed into a romanized Sanskrit word. If it had been translated by meaning, the meaning is now translated into English. The two exceptions are Bodhisattvas Samantabhadra and Avalokiteśvara, whose Sanskrit names are well known to Western Buddhists. In Chinese texts, Samantabhadra is translated as Universal Worthy (Puxian, 普賢).

Avalokiteśvara means Lord Who Looks Down, or Sovereign Watcher. In Sanskrit, *ava* means down; *lokita* means seen, beheld, or viewed; and *īśvara* means lord or capable of. However, in Chinese texts, the Bodhisattva bearing this name is called either Watching with Command (Guanzizai, 觀自在) or Watching the Sounds of the World (Guanshiyin, 觀世音). Watching with Command is probably an interpretation of sovereignty, which is free from interference and, thus, with command and ease. Watching the Sounds of the World is probably based on chapter 25 of the *Lotus Sūtra*, in which the Buddha explains this name. It is summarized as follows: *When people in distress call the name of this Bodhisattva who constantly watches the sounds of the world, they will immediately be rescued. Furthermore, Avalokiteśvara Bodhisattva assumes the most suitable form to deliver those who make a practice of uttering his name* (T09n0262, 0056c05–0057b21). As Chinese Buddhists perceive and portray Avalokiteśvara in female form, it is only natural that, in the twentieth century, Westerners saw him as a goddess and named him Goddess of Mercy.

Sanskrit Words Translated or Not Translated

Tathāgata, the first epithet of a Buddha, is conventionally translated as Thus-Come One. However, in some contexts Tathāgata refers to true suchness, the dharma body of a Buddha or a sentient being. Therefore, Tathāgata is not translated into English. Bhagavān, the tenth epithet of a Buddha, is translated as World-Honored One, as it is in Chinese texts. However, the compound word Buddha-Bhagavāns in the plural is kept as it is in Sanskrit.

The Sanskrit word *dharma* means anything (mental, physical, event). For example, a thought is a dharma, a human being is a dharma, and walking is also a dharma. Although law is one of its meanings in the dictionary, law certainly is not applicable to these three examples. The reader can draw an applicable meaning of *dharma* from its contexts within a sūtra. The upper-case Dharma is a collective noun for all the teachings of the Buddha, the Buddha Dharma. It is also used for specific teachings, for example, the Dharma of Emptiness. The words *dharma* and *Dharma* are not translated into various English words.

A saṁskṛta dharma means any dharma formed or made through causes and conditions; an asaṁskṛta dharma means something not formed or made through causes and conditions. There is no single English word that can correctly convey either meaning. Therefore, neither *saṁskṛta* nor *asaṁskṛta* is translated into English. It would be misleading to translate a saṁskṛta dharma as "a made dharma," "a conditioned dharma," or "a compounded dharma."

Upekṣa is one of the Seven Enlightenment Factors and the Four Immeasurable Minds, and this word also appears in other contexts. It is conventionally translated into English as equanimity, but into Chinese as letting go (捨). What one needs to let go of are extremes, such as joy and sorrow, excitement and boredom, favorable and unfavorable situations, and so forth. The word *upekṣa* means tranquility with a sense of equality, not indifferent composure, as *equanimity* suggests. Therefore, despite convention, *upekṣa* is translated as equability, which is more appropriate than equanimity.

Although the Sanskrit word *lakṣana* is translated into Chinese as appearance, it is conventionally translated into English as mark, as in the thirty-two major marks of the manifested body of a Buddha. In other contexts, however, appearance is used because it suggests that one's perceptions are illusory mental projections, whereas mark or sign might give the impression of an inherent quality.

The Sanskrit word *dhātu*, when used for different purposes, is translated into different nouns, such as realm for the Three Realms of Existence, sphere for the eighteen spheres, and domain for the six domains.

Translation of numbers can be tricky. The Sanskrit word *koṭi* means ten million, and it is left as it is in Sanskrit. The Sanskrit words *dvādaśa sahasrāṇi* can mean exactly 12,000 or thousands of 12. Following the Chinese text, I choose the former. The consecutive words "hundred, thousand, ten thousand" in Chinese are translated as "billion," simplicity overruling complexity or poetry.

The Glossary

To facilitate one's study of the sūtras, a glossary of Buddhist terms is provided. Learning these terms along with studying the sūtras will be rewarding in the long run. The Buddhist terms in this book are mainly based on *A Dictionary of Chinese Buddhist Terms* (Soothill and Hodous 1962); the *Foguang dacidian* 佛光大辭典 [Buddha's light dictionary 1988], and the *Online Buddhist Dictionary* 在線佛學辭典. Short biographies of the Buddha's disciples mentioned in the sūtras are included in the glossary, under the term *voice-hearers*.

Biographies of Ancient Translators

To show respect for, and to recognize the contribution of, the ancient Buddhist masters who translated from Sanskrit into Chinese the sūtras included in this book, their short biographies based on the dictionaries mentioned above and Wikipedia, the online encyclopedia, are presented in chronological order. From their stories, one may find a worthy role model for one's spiritual life and develop more appreciation of the sūtras now available to all.

Chinese characters for names, places, and book titles are also given, to facilitate study and research in Chinese. Chinese characters are especially helpful to Chinese readers because, strange as it may seem, romanized Chinese is Greek to them.

Reciting Mahāyāna Mantras in Sanskrit

One may choose to complement one's study and recitation of sūtras with mantra recitation. Mantras pronounced by Buddhas or holy Bodhisattvas are included in some sūtras, ceremonial practices, and mantra-only texts in the Chinese Canon. In the ancient past, Buddhist masters translated these mantras into Chinese by sound, based on pronunciations of the Chinese words of their time and place. Different translators of the same mantra chose their own words. Now, modern scholars have painstakingly restored some of the mantras in the Chinese Canon from Chinese back into Sanskrit. However, there are cases in which Sanskrit words are constructed, rather than restored, from the pronunciations of Chinese words. Understandably, there is no guarantee of the absolute accuracy in the restored version of a mantra. Still, one should be confident that any version sincerely recited can be just as efficacious and powerful as another because a mantra is in tune with one's own Buddha mind. This is confirmed by Mahāyāna Buddhists worldwide, who have been reciting mantras translated phonetically into their native languages from Sanskrit or another language. It is admirable that Western Buddhists, following their Eastern teachers, unflinchingly recite mantras in romanized Chinese, Japanese, Korean, Tibetan, Vietnamese, and so forth. This means that anyone who knows the English alphabet can learn to recite Buddhist mantras in romanized Sanskrit, thus uniting all in one universal tongue.

Of the eleven mantras included in this book, mantras 1, 2, 3, 6, 7, and 8 are taken from the *Zhencang fanwen zhouben* 珍藏梵文咒本, which means precious collection of Sanskrit mantras (Mahayana Vihara Press 2003). The mantras in that book are written in the Siddham script, with romanized Sanskrit as well as phonetic translations in Japanese and Chinese. Some of these mantras bear the text numbers in the Chinese Canon. For example, the Buddha-Crown Superb Victory Dhāraṇī in that book corresponds to the dhāraṇī in T19n0973, a text translated by Śubhakara-Siṁha (善無畏, 637–735), who went to China in 716, in the Tang Dynasty. This dhāraṇī is in Siddham, with a phonetic Chinese translation, which closely matches that in T19n0967, but not that in T19n0970. Mantra 5 is copied from Pang Huey Yong's (彭偉洋) website. Mantras 4 and 9 are copied from the website of the Digital Sanskrit Buddhist Canon (University of the West 2007). Mantra 10, the Great Compassion Mantra, is copied from Answers.com. Many words in this mantra are different from those in the popular Chinese version. Mantra 11 is the mantra in the well-known *Heart Sūtra.*

Although one can read or recite a sūtra or a mantra aloud, in a whisper, or silently, speaking it aloud has a distinct advantage. Not only does it involve all the sense organs, thereby purifying one's body, voice, and mind, but it may benefit an uninvited audience, visible or invisible to the human eye, planting a bodhi seed in their minds. For those who are inspired to recite a mantra in Sanskrit, the romanized Sanskrit alphabet and a guideline for pronunciation are provided in the appendix. The Devanāgarī letters of Sanskrit are not given because the appendix is intended to help one recite a mantra in virtual Sanskrit, not to teach anyone to read or write the Devanāgarī script. Finally, corrections of typographical or grammatical errors in the source texts of these mantras are bolded and italicized.

Saying Prayers Before and After Practice

The serious reader is recommended to say the Opening Sūtra Prayer before reciting a sūtra and, after reciting it, to say the Prayer for Transferring of Merit, followed by making the Four Vast Vows to conclude the practice. If one recites a mantra as a stand-alone practice, saying these prayers is also recommended.

A few other well-known prayers are also included for one's comfort and inspiration. For example, the Universally Worthy Vow of the Ten Great Actions, more elaborate than the Four Vast Vows, is a prayer that most Chinese Buddhists recite. The Prayer for the Bodhisattva Way summarizes the long-term training of a Bodhisattva on the Way to Buddhahood. The Repentance Prayer is for those who recognize their karma and seek purification and healing. Saying this prayer on one's knees, one needs to have sincere feelings of compassion for others who are in similar or even worse conditions. Included as well are four prayers from the Pure Land School, which specifically affirm one's resolve to be reborn in the Pure Land. One certainly may compose a prayer, expressing one's wish to alleviate poverty, epidemics, wars, and natural catastrophes, and to achieve peace, harmony, health, and prosperity in this world. Since the former events are a manifestation of our collective impure minds and the latter of our collective purified minds, this kind of prayer serves to remind us of the importance of our training aimed at transforming ourselves from within.

Translator's Introduction

At that time the Buddha universally observed all sentient beings in the dharma realm with His hindrance-free pure wisdom-eye and spoke these words: "Amazing! Amazing! Why do these sentient beings, deluded and confused, not know and not see that they have Tathāgata wisdom? I will teach them the holy Way, enabling them to discard the duality and fixation in their minds. Then they will be able to see within themselves the vast Tathāgata wisdom, no different from the Buddha's."

—*Mahāvaipulya Sūtra of Buddha Adornment*, fascicle 51
Translated from the Chinese Canon (T10n0279, 0272c25–0273a1)

The above passage in the 80-fascicle version of the *Mahāvaipulya Sūtra of Buddha Adornment* (Buddhāvataṁsaka-mahāvaipulya-sūtra) explains clearly why Śākyamuni Buddha (circa 563–483 BCE) appeared in this world. To suit the varied capacities and preferences of all sentient beings, the Buddha has taught 84,000 Dharma Doors. All Dharma Doors, or spiritual entrances, can be summarized into three holy vehicles (yāna). The first one is called the Voice-Hearer Vehicle, and the second one the Pratyekabuddha Vehicle. Together, they are called the Two Vehicles, and either of them can deliver one out of saṁsāra, the cycle of birth and death. A rider of the first vehicle, through hearing the teachings of the Buddha, can ultimately become a holy being called an Arhat; a rider of the second vehicle, who has realized the truth on his own, is a holy being called a Pratyekabuddha. A rider of the third vehicle, the Great Vehicle (Mahāyāna), is called a Bodhisattva (literally, enlightenment being), who will ultimately attain Buddhahood, becoming an all-knowing, all-compassionate holy teacher to all sentient beings. From the point of view of Mahāyāna teachings, the Two Vehicles are also called the Small Vehicle (Hīnayāna).

The Buddhist Canon

The Buddha Dharma, i.e., the teachings of the Buddha, is collected in the Buddhist Canon. The three collections of texts that constitute the Buddhist Canon are called the Tripiṭaka (three baskets), which includes (1) the Sūtra-piṭaka, discourses of the Buddha; (2) the Vinaya-piṭaka, rules of conduct; and (3) the Abhidharma-piṭaka, treatises on the Dharma.

After the Buddha's passing, three Buddhist Councils were convened in India, from the fifth to third centuries BCE, to collect the Buddha's teachings. In the first century BCE, these orally transmitted and preserved scriptures were committed to writing in the Fourth Council held in Sri Lanka, and became the first Pāli Canon.

The present-day voice-hearers (śrāvaka), as identified by Mahāyāna Buddhists, follow only the Hīnayāna Tripiṭaka in the Pāli Canon of the Theravāda (elder) School. This school is the survivor of twenty to twenty-four early

Buddhist sects that made and upheld different interpretations of the Dharma. The Sūtra-piṭaka in the Pāli Canon comprises the Five Nikāyas (collections). Therefore, Theravāda Buddhists, who are believers of these texts only, are also called Nikāya Buddhists. Spreading from Southeast Asia, Theravāda Buddhism now has a global following.

The origin of Mahāyāna teachings is mentioned in the *Sūtra of Immeasurable Meaning* (Sūtra 16). The Buddha states that, starting from the middle period of his teaching life, He has given Mahāyāna teachings. In addition, in the *Sūtra of the Bodhisattva in the Womb,* fascicle 7, Mahākāśyapa (Buddha's foremost disciple, the first patriarch in the Buddhist lineage), seven days after the Buddha's death, told Ānanda (Buddha's cousin and attendant, who became the second patriarch after Mahākāśyapa) to collect the Bodhisattva-piṭaka in one place, the Voice-hearer-piṭaka in one place, and the Vinaya-piṭaka in one place (T12n0384, 1058b13–16).

Although some Mahāyāna teachings are found in the Saṁyukta Āgama (connected discourses), which is one of the Five Āgamas (parallel but not identical to the Five Nikāyas) in the Chinese Canon, the majority of Mahāyāna texts began to emerge in India after the first century BCE. Translation of the Sanskrit texts taken to China began in the first century CE and continued for the following nine hundred years. The Mahāyāna Tripiṭaka in the Chinese Canon has evolved through tremendous efforts undertaken in successive dynasties down to the present day. The Buddha's teachings completely preserved in Chinese have come to be known as Chinese Buddhism.

Between 1998 and 2003 the Chinese Buddhist Electronic Text Association (CBETA) in Taiwan digitized the Chinese Canon. It is based on the Taishō Tripiṭaka (大正新脩大藏經), published in Tokyo in 1934, which in turn is based on the Tripiṭaka Koreana, carved on wooden blocks by Korean monks between 1236 and 1251. This collection includes 2,373 sūtras and other texts. Between 2004 and 2007 CBETA digitized the Shinsan Zokuzōkyō (卍續藏), the Extension of the Chinese Canon. This collection includes 1,229 sūtras and other texts. The entire CBETA digital collection includes the Taishō Tripiṭaka, T01–T55, T85, and the Shinsan Zokuzōkyō, X01–X88, where T and X stand for volume. Each text is identified by its volume and text numbers. For example, T10n0279 means volume 10, text 279, of the Taishō Tripiṭaka, and X74n1480 means volume 74, text 1480, of the Shinsan Zokuzōkyō. Any passage in a text can also be found by its page, column, and line numbers in the Taishō edition of the Chinese Canon. For example, 0272c25–0273a1 means from page 272, column c, line 25, to page 273, column a, line 1. The entire CBETA collection is posted on the Internet and available on DVD-ROM for free distribution. The 2008 version of their DVD-ROM also includes footnotes for alternative words in the texts, which are found in other editions of the Chinese Canon, compiled in the Song, Yuan, Ming, and Qing Dynasties. Making the Chinese Canon available to readers worldwide for study and research has been an ongoing contribution of CBETA.

In 2004 the University of the West and the Nagarjuna Institute of Exact Methods (NIEM) jointly launched the website for the Digital Sanskrit Buddhist Canon. Between 2004 and 2009 they posted on their site a few hundred sūtras and other Sanskrit texts for the benefit of the scholastic world.

The Tibetan Canon comprises texts translated from Sanskrit, Chinese, and other languages, which are divided into the Kangyur and the Tengyur. The Kangyur includes texts of sūtras and tantras, and the Tengyur includes treatises. Since the relocation of the Fourteenth Dalai Lama to India in 1950, Tibetan lamas from various sects and lineages have captivated the West and attracted a dominant following. Quite a few books on Tibetan Tantrism, the distinctive feature of Tibetan Buddhism, have been published by Tibetan lamas and Western scholars.

Introduction of Mahāyāna Buddhist teachings to the West is credited to the Japanese scholar Daisetz Teitaro Suzuki (1870–1966), who contributed greatly to the development of interest in Chan (Zen) Buddhism. Because the Chan School is known as a Dharma Door outside of the scriptures, the Chan life taught by the Japanese Soto School does not stress scriptural studies. Western students are satisfied with sitting meditation, listening to interesting Chan stories, routinely reciting the well-known *Heart Sūtra* (T08n0251), and possibly reading the *Diamond Sūtra* (T08n0235).

If the Buddha Dharma is to take root and flourish in the West, it is essential that Westerners have access to the teachings of the Buddha in their native languages and that some of them become learned teachers. However, while all the sūtras in the Pāli Canon have been translated into English, less than one hundred Mahāyāna sūtras are available in English.

The few Mahāyāna sūtras in this book, albeit a very small sample, show that the Buddha has given a wide range of teachings, addressing different concerns of His disciples. The following discussions are intended to help the reader gain, in an organized way, some understanding of the problems of sentient beings and the solutions given by the Buddha.

Sentient Beings and Their Environments

The Six Types of Sentient Beings

According to Buddhist doctrine, sentient beings, until enlightened through any of the Three Vehicles, endlessly transmigrate in a small world that comprises the Three Realms (trayo-dhātu) of Existence: desire realm, form realm, and formless realm. They can be broadly classified into six types of life forms living in the same or different dimensions. Driven by ignorance (avidyā) of the truth and thirsty love (tṛṣṇā) for being, every sentient being, after death, is reborn in a new body according to its karmas, to undergo another life and death. These six types of sentient beings can be graded in ascending order according to their quality of life.

In the first grade are hell-dwellers that undergo dreadful suffering in various hells to purge their sinful karmas. In the second grade are hungry ghosts that want but are unable to eat or drink. Some spirits are less unfortunate because people who follow folk religion worship spirits as deities, and the aroma of food offerings can relieve their hunger. Animals are in the third grade, and their biological life centers on survival and reproduction. Although some pets live an easy life with their devoted owners, animals, with their limited intelligence, are an unfortunate life form. In the fourth grade are humans, who experience both pleasures and pains in their lives. Because they can have a rich mental life and even a spiritual life, they are more fortunate than the preceding three life forms. Asuras, who are sub-gods or non-gods, are in the fifth grade, and they are often at war with gods. Finally, in the sixth grade are gods, the highest life form. Some gods are fortunate enough to receive teachings from a Buddha, while others indulge in the pleasures of celestial life. In terms of misfortune or fortune, the first three types of life forms take evil life-journeys while the last three take good life-journeys. However, asuras, who are given to anger and jealousy, are also considered to be taking an evil life-journey. These six life-journeys can be reduced to five because asuras can be born among gods, humans, animals, and hungry ghosts.

The Environments of Sentient Beings

According to ancient Indian cosmology, which the Buddha used in His teachings, these six types of life forms, because of their common karma, reside in a small world that rests on three wheels: a gold wheel, a water wheel, and a wind wheel at the bottom. In the center of this small world is Mount Sumeru. Orbiting Mount Sumeru at its mid height are the sun, the moon, and the stars. Mount Sumeru is encircled by eight concentric mountain ranges, and these nine mountains are separated by eight oceans.

The seven inner mountain ranges are called the Gold Mountains, and the outermost mountain range is called the Iron Mountain. Rising above the salty ocean between the Iron Mountain and the seventh inner mountain range are four large continents aligned with the four sides of Mount Sumeru. Between every two large continents are two medium-sized continents and five hundred small continents.

The first five types of life forms, with a full range of afflictions, principally greed, anger, and delusion, reside in the desire realm of a small world. They colonize the four large continents, the eight medium-sized continents, and some of the two thousand small continents. Jambudvīpa, the southern continent, is the large continent where reside all the humans and animals that we can know. Humans on this continent have no contact with those on the other three large continents. Ghosts share the same space with humans, but in another dimension, and they are visible only to some humans under certain conditions. According to the *Sūtra of the Rise of the World*, fascicle 2, the Iron Mountain is surrounded by the Great Iron Mountain, and many hells are situated between them (T01n0024, 0320b24–c5). A detailed description of various hells is given in the *Sūtra of the Original Vows of Earth Store Bodhisattva* (T13n0412). Although humans and animals must live in this four-dimensional space and time, hell-dwellers probably live in another dimension and experience suffering through their karmic perceptions (Sūtra 13).

Gods live in all three realms of a small world, in twenty-eight heavens in ascending order. According to their merit in past lives and their power of meditation, they have celestial bodies that are progressively more gigantic, ethereal, and luminous, and have increasingly longer lifespans. Gods with all afflictions reside in the six desire heavens in the desire realm. The first and lowest desire heaven is halfway up on Mount Sumeru, and the second desire heaven, consisting of thirty-three heavens at the same level, is on the top of Mount Sumeru. The remaining four desire heavens and the other twenty-two heavens are up in the sky. Brahma gods, who have only pure desires, reside in the Brahma World, i.e., the eighteen heavens in the form realm. Gods in the formless realm live a mental life in four heavens, which are four levels of long and deep meditative absorption. With bodies so ethereal, they are formless to humans.

A small world is formed by the force of the common karma of sentient beings. One thousand such small worlds constitute a Small Thousandfold World. One thousand Small Thousandfold Worlds constitute a Medium Thousandfold World. Finally, one thousand Medium Thousandfold Worlds constitute a Large Thousandfold World. This Large Thousandfold World is called the Three-Thousand Large Thousandfold World, where Three-Thousand does not mean 3,000 but means 1,000 raised to the power of three. This world, consisting of a billion small words, like a galaxy, is a Buddha Land, the education district of a Buddha.

Each sentient being is repeatedly reborn in the three realms of a small world according to its karmas, and causes and conditions. The specific life form of a karmic rebirth is the main requital of a sentient being, and the environment its life relies on is the reliance requital, which comes with the main requital as a package, like a birdcage keeping a bird or a fishbowl holding a fish (see stories in Sūtras 1 and 13). When the common karma of sentient beings is exhausted, a small world will perish. Sentient beings with remaining individual karmas will be reborn in another small world in this or some other Three-Thousand Large Thousandfold world.

Ordinary Beings and Holy Beings

These six types of ordinary beings are also called the six ordinary vehicles because in successive lives each sentient being changes body according to its karmas, like changing a vehicle for a corresponding life-journey. Therefore, there are nine vehicles: the first six are driven by sentient beings' karmas and the last three are propelled by their willing practice of the teachings of the Buddha. As told in a metaphor in the *Lotus Sūtra,* fascicle 2, these three holy vehicles are gifts from the Buddha to transport sentient beings out of saṁsāra, which is like a house on fire (T09n0262, 0012c8–11).

Some sentient beings, such as gods and humans, by riding the three holy vehicles, have become holy beings: holy voice-hearers, Pratyekabuddhas, and holy Bodhisattvas. Holy voice-hearers are those who have achieved any of the four voice-hearer fruits, becoming Srotāpannas, Sakradāgāmins, Anāgāmins, or Arhats (the fourth and highest voice-hearer fruit). Pratyekabuddhas, who are enlightened on their own, are by definition holy beings. Holy Bodhisattvas include those who have advanced to the Ten Grounds on the Bodhisattva Way and others who have completed the Tenth Ground and are in the holy position to demonstrate attainment of Buddhahood in their next life.

The Tiantai School of China proposes ten dharma realms, of which the first nine realms are of the six types of ordinary beings and the three types of holy beings, and the tenth realm is the realm of Buddhas, with the understanding that Buddhas are neither beings nor nonbeings. All ten realms are in effect the one dharma realm of true suchness (bhūta-tathātā).

The Structure and Functions of a Sentient Being

According to Buddhist doctrine, a sentient being is a set of interrelated processes dependent upon causes and conditions. These processes are broadly classified into categories called the aggregates (skandha), fields (āyatana), spheres (dhātu), and domains (dhātu). These four models of a sentient being are discussed below.

The Five Aggregates

In the first model, a sentient being is composed of five aggregates (pañca-skandha): form (rūpa), sensory reception (vedanā), perception (saṁjñā), mental processing (saṁskāra), and consciousness (vijñāna). The first aggregate is material and the other four are mental. Since these four are non-form, thus present in name only, the five aggregates are summarized as name and form or, in modern terms, mind-body. The word *skandha* means that which covers or conceals, and the regular working of the five aggregates conceals true reality from a sentient being.

The First and Fifth Aggregates

The first aggregate is form (rūpa), and its components are discussed under the second model, the twelve fields. The fifth aggregate is consciousness (vijñāna), which can be a general concept or may be classified into eight consciousnesses, as discussed under the third model, the eighteen spheres. There is unanimous agreement among translators to translate *rūpa* as form, and *vijñāna* as consciousness.

The Other Three Aggregates

However, translations of the other three aggregates vary significantly. Sampling from the Internet a few English versions of the *Heart Sūtra*, we can find vedanā variously translated as sensation, feelings, or perception; saṁjñā translated as perception, cognition, conception, or thought; and saṁskāra translated as formation, intention, volition, activity, impulse, or mental construction. Some words are taken from a Sanskrit-English dictionary, and other words from a Chinese-English dictionary. Translators have their own reasons for their choice of words.

For these three aggregates, the words chosen by this translator are based on the understanding that they are functions of a sentient being with a physiological system. According to modern neuroscience, when sense data, i.e., energy forms, such as photons, sound waves, and certain molecules in the air or food, come into contact with the receptor cells in one's sense organs—eye, ear, nose, tongue, and body—energy signals are converted into neural signals that are transmitted through sensory neurons to the brain. As these signals are processed in different cortical regions of the cerebellum, sense objects—sights, sounds, scents, flavors, and tactile sensations—are perceived together with their names. Through further mental processing, which incorporates emotions and past experiences, one then judges a sensory experience as pleasant, unpleasant, or neither.

Thus, sensory reception is at the initial stage of the perceptual process, and sensory experience is an interpretation that ensues. Therefore, sensory reception is the chosen translation for *vedanā*, the second aggregate, because it is a function that leads to a sensory experience.

According to Buddhist doctrine, *saṁjñā* means forming a percept and associating it with a name. Therefore, perception is the most suitable translation for *saṁjñā*, the third aggregate.

Saṁskāra, the fourth aggregate, is broadly translated as mental processing because a sentient being is a neurobiological being. Processing encompasses the full range of physiological processes, from the metabolism of each cell of the body to neural processing, which underlies all mental activities, including the preceding two aggregates. However, Buddhist doctrine is not concerned about physiology as such, and the kind of processing (行) found in the Mahāyāna doctrine includes only seventy-three mental functions or states, such as thinking, emotion, intention, and so forth. In particular, thinking (思) is considered the major aspect of mental processing, and it is broad enough to include dreaming, recollection, planning, volition, and so on, which are not listed in the seventy-three functions. Thinking is the most influential aspect of mental processing because thoughts are mental actions, which can be followed by further neural processing to use one's voice or take physical actions, resulting in karmic consequences.

The Twelve Fields

To understand how a sentient being is engaged in mind-body processes, we divide a sentient being into twelve fields (dvādaśa-āyatana). These twelve include the six faculties (ṣaḍ-indriya)—eye, ear, nose, tongue, body, and mental faculty (manas)—and their corresponding objects: sights, sounds, scents, flavors, tactile sensations, and mental objects. The six faculties, or six sense organs, are called the six internal fields, and their corresponding objects are called the six external fields.

The Six External Fields

In the *Sūtra of Detecting Good or Evil Karma and Requital* (Sūtra 9), these six external fields are called the external appearances of mind, a term in accord with the scientific understanding that they are the results of neural processing. The first five external fields, generally perceived as external, are also called the five desires because sentient beings pursue them for gratification. The sixth external field covers mental objects. Although most mental objects, such as thoughts and emotions, are internal, imagined sense objects are considered in Buddhist doctrine to be external.

A correspondence can be found between the first two models. Form, the first aggregate in the first model, includes eleven of the twelve fields in the second model: the first five sense organs, their five corresponding sense objects, and certain mental objects, such as imagined sense objects. The other four aggregates in the first model can be identified with mental faculty (manas), the sixth internal field, and its mental objects, excepting the imagined sense objects.

The Six Internal Fields

The first five faculties, or five sense organs, are also called the sensory entrances because it is their sensory receptors that convert the energy forms received and initiate the transmission of neural signals to the brain. It is obvious that the sense organs are not the perceivers of sense objects because they are only one of the conditions for perceptual processing.

Buddhist doctrine mentions five "inner" sense organs in one-to-one correspondence with the five sense organs. Before the twentieth century, Buddhists found these "inner" sense organs mystical and identified them as the perceivers of sense objects. Fortunately, they have been demystified by modern neuroscience because they can be understood as sensory cortical regions and neural circuits. Although perceptual processing has been identified with different cortical regions for visual functions, auditory functions, and so forth, these cortical regions are not the perceivers of sense objects. Nor are they the directors of such processing because cortical regions, neuronal circuits, and sensory entrances all are conditions of perceptual processing.

The sixth faculty is called *manas*, a Sanskrit word which can mean mind, intellect, or faculty. The word *manas* is translated into Chinese as yi (意), which can mean mind or intention. Any translation narrows the meaning of *manas*. With the understanding that manas is neither an internal organ, such as the brain, nor a sensory entrance, this translator ventures to translate it as mental faculty, and the reader, for want of a better English translation, may choose to use the Sanskrit word *manas*. Although one's mental faculty (the sixth internal field) and its mental objects (the sixth external field) seem broad enough to include the preceding five faculties and their corresponding objects, all twelve of them are listed as separate fields.

The Perceiver of a Sense Object

The six external fields are constructed through mental processing and dependent upon conditions. As mental processing and the resultant perception are indivisible, there are neither separate perceivers or directors for different sense objects nor a central perceiver or director. As we perceive a visual object, there is actually no seer, though we customarily say, "I see or my eyes see." Likewise, thoughts are played out through the thinking process, and there is no thinker of thoughts. Nor is there a watcher of thoughts because attention is also a function supported by mental processing. This is a scientific confirmation of an important truth that a sentient being has no self in command.

The Eighteen Spheres

In this third model, six consciousnesses are added to the twelve fields to define the eighteen spheres (aṣṭādaśa-dhātu). Each faculty and its object are likened to a field, from which a corresponding consciousness arises. To make eighteen, the twelve fields are renamed twelve spheres, and to them are added six corresponding spheres of consciousness, from eye consciousness to mental consciousness. The eighteen spheres group the faculties, objects, and consciousnesses into six sets of three. The three components of each set are interdependent, like the three legs of a tripod.

The First Five Consciousnesses

Consciousness implied in the second model is now listed in the third model. Each consciousness covers a number of mental processes. For example, one's visual faculty is to discern color, shape, stereoscopy, perspective, and motion, which are processed in different cortical regions of the brain. All these visual processes are now subsumed under the term *eye consciousness*. The other four perceptual consciousnesses (ear, nose, tongue, and body) are similarly named.

As the eye is the physical base from which eye consciousness arises, likewise manas (mental faculty) is the mental base from which the sixth consciousness (mental consciousness) arises. In the Mahāyāna doctrine, manas is also designated as the seventh consciousness (manas consciousness). In addition, the eighth consciousness, though not explicitly included in the eighteen spheres, is the root of them all.

The Eighth Consciousness

The eighth consciousness is called ādāna consciousness, the existence-grasping consciousness (有取識), because it enters a fertilized egg cell for karmic reasons. It is interesting that the body of a sentient being is considered an image of the eighth consciousness (Sūtra 13). Hence, it is consistent with the Mahāyāna doctrine to infer that the eighth consciousness is inseparable from each and every cell of a sentient being, from the first sign of life in a fertilized egg cell through the entire life of a sentient being until its death. Any biochemical processes before or after birth, whether at the level of cells, tissues, organs, or physiological systems, in the Buddhist view, are complex processes in the sphere of the eighth consciousness. An example is found in the regenerative process of the planarian (nonparasitic flatworm). Whether a planarian is cut lengthwise or crosswise, it will regenerate into two separate individuals. This shows that the existence-grasping force of the eighth consciousness can operate even without a fertilized egg cell. Animal cloning under scientifically-controlled conditions serves as another example.

The eighth consciousness is also called the root consciousness because it is the underlying mental processing that enables the functions classified under the preceding seven consciousnesses. Therefore, the eighth consciousness is called the mind field, from which grows the mental-physical life of a sentient being.

For an ordinary being, the eighth consciousness is also called ālaya consciousness, the store consciousness, because it can store seeds and is the stored seeds—all the pure, impure, and neutral seeds accumulated from past lives and acquired in the present life. A seed means a potential force that can manifest through causes and conditions. For example, one's memory is like a seed. When one recalls a name, a verbal thought arises from one's mind. As another example, the emotions and habits of a sentient being are like seeds which, triggered by conditions, can manifest as actions. These actions may become karmic seeds, which in turn drive a sentient being's rebirth under certain conditions.

When all the cells of one's body die, it is said that ālaya consciousness has abandoned the body (Sūtra 13). Then, driven by karmic force and thirsty love for being, ālaya consciousness, without any gap, may immediately develop the next karmic body through one of the four modes of birth: the womb, the egg, moisture, and miraculous formation. Or it may first produce an ethereal interim body, which can last up to forty-nine days, pending the right karmic conditions for a rebirth.

Because a new body is the ripening of the karmas of the previous body, ālaya consciousness is also called vipāka consciousness, the karma-ripening consciousness (異熟識). As an indifferent invisible carrier of seeds, not an autonomous entity, ālaya consciousness serves to answer the question as to how a sentient being transmigrates in saṁsāra. Upon attaining Buddhahood, the eighth consciousness holds only pure seeds, which will neither change nor manifest karmic rebirth. Shedding the names ālaya and vipāka, the eighth consciousness is given a new name, amala (stainless) consciousness, in honor of its purity.

The Seventh Consciousness

Certain mental processes attributed to the eighth consciousness contribute to the sense of an embodied self, distinct from its environment; for example, the instinct for self-preservation, the will to live, the thirsty love for being, exteroception, interoception, proprioception, and so forth. This sense of self is evident even in lower animal forms; for example, when a worm is touched, it feigns death or runs for its life. Such an inborn sense of self in a sentient being is assigned to the seventh consciousness (manas consciousness). It has four inborn defilements: self-delusion, self-love, self-view, and self-arrogance. Although all sentient beings have these four defilements, self-arrogance is especially prominent in humans and gods. With the implicit fixation on self, the seventh consciousness is the basis for the sixth consciousness to discriminate what is for or against self. While the first six consciousnesses are interrupted during anesthesia, dreamless sleep, or a coma, the seventh and eighth consciousnesses are always active.

The Sixth Consciousness

The sixth consciousness (mental consciousness) not only works together with the first five consciousnesses but also functions by itself. Its power lies in its analytical thinking process involving symbols and words, which is fully developed in humans. Through indoctrination and the discriminative power of the sixth consciousness, humans, in addition to the implicit fixation on self, can develop an explicit fixation on self by holding various wrong views.

Through underlying intricate mental processing and networking, all eight consciousnesses work together as one mind. While scientists concur that the mind is solely constructed by brain activities, in the Buddhist view, this is the tip of an iceberg. The entire body is an expression, but not the only expression, of the mind. Any physical process, from the division of a cell to the production of proteins, to unconsciously gesturing as one speaks, to shooting a ball into the basket, and to walking mindlessly like a robot, is also a mental process. In the flatworm case, growing a body from a severed head or growing a head and a brain from a severed body is a mental-physical process in the sphere of the eighth consciousness.

The Six Domains

According to ancient Indian philosophy, matter is made of the four domains (catur-dhātu)—earth, water, fire, and wind—which have four corresponding appearances: solid, liquid, heat, and mobility. Each domain's appearance is considered to be its self-essence (svabhāva), the changeless state. As building blocks of matter, the four domains are also called the great seeds (mahābhūta).

A non-sentient thing (plant or nonliving thing) is made of five domains: earth, water, fire, wind, and space, where space refers to the space within a form, including that within an atom. A sentient being is made of six domains, adding consciousness to the five domains. In this simplistic model, a sentient being is made up of matter and consciousness, i.e., body and mind.

The self-essence of earth, water, fire, and wind has been proven to be a fallacy because it is understood in modern science that the state of matter can be solid, liquid, plasma, or gas, according to prevailing conditions. However, it is descriptive to say that a sentient being appears to have these features: solid substance, fluid, heat, motion, space within the body, and consciousness.

Teachings Common to the Three Vehicles

Ignorance, Self-Essence, Self-View, Self-Love

Ignorance

Ignorance (avidyā) and thirsty love (tṛṣṇā) for being are the two driving forces for a sentient being to undergo birth and death endlessly. Ignorance includes not only ignorance of the truth but also belief in the wrong views. Some wrong views are inborn and others are learned.

Self-Essence

A fundamental wrong view is called the view of self-essence (svabhāva), where the Sanskrit word *svabhāva* (literally, own being) means an inherent state of being, self-made, self-determined, and changeless. This is a false reality that sentient beings intuitively attach to their perceptions of dharmas (things, mental objects, events), which they generally identify in polar opposites, mainly existence and nonexistence. Such false reality is strengthened by contrasting perceptions. Accepting that water in a mirage does not exist, they believe that water in a lake exists. Knowing that the moon in the water does not exist, they believe that moon in the sky exists. Accepting that events in a dream are unreal, they believe that events in their waking hours are real. Some believe that anything unreal must be founded upon something real. Early Buddhist sects taught that any composite thing, such as a ceramic pot or a sentient being composed of the five aggregates, was unreal, but that its atoms were real. Likewise, they believed that time was unreal, but that it could be split into nanoseconds, which were real.

People also have the ability to believe what they are told. Some of them can be indoctrinated to believe that bloody sacrifice is the key to pleasing their angry and jealous gods or God. When people see circles or fibrous strands in the air, which are projections of floaters in the vitreous body of their eyes, some of them can be taught to believe that these are evidence of their primordial wisdom.

Both commonly accepted realities, such as water in the lake and the moon in the sky, and fabricated realities, such as the merit of blood sacrifice, arise from the view of self-essence. Such realities will be examined in the light of Buddhist doctrine.

Self-View

People also have the ability to believe an imaginary entity to be real. A special case of the view of self-essence is the self-view that there exists a self within one. This self-view begins with an inborn sense of self that every sentient being has. It is then variously defined and fortified by religious or philosophical doctrines. The five aggregates that make up a sentient being are the material for the fabrication of an autonomous self (ātman). For example, in monotheism, there is the one God who is the creator and judge of human beings. In pantheism, this one God transcends as well as permeates human beings and things. From the Buddhist viewpoint, this God is just a version of self. In other words, monotheism holds that self is apart from one's five aggregates, and pantheism holds that a grand self contains one's five aggregates. One may intuitively choose form, the first aggregate, as self, the embodied self. Or one may be told that consciousness, the fifth aggregate, is the everlasting self. These are samples of the sixty-two self-views held by philosophers, which the Buddha refuted during His life. Any self-view alleging a self in command of one's present and future lives is based on self-delusion.

Self-Love

Once a version of self has established its boundary, non-self is considered the belongings of self. From the first-person point of view, the world of a sentient being is self and its belongings. Fortified with self-love and self-arrogance, one fervently loves and protects self and its belongings, such as one's body, space, territory, reputation, opinions, assets, guru, people, and so forth; and one righteously hates and destroys one's enemies, who trespass or are in the way. Of all the afflictions of a sentient being, such as greed, anger, and delusion, love is the strongest force. Love is a bondage because one seeks it, becomes attached to it, wants to protect it, disputes with others, triggers anger and hatred, and even resorts to violence, leading to suffering and karmic consequences. Embracing ignorance as a father and thirsty love for being as a mother, a sentient being is reborn again and again, in response to karmic forces.

The Four Dharma Seals

Buddhist teachings are summarized in Dharma Seals (dharma-mudrā). The Four Dharma Seals are these: (1) processes are impermanent; (2) experiences boil down to suffering; (3) dharmas have no selves; and (4) nirvāṇa is silence and stillness. Because suffering is the consequence of the impermanence of everything in the life of a sentient being, including itself, the second Dharma Seal can be omitted from the list to make Three Dharma Seals. Five Dharma Seals can be established by adding a fifth Dharma Seal: (5) dharmas are empty (śūnya). In the Mahāyāna doctrine, all these seals are integrated into one, the one true reality, emptiness (śūnyatā).

In the new-age movement, modern gurus can attract large followings as they talk and write eloquently on topics ranging from karma, rebirth, universal love, and world peace, to health, wealth, and how to find happiness in life. What sets such talks apart from Buddhist doctrine are the Dharma Seals.

They are called Dharma Seals because any text or doctrine can be measured against them to determine whether it is in accord with the Buddha Dharma. Four of the five Dharma Seals are discussed in the next section, and nirvāṇa is discussed in a later section.

Impermanence, Suffering

Every dharma in the world is a process with four appearances: arising, staying, changing, and perishing. In particular, every sentient being, a combination of the five aggregates, has these four appearances: birth, aging, illness, and death. These features of impermanence are usually summarized into birth and death.

Impermanence means change which is the common experience of all sentient beings in saṁsāra, and change means suffering, whether or not they know it. Impermanence is especially poignant for humans. Knowing the certainty of death is suffering; passing of pleasurable events is suffering; and even neutral experiences may turn into suffering (see "suffering" in the glossary). However, recognition of this fact can become the motivation for one to take the Buddhist path to find a solution for one's benefit.

Emptiness, No Self

Impermanence is the evidence against the presumed self-essence (svabhāva) of any dharma. According to Buddhist doctrine, nothing has self-essence, so everything is by definition empty (śūnya). This is called the emptiness (śūnyatā) of a dharma (法空). Just as any dharma, a sentient being is impermanent and therefore empty. This is called the emptiness of a sentient being (人空).

Suffering is the proof that a sentient being has no autonomous self (ātman), whether it is called a divine self or an everlasting soul, because such a self should be able to avoid suffering. However, the Buddha says in the *Sūtra of the Great Dharma Drum* (Sūtra 14) that "sentient beings each transmigrate through their cycle of birth and death without a commanding self." This understanding has nothing to do with the impermanence of anything because an autonomous self is simply a wrong view, a fixated imagination. So there is no self in a sentient being (人無我).

From the third-person point of view, sentient beings are part of all dharmas in the world, but each sentient being lives in a subjective world of an imaginary self and dharmas considered to be its belongings. These dharmas include the internal ones that make up one's mind-body, such as the five aggregates, the twelve fields, the eighteen spheres, and the six domains, and include the external ones in one's perception, such as one's space, territory, reputation, opinions, assets, gurus, enemies, people, and so forth. None of them is under the command of a self, separate or central. So there is no self in a dharma (法無我).

In summary, Buddhist doctrine distinguishes two emptinesses: the emptiness of a sentient being and the emptiness of a dharma. It also distinguishes two kinds of no self: no self in a sentient being and no self in a dharma.

Dependent Arising

Another important truth about dharmas of the world is their dependent arising. This is the Buddhist theory of general relativity without any mathematical equations. In the Saṁyukta Āgama (connected discourses), fascicle 10, Ānanda quotes the Buddha: "Because this exists, that exists; since this arises, that arises. . . . Because this exists not, that exists not; since this perishes, that perishes . . ." (T02n0099, 0067a4–8).

All dharmas are interdependent and relative to one another, but dependent arising does not dictate the one-to-one or one-to-many causation that people usually see. In fact, every dharma arises and perishes through the convergence of a number of conditions, known or unknown, and each condition in turn is a dharma conditioned upon a number of conditions. For example, a ceramic pot is made with clay, in a certain space and time, through the skill of a particular craftsman and use of equipment. Here the clay can be considered as the cause or the main condition, which is joined with other conditions, and the ceramic pot is the main effect of interest.

Dependent arising is why every dharma is impermanent and constantly changing. Whether considered as cause or effect, every dharma arises, stays, changes, and perishes through causes and conditions. Therefore, all dharmas are illusory.

On the surface, dependent arising seems consistent with common knowledge. But when people say that the cause of something is Mother Nature, it in effect means no cause. When people say that things occur by chance or out of one's good or bad luck, it in effect means no cause. Most people who accept causality believe that it applies only to one's present life. They disbelieve that karmic causes and effects run through one's past, present, and future lives. Another important difference is that most people embrace one-to-one or one-to-many causal models. An example is the Creator in monotheism, who is believed to be the causeless single cause that created and directs all things with divine will. A similar version is the causeless Big Bang in cosmological theory, which is believed to have created space, time, and matter in the universe available to human observation. Furthermore, unconsciously holding the view of self-essence, people mistakenly believe that all dharmas that appear or disappear through causes and conditions are real.

Karma, Requital

The principle of dependent arising is evident in one's cycle of birth and death. In each life, one does good, evil, and neutral karmas. Then, in the next life, one's new body and new environment are the corresponding requitals for the good and evil karmas in one's previous life or lives. For example, the death penalty for a murderer is a preliminary requital called the bloom of requital, and his next life in hell is the main requital called the fruition of requital (see stories in Sūtras 1 and 13). His subsequent unfortunate rebirths as hungry ghosts, animals, and deprived humans can be described as the residue of requital.

On the bright side, suppose a person wins a Nobel Prize for developing a cure for cancer, this preliminary requital is called the bloom of requital. Then, for the same good karma, this person may be reborn in heaven, and this main requital is called the fruition of requital. Taking the long view, through the good karma of spiritual training, one's rebirth in a pure Buddha Land is the bloom of requital, and one's eventual attainment of Buddhahood is the fruition of requital.

As one transmigrates in one's cycle of birth and death, each action taken becomes a karmic seed in one's mind, which will ripen into a corresponding requital in due time and under due conditions. Fortunately, one can help oneself by providing good conditions to avert or mitigate a dreadful requital before its fruition. The Buddha teaches in Sūtras 1–4 how one can avert or mitigate a painful requital through repentance and skillful means, such as recitation of mantras.

Therefore, a karmic requital does not mean fatalism, nor is it a punishment or reward ordered by an almighty judge. It is simply an event in response to one's karma according to the principle of dependent arising, like a ball rebounding from a wall, in one's present life and/or future lives.

The Twelve Links of Dependent Arising

A detailed explanation as to why and how a sentient being continues to be reborn according to karma is found in the Twelve Links of Dependent Arising. They include a series of causes and effects in a definite order, each being the main condition for the next one to arise. These twelve links are (1) ignorance, (2) karmic actions, (3) consciousness, (4) name and form, (5) six faculties, (6) contact with sense objects, (7) sensory reception, (8) love, (9) grasping, (10) karmic force for being, (11) birth, and (12) old age and death.

Ignorance refers to the condition, in one's past lives, of holding the wrong views and not knowing the truths, such as impermanence, suffering, no self, and emptiness. This condition fueled by one's afflictions triggers karmic actions. Karmic seeds are then stored in one's consciousness. For clarification, consciousness refers to the existence-grasping force that vitalizes a fertilized egg cell and, in the Mahāyāna doctrine, is called ālaya consciousness. Then the name and form of an embryo are developed. This condition leads to the development of the six faculties of a fetus, which, after its birth, can make contact with sense data.

Having received various sense stimulants, one loves the experience and desires to grasp more for gratification. Such karmas become the force that drives subsequent existence. Then the next birth in a new body will again be followed by old age and death, with anxiety, sorrow, pain, and distress.

Links 1–2 refer to the afflictions and karmic seeds from previous lives; links 3–7 refer to the karmic fruit in the present life; links 8–10 refer to karmas done in the present life; and links 11–12 refer to the karmic fruit in the next life. In this sequence, the twelve links connect one's lives from the past to the present, continuing to the future. With ignorance, one goes from affliction to karma to suffering, continuing the endless spiral of birth and death.

The Twelve Links of Dependent Arising is a profound truth that Śākyamuni Buddha realized in meditation. On the third night sitting under the bodhi (enlightenment) tree, He pondered these links in the reverse order, starting from old age and death. He identified the immediate cause of each link and successively reached the root cause, which is ignorance. He then saw that by ending ignorance one disengages the remaining eleven links and ends one's cycle of birth and death. The Buddha observed these twelve conditions in both directions. At early dawn, under the light of a star, He shattered the final hindrance to wisdom-knowledge and attained the unsurpassed perfect enlightenment.

Thus the Twelve Links of Dependant Arising can be used in two ways. If one continues one's ignorance, one will follow the sequence of the twelve links, transmigrating in saṁsāra, as cited above: "because this exists, that exists; since this arises, that arises." Alternatively, if one ends one's ignorance, the connection of the links will be broken, as cited above: "because this exists not, that exists not; since this perishes, that perishes." One transcends one's cycle of birth and death, realizing nirvāṇa.

The Four Noble Truths

In His first turning of the Dharma wheel, the Buddha taught the Four Noble Truths: (1) suffering (duḥkha), (2) accumulation (samudaya), (3) cessation (nirodha), and (4) the path (mārga). Suffering is the essence of repeated birth and death through the six life-journeys; accumulation of afflictions, especially thirsty love (tṛṣṇā), is the cause of suffering; cessation of suffering reveals nirvāṇa; and the Eightfold Right Path is the path to nirvāṇa.

These four truths summarize the process of continuing saṁsāra and the process of terminating saṁsāra, according to the principle of dependent arising. As a condensed version of the Twelve Links of Dependent Arising, the first two truths reveal that, for continuing the flow of saṁsāra, the cause is the accumulation of afflictions and the effect is suffering. The last two truths reveal that, for terminating the flow of saṁsāra, the cause is taking the Eightfold Right Path and the effect is cessation of suffering, realizing nirvāṇa.

All evil karmas are triggered by one's afflictions. Realization that one has no self is the key to the eradication of one's afflictions. Unburdened of an imaginary self with belongings, one no longer has the drive to grasp, to defend, and to attack, doing evil karmas to one's own detriment. Hence, shattering the self-view through observation and meditation on the Eightfold Right Path will gradually dry up one's thirsty love for being and other afflictions. When ignorance and afflictions are replaced by wisdom, one realizes nirvāṇa.

We can find in a dictionary extinction or cessation as the meaning of *nirvāṇa*. The usual interpretation is that the extinction of one's burning afflictions ends one's cycle of birth and death. In this sense, one's attainment of nirvāṇa is the fruit of the Liberation Path. Unfortunately, people often mistake nirvāṇa or the parinirvāṇa (death) of a holy one for "his extinction." A profound meaning of nirvāṇa is presented in the next section.

Emptiness, Nirvāṇa

Understanding Emptiness

The meaning of emptiness (śūnyatā) has been tackled since early Buddhism. For example, using the disassembly approach, an early Buddhist sect holds that a composite thing, which can be disassembled, is empty, but its atoms are real because what is unreal must be made of something real. They probably had difficulty disassembling a mental object. This disassembly approach is useful to a certain extent.

Then the perceptual approach has brought much understanding of emptiness as one recognizes the illusion of karmic perceptions of different sentient beings. For example, a color perceived by a human being as pink may be perceived differently by a cat, a frog, or a fly. While humans concur that the moon in the sky is real, a creature in deep sea would declare that it is entirely imaginary. The reality of liquid water, taken for granted by humans, is challenged because it is perceived as ice by gods, as dwelling by fish, and as ashes or feces by hungry ghosts. The reality of solid matter, which obstructs humans, is also challenged because ghosts walk through walls, as testified by those who have had encounters in haunted houses. This approach gradually blossomed into the Yogācāra School of India, later called in China the Consciousness-Only School.

The third approach is to penetrate the appearances of dharmas according to the principle of dependent arising. The definition of emptiness by this approach has become well established in the Mahāyāna doctrine because of Ācārya Nāgārjuna (circa 150–250), who wrote many treatises based on the tenets of the Āgamas and the *Mahāprajñā Sūtra* (T05–T07n0220a–o) in 600 fascicles.

As stated in a preceding paragraph, impermanence evidences that a dharma has no self-essence and is therefore empty. This statement can now be refined because dependent arising is the reason that dharmas are impermanent. It is through causes and conditions that a dharma arises, stays, changes, and perishes. Each cause or condition is also a dharma dependent on causes and conditions. Then it is more incisive to state that a dharma dependent on causes and conditions has no self-essence and is therefore empty. Hence, all things commonly accepted as real, including the water in a lake and the moon in the sky, are empty.

The Twofold Truth of Dharmas

Furthermore, emptiness is not merely a negation of self-essence in a dharma dependent upon causes and conditions. Emptiness reveals the twofold truth of such a dharma. First, the relative truth (worldly truth) recognizes that a dharma dependent upon causes and conditions exists in name only, and its birth and death as perceived are illusory appearances. Second, the absolute truth (supra-worldly truth) reveals that a dharma, in true reality, has neither birth nor death. In the absolute truth, the emptiness of a dharma and the no birth of a dharma are synonymous.

As an analogy, when a wave rises, the water of the ocean is neither born nor increased; when the wave falls, the water neither perishes nor decreases. As a wave appears to arise or to perish, the water in the ocean is changeless, as is the dharma realm. A wave is empty because, in true reality, it has neither birth nor death, though it appears and disappears, perceived as birth and death.

As another analogy, when a house is assembled on a vacant lot through causes and conditions, matter is neither born nor increased. When the house is destroyed, matter neither perishes nor decreases. In this analogy, emptiness does not refer to the open space before the construction of the house, then occupied by the house, and then recovered after the destruction of the house. The open space is but one of the conditions for the appearance of the house. It is the house that is empty throughout its illusory birth, existence, and destruction.

Note that emptiness, the true reality of dharmas, is not the first cause of the illusory birth of a dharma. However, because dharma nature (the nature of all dharmas) is emptiness, it is through causes and conditions that any dharma can manifest, such as the water in a mirage or in a lake, events in one's dream or during waking hours, the moon in the water or in the sky.

Emptiness, Inherent Nirvāṇa

Emptiness, the true reality of dharmas, is also called the inherent nirvāṇa. Despite the apparent commotion of births and deaths, the true nature of all dharmas is nirvāṇa, the silence and stillness of no birth and no death. Emptiness is also called the dharma body (dharmakāya) because the true body of all dharmas is not matter but emptiness. Other synonyms include reality state (bhūtakoṭi), true suchness (bhūtatathātā), the Tathāgata store (tathāgata-garbha), and the inherent pure mind. The inherent pure mind is in turn called the Buddha mind or the true mind.

In Sanskrit, a dharma formed or made through causes and conditions, as discussed above, is called a saṁskṛta dharma. Because causes and conditions are included in its definition, the twofold truth can now be restated succinctly. First, the relative truth recognizes that a saṁskṛta dharma exists in name only, and its perceived birth and death are illusory. Second, the absolute truth which penetrates the illusory birth and death of any saṁskṛta dharma reveals that dharmas, in true reality, have neither birth nor death.

In Sanskrit, a dharma not formed or made through causes and conditions is called an asaṁskṛta dharma. Although the words *saṁskṛta* and *asaṁskṛta* seem to be antonyms, that which is asaṁskṛta is the true reality of all saṁskṛta dharmas, not their opposite.

The Common Path of the Three Vehicles

Common to all Three Vehicles, the Eightfold Right Path is a balanced approach, led by the right views based on wisdom, not emotion or tradition. It can lead one out of one's cycle of birth and death. It includes (1) right views, (2) right thinking, (3) right speech, (4) right action, (5) right livelihood, (6) right effort, (7) right mindfulness, and (8) right meditative absorption (samādhi). Right views and right thinking provide one with the right understanding, which is an element of wisdom (prajñā). Right speech, right action, and right livelihood establish one on the ground of morality. Right mindfulness and right samādhi unfold one's wisdom, which in turn affirms one's right views and understanding. Right effort should be applied to the other seven paths.

The Eightfold Right Path is elaborated in the Thirty-seven Elements of Bodhi. They describe in detail how one can train one's mind for the development of wisdom.

One progresses on the Eightfold Right Path in four stages: faith, understanding, action, and verification (信解行證). Faith and understanding can be acquired through hearing and pondering the Dharma, by taking Paths 1–2. Action means carrying out the teachings through the Three Learnings (三學): observance of precepts (śīla), meditation (dhyāna), and development of wisdom (prajñā). Observance of precepts corresponds to Paths 3–5; meditation corresponds to Paths 7–8; and development of wisdom through the power of meditation affirms Paths 1–2 and enhances one's faith and understanding. Finally, verification of the truth is achieved by self-realization through the power of one's wisdom, which is also the goal of the Eightfold Right Path. Again, right effort should be applied to all these four stages.

For development of wisdom, Arhats, Pratyekabuddhas, and holy Bodhisattvas have all gone through the Three Liberation Doors, also called the Three Samādhis, which include (1) emptiness, (2) no appearance, and (3) no wish or no act. Through meditation, one realizes emptiness, penetrating the no birth of all dharmas. One also sees that one's perceptions of dharmas are illusory appearances, which are no appearance. And one makes no wish or does nothing for one's rebirth in the Three Realms of Existence.

Although there are Three Vehicles, the Buddha's teachings are not segregated among them. In the *Mahāyāna Vaipulya Sūtra of Total Retention* (Sūtra 15), the Buddha says that all His teachings should be retained. Voice-hearers should not reject Mahāyāna teachings. Likewise, riders of the Mahāyāna are not exempt from the teachings given at the beginning of the Buddha's teaching life. According to the 80-fascicle version of the *Mahāvaipulya Sūtra of Buddha Adornment*, as holy Bodhisattvas on the Ten Grounds cultivate the ten pāramitās, those on the Fifth Ground will verify the Four Noble Truths and those on the Sixth Ground will penetrate the Twelve Links of Dependent Arising.

The Holy Fruits of the First Two Vehicles

The Liberation Fruit

A voice-hearer goes through the Dharma Door of Impermanence and Suffering. With aversion for saṁsāra, through meditation and observation, a voice-hearer makes a breakthrough when he shatters his self-view. As a result, he also shatters his doubts and rejects useless precepts alleged to be the cause of liberation. Breaking away from these three bondages, he achieves the first voice-hearer fruit, becoming a Srotāpanna (Enterer of the Holy Stream). This first step is called seeing bodhi because he is sure to attain nirvāṇa. Realizing that there is no self in him, a Srotāpanna is enabled to gradually eradicate his afflictions. A Srotāpanna with even a low capacity can attain Arhatship after at most seven times being reborn as a god then a human, never again assuming any of the four evil life forms.

After a Srotāpanna has diminished his afflictions, he achieves the second holy fruit, becoming a Sakṛdāgāmin (Once Returner), who will be reborn as a human only once more before attaining Arhatship. After a Srotāpanna or a Sakṛdāgāmin has shattered the five bondages of the desire realm—doubts, useless precepts, greed, anger, and delusion—he achieves the third holy fruit, becoming an Anāgāmin (Never Returner), who will never be reborn in the human world, but will realize Arhatship in a heaven in the form realm.

Finally, after an Anāgāmin has shattered the five bondages of the two higher realms—greed for existence in the form realm, greed for existence in the formless realm, restlessness, arrogance, and ignorance—he achieves the fourth and highest voice-hearer fruit, becoming an Arhat (One Worthy of Offerings), who has destroyed all his foes, his afflictions. An Arhat has realized the inherent nirvāṇa of all dharmas, and his realization when he is alive is called the nirvāṇa with remnant. When an Arhat abandons his body, the karmic remnant, by entering profound samādhi, his death is called parinirvāṇa, also called the nirvāṇa without remnant.

These four voice-hearer fruits do not have to be achieved successively. In the days of the Buddha, many voice-hearers became Arhats in a few days or years after receiving His teachings. Having shattered his fixation on his self-view and eradicated all his afflictions, an Arhat has achieved the liberation fruit, completely freed from his cycle of birth and death, as he declares, "My rebirth is ended; my Brahma way of life is established; my undertaking is completed; I will not undergo subsequent existence."

A Pratyekabuddha has the extraordinary capacity to penetrate on his own the Twelve Links of Dependent Arising and realize the nirvāṇa with remnant, achieving the same liberation fruit as does an Arhat. He is also called a solitary Buddha because, living in solitude, he has realized the truth without receiving teachings from a Buddha. A Pratyekabuddha may occasionally give teachings (see story in Sūtra 1), but has little interest in delivering others.

The Bodhi Fruit

Like a jewel inseparable from its brilliance, nirvāṇa is the silence and stillness of true reality illuminated by the light of wisdom, the bodhi fruit. Both an Arhat and a Pratyekabuddha have achieved the bodhi fruit called the overall wisdom-knowledge (sarvajña, 一切智), realizing the emptiness of dharmas, though the bodhi of a Pratyekabuddha is said to be higher than that of an Arhat. It is controversial whether Arhats and Pratyekabuddhas have only realized the emptiness of a sentient being, a realization sufficient for achieving the liberation fruit of their only interest.

Although their liberation is equal to that of a Buddha, they have attained neither the great bodhi fruit nor the awesome powers of a Buddha. Nonetheless, they have achieved the six transcendental powers (see demonstration of powers in Sūtra 6).

The Path of the Third Vehicle, the Mahāyāna

The Mahāyāna is called the Great Vehicle because it has a great capacity for carrying sentient beings to Buddhahood. It is called the Bodhisattva Vehicle because its riders are Bodhisattvas. It is called the Buddha Vehicle because its destination is Buddhahood. And it is called the One Vehicle (ekayāna) because the Buddha teaches the ultimate equality of all sentient beings. He declares, for example, in the *Lotus Sūtra,* that not only the riders of the Two Vehicles but all sentient beings will eventually attain Buddhahood. Even an icchantika, one who has cut off one's roots of goodness in one's present life, may replant them through causes and conditions in a future life and eventually attain Buddhahood.

According to the 80-fascicle version of the *Mahāvaipulya Sūtra of Buddha Adornment,* a Bodhisattva advances on the Bodhisattva Way toward Buddhahood through fifty-two levels, which are grouped into seven stages: (1) ten faithful minds, (2) ten levels of abiding, (3) ten levels of action, (4) ten levels of transference of merit, (5) Ten Grounds, (6) virtually perfect enlightenment, and (7) perfect enlightenment (Buddhahood).

A Bodhisattva will continue to be an ordinary being as he cultivates, in ten thousand kalpas, the ten faithful minds. Then, in the first great asaṁkhyeya kalpa, he will become a sage on the Training Ground for Excellent Understanding (勝解行地) as he repeatedly practices the ten pāramitās, passing through the ten levels of abiding, the ten levels of action, and the ten levels of transference of merit. In the second great asaṁkhyeya kalpa, he will become a holy being as he successively trains on the first seven Grounds. In the third great asaṁkhyeya kalpa, he will ascend to higher Grounds, progressing from the Eighth to the Tenth Ground. Upon completion of the Tenth Ground, his enlightenment being virtually perfect, he will be in the holy position of waiting to become a Buddha in his next life. Finally, sitting under a bodhi tree, he will demonstrate the perfect enlightenment of a Buddha, the ultimate fruit of the aspiration and training of a Bodhisattva.

The Holy Fruits of the Mahāyāna

The Liberation Fruit

According to the sūtra above, upon completion of his training on the Seventh Ground, a Bodhisattva has achieved the liberation fruit. However, unlike an Arhat, he chooses not to enter parinirvāṇa. Instead, he ascends to the Eighth Ground, from which he will never regress, and his attainment is called the Endurance in the Realization of the No Birth of Dharmas (無生法忍). He will continue to accumulate merit and develop his discriminatory wisdom-knowledge (道種智) for the sake of delivering sentient beings, as he progresses to higher Grounds until attainment of Buddhahood.

While an ordinary being, whose lifespan and life form are governed by the law of karma, repeatedly undergoes karmic birth and death (分段生死), a holy Bodhisattva on any of the Ten Grounds, whose lifespan and mind-created body (意生身) are changeable at will, undergoes changeable birth and death (變易生死). Only a Buddha has ended both types of birth and death. He has eradicated not only all the afflictions and their subtle traces as habits, but also the ground-abiding ignorance (住地無明), which is the original hindrance to wisdom-knowledge. The liberation fruit achieved by a Buddha is called the nirvāṇa that abides nowhere, beyond the distinction between nirvāṇa and saṁsāra.

The Great Bodhi Fruit

The great bodhi fruit achieved by a Buddha is omniscience (sarvajñatā), also called knowledge of all knowledge (sarvajña-jñāna, 一切種智). The adornment of a Buddha is His completely fulfilled merit and wisdom. Standing firmly on two feet—merit and wisdom—He is hailed the Two-Footed Honored One and honored with His ten epithets.

He has also achieved the Eighteen Exclusive Dharmas, the Ten Powers, the Four Fearlessnesses, and the Command of the Eight Great Displays, all of which are unattained by Arhats and Pratyekabuddhas.

The Anuttara-Samyak-Saṁbuddha

A Buddha is called Anuttara-Samyak-Saṁbuddha (Unsurpassed, equally, perfectly enlightened one). *Anuttara* means unsurpassed; *samyak* is derived from the stem *samyañc,* which means same or identical; *saṁbuddha* means perfectly enlightened one. A passage in the 4-fascicle version of the *Laṅkāvatāra Sūtra* states that Buddhas are equal in four aspects: their epithets, their words spoken with the Brahma tone, the truth they have realized, and their dharma body and manifested bodies (T16n0670, 0498b29–c12). Beyond diametric discriminations, such as same and different, held by sentient beings, a Buddha manifests various forms and assumes different names to suit the needs of sentient beings.

The first of the ten epithets of a Buddha is Tathāgata, which is usually translated as Thus-Come One. Tathāgata is true suchness, the dharma body, free from appearance and motion, though a Buddha appears to have come and gone in the same way as have past Buddhas.

In Mahāyāna sūtras, Śākyamuni Buddha has introduced many Buddhas and holy Bodhisattvas. Some scholars might ascribe pantheism to Mahāyāna Buddhism, equating Buddhas to gods, and Bodhisattvas to goddesses. In truth, neither rulers nor objects of worship or fear, Buddhas and Bodhisattvas are teachers and role models for their students. Buddhas are physicians who give the right prescriptions of medicine to suffering sentient beings. If one can recognize one's problems, as diagnosed by a Buddha, and is willing to take the medicine, one can set off on the right path to Buddhahood. Scholarly argument over isms has nothing to do with His teachings. Buddhism is already one ism too many.

Dharma Doors of the Mahāyāna

The Dharma Door of Lovingkindness and Compassion

A Bodhisattva (literally, enlightenment being) is resolved to attain anuttara-samyak-saṁbodhi (unsurpassed, equally perfect enlightenment) and, out of lovingkindness and compassion, to enlighten others. Although all sentient beings will eventually attain Buddhahood, not all of them are presently Bodhisattvas. Only those who have activated their resolve to attain Buddhahood are called Bodhisattvas. This resolve is called the anuttara-samyak-saṁbodhi mind or, for short, the bodhi mind (bodhicitta).

The Bodhisattva Way to Buddhahood is a very long endeavor. As described in the *Sūtra of Immeasurable Meaning* (Sūtra 16), even a novice Bodhisattva, out of lovingkindness and compassion, will give his ship to others to sail across to the shore of liberation while he remains on this shore of birth and death, because he considers benefits to others as benefits to himself. For those who might feel discouraged, the good news is that both space and time are illusions. In the *Sūtra of the Great Compassion-Mind Dhāraṇī,* Avalokiteśvara Bodhisattva recalls that, upon hearing the Great Compassion-Mind Mantra, he instantly ascended from the First Ground to the Eighth Ground (T20n1060, 0106c3–4).

The spirit of the Mahāyāna is best described by Samantabhadra Bodhisattva. In the 40-fascicle version of the *Mahāvaipulya Sūtra of Buddha Adornment,* he says, "Sentient beings are the tree roots, and Bodhisattvas and Buddhas are respectively the flowers and fruits. If one benefits sentient beings with the water of great compassion, one can develop the flowers and fruits of wisdom, becoming a Bodhisattva then a Buddha. Why? Because if Bodhisattvas benefit sentient beings with the water of great compassion, they can attain anuttara-samyak-saṁbodhi. Therefore, bodhi belongs to sentient beings. Without sentient beings, Bodhisattvas can never attain the unsurpassed saṁbodhi" (T10n0293, 0846a17–

22). Based on this conviction, Samantabhadra recommends the Ten Great Actions (Prayer 4) as essential training for a Bodhisattva.

The Middle Way through the Dharma Door of Emptiness

As mentioned above, ordinary people perceive dharmas in terms of opposites, such as birth and death, perpetuity and cessation, same and different, and coming and going. More pairs of opposites can be readily added to the list, such as existence and nonexistence, subject and object, and good and evil. Note that perpetuity and cessation are temporal extensions of existence and nonexistence. Those who take existence as real mistakenly believe in perpetuity; those who take nonexistence as real mistakenly believe in cessation. Many monotheists mistakenly believe that *absolute* good will one day annihilate *absolute* evil, unaware that the concepts of good and evil, and subject and object, depend on each other.

Dharmas appear paradoxical because they all are relative to one another. Thus, birth is destined for death, and death is certain because of birth. The existence of a sentient being seems to cease at death. However, its cessation seems to be contradicted by its rebirth. Whether dharmas are classified as same or different depends on comparing two or more dharmas according to some criteria. Whether a dharma is coming or going depends on the designation of a point of departure or arrival.

By showing the Middle Way (madhyamaka), the Mahāyāna doctrine refutes all fixations on opposites, which arise from the view of self-essence. This is the way to understand both the relative truth and the absolute truth.

In the relative truth, the principle of dependent arising is the Middle Way, or the Middle Observation. In the Saṁyukta Āgama (connected discourses), Ānanda quotes the Buddha: "People of the world are deluded, and they believe in opposites, either existence or nonexistence. . . . Those who correctly observe the arising of anything in the world do not hold the view of nonexistence. Those who correctly observe the perishing of anything in the world do not hold the view of existence. . . . Staying away from the opposites, the Tathāgata expounds the Middle Way: Because this exists, that exists; since this arises, that arises. . . . Because this exists not, that exists not; since this perishes, that perishes. . . ." (T02n0099, 0066c25–0067a8).

In the absolute truth, emptiness is the Middle Way. Emptiness is the true reality of all dharmas because they are illusory appearances through causes and conditions. Hence, in true reality, dharmas have neither birth nor death; they are neither perpetual nor ceasing, neither same nor different, neither coming nor going. These eight negations in four pairs of opposites are the theme of the *Middle Treatise* (T30n1564, 0001b14–15) authored by Ācārya Nāgārjuna, who is recognized as the first patriarch of the Emptiness School. The essence of emptiness lies in the first pair of negations, no birth and no death, and its corollaries are the other three pairs of negations. Further simplified, the emptiness of all dharmas means no birth, which underlies the other seven negations.

The word *middle* does not mean that emptiness is a midpoint or a compromise between opposites, nor is it their union. The Middle Way means that emptiness is non-dual, above the plane of polar opposites, which are illusory manifestations of dharmas through illusory causes and conditions, all under false names. Emptiness is also a false name. Although the Buddha often likens emptiness to space, one should not take emptiness as nothingness or as a metaphysical base for saṁskṛta dharmas.

With the understanding that emptiness as a concept is also empty, one can call emptiness the ultimate emptiness, nirvāṇa, Tathāgata, or dharma body. Because emptiness, not self-essence, is dharma nature, myriad illusory dharmas are vividly perceived through causes and conditions. As stated in the *Heart Sūtra* (Sūtras 10–12), "Form is no different from emptiness; emptiness is no different from form. In effect, form is emptiness and emptiness is form. The same is true for sensory reception, perception, mental processing, and consciousness."

Although the five aggregates are empty, it is never obvious to ordinary beings because emptiness is the realization of holy beings, such as Arhats, who have realized the nirvāṇa with remnant, and holy Bodhisattvas, who have achieved the Endurance in the Realization of the No Birth of Dharmas. Therefore, unless one has realized nirvāṇa through the right path, to celebrate that everyone in saṁsāra is already in nirvāṇa is meaningless.

Riders of the Voice-Hear Vehicle go through the Dharma Door of Impermanence and Suffering, believing that there are afflictions to annihilate, saṁsāra to leave, and nirvāṇa to attain. By contrast, riders of the Mahāyāna take the Middle Way through the Door of Emptiness, knowing that there are no afflictions to annihilate, no saṁsāra to leave, and no nirvāṇa to attain. Although nothing to attain is the right observation of the Middle Way, one must verify it through self-realization.

The Dharma Door of Consciousness-Only

The foundation of Yogācāra doctrine, also called the consciousness-only doctrine, was laid down in the fourth century by two Indian masters, Asaṅga and his younger brother Vasubandhu, who wrote several treatises. This doctrine is based on six Mahāyāna sūtras and eleven treatises. A major work of Asaṅga titled *Yogācārya-bhūmi-śāstra* (T30n1579) is reputed to have been imparted by Maitreya, the next Buddha to come.

Vasubandhu authored many treatises, including the *Abdhidharma-kośa-bhāṣya* (T31n1605), the *Mahāyāna-saṅgraha-bhāṣya* (T31n1596), and the *Thirty Verses on Consciousness-Only* (T31n1586). The commentaries by ten Indian masters, including Dharmapāla as the principal commentator, on these thirty verses were integrated and translated into Chinese by the Chinese master Xuanzang (玄奘, 600– or 602–664). His book *Cheng weishi lun* 成唯識論 (T31n1585), which means completing the doctrine of consciousness-only, is an important text for the Faxiang (dharma appearance) School of China.

The basic tenet of this school is that myriads of internal or external objects in the subjective world of a sentient being are constructions of its eight consciousnesses. In brief, all saṁskṛta dharmas in one's life arise from the pure, impure, and neutral seeds stored in one's ālaya consciousness (the eighth consciousness), which is the root of the first seven consciousnesses. The seventh consciousness misidentifies the working of the eighth consciousness as the image of a self, giving one an inborn sense of self. The sixth consciousness not only does thinking, dreaming, and reasoning, but also supports the five sense consciousnesses to differentiate the sense objects they construct.

Having declared that consciousnesses are agents that both construct and perceive mental objects, this school proposes that one should undertake the Four Preparatory Trainings in meditation. This stage is added to the seven-stage Bodhisattva Way and placed between the ten levels of transference of merit and the Ten Grounds. Through these Four Preparatory Trainings in meditation, one should realize first that the mentally constructed objects are empty, then that consciousnesses, as constructor-perceivers, are also empty. Upon realizing that there is neither object nor subject, one ascends to the First Ground, becoming a holy Bodhisattva.

Ālaya consciousness, also called ādāna consciousness, is mentioned but not explained in the Āgamas. But it plays an important role in the Mahāyāna doctrine as the store of changing seeds being transferred from one life to the next. In the *Sandhinirmocana Sūtra,* fascicle 1, the Buddha says, "Ādāna consciousness is profound and imperceptible, and I do not reveal it to the ordinary and the foolish. As its seeds churn like raging rapids, I am concerned that they would fixate on it as a self" (T16n0676, 0692c22–23). This is the reason ālaya consciousness was not explained early on.

Mahāyāna Schools of China

The story in China began with Emperor Ming (漢明帝, 28–75) of the Eastern Han Dynasty, who dreamed of a golden man with a halo of sun-moon light. Informed by his ministers, he sent two agents to India to seek the teachings of the Buddha. In 67, the tenth year of the Yongping (永平) years, they came back with Dharmāraṇya (竺法蘭) and Kāśyapamātaṅga (竺攝摩騰). Carrying Sanskrit texts on a white horse, these two Indian monks arrived in Luoyang, China's capital. They stayed at the White Horse Temple, built for them, and translated the *Sūtra in Forty-two Sections* (T17n0784), thus beginning the transmittal of the Buddha Dharma to China.

Based on Indian Buddhism, eight Mahāyāna Schools have emerged in China: (1) the Three Treatises School, extended from the Emptiness School; (2) the Faxiang (dharma appearance) School, extended from the Yogācāra School; (3) the Pure Land School, founded on Pure Land sūtras; (4) the Tiantai School, founded on the *Lotus Sūtra;* (4) the Huayan School, founded on the *Mahāvaipulya Sūtra of Buddha Adornment;* (5) the Chan School, emphasizing the experience of seeing one's Buddha nature; (7) the Vinaya School, emphasizing observance of precepts; and (8) the Esoteric School, emphasizing visualization and mantra recitation.

These schools are not sectarian because they all revere Śākyamuni Buddha as the original teacher and recognize Ācārya Nāgārjuna as their distant, common originating patriarch. Since early Qing Dynasty (1644–1912), all Chinese Buddhist temples have adopted the practice lessons compiled by the Imperial Teacher, Dharma Master Yulin (玉琳國師, 1613–76), to recite the same sūtras, mantras, and prayers in their morning and evening chanting practices.

Through meditation and concentrated study of a few sūtras and treatises, the founders and successors of these Chinese schools acquired profound understanding of the Buddha Dharma. The works of these Chinese masters can be found in the Chinese Canon or the Extension of the Chinese Canon. With equal respect, modern Chinese Buddhists study the sūtras and works valued by all eight schools.

Dharma Master Zhiyi (智顗, 538–97), founder of the Tiantai School, classified all Dharma Doors by five chronological periods: (1) the Buddha adornment period of the first three weeks after the Buddha's enlightenment, during which He pronounced the *Mahāvaipulya Sūtra of Buddha Adornment* to teach advanced Bodhisattvas the Way to Buddhahood; (2) the Āgamas period of twelve years, during which He pronounced the Āgamas to voice-hearers; (3) the vaipulya period of eight years, during which He pronounced the vaipulya (vast and extensive) sūtras, directing voice-hearers to the Mahāyāna; (4) the prajñā period of twenty-two years, during which He pronounced the prajñā sūtras to teach emptiness and to end people's emotional attachment to the Small Vehicle; and (5) the Dharma flower and nirvāṇa period, during which He pronounced the *Lotus Sūtra* in His last eight years of life, and the *Mahāparinirvāṇa Sūtra* before entering parinirvāṇa. The former reveals the One Vehicle for all, and the latter reveals Buddha nature in all, thus perfectly concluding the Buddha's teachings.

The Development of a Bodhisattva

The Four Immeasurable Minds

The predisposition of a sentient being is self-love and self-interest, not lovingkindness and compassion for others. Therefore, spiritual training is essential to the development of a Bodhisattva. A Bodhisattva needs to cultivate the Four Immeasurable Minds: lovingkindness, compassion, sympathetic joy, and equability. It is with lovingkindness that a Bodhisattva gives happiness to others. It is out of compassion that a Bodhisattva rescues others from suffering. It is with sympathetic joy, not jealousy or arrogance, that a Bodhisattva recognizes others' merit. It is with equability that a Bodhisattva faces favorable and unfavorable situations and handles his emotions. These Four Immeasurable Minds will be fully developed in a Bodhisattva when he completes his training on the Third Ground.

The Ten Pāramitās

Furthermore, a Bodhisattva practices the pāramitās on the Bodhisattva Way. The Sanskrit word *pāramita* means gone across to the opposite shore. To succeed in crossing over to that shore of nirvāṇa, opposite this shore of saṁsāra, one needs to achieve the six pāramitās and the four extensions that spontaneously flow out from the sixth pāramitā. These ten pāramitās are (1) almsgiving (dāna), (2) observance of precepts (śīla), (3) endurance of adversity (kṣānti), (4) energetic progress (vīrya), (5) meditation (dhyāna), (6) development of wisdom (prajñā), (7) skillful means (upāya), (8) earnest wish (praṇidhāna), (9) power (bala), and (10) wisdom-knowledge (jñāna). On the Bodhisattva Way, a Bodhisattva repeatedly practices these ten pāramitās through the ten levels of abiding, the ten levels of action, and the ten levels of transference of merit, and finally achieves them on the Ten Grounds.

He cultivates generosity by giving others (1) things, (2) fearlessness, and (3) the Dharma, as he observes the emptiness of the giver, the recipient, and the act of giving or the object given. He observes the Bodhisattva precepts extended from the ten good karmas. He undauntedly endures adversity, tribulation, and persecution. As he boldly makes energetic progress, he continues his meditation in stillness and in motion. He unfolds his wisdom, which affirms his right views. Then, with skillful means, the earnest wish to attain bodhi and transform others, the power to accomplish deeds, and myriads of wisdom-knowledge, he spontaneously delivers sentient beings.

Through perfection in these ten trainings, a Bodhisattva eventually attains Buddhahood. While sentient beings embrace thirsty love for being as their mother and ignorance as their father, the mother of a Buddha is wisdom (prajñā) and the father is skillful means (upāya) for delivering sentient beings.

The Four Drawing-in Dharmas

As a Bodhisattva develops wisdom and accumulates merit on the Bodhisattva Way, he also needs to develop people skills to draw others into the Dharma. To this end, he carries out the Four Drawing-in Dharmas, which include (1) almsgiving, (2) loving words, (3) beneficial actions, and (4) collaborative work. In addition, the Buddha teaches us to expound the Dharma cautiously to five groups of people so that they will not react with anger, malign the Dharma, and suffer unfortunate consequences. In the *Mahāparinirvāṇa Sūtra,* fascicle 33, the Buddha says, "To nonbelievers, do not praise true faith. To offenders of morality, do not praise observance of precepts. To misers, do not praise generosity. To the indolent, do not praise hearing much of the Dharma. To the foolish, do not praise wisdom" (T12n0374, 0564b6–13).

The Promise of One's Buddha Nature

Buddha Nature, Tathāgata Store, Ālaya Consciousness

Buddhahood is the goal that sets the Mahāyāna apart from the Two Vehicles. To assure timid sentient beings of their Buddhahood, the Buddha reveals Buddha nature (buddha-gotra). In the *Mahāparinirvāṇa Sūtra,* fascicle 28, He says, "Those who see Buddha nature in all sentient beings are Buddhas, and Bodhisattvas on the tenth level of abiding and above; those who do not see Buddha nature are sentient beings . . . [that] only hear about it. . . . Never lost or destroyed, Buddha nature is in every sentient being" (T12n0374, 0530nb4–16).

Buddha nature is also called the Tathāgata store (tathāgata-garbha), which is the theme of two Mahāyāna sūtras (T16n0666–67). Each sūtra uses nine analogies to explain that every sentient being is the Tathāgata unrealized. Furthermore, the Tathāgata store and ālaya consciousness are united in the 4-fascicle version of the *Laṅkāvatāra Sūtra*. In fascicle 4, the Buddha explains, "The Tathāgata store . . . , conditioned by fabrications and habits since time without a beginning, is also called the store consciousness. Together with the other seven consciousnesses, it is led by the ground-abiding ignorance. Though mistaken for a self, it is inherently pure. Like the substance of ocean waves, it continues unceasingly, free from the appearance of impermanence, while the other consciousnesses arise and perish, thought after thought" (T16n0670, 0510b4–10).

Buddha Nature Fully Realized

All sentient beings can attain Buddhahood through causes and conditions because Buddha nature is likened to gold mixed with dirt. While one can never find gold by digging in a coal mine, one can surely extract gold by refining gold ore. When one's Buddha nature is fully revealed through self-realization, it is called the Tathāgata, the great nirvāṇa. People may question whether ignorance may one day arise in a Buddha's mind and turn Him back into a sentient being. The answer is negative. The gold extracted from dirt will never be mixed with dirt again.

In the *Mahāparinirvāṇa Sūtra,* fascicle 21, the Buddha distinguishes between producing causes and revealing causes: "For example, a potter and his equipment are called the producing cause of a ceramic pot. The lamplight and candlelight are called the revealing cause of things in the dark. Good man, the great nirvāṇa is attained not through producing causes, but through revealing causes, such as the Thirty-seven Bodhi Elements and the six pāramitās" (T12n0374, 0492c2–7).

Dharmas born from producing causes are saṁskṛta dharmas, such as a ceramic pot or a sentient being, which will definitely perish. By contrast, a revealing cause is like a light shining on a treasure stored in a dark room. The light enables one to see what is already there. The spiritual training of a Bodhisattva, which unfolds his wisdom that penetrates the emptiness of the dirt on the gold, is a revealing cause of his great nirvāṇa, not a producing cause.

Self, No Self, Nominal Self, True Self

In the days of the Buddha, most Hindus believed, as they still do today, in an individual soul (ātman), who "is the inner controller, the immortal" (Olivelle 2008, 41–45), whether distinct or indistinct from the universal spirit (brahman). By contrast, the Buddha teaches that a sentient being composed of the five aggregates is a mental-physical process, which means impermanence, suffering, no self, and impurity. In Buddhist doctrine, while the self-view that there exists an autonomous self is refuted, the use of a nominal self for referring to a sentient being composed of the five aggregates is accepted. The Buddha often tells stories of His past lives, using the pronouns *I, me,* and *my.*

In the *Mahāparinirvāṇa Sūtra,* the Buddha describes the Tathāgata with four words: eternity, bliss, self, and purity. What kind of self is this one? In fascicle 30, the Buddha distinguishes between no self and true self: "If self is a doer, how can it be eternal? If it is eternal, how can it sometimes do good and sometimes do evil? If it sometimes does good and sometimes does evil, how can it be said to be boundless? Therefore, there is no self in a sentient being. . . . If there is a self, it must be the Tathāgata. Why? Because there is no doubt about its boundlessness. It is called eternity because it neither does nor experiences anything. It is called bliss because it has neither birth nor death. It is called purity because it has no afflictions. It is called emptiness because it does not have the ten appearances. Therefore, the Tathāgata is eternity, bliss, self, and purity, free from appearances" (T12n0374, 0544c11–19).

The eternity of the Tathāgata and the significance of true self are also discussed in the *Sūtra of the Great Dharma Drum* (Sūtra 14). To those who fear the mention of no self and those who fear that parinirvāṇa would mean the extinction of a holy being, the Buddha introduces the true self. However, it is neither an autonomous self nor a nominal self denoting a sentient being. In the above passage, the true self is equated to the Tathāgata, the great nirvāṇa, the dharma body, and ultimate emptiness. Different terms carrying their own meanings find their common ground in emptiness. In emptiness, the great nirvāṇa is neither being nor nonbeing. The eternity of the true self is neither eternity nor extinction; its bliss is neither bliss nor suffering; its purity is neither purity nor impurity.

Seeing One's Buddha Nature

In the *Mahāparinirvāṇa Sūtra,* fascicle 32, the Buddha teaches that it is possible to see one's Buddha nature: "Sentient beings' Buddha nature . . . is neither internal nor external, neither something nor nothing, neither this nor that, nor coming from elsewhere . . . ; nor is it invisible to all sentient beings. Bodhisattvas, at the convergence of timing, and causes and conditions, will be able to see it" (T12n0374, 0555c1–6).

Then the Buddha says that if a Bodhisattva on the Eightfold Right Path has acquired the mind of equality toward sentient beings, he can see his Buddha nature. He is then called a sage at the tenth level of abiding on the Bodhisattva Way.

Seeing one's Buddha nature is a breakthrough for a Bodhisattva below the First Ground. It is well documented in the Chan School (Chan is the phonetic translation of the Sanskrit word *dhyāna,* which means meditation) that, in a flash of attunement, one can suddenly enter a non-dual state, realizing one's true mind and seeing one's Buddha nature, passing the gateless gate. Without this significant experience, one's understanding of true reality is only a conceptual one. How a

Chan master can help a student open his wisdom-eye depends on the causes and conditions between them.

Contrary to the general impression that a Chan master will just gesture, shout, tell riddles, hit students, and shun scriptural studies, Huineng (惠能, 638–713), the sixth patriarch of the Chan School, for example, suddenly came to see his Buddha nature while listening to the explanation of the *Diamond Sūtra* by the fifth patriarch. As a result, the *Diamond Sūtra* became the principal text for the Chan School, outweighing the status of the 4-fascicle version of the *Laṅkāvatāra Sūtra*, which was taken from India to China by Bodhidharma (菩提達摩, early 5th century), the twenty-eighth and last patriarch of the Indian Buddhist lineage, who is recognized as the first patriarch of the Chan School of China.

Buddhist Training in Knowledge and Meditation

Study of Buddhist Sūtras

The Buddha teaches that words and names are fabrications of the mind, but His words are a finger pointing to the truth, which one must realize on one's own. Therefore, one needs to learn the right views from the right source, the Buddha's words. Whichever Dharma Door one uses to train one's mind, it is essential to study the sūtras to enforce and reinforce one's faith, understanding, and endeavor. The best offering one can make to a sūtra is to penetrate its meanings and carry out its teachings, because one develops wisdom through (1) hearing the Dharma, (2) pondering its meanings, and (3) training accordingly.

Furthermore, the Buddha, having foreseen the problems that students of the Dharma will encounter in this Dharma-ending age, has instructed us to follow, under all circumstances, the Four Dharmas to Rely Upon. Therefore, to ensure the purity and correctness of understanding, with the trust that only the Buddha is completely correct in His Dharma, one needs to recite and study the sūtras online or in print. To do so is to receive the teachings and blessings from the Buddha, the only perfectly enlightened teacher in this age. Subject to neither authorization nor regulation of exclusive sects and lineages, the Buddha, with unconditional lovingkindness and compassion, bestows his teachings and blessings upon all who are receptive.

Training in Meditation

Riders of the Three Vehicles train in meditation through śamatha (meditative concentration) and vipaśyanā (correct observation) but with different approaches. Practicing śamatha to quiet his mind, a voice-hearer notes his breathing or visualizes a decomposing corpse to foster aversion for saṁsāra. To develop insight, he concurrently practices vipaśyanā according to the Four Foundations of Mindfulness, paying nonjudgmental attention to his (1) physical movements, (2) sensory feelings, (3) greed, anger, and delusion, and (4) other mental objects. He recognizes these events as impermanent but real. Through this Dharma Door of Impermanence, he can shatter his self-view and enter the holy stream.

Counting or noting one's breaths is a practice of śamatha common to all meditators, Buddhists or non-Buddhists. Mahāyāna Buddhists certainly use this method as well. However, their distinctive approach is to go through the Door of Emptiness to practice śamatha and vipaśyanā as described in, for example, the *Sūtra of Detecting Good or Evil Karma and Requital* (Sūtra 9). Thus one can meditate on emptiness to quiet one's mind as one observes the objects perceived as internal or external, with the understanding that they are mental projections and that, in true reality, nothing is born.

One's power of meditation is developed from a pure mind. In the *Mahāyāna Vaipulya Sūtra of Total Retention* (Sūtra 15), the Buddha says, "For seven years in the distant past, day and night in the six periods, I repented of the grave sins I had committed with my body, voice, and mind. After being purified, it took me ten kalpas to acquire the Endurance in Dharmas." Indeed, purification through repentance provides a favorable condition for one's spiritual progress.

One of the favorite repentance prayers Chinese Buddhists recite in group practice is called the Precious Repentance Prayer to Medicine Buddha. The text in the Extension of the Chinese Canon (Shinsan Zokuzōkyō) includes a passage on meditation as a form of repentance. This Mahāyāna approach to vipaśyanā meditation is paraphrased below.

> With the mind of lovingkindness, compassion, sympathetic joy, and equability toward all sentient beings, mindfully observe that all dharmas, in true reality, are empty. This present mind arises as a false mind that presents its objects. Is it a causal mind, non-causal mind, both, or neither? Is it of the past, present, or future? Is it internal or external, or in-between? Does it have a trace or place? Active through various causes and conditions, the mind ultimately cannot be captured, like a dream or an illusion. The meditator sees the mind as neither saṁsāra nor nirvāṇa, and he finds neither the object of observation nor the observer. He neither accepts nor rejects anything, neither relies on nor is captivated by anything, nor is he lost in a blank state. When the way of words is interrupted, nothing can be expressed. Seeing that the mind is no mind, he knows that virtue and sin have no acquirer. As virtue and sin are empty, so too are all dharmas. This repentance is called the great repentance. (X74n1484, 0576b16–c3)

The text goes on to say that one should continue to observe the emptiness of one's mind in daily activities, whether walking or sitting, eating or excreting, seeing or hearing.

Meditation is Paths 7–8 of the Eightfold Right Path. The aim is to unfold one's wisdom (prajñā), which is the sixth of the ten pāramitās. One's spiritual journey is initiated and guided by the right views and culminates in enlightenment, the unsurpassed wisdom. Indeed, prajñā is the mother of all Buddhas.

Meditation on Amitābha Buddha

The possibility of seeing one's Buddha nature is available not just to Chan students using Chan methods under a Chan master who has seen his Buddha nature. In the *Śūraṅgama Sūtra,* fascicle 5, Mahāsthāmaprāpta (Great Might Arrived) Bodhisattva says, "If sentient beings' minds remember and think of Buddhas, in the present or a future life, they will definitely see Buddhas and will never be far from Buddhas" (T19n0945, 0128a29-b2). Therefore, thinking of a Buddha is an efficacious meditation through which one can see one's Buddha nature in due time. This teaching is followed by the Pure Land School, originated in China.

This school upholds the teachings in five sūtras and one treatise. For example, in the *Amitābha Sūtra,* the Buddha says, "Therefore, Śāriputra, if, among good men and good women, there are those who believe [my words], they should resolve to be reborn in that land" (T12n0366, 0348a16-17).

Taking the Buddha's instruction to heart, most devotees of this school, putting aside the possibility of seeing their Buddha nature, strive, as their immediate goal, to be reborn in Sukhāvatī, Amitābha Buddha's Land of Ultimate Bliss. In that splendid environment and in the excellent company of advanced Bodhisattvas, one will attain Buddhahood with Amitābha's training and support, bypassing the long Way to Buddhahood through one's cycle of birth and death in the Three Realms of Existence. However, one has the choice to return to this impure world any time for delivering sentient beings, if one feels compelled and able to do so.

The Pure Land School does not claim that rebirth in Amitābha Buddha's Pure Land can be achieved through faith only. There are three requirements: faith, resolve, and training. Their Meditation Door involves thinking of Amitābha Buddha by means of appearance, such as saying His name, visualizing His image and His land, and reciting His mantra (Mantra 5 or 6), or thinking of Him in the back of one's mind without appearance. Thinking of Amitābha Buddha is their way to practice śamatha; being vigilant in their thinking is their way to practice vipaśyanā.

Texts 1549-50 (X78n1549-50) in the Extension of the Chinese Canon document that many adherents of the Pure Land School, including most of its thirteen patriarchs and some of their disciples, had realized their true mind and seen their Buddha nature before abandoning their bodies for rebirth in the Pure Land. In the terminology of the Chan School, these two realizations are respectively labeled the first gate and the second gate. Therefore, passing these two gateless gates is not achieved exclusively by Chan Buddhists through the Chan Door. Constantly remembering and thinking of Amitābha Buddha is a great Dharma Door, through which one may achieve not only realization of the truth during one's life, as taught by Great Might Arrived Bodhisattva, but also rebirth in the Pure Land for advanced training toward Buddhahood—a double accomplishment.

Becoming a Novice Bodhisattva

The Three Refuges and the Five Precepts

One formally becomes a lay Buddhist after taking refuge in the Three Jewels: (1) the Buddha, the enlightened teacher; (2) the Dharma, His teachings; and (3) the Saṅgha, the Buddhist community comprising monks, nuns, laymen, and laywomen. A lay Buddhist also accepts the five precepts, which prohibit (1) killing, (2) stealing, (3) sexual misconduct, (4) lying, and (5) drinking alcohol. The first four precepts prohibit committing the four root sins, and the fifth precept is a preventive precept, which helps one to observe the first four precepts.

Accepting the Bodhisattva Precepts

When Chinese Buddhist monks and nuns are ordained, they accept not only their monastic precepts but also the Bodhisattva precepts in the *Brahma Net Sūtra* (T24n1484). While Chinese monks and nuns are vegetarians, lay Buddhists are only gently encouraged to be vegetarians. However, if they accept the Bodhisattva precepts, they will become vegetarians, as a practice of compassion. Those who accept the Bodhisattva precepts in the *Brahma Net Sūtra* also observe celibacy, even in married life. Husband and wife will live and train together as Dharma companions. Others who choose to accept the Bodhisattva precepts in the *Sūtra of the Upāsaka Precepts* (T24n1488) only need to observe the precept of no sexual misconduct.

However, acceptance of the Bodhisattva precepts is only as good as how well one observes them. Delivering a public talk on compassion, a speaker may move himself to tears, then, in the privacy of his dining room, comfort himself with a bloody beef steak. By contrast, suppose a person saves someone's life, or becomes a vegetarian, not for the benefit of his own health, but out of compassion and respect for all life forms. Such a person is considered a Bodhisattva regardless of his religion, because he will eventually walk the Bodhisattva Way toward Buddhahood.

The God Vehicle and the Human Vehicle

The Three-Thousand Large Thousandfold World is also called the Sahā (endurance) World because its inhabitants are able to endure their suffering and may even find their lives enjoyable. Understandably, ordinary beings may not be motivated to ride the three holy vehicles. Aside from nonbelievers, there are those who are pleased with their present lives and consciously or unconsciously wish to be reborn as humans again. Then there are those who aspire to be reborn as gods to enjoy the pleasures in heaven. In comparison with the four vehicles that take unfortunate life-journeys, both the God Vehicle and the Human Vehicle take fortunate life-journeys and well deserve one's consideration.

The God Vehicle

One who aspires to ride the God Vehicle in one's next life should do the ten good karmas. In addition to observing the first four of the five precepts, one should avoid (5) divisive speech, (6) abusive speech, (7) suggestive speech, (8) greed, (9) anger, and (10) delusion (the wrong views). A celestial life is a pleasurable long vacation financed by one's merit in previous lives. When that merit is spent, one can see with one's god-eye the next life form one will assume. It will be extremely painful when one sees that it will be an unfortunate one.

The Human Vehicle

According to Buddhist doctrine, the population of those in evil life forms is as massive as the dirt on Earth, whereas the population of humans is like the dirt under a finger nail. It is a rare privilege and fortune to live a human life no matter how hard it may be, and one should by all means avoid rebirth in one of the four evil life forms. To prepare the Human Vehicle for one's next life, one should observe the five precepts, whether or not one is a Buddhist.

The Buddhist view of life is far from the existentialist view of an absurd, meaningless human life in a *concrete* human world. While existentialism claims that suicide is the way to end one's agony and distress, Buddhist doctrine prohibits the killing of sentient beings, including oneself. Taking one's own life as if it were the owner's right is the wrong view and action because there is neither a self nor an owner, only a living sentient being. Furthermore, in each life one has karmic debts to repay, merits to earn, and lessons to learn. Suicide merely postpones one's present agenda, and its severe karmic consequence worsens one's tribulations in one's next life or lives.

As one gratifies one's desires for the five sense objects, it would be advisable to loosen one's hold of deep-seated wrong views and heed the Buddha's teachings. A worthy reminder is given in the last four verses in the *Diamond Sūtra* (T08n0235, 0752b28–29):

> All saṁskṛta dharmas are
> Like dreams, illusions, bubbles, and reflections,
> Like dew, also like lightning.
> Regard them as such.

As long as one lingers in one's cycle of birth and death, it would be wise to view the adversities of life through the perspective of one's karmic requital and to stop blaming others. Because dharmas are empty, with the right views, through causes and conditions, one can take the right actions to change one's karmic situations for the better.

Therefore, it would be sensible to do one's best for oneself and others in one's saṁsāric dream. A simple down-to-earth instruction given by the Buddha is found in the *Dharmapada Sūtra* (T04n0210, 0567b1–2), fascicle 2:

Never do any evil.
Do all that is good.
Purify your mind.
These are taught by Buddhas.

PART I

Mahāyāna Sūtras Selected from Six Sections of the Chinese Canon

From the Esoteric Teachings Section

1 Sūtra of the Buddha-Crown Superb Victory Dhāraṇī

Texts 967–71 (T19n0967–71) are five Chinese versions of this sūtra, each translated from a different Sanskrit text. Two of them were translated by Divākara (地婆訶羅, 613–87). Sūtra 1 is an English translation of text 970, Divākara's second translation, in which the Buddha tells a past life of the god-son Well Established (Supratiṣṭhita), the principal character. He also explains which of the god-son's past karmas had led to the pleasant requitals and which ones were about to result in painful requitals. Text 967, the version translated by Buddhapāla (佛陀波利, dates unknown), includes a story written by a monk named Zhijing (志靜), which tells why Buddhapāla took this sūtra to China. For the reader's interest, this story (T19n0967, 0349b4–c19) is also translated into English to serve as a foreword to Sūtra 1. The Buddha usually gives several names for a sūtra and, for brevity, the shorter name of the sūtra in text 967 is adopted.

One can learn from the story of the god-son, whose good karmas and bad karmas done with his body, voice, and mind do not offset or mitigate each other. As one transmigrates in one's cycle of birth and death, each action taken becomes a karmic seed in one's mind, which will ripen into a corresponding requital in due time and under due conditions. Fortunately, one can help oneself by providing good conditions to mitigate or avert a dreadful requital before its fruition. The best condition one can use against any dreadful requital is sincere repentance. Moreover, in this sūtra, the Buddha imparts a special mantra as a skillful means to purify the karmic seeds in one's mind. One can also recite this mantra to rescue others who are in the midst of their suffering.

This special mantra is the Buddha-Crown Superb Victory Dhāraṇī (Uṣṇīṣa vijaya dhāraṇī). In 776, the eleventh year of the Dali (大曆) years of the Tang Dynasty, Emperor Daizong (唐代宗) decreed that all Buddhist monks and nuns in China should learn this mantra in a month's time, and that they should recite it twenty-one times every day and report their compliance to the Imperial Court on the lunar New Year's Day each year. In the fourth month of 860, Heavenly Emperor Qinghe (清河天皇) of Japan also decreed that recitation of this mantra twenty-one times a day should be a mandatory practice of the monastic community. This mantra has been widely recognized and recited in China, Japan, and Tibet, and stories of its power have been documented. Timeless in its power, recitation of this mantra is especially appropriate and needed in the present age of greed, anger, and delusion.

2 Buddha Pronounces the Sūtra of the Great Cundī Dhāraṇī

Texts 1075–77 (T21n1075–77) are three Chinese versions of this sūtra, each translated from a different Sanskrit text. They all include the same mantra, the heart of Cundī Bodhisattva, who is hailed mother of seven koṭi Buddhas. Sūtra 2 is an English translation of text 1077, which is the shortest of the three texts, and it was translated into Chinese by Divākara.

Cundī Bodhisattva is one of the six special forms of Avalokiteśvara Bodhisattva (Guanyin in Chinese), who is forever active in delivering sentient beings that transmigrate through the six life-journeys. Cundī is portrayed in female form with three eyes and eighteen arms, adorned with a white conch shell on her wrist.

In this sūtra the Buddha teaches that one should recite the Cundī Mantra thousands or tens of thousands of times as a form of meditation, to purify one's evil karma and remove karma hindrances. The Cundī Mantra is one of the ten short mantras that Chinese Buddhists recite in their morning recitation practice.

Text 1076, translated into Chinese by Amoghavajra (不空金剛, 705–74), includes a ritualistic practice for using the Cundī Mantra. In this text, the Buddha reveals the absolute truth as He explains the meaning of the name Cundī. He states that *cun* means the unsurpassed enlightenment; *di* means that all things are illusions, irrelevant to being accepted or rejected; *Cundī* means the inherent purity of the nature of one's true mind.

Text 1076 also gives the meanings of the syllables of this mantra, which are translated into English for one's meditation.

> *Oṁ*, signifying the three bodies of a Buddha, means that dharmas have never been born.
> *Ca* means that dharmas are never born, nor do they die.
> *Le* means that the appearances of dharmas cannot be captured.
> *Cu* means that dharmas neither have been born nor have they died.
> *Le* means that dharmas have no defilements.
> *Cun* means that dharmas are in the unsurpassed enlightenment state.
> *Di* means that dharmas can be neither accepted nor rejected.
> *Svā* means that dharmas are equal and free from concepts.
> *Hā* means that dharmas [in true suchness] have no causations.
>
> Because dharmas have never been born, they neither arise nor perish.
> Because dharmas neither arise nor perish, their appearances cannot be captured.
> Because their appearances cannot be captured, dharmas must have neither arisen nor perished.
> Because dharmas have neither arisen nor perished, they have no defilements.
> Because there are no defilements, one attains the unsurpassed enlightenment.
> Because one has attained the unsurpassed enlightenment, one does not accept or reject anything.
> Because one neither accepts nor rejects anything, one attains equality, free from concepts.
> Because there is equality, free from concepts, one understands that [in true suchness] there are neither causes nor effects.

In accord with the wisdom that there is nothing to attain, one penetrates the ultimate reality and verifies the true suchness of the dharma realm. With this understanding, recite the mantra with meditative concentration, holding the root mudrā.

3 Sūtra of the Whole-Body Relic Treasure Chest Seal Dhāraṇī

Texts 1022A, 1022B, and 1023 (T19n1022A–23) are three Chinese versions of this sūtra, each translated from a different Sanskrit text. Text 1023 was translated by Dānapāla (施護, dates unknown) from Udyāna in northern India, who went to China in 980, during the Northern Song Dynasty. Both texts 1022A and 1022B were translated by Amoghavajra (不空金剛, 705–74). Sūtra 3 is based on text 1022B, the longest of the three texts.

In this sūtra the Buddha visits a ruined pagoda, which contains the whole-body relics of innumerable Tathāgatas and even the store of 84,000 Dharmas. The Buddha weeps because sentient beings, blinded and obstructed by their delusion, leave this treasure pagoda buried. He weeps because this treasure pagoda is none other than the Tathāgata store, one's Buddha mind. With great compassion, the Buddha imparts a mantra as a skillful means to remove one's karma hindrances and to unearth the treasure pagoda, one's Buddha mind. If one says one's ancestor's name then recites this spiritual mantra, upon completion of only seven repetitions, one's ancestor in hell will quickly be reborn in a lotus flower in the Pure Land of Ultimate Bliss.

4 Buddha Pronounces the Mahāyāna Sūtra of the Dhāraṇī of Infinite-Life Resolute Radiance King Tathāgata

Texts 936–37 (T19n0936–37) are two Chinese versions of this sūtra, each translated from a different Sanskrit text. Sūtra 4 is based on text 937, the longer version, which was translated into Chinese by Fatian (法天, ?–1001). In this sūtra the Buddha imparts the mantra of Infinite-Life Resolute Radiance King Tathāgata, who resides in His Pure Land. This mantra is one of the ten short mantras that Chinese Buddhists recite in their morning recitation practice.

The Sanskrit text of this mantra is copied from the website of the Digital Sanskrit Buddhist Canon, posted by the University of the West, Rosemead, California. It includes a few phrases not in the Chinese text. However, these phrases, enclosed in brackets, are needed because the Buddha says that this mantra comprises 108 syllables.

The Buddha says that recitation of this mantra and this sūtra can lengthen one's lifespan and support one's eventual attainment of Buddhahood. A lengthened lifespan may sound especially attractive to humans. However, even a 100-year human life must end. A more significant benefit of one's practice is being reborn in that Tathāgata's Pure Land, which is comparable to Amitābha Buddha's Pure Land of Ultimate Bliss.

The set of verses at the end of this sūtra praises one's practice of the six pāramitās, which can deliver one to the shore of enlightenment, opposite this shore of birth and death. The Buddha teaches that when one practices in the fine chamber of great compassion, one will quickly attain Buddhahood though one has not yet achieved the six pāramitās. In the *Lotus Sūtra,* fascicle 4, chapter 10, this chamber is called the Tathāgata's chamber, and it is none other than one's own mind of great compassion (T09n0262, 0031c21–28). Therefore, the right path to Buddhahood is one's compassion for all sentient beings, which is the ground of the six pāramitās.

Foreword to Sūtra 1: The Story of Buddhapāla

Written by Zhijing, Head Monk of the Dingjue Temple

The advent of this *Sūtra of the Buddha-Crown Superb Victory Dhāraṇī* (Uṣṇīṣa-vijaya-dhāraṇī-sūtra) is credited to the Brahmin monk Buddhapāla, who came from India to China in 676, the first year of the Yifeng (儀鳳) years of the Tang Dynasty. He came to Wutaishan (五臺山), the Wutai (five-platform) Mountain, and prostrated himself on the ground, paying homage to the mountain. He said, "Since the Buddha's parinirvāṇa, holy beings have been hidden from view, except for the great one Mañjuśrī, who remains in this mountain to draw in sentient beings and to teach Bodhisattvas. I lament that I was born in this age of the eight difficulties and that I am unable to see your holy visage. Having trudged across rugged territories from afar, I have come with the purpose of paying homage to you. I humbly beg for your response of great lovingkindness and compassion. Please let me see your dignified appearance."

Having spoken these words, Buddhapāla wept tears of sorrow as he made obeisance to the mountain. When he raised his head after bowing, he suddenly saw an old man coming out of the mountain. The old man spoke to Buddhapāla in the Brahmin language: "Dharma Master, with earnest aspirations for the Way, you have followed the tracks of the holy beings. Without any fear of arduous toil, you have traveled far in quest of their traces. However, many sentient beings in China have done sinful karma. Even many of those who have renounced family life have violated their monastic precepts. Only the *Sūtra of the Buddha-Crown Superb Victory Dhāraṇī* can obliterate all the evil karma of sentient beings. I don't know whether or not you have brought this sūtra with you."

"This poor monk has simply come to pay homage and did not bring this sūtra," Buddhapāla replied.

The old man said, "Without bringing the sūtra, what can you benefit from this futile visit? Even if you saw Mañjuśrī, how would you recognize him? You should go to the Western Nation to acquire the sūtra and let it circulate in China. To requite the kindness of all Buddhas in this way is to make offerings to all holy ones, benefit all sentient beings, and rescue all those in the underworld. Dharma Master, once you bring the sūtra here, I, the disciple, will certainly show you the whereabouts of Mañjuśrī Bodhisattva."

Upon hearing these words, Buddhapāla was so joyful that he held back his tears of sorrow and bowed to the old man. When he raised his head, to his amazement, the old man had vanished.

Even more devout than before, Buddhapāla kept his mission in mind with total dedication, and he hastened to return to India for the sūtra. In 683, the second year of the Yongchun (永淳) years, he brought the sūtra to Chang-an (長安), China's western capital, and reported what he had encountered to Emperor

Gaozong (唐高宗). The Emperor took the sūtra and kept it in the palace. He then commissioned the Indian Tripiṭaka master Rizhao (日照, Divākara), Du Xinyi (杜行顗), and those who were chosen by the guest-welcoming representative of the Sibin Temple (司賓寺), to translate this sūtra into Chinese. The Emperor bestowed upon Buddhapāla thirty bolts of silk fabric but forbade the sūtra to be taken out of the palace.

Shedding tears of sorrow, Buddhapāla entreated the Emperor, "This poor monk has been entrusted to bring this sūtra from afar even at the risk of his life. Without any thought of wealth or concern for fame, I earnestly hope to help all sentient beings and to rescue them from suffering and tribulations. Your Majesty, please allow this sūtra to circulate everywhere so that all sentient beings will equally benefit."

Hence the Emperor kept only the translation of the sūtra in the palace and returned the original Sanskrit text to Buddhapāla, who then went to the Ximing Temple (西明寺). There he found a Chinese monk named Shunzhen (順貞), who was proficient in Sanskrit. Buddhapāla requested permission for him and Shunzhen to translate the sūtra, and the Emperor granted his wish. Buddhapāla completed the translation with Shunzhen in the presence of other eminent monks. He then took the Sanskrit text and went to the Wutai Mountain. He was never seen again.

Therefore, there are two translations of the sūtra, both circulating in China. It should not be surprising that there are minor differences in these two translations.

In 687, the third year of the Chuigong (垂拱) years, I, Zhijing (志靜), head monk of the Dingjue Temple (定覺寺), happened to stay at the Weiguodong Temple (魏國東寺) in the capital city of Luoyang (洛陽). I saw the Tripiṭaka Dharma master Rizhao (Divākara) and asked him about Buddhapāla's visit. The story told by Master Rizhao is exactly [retold by me] as above. Then I requested Master Rizhao to teach me this spiritual mantra. For fourteen days, he pronounced the Sanskrit words and instructed me phrase by phrase until I learned all the Sanskrit pronunciations without making any mistakes. Furthermore, he proofread the old translation of the Sanskrit text and corrected the errors and omissions. This edited mantra bears a note up front, designating it as the latest different translation. The mantra words are somewhat different from Du Xinyi's translation because this newly revised mantra is based on Master Rizhao's phonetic translation. Future students will be fortunate to know this.

In the eighth month of 689, the first year of the Yongchang (永昌) years, I met in the Dajing-ai Temple (大敬愛寺) the senior Dharma master Cheng (澄) of the Ximing Temple. I also asked him about Buddhapāla's visit because the monk Shunzhen, who had translated the sūtra with Buddhapāla, was then still residing at the Ximing Temple. Master Cheng confirmed the story that I have stated above.

This most dignified and most victorious sūtra can rescue and deliver all sentient beings in this world or in the underworld. Its spiritual power is totally inconceivable. Because some students may not know this, the details about the arrival of the sūtra are recorded here for their interest.

1 最勝佛頂陀羅尼淨除業障咒經
Sūtra of the Buddha-Crown Superb Victory Dhāraṇī

Translated from Sanskrit into Chinese in the Tang Dynasty
by
The Tripiṭaka Master Divākara from India

Thus I have heard:

At one time the Bhagavān was staying in the Anāthapiṇḍika Garden of Jetavana Park in the city kingdom of Śrāvastī, together with 8,000 great bhikṣus. As recognized by the multitudes, all of them were venerable voice-hearers, or great Arhats. At the head of this group were great voice-hearers, such as the venerable Śāriputra, Mahāmaudgalyāyana, Mahākāśyapa, Aniruddha, and others. Also present was an innumerable multitude of Bodhisattva-Mahāsattvas, adorned with immeasurable virtues, all standing on the Ground of No Regress. Among them were Avalokiteśvara Bodhisattva, Mañjuśrī Bodhisattva, Great Might Arrived Bodhisattva, Maitreya Bodhisattva, Sublime Lotus Store Bodhisattva, Annihilating All Hindrance Bodhisattva, and Samantabhadra Bodhisattva. Bodhisattva-Mahāsattvas such as these, seated with the multitude in the assembly, were at the head of 32,000 Bodhisattva-Mahāsattvas. At the head of the Brahma group were god-kings from Brahma Multitude Heaven, Great Brahma Heaven, and Sudarśana Heaven, and at the head of 12,000 gods was the god-king Śakro-Devānām-Indra. Also seated in the assembly was an innumerable multitude of gods, dragons, yakṣas, gandharvas, asuras, garuḍas, kiṁnaras, mahoragas, kumbhāṇḍas, piśācas, humans, nonhumans, and others. At that time, surrounding the World-Honored One with reverence and gazing at Him with adoration, His four groups of disciples and others listened single-mindedly to the Dharma.

Meanwhile, the gods in Trayastriṁśa Heaven, or the Thirty-three Heavens, met in the Good Dharma Hall, and among them was a god-son named [Supratiṣṭhita] Well Established. Accompanied by goddess-daughters and attendants from the Great Jewel Palace, he frolicked indulgently with those surrounding him and amused himself with those goddess playmates. In the post-midnight period, he suddenly heard a voice in the sky pronouncing these words:

"God-Son Well Established, after seven days, you will die and fall to the southern continent, Jambudvīpa, to be reborn seven times as animals of different species, which eat filthy, impure food. Then you will fall into hell to undergo all kinds of suffering. Only after many kalpas will you become a human. Although you will have a human body, you will be born incomplete, eyeless, looking gross and ugly. Your breath will constantly be foul, and you will always lack food and clothing. You will be poor, sordid, and repulsive."

The god-son Well Established was terrified, and the hair on his entire body stood on end. Forthwith, he and his well-adorned palace attendants, carrying incense, flowers, and other objects of offering, went to the god-king Śakra. After kneeling and bowing down at the god-king's feet, he cried in sorrow and said to the god-king, "Please hear me. While I was making merry in the Good Dharma Hall with a multitude of gods and goddesses, I suddenly heard a voice in the sky calling my name. It said that my life would end after seven days, and that I would descend to Jambudvīpa to be reborn in animal form for seven lives, eating impure, filthy food. I would then enter into hell and suffer for many kalpas. Afterward, I would gain a human body without eyes. I would live in destitution with a gross, ugly appearance. My breath would be foul, and I would be poor and sordid, fettered by afflictions and detested by others. God-King, how would you save me from this fate?"

At that time the god-king Śakra was astonished to hear these words, and he pondered what merit had caused the god-son Well Established to be reborn in heaven, enjoying wonderful pleasures for many kalpas. He also pondered what evil karma would cause his celestial-life requital to end suddenly and cause him to be reborn in Jambudvīpa in animal form for seven lives, to enter into hell to undergo a great deal of suffering, and then to become a human without eyes, living under wretched conditions. After those thoughts, he thought about what animal forms Well Established would assume. Using his god-eye to scan these prospective requitals, Śakra saw in a momentary samādhi the seven animal forms that the god-son Well Established would assume. They would be pig, dog, jackal, monkey, python, raven, and vulture, all of which eat very foul, filthy things. What he had just seen aggravated his concern, making his heart ache with sorrow and anguish. Śakra then thought: "I have only seen a small part of his requitals. Matters responding to causes deep and far are beyond my ability to conjecture. Only the Tathāgata, the Ocean of True Omniscience, knows the good and evil causations such as these. I should go consult Him about this matter. The World-Honored One, out of His great lovingkindness, would tell us the reasons and even help Well Established to avoid such suffering."

Immediately, the god-king Śakra commanded his multitude of gods that each should have his palace attendants well adorned and carry offerings, such as garlands, necklaces, powdered incense, incense for burning, and various kinds of solid perfumes, as well as celestial garments hovering over all. Accompanied by his retinue, the god-king Śakra came swiftly to Jetavana Park. Upon arrival, he bowed down to the Buddha, circled Him clockwise seven times, and made his enormous offerings before the Buddha. Having completed such Dharma decorum, he stepped back to one side.

At the Buddha's holy command, he said, "World-Honored One, the god-son Well Established was enjoying himself frolicking with a multitude of gods and goddesses in the Good Dharma Hall when he suddenly heard a voice in the sky. It announced that after seven days the celestial life of the god-son Well Established would end, and that he would assume various animal forms, then enter into hell, and then become a human with incomplete faculties, undergoing a great deal of suffering. Having reported everything to Buddha, I pray only that the World-

Honored One, for the sake of His four groups of disciples and all of us, will explain the causes and conditions in the past lives of Well Established. What meritorious karma had he done, which has brought about his rebirth in heaven to enjoy pleasures for many kalpas? And through what causes and conditions would he fall after death to become those seven animals as stated before, eating filth as food; then to enter into hell to undergo suffering for many kalpas; and then to gain a human form, eyeless, dwarfish and sordid, gross and ugly, poor and filthy, entangled in evils, and despised by others? Also, what merit had he achieved, which moved the one who spoke in the sky, forewarning him of his future requitals? I pray only that the World-Honored One, out of sympathy for Well Established and all of us, will tell the origin of these causes, conditions, and deserved requitals. Please save him with lovingkindness and compassion and enable him to achieve liberation."

The World-Honored One told the god-king Śakra, "Good man, out of great lovingkindness, you are able to ask for Well Established's sake about matters related to the causes and conditions in his past, which would have resulted in good and evil requitals. You are also able to ask me to save him from future suffering. Very Good! Hugely Good! Hearken! Hearken! I will explain to you."

Then the World-Honored One emitted vast bright light from the crown of His head, illuminating all Buddha Lands in the ten directions. The light consisted of five colors—blue, red, yellow, white, and black—which reflected one another and circled clockwise. It returned to the Buddha, circled Him three times, and entered His mouth.

After drawing in the light, the Buddha smiled and told the god-king Śakra, "Hearken! Hearken! Innumerable asaṁkhyeya kalpas ago, there was a Buddha called Vipaśyin, the Tathāgata, Arhat, Samyak-Saṁbuddha, Knowledge and Action Perfected, Sugata, Understanding the World, Unsurpassed One, Tamer of Men, Teacher to Gods and Humans, Buddha the World-Honored One. After the conditions for Him to transform the world had ended, He entered parinirvāṇa. In the subsequent Dharma-likeness age, there was a city kingdom called Vārāṇasī, where a Brahmin had an only son born to him and died soon afterward. The son was raised only by his mother. As he was growing up, he worked in the fields planting crops, and his poor mother went about begging for food from place to place. When it was past mealtime and food did not arrive, hungry, thirsty, and angry with his mother, the son would speak malicious words, grumbling about why she had not yet brought him food that day. With annoyance and resentment, he would go on and on. One day, he spoke angry words about her: 'My mother is less than an animal. I have seen pigs, dogs, jackals, monkeys, ravens, vultures, and the like raising their young. Even an animal, raising and caring for its young, would not let them go hungry and thirsty or leave them alone even temporarily. Why does my mother not come to see me? I am so hungry and thirsty, but she does not bring me food.'

"While the son was harboring hatred, his mother had received food by begging, with which she immediately arrived. She comforted her son and made him happy. As they sat down to eat, they suddenly saw a Solitary Buddha, in the appearance of a monk, flying in the sky from the south to the north. When the son saw him, feelings of reverence arose in his heart. At once he stood up, joined his palms, and bowed his head, asking the monk to descend. The Pratyekabuddha accepted the invitation. Joyfully, the son prepared a white-grass seat, gathered beautiful flowers, and took a portion of his food. He offered these to the monk, who, after finishing eating, taught him the essentials of the Dharma, which brought him benefit and delight.

"Later on, the son was able to renounce family life, and was assigned to be the taskmaster in a temple. About that time, a Brahmin had living quarters built for the monks, and donors had offered a lot of butter and oil. It happened that some visiting monks were eating in the temple. The taskmaster, stingy and antagonistic, saw the visitors eating and regarded them as trouble. He did not give them butter, oil, or other food. One of the visiting monks asked, 'It is customary to give food to visiting monks. Why do you save it and not give it to us?' The ill-natured director exploded, shouting at the visiting monks: 'Why don't you eat feces and urine, instead of asking for butter? Your eyes are blind? Did you see me hide the butter?'"

The Buddha told the god-king Śakra, "The Brahmin's son of the past is the god-son Well Established now. Because he used angry words comparing his mother to animals, he has drawn an animal's body for himself for the next seven lives. Because he, as the taskmaster, spoke of eating filth, the karmic response is that he himself would eat filthy things. Because he was too stingy to offer food to those monks, he was bound to fall into hell to undergo suffering. Because he scolded the monks as being blind, he would receive the requital of having no eyes for seven hundred lives, staying in darkness for a long time, undergoing tremendous misery. God-King, such sinful karmas never fail to bring corresponding requitals.

"Moreover, God-King, the god-son Well Established has been reborn in heaven because he made offerings to a Pratyekabuddha in the past and, specifically, because of the karmic force generated from his having prepared a seat, respectfully offered flowers and food, and listened to the teachings. Therefore, he has received the heaven-fortune for several kalpas, continuously enjoying wonderful pleasures. Besides, he looked up in admiration at the Pratyekabudhha flying across the sky, and then sincerely bowed his head down, paying respects. In response to this merit, the divine voice in the sky declaring the god-son's future requitals was from his palace-guardian god."

Accepting what the Buddha had said, Well Established acknowledged that his karmas originated from past conditions. He severely reproached himself before the Buddha: "In the past, I had been angry with my mother and scolded the monks out of hatred and stinginess. Those karmas would bring me future horrendous requitals. Accepting His holy finding, I now repent with my life."

Well Established then threw himself to the ground. Blood all over his body, he stayed unconscious for a long time. When he gradually came to, overcome by anguish, he cried loudly, tears falling like rain.

The Buddha told Well Established and the god-king Śakra: "Of the ten evil karmas, abusive speech is the worst. Malicious scolding is stronger than a blazing fire. While a blazing fire can burn the wealth of the seven treasures, which are only worldly playthings, the flames of an abusive mouth can burn the wealth of the seven noble treasures. They can completely burn out all the merit needed for transcending the world, and can swiftly bring evil requitals. In your case, Well Established, your words of hate about your mother and abusive language to the monks have completely burned out your heaven-reward, sending you to hell.

"You should not insult god-kings, parents, or monks. Instead, you should respect, honor, and make offerings to them. You should praise them with gentle words and constantly remember their lovingkindness. Remember that lovingkindness in the Three Realms of Existence comes only from your parents. The fields, encountered in your past, present, and future lives, for planting seeds of fortune do not outweigh the monks as such. For example, making offerings to monks in the eight holy ranks, to the twelve sages, and to holy beings will never be in vain, because such merit can support you to transcend the world and, furthermore, to attain bodhi. How could you ever use abusive language to the monks?

"It is arduous toil for parents to bear and rear a child. It takes ten months of gestation and three years of nursing. As parents spend years of worries and hardships, rearing and educating their child, they hope that the child will develop outstanding abilities. They also hope that their child will renounce family life and transcend his cycle of birth and death. Their kind concern is too great to requite. Therefore, as I have told Ānanda, even if you carried your father on your left shoulder and your mother on your right to circle Mount Sumeru a billion times, shedding blood ankle deep, it would not be enough to requite their lovingkindness in nurturing you for one day. How could you ever think evil thoughts and speak angry words about them?"

The Buddha said to the god-king Śakra and the god-son Well Established: "Because you have seen me today, your five eyes are purified. Because your repentance is thorough, your sins have been expunged."

Looking at Well Established, the Buddha said, "You can stop crying now because I have a Dharma Door called the Superb Victory Buddha-Crown Dhāraṇī Mantra. Those who recite this mantra can be liberated from their suffering. Well Established, this Superb Victory Buddha-Crown Dhāraṇī Mantra of mine is pronounced by a billion koṭi Buddhas. This dhāraṇī, which I will soon pronounce, can be compared to all the Buddha-crowns and is most dignified and most victorious. It can annihilate all karma hindrances and bring purity; pull sentient beings out of their life-journeys in hell, as animals, and in King Yama's dominion; and eradicate the afflictions of birth and death for all sentient beings."

The Buddha then told the god-king, "If, among good men, good women, bhikṣus, and bhikṣuṇīs, there are those who can accept and uphold this pure Buddha-Crown Superb Victory Dhāraṇī Mantra, reading and reciting it, this merit can obliterate their ten evil karmas and their five rebellious acts done in a billion kalpas, and can prepare them to attain anuttara-samyak-saṁbodhi. They will have past-life knowledge without changing their present bodies, and they will be reborn in one Buddha Land after another. They will constantly encounter Bodhisattvas Samantabhadra, Mañjuśrī, Avalokiteśvara, and Great Might Arrived, who will rub their heads and proffer them a guiding hand, recognizing them as Bodhisattvas. They will constantly hear and uphold the true Dharma in a bodhimaṇḍa and acquire sarvajña. Their lifespan will be lengthened, and they will not die accidental deaths because their body, voice, and mind will be pure.

With their bodies pleasantly tingly, they will feel very clean, light, and tranquil anywhere and anytime. If they remember this dhāraṇī upon dying, they will be reborn in Buddha Lands."

When the god-king Śakra heard the Buddha praise the inconceivable virtue of this Superb Victory Dhāraṇī, he was filled with joyful appreciation and wholehearted longing. He said, "World-Honored One, I pray only that the Tathāgata, taking sympathetic consideration of Well Established and the rest of us as well as sentient beings in the expected Dharma-ending age, will pronounce this Superb Victory Buddha-Crown Dhāraṇī Mantra. I should train myself to have all sentient beings forever avoid the suffering of the eight difficulties."

Then the World-Honored One, for the sake of the god-king, the god-son Well Established, His four groups of disciples, and others, pronounced the mantra:

> namo bhagavate trai-lokya prativiśiṣṭāya buddhāya bhagavate | tad-yathā oṁ viśodhaya viśodhaya | asamasama samanta-avabhāsa spharaṇa gati gahana svabhāva viśuddhe | abhiṣiñcatu māṁ | sugata vara vacana | amṛta-abhi***ṣeke*** mahāmantra ***pāne*** | āhara āhara āyuḥ sandhāraṇi | śodhaya śodhaya gagana viśuddhe | uṣṇīṣa vijaya viśuddhe | sahasra-raśmi saṁcodite | sarva tathāgata-avaloka***na*** ṣaṭ-pāramitā paripūraṇi | sarva tathāgata hṛdaya-adhiṣṭhāna-adhiṣṭhita mahāmudre | vajra-kāya saṁha***ra***ṇa viśuddhe | sarva-āvaraṇa-apāya-durgati pari-viśuddhe | prati-nivartaya-āyuḥ śuddhe | samaya-adhiṣṭhite maṇi maṇi mahāmaṇi | ta***thātā*** bhūta koṭi pariśuddhe | visphuṭa buddhi śuddhe | jaya jaya vijaya vijaya smara smara | sarva buddha-adhiṣṭhita śuddhe | vajre vajra-garbhe vajraṁ bhavatu mama śarīraṁ | sarva sattvānāṁ ca kāya pari-viśuddhe | sarva gati pariśuddhe | sarva tathāgatāśca me sama-āśvāsayantu | sarva tathāgata sama-āśvāsa-adhiṣṭhite | budhya budhya vibudhya vibudhya | bodhaya bodhaya vibodhaya vibodhaya | samanta pariśuddhe | sarva tathāgata hṛdaya-adhiṣṭhāna-adhiṣṭhita mahāmudre svāhā ||

The Buddha said to the god-king, "This Purifying Life-Journey Superb Victory Buddha-Crown Dhāraṇī Mantra of mine can annihilate the hindrances caused by sinful karma and end the suffering of the three evil life-paths. This dhāraṇī mantra is pronounced by all Buddhas, as numerous as the sands of eighty-eight koṭi Ganges Rivers. They all remember, safeguard, delight in, and praise it. It bears the seal of sanctification of all Tathāgatas because it can expunge for all sentient beings their sins of the ten evil karmas, and can rescue those that are taking life-journeys in hell, as animals, as hungry ghosts, and in King Yama's dominion. Suppose the meritorious karma of all sentient beings is diminishing, and some of them should receive the requital of a short lifespan or of being handicapped, sickly, ugly, dwarfish, destitute, blind, deaf, or mute, or should fall into hell or assume animal form to undergo suffering. If they hear me speak the name of this dhāraṇī, their evil requitals will be revoked and they will be liberated. Even sentient beings that have accumulated evil karmas, including the ten evil karmas and the five rebellious acts, will benefit. All their hindrances caused by sin, whether severe or slight, will be annihilated. They will eventually attain anuttara-samyak-saṁbodhi, forever leaving behind all suffering, forever free from King Yama's dominion and from taking life-journeys as animals or even asuras, yakṣas, rakṣasas, pūtanas, kaṭa-pūtanas, apasamāras, and the like."

The Buddha said to the god-king, "If there are those who can accept and recite this mantra, once they have kept reciting it, they will be forever free from the evil life-journeys and will always be with Buddhas [in worlds] in the ten directions. They will be reborn in the excellent company of Bodhisattvas, or they will be reborn into the noble Brahmin caste. They will always be in the bodhimaṇḍas of Buddhas' Pure Lands, and they will even attain the unsurpassed bodhi and achieve the liberation body in the ocean of Tathāgata-Saṁbuddhas."

The Buddha said to the god-king and the god-son Well Established: "This Purifying Life-journey Superb Victory Dhāraṇī Mantra of mine has vast spiritual power, great virtue, and awesome might. It is like the auspicious sun and like a precious jewel. It is pure and immaculate like the sky. From its site, it illuminates the world, like the superb seven treasures of the world. Among all sentient beings, including kings, queens, princes, prime ministers, and state officials, whoever has seen it will treasure it and never tire of seeing it because this wonderful jewel is never tainted by filth. God-King, this dhāraṇī is like the jewel I just described. Whoever accepts and upholds, reads and recites, or copies this dhāraṇī, or makes offerings to it, the eight classes of Dharma protectors, such as gods and dragons, will treasure his merit as they do that wonderful jewel, which they would not want to part with even temporarily. Why? Because the power of this dhāraṇī can expunge the grave sins of all hell-dwellers, animals, and hungry ghosts! Furthermore, its power will enable its upholder to attain anuttara-samyak-saṁbodhi."

The Buddha told the god-king and the god-son Well Established: "Suppose, among kings, queens, crown-princes, princes, prime ministers, state officials, bhikṣus, bhikṣuṇīs, good men, and good women, there are those who, as an offering, copy this dhāraṇī mantra and enshrine the copy, whether in a pagoda made of the seven treasures, on a jeweled lion-throne, on a vajra pedestal, in a pagoda containing holy relics, or on the top of a cylindrical banner. Then suppose, among sentient beings born through the four modes of birth, bhikṣus, bhikṣuṇīs, upāsakas, and upāsikās, there are those who have committed grave sins, such as the ten evil karmas, the five rebellious acts, or violations of the four grave prohibitions, and therefore should be reborn in King Yama's dominion or even journey the six life-paths, suffering along the way. Should these sinners walk by the pagoda containing this dhāraṇī and should the dust of the pagoda fall on them, their sins would all be expunged. Even if the wind sweeps across the pagoda then blows a little on them, they will be reborn in heaven to enjoy splendid pleasures or reborn in a Pure Land according to their wishes. Should a person who upholds this dhāraṇī wash his hands and drip water from his hands to the ground, even ants and insects touched by the water would be reborn in heaven. Therefore if, among bhikṣus, bhikṣuṇīs, upāsakas, upāsikās, men, and women, there are those who can observe their precepts day and night in the six periods and keep reciting this dhāraṇī without interruption, their grave sins in the past and present, such as the five rebellious acts, violations of the four grave prohibitions, and the ten evil karmas, will all be expunged. Moreover, Bodhisattvas and Tathāgatas will rub their heads, recognizing them as

Bodhisattvas, and say to them, 'Good men, because you can accept and uphold the Superb Victory Buddha-Crown Dhāraṇī Mantra, you will certainly attain anuttara-samyak-saṁbodhi in a future life.'"

The Buddha said to the god-king, "If someone can at crossroads build a treasure pagoda or erect a high cylindrical banner to enshrine this dhāraṇī sūtra, and can make offerings of flowers, incense, necklaces, adornments made of the seven treasures, wonderful garments, food and drink, and medicinal potion, his merit will be immeasurable and boundless, and his fortune and wisdom incalculable. This person is truly a Bodhisattva-Mahāsattva and a Buddha-son. Why? Because he is saving and benefiting innumerable sentient beings that pass by under the pagoda."

In the post-midnight period, Yama, king of the underworld, accompanied by his retinue in the billions of koṭis, carrying flowers, incense, and various kinds of adornments, came to the Buddha to make offerings. He circled the Buddha clockwise seven times, bowed down at the Buddha's feet, and offered Him flowers, incense, and other things. He said, "World-Honored One, I have heard that the World-Honored One is pronouncing the Superb Victory Buddha-Crown Dhāraṇī Mantra. Therefore, I now have come to hear, accept, and follow His oral teachings, and to safeguard them."

At the same time, the four god-kings, who protect the world, the god-king Śakro-Devānām-Indra of Trayastriṁśa Heaven, and the god-kings of Suyāma Heaven, Saṁtuṣita Heaven, Sunirmita Heaven, Vaśavartti Heaven, Brahma Heaven, Great Brahma Heaven, and other heavens, accompanied by their retinues, carrying incense, flowers, and necklaces, came to the Buddha to make offerings. They circled the Buddha clockwise seven times and said, "We pray only that the World-Honored One will pronounce the Dharma procedure for upholding this Superb Victory Buddha-Crown Dhāraṇī Mantra, so that we can know how to perform the rite of offering."

The Buddha said to the world protectors, the great Brahma-kings, King Yama, and others: "Hearken! Hearken! I speak at your request. If there is a suffering sentient being with grave sins and with no one to rescue him, he should, on the fifteenth day of a waxing moon, bathe, wear clean clothes, and accept the eight precepts. He should mindfully kneel on his right knee, facing the image of an enlightened being, and recite this mantra 1,080 times. Then all his sins and karma hindrances will be removed. He will be able to retain all the meanings of this Dhāraṇī Door and to command unimpeded eloquence, and he will be purified and liberated."

The Buddha told the god-kings, "If a person hears this dhāraṇī, though he himself does not recite it, the sound, once it enters the ear, can condition his ālaya consciousness and become the Buddha seed. As an analogy, when a small adamantine substance falls to the ground, it can penetrate deep into the earth. Unobstructed by the thickness of the earth, it will reach the core and stay there. In the same way, the sound of this mantra, once heard, can condition the person's habitual nature into a resolve to attain the perfect enlightenment, unhindered by his afflictions, however severe they may be. Even if he becomes a hell-dweller, an animal, or a hungry ghost, he will not be stopped by his karmic requitals. By the power of this mantra, he will progress and eventually arrive at the Buddha Ground.

"God-Kings, once sentient beings born through the four modes of birth have heard this dhāraṇī, they will not have more troubles or repeat their old troubles in their present lives. Instead of assuming the form of an embryo again, they will be reborn with miraculously formed bodies in lotus flowers, and all shackles of their afflictions will be broken forever. Their five eyes becoming pure, they will have past-life knowledge and will eventually attain anuttara-samyak-saṁbodhi."

The Buddha said to the god-kings, "If a person recites this dhāraṇī mantra twenty-one times to a handful of yellow soil and scatters the soil on the remains of someone who is just deceased or has been deceased for a long time, the deceased will be reborn in any of the Pure Lands in the ten directions. If the consciousness of the deceased has already begun his life-journey in hell, as an animal, as a hungry ghost, or in King Yama's dominion, when the mantra soil touches the bones, he will be liberated and reborn in heaven, abandoning the evil life-journey.

"If a person expecting a short life desires longevity, on the fifteenth day of a waxing moon, he should bathe, wear clean clothes, observe the precepts single-mindedly, and recite this dhāraṇī mantra 1,080 times. This person expecting a short life will thus gain longevity, and all his karma hindrances will be annihilated.

"Moreover, if a person recites this dhāraṇī mantra only once into the ears of an animal, this animal, having heard this mantra once, will not assume animal form again after this life. Even if the animal is supposed to enter hell, it will be exempted.

"If a person who is suffering immensely from an evil disease hears only the sound of this dhāraṇī mantra, his hindrances caused by sin will be annihilated, and he will be able to leave his suffering behind. Even sentient beings born through the four modes of birth, having heard this mantra, will be freed from illness, suffering, and their modes of birth. Through miraculously formation, they will be reborn in lotus flowers, and they will know their past lives and not forget their birthplaces.

"If a person since birth has done any of the ten evil karmas, or committed any of the five rebellious sins or the four grave root-sins, he knows that, because of his evil karma, after death, he will fall into Avīci Hell to undergo dreadful suffering for many kalpas, and will repeatedly be reborn there, kalpa after kalpa, for thousands of kalpas. He also knows that if he goes down the life-path as an animal, he will repeatedly take that evil life-path without reprieve. On the fifteenth day of a waxing moon, before the image of an enlightened being, this person should place in the maṇḍala one liter of pure water in a gold or silver container, accept the Bodhisattva precepts, and observe the precept of not eating food after lunch. He should stay on the west side of the maṇḍala, facing the holy image on the east side. He should burn incense, do prostrations, and pray with utmost sincerity, mindfully kneeling on his right knee. He should recite this dhāraṇī mantra 1,080 times without interruption. Then he should sprinkle the water in all four directions, also up and down, praying that all sentient beings be purified. After he has performed this rite, his evil karma, which would cause him to fall into hell or become an animal or a hungry ghost, will be obliterated, and he will be liberated. King Yama's exoneration officer, not angered but respectful, will joyfully join his palms and praise this person's merit. After death, he will be reborn in a Buddha Land and, as he may wish, he can visit Pure Lands in the ten directions. In addition, on the fifteen day of a waxing moon, one may recite the mantra to pippala figs in butter-honey 1,080 times and let the sinner eat them. Having eaten, his sins of the ten evil karmas and the five rebellious acts will all be expunged. Furthermore, he will eventually attain anuttara-samyak-saṁbodhi.

"Those who desire to perform this maṇḍala rite should, on the fifteenth day of a waxing moon, mix perfumed water with yellow soil and cow dung and smear the ground with this mixture. The square maṇḍala measures four elbow lengths on each side, and it should be surrounded by three tiers of gemstones from the Laṅkā Mountain, which are in five colors. An ancillary tier of white Laṅkā gemstones marks the boundary on the four sides. Scatter flowers inside the maṇḍala and place four vessels of water on the lotus flowers painted in the four corners. The vessels should be the same in size. Reverently place a bottle of holy relics and cow's bezoar on the center lotus flower. In the maṇḍala, scatter various flowers and burn incense and various kinds of fragrances, such as camphor, saffron, agalloch, and so forth. Light various kinds of lamps, such as butter lamps, oil lamps, and scented lamps. As an offering in the maṇḍala, place grape and pomegranate juices and various kinds of food, such as rice, milk, cream, butter, oil, and cane sugar, in a container made of the seven treasures. Then the spiritual trainee should observe the Bodhisattva precepts to purify his conduct, and eat the three white foods as a meal. He should wear clean clothes and stay on the west side of the maṇḍala. After praying with his palms joined, kneeling on his right knee, he should first make the mudrā of Buddha protection then perform the Buddha-mind maṇḍala rite by reciting this Superb Victory Buddha-Crown Dhāraṇī Mantra 1,080 times. All his sins, such as the ten evil karmas, will thus be expunged, and he will eventually attain anuttara-samyak-saṁbodhi. Buddhas and Bodhisattvas will rub his head, personally bestowing upon him the prophecy of his attaining bodhi. If he wants to visit the abode of Bodhisattvas, they will take him to their own palaces, traveling to and fro among Buddha Lands in the ten directions."

Finally, The Buddha said to the god-kings, "Such is the Superb Victory Buddha-Crown Dhāraṇī Mantra! In the Dharma-ending age, if, among bhikṣus, bhikṣuṇīs, upāsakas, and upāsikās, or among kings, queens, queen-mothers, crown princes, princes, princes' wives, prime ministers, state officials, humans, and nonhumans, or even among sentient beings that understand the human language, there is someone who can perform this maṇḍala rite, he should smear the ground with a mixture of water or perfumed water, soil, and cow dung to purify the ground. When he adorns the maṇḍala with scattered flowers, burning incense, cylindrical banners, canopies, and lanterns, and makes an offering of various kinds of precious jewels, food, and drink, this is called dāna-pāramitā. When he maintains the maṇḍala without any resentment at disturbances, it is called kṣānti-pāramitā. When he performs this maṇḍala rite diligently and bravely without negligence or indolence, it is called vīrya-pāramitā. When he follows the rules single-mindedly without being distracted, it is called dhyāna-pāramitā. When he arranges things straight and proper, knowing the difference between right and wrong, it is called prajñā-pāramitā. God-Kings, if you follow my oral teachings to conduct Dharma affairs, you will naturally practice the six pāramitās. Therefore, you should in turn pronounce these teachings to all sentient beings to benefit them and enable them to attain bodhi."

After the Buddha finished expounding this sūtra, the god-king Śakra and the god-son Well Established returned to their own palaces. Well Established recited the mantra according to the instruction for seven consecutive days, then he saw that the requitals for his sins had all been revoked. Moreover, his celestial lifespan was lengthened immeasurably. Forthwith, he and the god-king Śakra, along with other gods, carrying incense, flowers, and various kinds of wonderful celestial garments and necklaces, came to make offerings. They bowed down to the Buddha in celebration of His great lovingkindness and compassion, and they joyfully and exuberantly circled Him thousands of times.

Then the World-Honored One opened His golden hand and rubbed the god-son's head, bestowing upon him the prophecy of his attaining bodhi. The Buddha said to him, "This sūtra is called *The Superb Victory Buddha-Crown Dhāraṇī Mantra That Annihilates Karma Hindrances*. All of you and my four groups of disciples should accept and uphold it."

The four groups of disciples, Bodhisattva-Mahāsattvas, and the eight classes of Dharma protectors—gods, dragons, gandharvas, asuras, yakṣas, garuḍas, kiṁnaras, and mahoragas—together with kumbhāṇḍas, piśācas, humans, nonhumans, and others, having heard the Buddha's words, greatly rejoiced. With faith, acceptance, and determination to carry out the teachings, they made obeisance and departed.

2 佛說七俱胝佛母心大准提陀羅尼經
Buddha Pronounces the Sūtra of the Great Cundī Dhāraṇī, the Heart of the Mother of Seven Koṭi Buddhas

Translated from Sanskrit into Chinese in the Tang Dynasty
by
The Tripiṭaka Master Divākara from India

At one time the Buddha was dwelling in the Anāthapiṇḍika Garden of Jetavana Park in the city kingdom of Śrāvastī. The World-Honored One meditated, observing sentient beings of the future. Feeling sympathy with them, He expounded the Dharma of the Cundī Dhāraṇī, the heart of the mother of seven koṭi Buddhas. The Buddha then pronounced the mantra:

> namaḥ saptānāṁ samyak-saṁbuddha koṭīnāṁ | tad-yathā oṁ cale cule cundi svāhā ||

"If, among bhikṣus, bhikṣuṇīs, upāsakas, and upāsikās, there are those who uphold this dhāraṇī and recite it 800,000 times, their sins, such as the five rebellious sins, accumulated over innumerable kalpas will all be expunged. They will be reborn at places where they will meet Buddhas and Bodhisattvas. They will have all the material goods they wish. They can choose to renounce family life in successive future lives, and they will be able to observe the pure Bodhisattva precepts completely. They will be reborn either in the human world or in heaven, having ended forever the evil life-journeys. They will always be protected by gods. If there are good laymen and laywomen who keep reciting this dhāraṇī, their homes will not be ravaged by catastrophes or diseases. Their work will be smooth and harmonious, and others will believe and accept what they say.

"If one has recited this dhāraṇī mantra 100,000 times, one will see in one's dreams Buddhas, Bodhisattvas, voice-hearers, or Pratyekabuddhas, and see oneself vomit black things. For graver sins, one should recite the mantra 200,000 times. Then one will also see in one's dreams Buddhas and Bodhisattvas as well as oneself vomit black things. If one is unable to get such good dreams because of having committed any of the five rebellious sins, one should further recite the mantra 700,000 times. Then one should have these good dreams and even see oneself vomit white things, such as creamy rice. These are signs of purification, indicating that this person's sins have been expunged.

"Next, I will now explain the procedure for using this great dhāraṇī. In front of a Buddha image or a pagoda, smear the ground of a clean area with cow dung, making a large or small square maṇḍala. According to your ability, decorate it with offerings of flowers, incense, banners, canopies, food, drink, lamps, and candles. To mark the boundary, recite the mantra to perfumed water in a vessel and sprinkle it in all four directions, also up and down. Then place a vessel of perfumed water in the center and in each of the four corners of the maṇḍala. You, the mantra reciter, staying inside the maṇḍala, should face east, kneel on your right knee, and recite the mantra 1,080 times. Afterward, the vessels of perfumed water should swivel by themselves. Next, hold a bunch of flowers in both hands, recite the mantra 1,080 times, and scatter them all on the face of a mirror. Looking straight into the mirror in front of you, recite the mantra 1,080 times. Then you should see images of Buddhas and Bodhisattvas in the mirror. Again, recite the mantra 1,080 times to another bunch of flowers and scatter them around as offerings to Buddhas and Bodhisattvas. Then you should receive answers to any questions you ask.

"To treat illness caused by a ghost, brush the patient with kuśa grass to which you have recited the mantra. Then he should be cured. For a child possessed by a ghost, have a young maiden twist five threads of different colors into a string. Recite the mantra once each time you tie a knot in the string as you tie twenty-one knots. Tie the knotted string around the neck of the child. Recite the mantra seven times to a few mustard seeds and sprinkle them at his face. Then the condition should be removed.

"Another dharma is to draw a picture of the patient on a piece of paper. Strike it in front of the patient with a willow branch to which you have recited the mantra. This should also remove the condition.

"Another dharma is for a possessed patient who lives far away. Recite the mantra seven times to a willow branch. Send the willow branch to someone to strike the picture of the patient in his presence. This should also remove the condition.

"Another dharma is to recite the mantra as you travel. Then you should be free from fear of bandits and ferocious animals.

"Another dharma is to keep reciting this mantra in order that you will win any disputes or lawsuits. In crossing a river or an ocean, continuous recitation of the mantra will keep you safe from aquatic animals.

"Another dharma is for a person who is in shackles or in prison. If he keeps reciting the mantra, he will be freed.

"Another dharma is for a country troubled by flood, drought, or ongoing epidemics. You should mix some butter, sesame seeds, and white rice. Take a pinch of the mixture with three fingers, recite the mantra once to it, and throw it in the fire. Repeat this procedure continuously day and night in the six periods for seven days and seven nights. All catastrophes or epidemics should thus be eliminated.

"Another dharma is to imprint with a stamp on riverbanks or sandy beaches the image of a pagoda. Recite the mantra 600,000 times, imprinting a pagoda each time. You will then see Avalokiteśvara Bodhisattva, Tara Bodhisattva, or Vajrapāṇi Bodhisattva. Any one of them can fulfill your wishes, give you divine medicine, or bestow upon you the prophecy of future enlightenment.

"Another dharma is to circle the picture of the bodhi tree clockwise as you recite the mantra 10,000,000 times. You should then have a vision of a [holy] Bodhisattva teaching you the Dharma, and you may choose to follow him.

"Another dharma is to recite the mantra as you beg for food. Then you will not be harmed or harassed by villains, vicious dogs, or the like.

"Another dharma is to recite the mantra 300,000 times in front of a pagoda, a Buddha image, or a pagoda containing holy relics. Furthermore, on the fifteenth day of a waxing moon, make a large offering and recite the mantra mindfully without eating food for one day and one night. You will even be able to see Vajrapāṇi Bodhisattva, and he can take you to his palace.

"Another dharma is to go to the pagoda where the Buddha first turned the Dharma wheel, the pagoda at the Buddha's birthplace, or the pagoda where the Buddha descended the jeweled steps from Trayastriṁśa Heaven, or a pagoda containing holy relics. If you recite the mantra as you circle the pagoda clockwise, then you should see Aparājitā Bodhisattva and Hāritī Bodhisattva. They can grant your wishes, give you divine medicine if you need it, and show you the Bodhisattva Way by teaching you the Dharma. Whoever recites this dhāraṇī, though he is not yet in a bodhimaṇḍa, will have all Bodhisattvas as his beneficent friends.

"Moreover, this Great Cundī Dhāraṇī, the great illumination mantra, was pronounced by all Buddhas of the past, will be pronounced by all Buddhas of the future, and is pronounced by all Buddhas of the present. I too now pronounce it for the benefit of all sentient beings, helping them to attain the unsurpassed bodhi. There are sentient beings with a meager store of merits, without roots of goodness, without the right capacity, and without the [Seven] Bodhi Factors. If they are so fortunate as to hear the Dharma of this Cundī Dhāraṇī, they will quickly attain anuttara-samyak-saṁbodhi. If a person always remembers to recite this mantra diligently, he will develop immeasurable roots of goodness."

As the Buddha was expounding this Dharma of the Great Cundī Dhāraṇī, innumerable sentient beings shunned dust and filth [their afflictions], and gained the virtue of the Great Cundī Dhāraṇī, the great illumination mantra. They were able to see Buddhas, Bodhisattvas, and other holy beings [in worlds] in the ten directions. [The listeners] made obeisance to the Buddha and departed.

3 一切如來心祕密全身舍利寶篋印陀羅尼經
Sūtra of the Whole-Body Relic Treasure Chest Seal Dhāraṇī, the Heart Secret of All Tathāgatas

Translated from Sanskrit into Chinese in the Tang Dynasty
by
The Tripiṭaka Master Amoghavajra from India

Thus I have heard:

At one time the Buddha was at the Jewel Brilliance Pond in the Immaculate Garden of the kingdom of Magadha. Surrounding Him were hundreds of thousands of Mahāsattvas, great voice-hearers, gods, dragons, yakṣas, gandharvas, asuras, garuḍas, kiṁnaras, mahoragas, human, nonhumans, and others. At that time, in the assembly was a great Brahmin named Immaculate Light, who was well educated and intelligent. People delighted in seeing him. Having taken refuge in the Three Jewels, he persistently did the ten good karmas. Benevolent, wealthy, and wise, he intended that other people acquire benefits, great fortune, and prosperity.

Immaculate Light rose from his seat, came to the Buddha, circled Him seven times, and offered the World-Honored One incense and flowers. He also covered the Buddha with priceless wonderful garments, necklaces, and tiaras of gems. After bowing down at the Buddha's feet, he stepped back to one side and said, "I pray that the World-Honored One and the huge assembly will come to my house tomorrow morning to accept my offerings."

The Buddha gave him permission in silence. Knowing that the Buddha had accepted his invitation, the Brahmin hurried home. In the evening, he ordered extensive preparation of food and drink of one hundred flavors for the banquet. Water was sprinkled, the halls were swept clean, and canopies and banners were set up.

In the next morning, carrying incense, flowers, and musical instruments, together with his retinue, the Brahmin came to the Buddha. He said, "The time has come, and I pray that the World-Honored One will grace my house."

The Buddha greeted the Brahmin Immaculate Light with kind words and made an announcement to the huge assembly: "All of you should go to this Brahmin's home to accept his offerings, for the purpose of letting him receive great benefits."

Then the World-Honored One rose from His seat. As the Buddha stood up, His body emitted all kinds of radiance with intermingled wonderful colors, illuminating and filling the space in the ten directions. Being thus alerted, all set off on the road. Respectfully escorting the Buddha, the Brahmin carried wonderful incense and flowers with a reverent heart. He led the way, along with his retinue, the Brahma-kings, the god-king Śakra, the four god-kings, and the eight classes of Dharma protectors, such as gods and dragons.

The World-Honored One, having traveled not too far on the road, came to a garden called Abundant Wealth. In that garden were the ruins of an ancient pagoda, dilapidated and collapsed. With the courtyard covered by thistles and the doors sealed by creeping weeds, the rubble resembled a mound of dirt. The Buddha went straight to the pagoda. Forthwith, the pagoda issued vast, bright light, illuminating and glowing. A voice from the heap of earth praised, "Very good! Very good! Śākyamuni, Your action today is excellent! And you, Brahmin, will receive great benefits today!"

The World-Honored One paid respects to the ruined pagoda by circling it clockwise three times. He took off His upper garment, placed it over the pagoda, and wept tears with blood. He then smiled. Meanwhile, all Buddhas [in worlds] in the ten directions, looking on together, also shed tears, each emitting light to illuminate this pagoda. The multitude was so astonished as to lose their color, and they all wanted to resolve their bewilderment.

Vajrapāṇi and other Bodhisattvas also shed tears. Twirling his vajra in glowing flames, he came to the Buddha. He asked, "World-Honored One, through what causes and conditions does this radiance manifest? Why did the Tathāgata's eyes shed these tears? And why do Buddhas [in worlds] in the ten directions emit vast auspicious light? I pray that the Tathāgata will resolve my bewilderment."

The World-Honored One replied to Vajrapāṇi, "This great treasure pagoda of accumulated whole-body relics of Tathāgatas contains innumerable koṭis of the heart dhāraṇīs, the secret seal of the essentials of the Dharma of all Tathāgatas. Vajrapāṇi, because of the essentials of the Dharma contained in it, the pagoda has become tiered seamlessly like sesame seeds. The bodies of 100,000 koṭi Tathāgatas are also like sesame seeds. Contained in the pagoda is the accumulation of the whole-body relics of 100,000 koṭi Tathāgatas and even the store of 84,000 Dharmas. Also contained in it are 99 billion koṭi Tathāgata-crowns. Because of these wondrous things, the site of this pagoda has superb, awesome virtue and serves as a spiritual testament. It can fill the entire world with auspicious events."

When the multitude heard the Buddha's words, they shunned dust and filth [their afflictions] and acquired the pure dharma-eye. Because the capacities of the multitude were so varied, each received a different benefit. Some became Pratyekabuddhas; some achieved voice-hearer fruits, becoming Srotāpannas, Sakṛdāgāmins, Anāgāmins, or Arhats. On the Bodhisattva Way, some achieved the level of avinivartanīya or acquired sarvajña; some attained the First Ground, Second Ground, or even the Tenth Ground; and some achieved the six pāramitās. The Brahmin shunned dust and filth [his afflictions], and acquired the five transcendental powers.

Witnessing these unprecedented occurrences, Vajrapāṇi exclaimed, "World-Honored One, how wonderful and how extraordinary! If people acquire such excellent merit by merely hearing about this matter, how much more merit will they acquire if they hear the profound truth and elicit their faith with an earnest mind?"

The Buddha replied, "Hearken, Vajrapāṇi. In future times, if, among male believers, female believers, and my four groups of disciples, there are those who are inspired to copy this sūtra, they in effect copy all the sūtras pronounced by 99 billion koṭi Tathāgatas. Their merit will surpass the roots of goodness they have been planting for a long time in the presence of 99 billion koṭi Tathāgatas. All Tathāgatas will support, protect, and remember them in the same way as they cherish their own eyes or as loving mothers care for their young children. If a person recites this short sūtra, he in effect recites all the sūtras pronounced by Buddhas of the past, present, and future. For this reason, 99 billion koṭi Tathāgatas, also called Arhats, Samyak-Saṁbuddhas, will come, jam-packed sideways without any gap between them, like sesame seeds in a pile. Day and night they will appear and support that person. Thus, all Buddha-Tathāgatas, who are as numerous as the sands of the Ganges, will come. The first group of them has not yet left, and the next has arrived. They all instantly move away and return again, like fine sands whirling in quick water. Incessantly, they come again as soon as they turn away. If a person makes offerings of incense, flowers, solid perfumes, garlands, garments, and wonderful ornaments to this sūtra, he in effect makes an entire offering, before 99 billion koṭi Tathāgatas [in worlds] in the ten directions, of divine incense, flowers, garments, and ornaments made of the seven treasures, all piled high like Mount Sumeru. Planting one's roots of goodness can be accomplished in the same way."

Having heard these words, the eight classes of Dharma protectors, such as gods and dragons, as well as humans, nonhumans, and others, filled with wonder, said to one another, "How marvelous is the awesome virtue of this old pile of earth! Its miraculous manifestation must have been caused by the spiritual power of the Tathāgata."

Vajrapāṇi next asked the Buddha, "World-Honored One, through what causes and conditions does this pagoda made of the seven treasures now manifest as a pile of dirt?"

The Buddha replied to Vajrapāṇi, "This is not a pile of dirt, but a wonderful, great treasure pagoda. It is hidden because of the inferiority of sentient beings' karmic fruits. Although the pagoda is hidden, the bodies of the Tathāgatas are indestructible. How could the vajra store of the bodies of the Tathāgatas be destroyed? After I have abandoned my body, the ending of the Dharma will be unrelenting in future times. Sentient beings that act against the Dharma are bound to fall into hell because they neither believe in the Three Jewels nor plant any roots of goodness. For this reason, the Buddha Dharma should be hidden. But this pagoda will still be solid and will not be demolished because it is supported by the spiritual power of all Tathāgatas. However, ignorant sentient beings, covered and obstructed by their delusion, not knowing how to unearth and use the treasure, simply leave it buried. For this reason, I now shed tears, and other Tathāgatas shed tears as well."

The Buddha then told Vajrapāṇi, "If a person copies this sūtra and enshrines the copy in a pagoda, this pagoda will become the stūpa of the vajra store of all Tathāgatas and the stūpa supported by the heart secret of the dhāraṇī of all Tathāgatas. It will become the stūpa of 99 billion koṭi Tathāgatas and the stūpa of the Buddha-crown and Buddha-eye of all Tathāgatas, and it will be protected by their spiritual power. If you enshrine this sūtra inside a Buddha statue in a stūpa, the statue will in effect be made of the seven treasures. This statue will be so efficacious and responsive that one's wishes will be fulfilled without exception.

"According to your ability, construct for a stūpa these things: canopies, nets, columns, dew-catching wheels, fine eaves, bells, foundations, or steps. Whether you use earth, wood, stones, or bricks, they will turn into the seven treasures because of the awesome power of this sūtra. Moreover, all Tathāgatas will increase the power of this sūtra. Keeping a sincere promise, they support it incessantly.

"If a sentient being makes obeisance and gives an offering of only a little incense and one flower to this pagoda, his grave sins, which would entail 80 koṭi kalpas of birth and death, will all be expunged at once. He will be free from catastrophes during his life and, after death, be reborn in a Buddha family. Even for a person who should fall into Avīci Hell, if he only makes one obeisance to the pagoda or circles it clockwise once, the door to hell will be blocked and the bodhi road will be opened.

"Furthermore, the place of the pagoda or of its image will be protected by the spiritual power of all Tathāgatas. The place will not be damaged by hurricanes and lightning bolts. It will be neither disturbed by venomous snakes, vipers, scorpion, or other poisonous insects, nor harmed by lions, rampaging elephants, tigers, wolves, jackals, or other animals. It will be free from the terror of yakṣas, rakṣasas, pūtanas, piśācas, spirits, monsters, and epilepsy. It will not be troubled by diseases, such as chills, fevers, skin ulcers, carbuncles, scabies, or psoriasis. One can avert all disasters by seeing the pagoda briefly. At the place of the pagoda, horses, six kinds of livestock, and people, including young boys and girls, will not be plagued by epidemics. They will not die unnatural, accidental deaths, nor be harmed by knives, clubs, flood, or fire. They will not be attacked by bandits or enemies, and they will have no worries about famine or poverty. They will not be subject to the power of sorcery or curses. The four great god-kings and their retinues will protect them day and night. In addition, the yakṣa generals of the twenty-eight brigades of spirits, the sun, the moon, the five planets, and cloudlike comets will protect them day and night. All dragon-kings will increase their vital energy and bring rainfall at the right time. All gods, including those in Trayastriṁśa Heaven, will descend during the three periods of the day to make offerings. All fairies will gather during the three periods to circle the pagoda, sing songs of praise, give thanks, and pay respects. The god-king Śakra and goddesses will descend during the three periods of the day to make offerings. The place will be remembered and supported by all Tathāgatas. Such will be the pagoda because it contains this sūtra.

"If people build a pagoda using earth, stone, wood, gold, silver, bronze, and lead, and if they copy this spiritual mantra and enshrine the copy in the pagoda, then as soon as it is enshrined, the pagoda will in effect be made of the seven treasures. The upper and lower steps, dew-catching wheels, canopies, bells, and columns will all be made of the seven treasures. Also, the four sides of the pagoda will have the images of Tathāgatas. Because of the essentials of the Dharma, all Tathāgatas will firmly protect and support the pagoda, staying in it day and night without departing. Because of the awesome power of the mantra, the pagoda made of the seven treasures, which contains the wonderful treasure of the whole-body relics, will soar up into the midst of the palaces in Akaniṣṭha Heaven. Wherever a pagoda stands like a mountain, all gods will view it with reverence, stand guard, and make offerings day and night."

Vajrapāṇi asked, "Through what causes and conditions has this Dharma such superb virtue?"

The Buddha replied, "Because of the spiritual power of this Treasure Chest Seal Dhāraṇī."

Vajrapāṇi said, "I pray that the Tathāgata, out of compassion for us all, will pronounce this dhāraṇī."

The Buddha responded, "Hearken, contemplate, and do not forget it! The radiance of the copies of the bodies of all Tathāgatas of the present and the whole-body relics of all Buddhas of the past are contained in this Treasure Chest Seal Dhāraṇī. The three bodies of every Tathāgata are also in it."

Then the Buddha pronounced the dhāraṇī:

> namas tryadhvikānāṁ sarva tathāgatānāṁ | oṁ bhuvi-bhavana-vare vaca*na*-vaca*ti* | suru suru dhara dhara | sarva tathāgata dhātu dhare padmaṁ bhavati | jaya vare mudre | smara tathāgata dharma-cakra pravartana vajre bodhimaṇḍa-alaṁkāra-alaṁkṛte | sarva tathāgata-adhiṣṭhite | bodhaya bodhaya bodhi bodhi budhya budhya | saṁbodhani saṁbodhaya | cala cala calantu sarva-āvaraṇāni | sarva pāpa vigate | huru huru sarva śoka vigate | sarva tathāgata hṛdaya vajriṇi | saṁbhāra saṁbhāra | sarva tathāgata guhya dhāraṇī mudre | bhūte subhūte | sarva tathāgata-adhiṣṭhita dhātu garbhe svāhā | samaya-adhiṣṭhite svāhā | sarva tathāgata hṛdaya dhātu mudre svāhā | supratiṣṭhita stūpe tathāgata-adhiṣṭhite huru huru hūṁ hūṁ svāhā | oṁ sarva tathāgatoṣṇīṣa dhātu mudrāṇi sarva tathāgata sadhātu vibhūṣita-adhiṣṭhite hūṁ hūṁ svāhā ||

After the Buddha finished reciting this spiritual mantra, all the Buddha-Tathāgatas in the pile of earth voiced their praises: "Very good! Very good! Śākya the World-Honored One, You have appeared in this turbid, evil world to expound the profound Dharma for the benefit of sentient beings that have nothing and nobody to depend upon. Therefore, the essentials of the Dharma will long remain in the world, bringing wide, abundant benefits and joyful peace."

Then the Buddha told Vajrapāṇi, "Hearken! Hearken! The essentials of this Dharma have inexhaustible spiritual power and boundless benefits! It is like a wish-fulfilling jewel atop a cylindrical banner, constantly raining down treasures and fulfilling all wishes. Next, I will briefly describe one ten-thousandth of these boundless benefits. You should remember and uphold it for benefiting all sentient beings.

"If an evil man after death falls into hell, he must suffer uninterruptedly, not knowing when release will come. However, if his descendants say his name and then recite this spiritual mantra, upon completion of only seven repetitions, the molten copper and burning iron in hell will suddenly change into pond water with the eight virtues. This man will have a lotus flower supporting his feet and a jeweled canopy over his head. The door of hell will break and the Bodhi Way will open. His lotus flower will fly him to the Land of Ultimate Bliss. There, his knowledge of all knowledge will spontaneously unfold. Delighting in expounding the Dharma endlessly, he will be ready to attain Buddhahood in his next life.

"Moreover, a person who, with a heavy heart, suffers from 100 diseases as requital for his grave sins should recite this spiritual mantra twenty-one times. Then 100 diseases and 10,000 distresses will be eliminated at once. His lifespan will be lengthened, and his fortune and merit will become immeasurable.

"Suppose a person has been born into a poor family because of his karma of greed and stinginess. His clothes cannot cover his body and his food cannot sustain his life. Emaciated and haggard, he is despicable to others. This person, ashamed of himself, goes to the mountain and plucks wild flowers not owned by anyone. He grates rotten wood for incense powder. Then he goes to the pagoda to make obeisance and offerings, circling it seven times, repenting in tears. Because of the power of this spiritual mantra and the awesome virtue of the pagoda, his poverty requital will end and fortune will suddenly arrive. The seven treasures will appear like abundant rain. However, at this time, he should give to the poor and needy, completely honoring the Buddha Dharma. If he is reluctant to give, his riches will suddenly vanish.

"Suppose a person, planting roots of goodness for himself, builds a pagoda at his pleasure, using earth or bricks that he can afford. The pagoda is as big as a mango, its height about four finger lengths. He copies this spiritual mantra and enshrines the copy in the pagoda. Then he makes obeisance and offers incense and flowers. Because of the power of the mantra and his faithful heart, vast, fragrant clouds will come out of the little pagoda. The fragrance and the light of the clouds will pervade the dharma realm, widely doing Buddha work with fragrance and radiant clouds. The benefits he will receive are as I have just stated. In sum, all his wishes will be fulfilled without exception. During the Dharma-ending age, if, among my four groups of disciples, good men, and good women, there are those who, following the unsurpassed Way, do their best to build pagodas and enshrine this mantra in them, I cannot finish describing the merit they will acquire.

"If a person goes to the pagoda to ask for fortune, he should make obeisance and offer a flower and a little incense to the pagoda, and circle it clockwise. Because of his virtuous act, rank and glory will arrive unsought. Longevity and prosperity will increase without effort. Foes and bandits will fall without being subjugated. Vengeful thoughts and curses will return to their source without resistance. Epidemics and evil forces will be turned away without need of being purged. A good husband or good wife will come without being persuaded. Beautiful good children will be born without being prayed for. All wishes will be fulfilled at will.

"Even for ravens, owls, turtledoves, hawks, wolves, jackals, mosquitoes, ants, and the like, which momentarily come into the shadow of the pagoda and step on the grass there, their affliction-hindrances will be annihilated, and they will recognize their ignorance. They will suddenly enter a Buddha family and freely receive Dharma wealth. Even more are the benefits to humans who have seen the form of the pagoda, heard its bell tolling, heard its name, or been in its shadow. Their hindrances caused by sin will all be annihilated, and their wishes fulfilled.

Their present lives will be peaceful, and they will be reborn in the Pure Land of Ultimate Bliss.

"If a person, without extra effort, applies a glob of mud to the damaged wall of a pagoda or uses a fist-sized stone to support a leaning pagoda, because of this virtuous act, his fortune will increase and his lifespan will be lengthened. After death, he will be reborn as a Wheel-Turning King.

"After I have abandoned my body, my four groups of disciples, in order to rescue sentient beings in miserable existence, should come before this pagoda, make offerings of incense and flowers, and recite this spiritual mantra, making vows in earnest. Each and every mantra word and phrase [they utter] will radiate vast, bright light, illuminating the three evil life-journeys to end all suffering. Once those sentient beings are delivered from suffering, their Buddha seed will germinate, and they will be reborn as they wish in Pure Lands in the ten directions.

"If a person recites this mantra earnestly on the top of a high mountain, all sentient beings within the scope of his sight, including those in furs, feathers, scales, and shells, residing near and far in mountain valleys, forests, streams, lakes, rivers, and oceans, will annihilate their affliction-hindrance and recognize their ignorance. They will realize their three Buddha natures and eventually attain the great nirvāṇa. If people walking the same road as this person are touched by the wind blown through his clothes, step on his footprints, see his face, or converse with him briefly, their grave sins will all be expunged and their siddhis perfected."

The Buddha then said to Vajrapāṇi, "I now entrust this secret spiritual mantra and this sūtra to you all. Protect, uphold, and disseminate them in the world. Do not allow the transmittal [of the Dharma] to end for sentient beings."

Vajrapāṇi said, "I am honored to receive the trust of the World-Honored One. I pray only that we will requite the World-Honored One for his profound grace, day and night protecting, upholding, disseminating, and pronouncing [the mantra and the sūtra] to the world. If there are sentient beings that copy, uphold, and remember them unceasingly, we will command the Brahma-kings, the god-king Śakra, the four great god-kings, and the eight classes of Dharma protectors to protect them day and night without leaving even temporarily."

The Buddha said, "Very good, Vajrapāṇi. For the benefit of all sentient beings of the future, protect and uphold this Dharma, and make it endless."

After the World-Honored One pronounced this Treasure Chest Seal Dhāraṇī and widely did His Buddha work, He went to the Brahmin's home and accepted his offerings, causing humans and gods to receive great benefits. Then He returned to the place where He was staying.

During that time the bhikṣus, bhikṣuṇīs, upāsakas, upāsikās, gods, dragons, yakṣas, gandharvas, asuras, garuḍas, kiṁnaras, mahoragas, humans, nonhumans, and others in the assembly greatly rejoiced. They all believed in, accepted, and reverently carried out the teachings.

4 佛說大乘聖無量壽決定光明王如來陀羅尼經
Buddha Pronounces the Mahāyāna Sūtra of the Dhāraṇī of Infinite-Life Resolute Radiance King Tathāgata

Translated from Sanskrit into Chinese in the Northern Song Dynasty
by
The Dharma Master Fatian from India

Thus I have heard:

At one time the World-Honored One was dwelling in the Anāthapiṇḍika Garden of Jetavana Park in the city kingdom of Śrāvastī, together with 1,250 great bhikṣus. As recognized by the multitudes, all of them were great Arhats, who had ended their afflictions and the discharges thereof, acquired benefits for themselves, and completely liberated their minds. Honored Bodhisattva-Mahāsattvas with vast wisdom and merit, complete in their majestic deportment, also came to the assembly to hear the Dharma. At the head of the assembly was Great Wisdom Mañjuśrī Bodhisattva-Mahāsattva.

At that time Śākyamuni Buddha sympathetically considered all sentient beings that would live a short life in future times. In order to let them acquire the great benefit of lengthened lifespan, He decided to expound the inconceivable, secret, profound, wondrous, victorious Dharma.

The World-Honored One told Great Wisdom Mañjuśrī Bodhisattva, "All of you, hearken! West of Jambudvīpa, this southern continent, beyond countless Buddha Lands, there is a land called Immeasurable Merit Store. That land is magnificent, adorned with multitudinous treasures, pure and superb, peaceful and joyous, foremost in exquisiteness, surpassing all worlds in the ten directions. In that land of Immeasurable Merit Store resides a Buddha called Infinite-Life Resolute Radiance King Tathāgata, who has attained anuttara-samyak-saṁbodhi. He is now staying in that land. Exuding great lovingkindness and compassion, He expounds the true Dharma for the sake of sentient beings, enabling them to acquire excellent benefits, peace, and joy."

The Buddha next told Mañjuśrī Bodhisattva, "Now in this world of Jambudvīpa, human lifespan is one hundred years, but many do evil karma and die prematurely. Mañjuśrī Bodhisattva, if there are sentient beings that have seen this *Sūtra of the Dhāraṇī of Infinite-Life Resolute Radiance King Tathāgata* and heard this Tathāgata's name, their merit will be excellent. After they copy or have others copy this sūtra, they will enshrine the copies in their homes, in high towers, or in the halls of ashrams. They will accept and uphold this *Sūtra of the Dhāraṇī of Infinite-Life Resolute Radiance King Tathāgata* as they read and recite it, make obeisance to it, and offer various kinds of flowers, incense for burning, powdered incense, solid perfumes, necklaces, and so forth. If those who expect to live a short life earnestly copy and uphold this sūtra, read and recite it, and make offerings and obeisance, they will have their lifespans lengthened to one hundred years.

"Mañjuśrī Bodhisattva, if sentient beings that have heard the name of Infinite-Life Resolute Radiance King Tathāgata earnestly say His name 108 times, their short lifespans will be lengthened. If those who have only heard His name earnestly believe, accept, and honor it, they too will have their lifespans lengthened.

"Moreover, Mañjuśrī Bodhisattva, suppose there are those who, without momentary wavering, constantly and earnestly think of and seek the true Dharma. Good men and good women, all of you should hearken. For your sake, I now pronounce the 108-syllable dhāraṇī of Infinite-Life Resolute Radiance King Tathāgata:

> namo bhagavate aparimita-āyur-jñāna-suviniścita-tejorājāya | tathāgatāya-arhate samyak-saṁbuddhāya | tad-yathā [oṁ puṇya mahā-puṇya | aparimita-puṇya | aparimita-āyuḥ-puṇya-jñāna-saṁbhāropacite |] oṁ sarva saṁskāra pariśuddha dharmate gagana samudgate | svabhāva viśuddhe mahānaya parivāre svāhā ||

"Mañjuśrī Bodhisattva, for those who expect to live a short life, if they copy or have others copy this 108-syllable dhāraṇī of Infinite-Life Resolute Radiance King Tathāgata, enshrine the copies on the tops of high towers or in clean places in the halls [of ashrams], adorn them in accordance with the Dharma, and make various kinds of offerings, they will gain longevity, living one hundred years. After their lives end here, they will be reborn in Immeasurable Merit Store, the land of Infinite-Life Resolute Radiance King Tathāgata."

While Śākyamuni Buddha was pronouncing this *Sūtra of the Dhāraṇī of Infinite-Life Resolute Radiance King Tathāgata,* 99 koṭi Buddhas, with one mind and one voice, also pronounced this *Sūtra of the Dhāraṇī of Infinite-Life Resolute Radiance King Tathāgata.* Meanwhile, 84 koṭi Buddhas, with one mind and one voice, also pronounced this *Sūtra of the Dhāraṇī of Infinite-Life Resolute Radiance King Tathāgata.* Meanwhile, 77 koṭi Buddhas, with one mind and one voice, also pronounced this *Sūtra of the Dhāraṇī of Infinite-Life Resolute Radiance King Tathāgata.* Meanwhile, 66 koṭi Buddhas, with one mind and one voice, also pronounced this *Sūtra of the Dhāraṇī of Infinite-Life Resolute Radiance King Tathāgata.* Meanwhile, 55 koṭi Buddhas, with one mind and one voice, also pronounced this *Sūtra of the Dhāraṇī of Infinite-Life Resolute Radiance King Tathāgata.* Meanwhile, 44 koṭi Buddhas, with one mind and one voice, also pronounced this *Sūtra of the Dhāraṇī of Infinite-Life Resolute Radiance King Tathāgata.* Meanwhile, 36 koṭi Buddhas, with one mind and one voice, also pronounced this *Sūtra of the Dhāraṇī of Infinite-Life Resolute Radiance King Tathāgata.* Meanwhile, 25 koṭi Buddhas, with one mind and one voice, also pronounced this *Sūtra of the Dhāraṇī of Infinite-Life Resolute Radiance King Tathāgata.* Meanwhile, koṭis of Buddhas, as numerous as the sands of ten Ganges Rivers, with one mind and one voice, also pronounced this *Sūtra of the Dhāraṇī of Infinite-Life Resolute Radiance King Tathāgata.*

[The Buddha continued] "If there are those who copy or have others copy this dhāraṇī sūtra, they will never be reborn in hell, the ghost world, the animal kingdom, or the dominion of Yama, king of the underworld. They will never again take those evil life-paths in acceptance of evil requitals. Because of their merit acquired from copying this *Sūtra of the Dhāraṇī of Infinite-Life Resolute Radiance King Tathāgata*, they will have past-life knowledge, rebirth after rebirth, life after life, wherever they are reborn. If there are those who copy or have others copy this *Sūtra of the Dhāraṇī of Infinite-Life Resolute Radiance King Tathāgata,* their merit will be the same as that from copying texts in 84,000 Dharma stores. If there are those who copy or have others copy this *Sūtra of the Dhāraṇī of Infinite-Life Resolute Radiance King Tathāgata,* their merit will be the same as that from constructing 84,000 treasure pagodas.

"If there are those who copy or have others copy this *Sūtra of the Dhāraṇī of Infinite-Life Resolute Radiance King Tathāgata,* because of this merit, their [evil] karmas, which would drive them into the hell of uninterrupted suffering, will all be obliterated. If there are those who copy or have others copy this *Sūtra of the Dhāraṇī of Infinite-Life Resolute Radiance King Tathāgata,* they will neither fall under the rule of the māra-king and his retinue nor take the life-paths of yakṣas or rakṣasas. They will not die an accidental death and will never receive those evil requitals mentioned before. If there are those who copy or have others copy this *Sūtra of the Dhāraṇī of Infinite-Life Resolute Radiance King Tathāgata,* at the end of their lives, 99 koṭi Buddhas will appear before them to receive them to be reborn in that Buddha's land. You all should not doubt what I say. If there are those who copy or have others copy this *Sūtra of the Dhāraṇī of Infinite-Life Resolute Radiance King Tathāgata,* they will never assume female form in their future lives. If there are those who copy or have others copy this *Sūtra of the Dhāraṇī of Infinite-Life Resolute Radiance King Tathāgata,* they will always be secretly followed and protected by the four god-kings. In the east is the god-king Upholding the Kingdom, lord of gandharvas; in the south is the god-king Increase and Growth, lord of kumbhāṇḍas; in the west is the god-king Broad Eye, lord of great dragons; and in the north is the god-king Hearing Much, lord of yakṣas.

"If there are those who, for this sūtra, give away a small portion of their wealth as alms, they in effect give others all of the seven treasures—gold, silver, aquamarine, conch shell, emerald, coral, and amber—filling up this Three-Thousand Large Thousandfold World. Furthermore, if there are those who make offerings to this sūtra, they in effect make offerings to the entire store of the true Dharma. If there are those who present the superb seven treasures as an offering to the past seven Buddha-Tathāgatas, also called Arhats, Samyak-Saṁbuddhas—Vipaśyin, Śikhin, Viśvabhū, Krakucchanda, Kanakamuni, Kāśyapa, and Śākyamuni—the quantity of merit they acquire can never be known by measurement. Similarly, if there are those who make offerings to this *Sūtra of the Dhāraṇī of Infinite-Life Resolute Radiance King Tathāgata,* the limit of their merit can never be known by measurement.

"As the number of drops of water in the four great oceans can never be known, likewise, if there are those who copy this *Sūtra of the Dhāraṇī of Infinite-Life Resolute Radiance King Tathāgata*, uphold it, read and recite it, and make offerings, the limit of their merit cannot be known by measurement. If there are those who copy this *Sūtra of the Dhāraṇī of Infinite-Life Resolute Radiance King Tathāgata,* their place has the status of a treasure pagoda containing the holy relics of Buddhas. Their place is worthy of paying respects and making obeisance. If there are sentient beings that have heard this dhāraṇī, they will never again assume unfortunate life forms, such as birds, four-legged creatures, or multi-legged creatures. They will quickly attain anuttara-samyak-saṁbodhi, from which they will never regress.

"If those who have accumulated the seven treasures—gold, silver, aquamarine, conch shell, emerald, coral, and amber—piled high like a wonderful mountain, give them all away as alms, the quantity of merit they acquire cannot be known by measurement. Similarly, if there are those who, for this *Sūtra of the Dhāraṇī of Infinite-Life Resolute Radiance King Tathāgata,* give alms, the limit of their merit cannot be known by measurement. Moreover, if there are those who copy this *Sūtra of the Dhāraṇī of Infinite-Life Resolute Radiance King Tathāgata,* and make obeisance and offerings to it, they in effect make obeisance and offerings to all Tathāgatas in Buddha Lands in the ten directions. There is no difference."

Then Śākyamuni the World-Honored One spoke in verse:

Through training acquire the power of almsgiving.
By virtue of the power of almsgiving, one attains Buddhahood.
If one enters the fine chamber of great compassion
And one's ear briefly hears this dhāraṇī,
Although almsgiving is not yet fully achieved,
One will soon become the teacher to gods and humans.

Through training acquire the power of observing the precepts.
By virtue of the power of observing the precepts, one attains Buddhahood.
If one enters the fine chamber of great compassion
And one's ear briefly hears this dhāraṇī,
Although observing the precepts is not yet fully achieved,
One will soon become the teacher to gods and humans.

Through training acquire the power of endurance.
By virtue of the power of endurance, one attains Buddhahood.
If one enters the fine chamber of great compassion
And one's ear briefly hears this dhāraṇī,
Although endurance is not yet fully achieved,
One will soon become the teacher to gods and humans.

Through training acquire the power of energetic progress.
By virtue of the power of energetic progress, one attains Buddhahood.
If one enters the fine chamber of great compassion
And one's ear briefly hears this dhāraṇī,
Although energetic progress is not yet fully achieved,
One will soon become the teacher to gods and humans.

Through training acquire the power of meditation.
By virtue of the power of meditation, one attains Buddhahood.
If one enters the fine chamber of great compassion
And one's ear briefly hears this dhāraṇī,
Although meditation is not yet fully achieved,
One will soon become the teacher to gods and humans.

Through training acquire the power of wisdom.
By virtue of the power of wisdom, one attains Buddhahood.
If one enters the fine chamber of great compassion,
And one's ear briefly hears this dhāraṇī,
Although wisdom is not yet fully achieved,
One will soon become the teacher to gods and humans.

After the Buddha pronounced this sūtra, the great bhikṣus, Bodhisattvas, gods, humans, asuras, gandharvas, and others in the assembly, having heard the Buddha's words, greatly rejoiced. They all believed in, accepted, and reverently carried out the teachings.

From the Nirvāṇa Section

5 Buddha Pronounces the Sūtra of the Total Annihilation of the Dharma

In this world, the Dharma of Śākyamuni Buddha will end after three periods. (1) The true Dharma age lasted 500 to 1,000 years after His passing. During this period, there were teachings, carrying out of the teachings, and attaining of fruits. (2) The Dharma-likeness age lasted 500 to 1,000 years. During this period, there were teachings and carrying out of the teachings, but no attaining of fruits. (3) The Dharma-ending age will last 10,000 years. During this period, the teachings will gradually vanish, and there will be neither carrying out of the teachings nor attaining of fruits. Thereafter, the Dharma will be gone until the advent of the next Buddha.

Sūtra 5 is an English translation of text 396 (T12n0396), which was translated from Sanskrit into Chinese by an unknown person. In this sūtra the Buddha prophesies the degeneration of Buddhist monks in the Dharma-ending age. Māras disguised as monks will drink alcohol, eat flesh, and kill sentient beings. Devoid of morality, they will engage in sexual debauchery and perversion, whether with men or women. They will not observe the precepts or regulations. They will glorify themselves with fake elegant ways, expecting offerings from others.

As the Dharma is ending, the world will be ravaged by flood, drought, famine, and epidemics. Human lifespan will shorten, and many will perish in a massive flood. All the sūtras will be destroyed, and the words of the Buddha will not be seen again.

In the *Bodhisattva in the Womb Sūtra*, fascicle 2, the Buddha prophesies that, after 56 koṭi and 70 million years, which means 630 million years (if a koṭi is 10 million), Maitreya Bodhisattva will descend from Tuṣita Heaven and become the next Buddha, bringing the Dharma to a renewed world (T12n0384, 1025c15–19).

5 佛說法滅盡經
Buddha Pronounces the Sūtra of the Total Annihilation of the Dharma

Translated from Sanskrit into Chinese
by
An Unknown Person

Thus I have heard:

At one time the Buddha, together with bhikṣus and Bodhisattvas, was staying in the city kingdom of Kuśinagara, where He would enter parinirvāṇa in three months. Countless multitudes came to the Buddha and bowed their heads down to the ground. Surrounded by His devotees longing to hear the Dharma, the World-Honored One remained silent, and His radiance did not manifest.

The venerable Ānanda made obeisance to the Buddha and asked Him, "When the World-Honored One pronounces the Dharma, His awesome radiance is always displayed before and after. Now in this huge assembly, His radiance does not appear. Why is this so? There must be a reason. I pray to hear its implication."

The Buddha remained silent, not responding. After Ānanda asked this question for the third time, the Buddha told Ānanda, "After my parinirvāṇa, as the Dharma comes to an end, the way of the māras will thrive in this world of the five turbidities. Māras will appear as śramaṇas so as to undermine and destroy my Way. They will wear lay clothes and delight in the monk's robe dyed with a mixture of five colors. To gratify ravenous appetites, they will drink alcohol, eat flesh, and kill sentient beings. Devoid of lovingkindness, they will hate and envy others.

"At that time, there will be Bodhisattvas, Pratyekabuddhas, and Arhats, who energetically cultivate virtue and treat all with respect. Esteemed by all, they will teach and transform others impartially. They will pity the poor and old, and help the needy and unfortunate. They will teach others to revere and uphold the sūtras and the holy images. Kind and benevolent in nature, they will do meritorious karmas. Never harming others, they will disregard any harm to themselves in order to help others. Kind and friendly, they will endure abuse, not protecting themselves.

"Although there will be such good people, all māra bhikṣus will be jealous of them. They will slander, malign, and banish them. Afterward, individually and as a group, the māra bhikṣus will not cultivate virtue. Temples will be deserted, falling into disrepair then into ruins. Greedy for material wealth, they will accumulate things, not using them to acquire merit. They will sell slaves to work in the fields. Devoid of lovingkindness, they will burn mountain forests, harming sentient beings. Male slaves will become bhikṣus, and female slaves will become bhikṣuṇīs. Devoid of morality, they will engage in sexual debauchery and perversion, whether with men or women. Such people will cause my Way to fade away.

"Some of them will seek sanctuary in my Order to escape prosecution by the law. They will become śramaṇas but will not observe the precepts or regulations. Although they will, in appearance, recite the precepts on new-moon and full-moon days, they will be reluctant and indolent, not wanting to hear the recitation. They will omit some precepts, not wanting to recite all of them. They will not recite or study the sūtras. If there are readers who do not know the words [in the sūtras], they claim that they know them. They will not consult the learned ones, but will instead seek fame for self-elevation. They will glorify themselves with fake elegant ways, expecting offerings from others. For committing [any of] the five rebellious sins, after death, these māra bhikṣus will fall into the hell of uninterrupted suffering. They will then be reborn as animals or hungry ghosts for as many kalpas as the sands of the Ganges. After their sins have been purged, they will be reborn [as humans] in a fringe country where the Three Jewels will not be accessible.

"When the Dharma is ending, women will diligently do meritorious karmas while men will be indolent and arrogant. Men, having no faith, will not use the words in the Dharma, but will regard śramaṇas as feces and dirt. When the Dharma is ending, gods will shed tears. Flood and drought will ravage, and five kinds of grain will not ripen. Epidemics will be prevalent and many will die. People will endure a hard life, and government officials will exploit them. People will not follow good principles, thinking only of pleasure and strife. The evil ones will become as numerous as the sands in the sea. The good ones will decrease to one or two. As a kalpa is ending, the sun and the moon will be unstable and human lifespan will shorten. At the age of 40, one's hair will turn white. Men indulging in sexual acts may die prematurely from depletion of their semen, or may live to only 60. While men will live short lives, women will live long, to 70, 80, 90, or even 100 years. Faithless people will say that the situation can be permanent.

"A massive flood will suddenly rise, lasting endlessly. Various species of sentient beings, lofty or lowly, will drown or drift in the waters, and they will be eaten by fish and other sea creatures. Bodhisattvas, Pratyekabuddhas, and Arhats, driven away by the māras, will not convene. [These holy beings of] the Three Vehicles will enter the meritorious grounds in the mountains. There they will live a long life, tranquilly biding their time. They will meet with one another when the god-kings escort Moonlight Bodhisattva to appear in the world. Together they will revitalize my Dharma for fifty-two years.

"Then the *Śūraṅgama Sūtra* and the *Pratyutpanna Buddha Sammukhāvasthita Samādhi Sūtra* will be destroyed, to be followed by all other sūtras in the twelve categories. Their words will not be seen again. The monk's robe will naturally turn white. When my Dharma perishes, it will be like [the flame of] an oil lamp. When it is dying, its light becomes brighter for a while then dies out. When my Dharma perishes, it will be like the extinction of a lamp. What will happen afterward is hard to describe. Eventually, after tens of millions of years, Maitreya Bodhisattva will descend to this world to become a Buddha. All toxic gases will then be eliminated, and the world will be safe and peaceful. The rains will be harmonious and the five grains will thrive. The trees will be tall, and humans will each be eighty feet tall, with a lifespan of 84,000 years. Innumerable sentient beings will be delivered."

The venerable Ānanda made obeisance to the Buddha and asked Him, "What should we call this sūtra? How should we uphold it?"

The Buddha replied, "Ānanda, this sūtra is called *Total Annihilation of the Dharma*. Pronounce it to all and let them know its significance. Your merit will be immeasurable, beyond reckoning."

The four groups of disciples, having heard this sūtra, were distressed and downcast, but they all activated their resolve to attain the unsurpassed bodhi. Then they made obeisance to the Buddha and departed.

From the Sūtra Collection Section

6 Buddha Pronounces the Sūtra of Maitreya Bodhisattva's Attainment of Buddhahood

Texts 453–57 (T14n0453–57) are five Chinese versions of this sūtra. Sūtra 6 is an English translation of text 456, the longest of the five versions. This text was translated from Sanskrit into Chinese by Kumārajīva (鳩摩羅什, 344–413) from Kucha.

Preceded by Krakucchanda, Kanakamuni, and Kāśyapa, Śākyamuni Buddha is the fourth of the one thousand Buddhas in this kalpa called Worthy Kalpa (賢劫). Maitreya Bodhisattva will be the fifth Buddha, and he is presently staying in the inner court of Tuṣita Heaven, the fourth of the six heavens in the desire realm, teaching the gods there. As described in Sūtra 5, after the Dharma of Śākyamuni Buddha is destroyed, humanity will undergo a long period of suffering until the world is transformed into a virtual Pure Land. Then Maitreya Bodhisattva will descend from Tuṣita Heaven to teach a new race of giant humans with a long lifespan.

In this sūtra the Buddha describes the magnificence and prosperity of the human world in the distant future, when Maitreya will be born. Humans, although still in the desire realm, will have no greed, anger, or delusion because they all will have lovingkindness and the power of meditation. Maitreya will demonstrate attainment of Buddhahood, sitting under the bodhi tree, the dragon-flower tree, in His bodhimaṇḍa. He will turn the Dharma wheel three times, pronouncing the Dharma just as Śākyamuni Buddha did.

The word *maitreya* means lovingkindness. The disciples and followers of Maitreya Buddha will be those who have planted their roots of goodness, especially lovingkindness, under Śākyamuni Buddha. Another name of this sūtra is *The Mind of Lovingkindness, No Killing and No Eating Flesh*.

7 Buddha Pronounces the Sūtra of Neither Increase Nor Decrease

Sūtra 7 is an English translation of text 668 (T16n0668), which was translated from Sanskrit into Chinese by Bodhiruci (菩提留支, 5th–6th centuries) from northern India. In response to Śāriputra's question as to whether sentient beings that endlessly undergo birth and death in the Three Realms of Existence are increasing or decreasing in number, the Buddha expounds the absolute truth, using these three terms: the dharma body, the Tathāgata store, and the inherent pure mind. All of them in effect are the realm of sentient beings.

In the absolute truth, dharmas have neither birth nor death, and there can never be increase or decrease in their numbers. Hence the view of increase or decrease is a wrong view which can develop into many other wrong views. For example, the view of decrease can lead to the wrong view of cessation, extinction, or nirvāṇa as a void. The view of increase can lead to the wrong view that nirvāṇa is formed or that nirvāṇa suddenly comes about without causes or conditions.

The Buddha teaches that the dharma body that drifts in the ocean of birth and death, fettered by endless afflictions, is called a sentient being. The dharma body that, tired of the suffering of repeated birth and death, cultivates the six pāramitās through Dharma Doors is called a Bodhisattva. Finally, the dharma body that, breaking the bondage of afflictions, attains the unexcelled, ultimate insight into the realm of dharmas is called a Tathāgata, the Samyak-Saṁbuddha.

The Buddha introduces the inherent pure mind, which is another name of the Tathāgata store. It is always responsive to pure dharmas, but is covered up by afflictions, which are like dust particles that have become long-term visitors. However, afflictions accumulated in one's mind, though empty by nature, are not *adventitious* visitors who may leave. Afflictions can be subjugated by meditation and eradicated only by wisdom.

8 Mahāyāna Sūtra of the Illuminating Everywhere Radiance-Store Wordless Dharma Door

Texts 828–30 (T17n0828–30) are three Chinese versions of this sūtra, each translated from a different Sanskrit text. Text 828 was translated by Bodhiruci (菩提留支, 5th–6th centuries), and texts 829 and 830 were both translated by Divākara (地婆訶羅, 613–687). Sūtra 8 is an English translation of text 830, the longest of the three texts.

This short sūtra presents the gist of the teachings of the Buddha. First, the Buddha gives specific instructions that Bodhisattvas should eradicate their afflictions and observe the precepts. Next, He expounds the relative truth that dharmas are born through causes and conditions. These causes and conditions change from kṣaṇa to kṣaṇa, like a flash of lightning. Hence all dharmas are like illusions, like mirages, and like the moon in the water.

The Buddha then reveals the absolute truth that dharmas have never come into existence, nor can they go into nonexistence, because the true nature of dharmas is apart from birth and death, existence and nonexistence. Dharmas by nature are in the one flavor of liberation, the flavor of emptiness, and dharma nature is called the Illuminating Everywhere Radiance Store. Note that the Radiance Store and the dharma nature of a sentient being in this sūtra are called, in other sūtras, respectively, the Tathāgāta store or Buddha store, and Buddha nature.

9 Sūtra of Detecting Good or Evil Karma and Requital, fascicle 2

Sūtra 9 is an English translation of the second fascicle of text 839 (T17n0839), which comprises two fascicles. In the first fascicle, Earth Store Bodhisattva skillfully induces those who delight in divination for worldly matters to turn their interest to the Dharma. To detect one's good or evil karma and requital, he teaches a procedure that involves successively tossing three sets of wooden blocks inscribed with corresponding words, lines, and numbers. Tossing the first two sets reveals one's ten good or evil karmas done by one's body, voice, or mind. Tossing the third set reveals one's good or evil requital, according to a given list. Once the problem is identified, one should prepare oneself for spiritual training by purifying one's evil karma through repentance.

On the assumption that those who recognize themselves as ordinary beings do not need to toss wooden blocks to confirm that their karmas and requitals are less than desirable, the first fascicle is not translated here.

In fascicle 2, Kṣitigarbha (earth store) Bodhisattva teaches that sense objects, such as sights, sounds, scents, flavors, and tactile sensations, are called "external appearances of mind" (心外相). The Consciousness-Only School calls them "projected appearances" (影像相分). And modern neurologists recognize that percepts are "brain representations." These three names reflect the common understanding of sense objects.

He then introduces the false mind, which encompasses mental functions that perceive, differentiate, and recollect objects it constructs. The true reality of the false mind is called true suchness, the dharma body, the Tathāgata store, the true mind, or the inherent pure mind. Those who are aware of only their false mind, which accords with delusion, are called sentient beings. Those who walk the Bodhisattva Way to realize their dharma body are called Bodhisattvas. Those who fully realize their dharma body are called Buddhas. Throughout one's journey to Buddhahood, the dharma body remains the same, silent and still, without birth or death, coming or going.

Central to Buddhist doctrine is the emptiness of dharmas, which is beyond the concept of existence or nonexistence, but no different from dharmas in manifestation, holy or karmic. To comfort those who fear that the dharma body might mean nothingness, Earth Store Bodhisattva says that "the true nature of the Tathāgata's dharma body is 'not empty' because it in essence is complete with immeasurable pure, meritorious karmas." Then he reminds us that "because the nature of the dharma body, neither empty nor not empty, is free from differentiation, free from the distinction between self and others, and between all appearances, one can say that the essence of the dharma body is ultimate emptiness."

6 佛說彌勒大成佛經
Buddha Pronounces the Sūtra of Maitreya Bodhisattva's Attainment of Buddhahood

Translated from Sanskrit into Chinese in the Later Qin Dynasty
by
The Tripiṭaka Master Kumārajīva from Kucha

Thus I have heard:

At one time the Buddha was staying in the kingdom of Magadha, near the Pāśa Mountain, where past Buddhas had subjugated the māras. It was during the summer meditation retreat, when the Buddha was doing walking meditation on the mountaintop with Śāriputra, that He spoke in verse:

> Hearken single-mindedly!
> In radiant great samādhi,
> The one with unsurpassed merit
> Will rightfully appear in the world.
>
> He will pronounce the true Dharma,
> And all will be infused with it,
> Like the thirsty drinking sweet nectar.
> All will swiftly set off on the Liberation Path.

At that time the Buddha's four groups of disciples repaired and leveled the roads. They sprinkled water, swept the streets, and burned incense. [A huge multitude] carrying objects of offering, came to the assembly to make offerings to the Tathāgata and the bhikṣus. Intently gazing at the Tathāgata, they were like filial sons beholding their father, or like the thirsty longing for a drink [of water]. In the same way they loved and thought of their Dharma father. With one mind they all wanted to ask the Dharma King to turn the wheel of the true Dharma. With their senses undistracted, one by one, their minds flowed toward the Buddha. At that time bhikṣus, bhikṣuṇīs, upāsakas, and upāsikās, as well as gods, dragons, spirits, gandharvas, asuras, garuḍas, kiṁnaras, mahoragas, humans, nonhumans, and others, all rose from their seats and circled the Buddha clockwise. Then they prostrated themselves on the ground, shedding tears before the Buddha.

Śāriputra the Wise arranged his robe and bared his right shoulder. Having followed the Buddha, the Dharma King, to turn the wheel of the true Dharma, he was the Buddha's minister, and a great general upholding the Dharma. Out of sympathy for sentient beings, he wanted them to be liberated from the bondage of suffering. Knowing that the Dharma King's mind would be responsive, he said to the Buddha, "World-Honored One, just now the Tathāgata spoke in verse on the mountaintop, praising the one with the foremost wisdom. This was never mentioned in previous sūtras. The minds of this huge multitude are now filled with expectation. They shed tears like heavy rain, hoping to hear the Tathāgata speak of the next Buddha, who will open the Sweet Nectar Path, to hear His name, Maitreya, and to hear of His merit, His spiritual power, and His splendid land. Based on what roots of goodness, almsgiving, virtuous conduct, meditation, wisdom, and intellect will one be able to see Maitreya Buddha? With what mindset should one walk the Eightfold Right Path?"

While Śāriputra asked this question, hundreds of thousands of god-sons and innumerable Brahma-kings, joining their palms reverently, with one voice said to the Buddha, "We pray that the World-Honored One will enable us in a future life to see Maitreya Buddha, the fruition of the greatest requital among men, the luminous eye of the Three Realms of Existence, who will teach great lovingkindness and compassion to all sentient beings."

The eight classes of Dharma protectors, joining their palms reverently, also made their request to the Tathāgata in the same way. Brahma-kings and a multitude of Brahma gods, joining their palms, with one voice sang their praise in verse:

Namo the Full Moon!
Complete with the Ten Powers,
Great leader of energetic progress,
Valiant and fearless,

The one with knowledge of all knowledge,
Having transcended the Three Realms of Existence,
Having acquired the Three Thorough Clarities,
Having subjugated the four māras,

His body being a Dharma vessel,
His mind like open sky,
Quiet and unmoved
Toward existence or no existence,
Toward nonexistence or no nonexistence,
With perfect understanding of emptiness,
One who is praised by the world!

With one mind,
Simultaneously we all take refuge,
Praying that He will turn the Dharma wheel.

Then the World-Honored One told Śāriputra, "I will expound broadly to you. Hearken, hearken, and ponder it well! All of you today, with a truly good intention, want to ask the Tathāgata about the unsurpassed Way to mahā-prajñā, which the Tathāgata sees as clearly as a mango in His palm. Śāriputra, if one, under the past seven Buddhas, has heard the names of Buddhas and made obeisance and offerings, one's karma hindrances will all be annihilated. If one has also heard of Maitreya Buddha's great lovingkindness, one will achieve a pure mind. You all should join your palms single-mindedly and take refuge in the great loving-kind, compassionate one to come. I will expound broadly to you.

"The land of Maitreya Buddha will be a land of pure life, with no sycophancy or deceit, because He neither embraces nor clings to his achievement of dāna-pāramitā, śīla-pāramitā, or prajñā-pāramitā. It will be splendid because of His ten wonderful vows. When sentient beings, drawn by His great lovingkindness, invoke their gentle minds, they will see Maitreya Buddha. They will be reborn in this Buddha's land, tame their faculties, and follow His teachings.

"Śāriputra, the surface of each of the four great oceans will be reduced by 3,000 yojanas. The ground of Jambudvīpa will be 10,000 yojanas in length and width. It will be level and clean, like a crystal mirror. There will be large flowers that suit one's fancy, pleasing flowers, huge fragrant flowers, utpala flowers, flowers with large golden petals, flowers with petals made of the seven treasures, and flowers with silver petals. The stamens of these flowers will be soft like celestial silk. They will bear auspicious fruits, soft like celestial cotton and full of aroma and flavor. In the forests, there will be abundant wonderful flowers and sweet fruits, surpassing those in the garden favored by the god-king Śakra. The trees will be thirty lis tall.

"The adjacent cities will be only a rooster's flight apart. Those who have planted their roots of goodness under [me] the present Buddha, will be reborn in that world as the requital for their practice of lovingkindness. They will have wisdom, virtue, joy, and peace, as they gratify their five desires. They will not have illnesses caused by cold, heat, wind, or fire, nor will they suffer from the nine afflictions. They will each live 84,000 years, and no one will die a premature death. Their bodies will be 160 feet tall. Every day they will enjoy wonderful peace and bliss, experiencing deep meditation as their instrument of happiness. They will have only three troubles: first, need to eat and drink; second, need to discharge bodily wastes; and third, need to grow old. Women will marry when they are 500 years old.

"There will be a great city called Ketuma, 1,200 yojanas in length and width, 7 yojanas in elevation, and adorned with the seven treasures. In the city will be magically created towers made of the seven treasures, and they will be majestic, wonderful, august, and pure. Through the windows will be seen fair maidens, holding nets made with precious gems. These towers will be covered with various treasures as adornment and hung with jeweled bells, the sound of which resembles celestial music. Among the lines of trees made of the seven treasures will be waterways and fountains, also made of the seven treasures. The streams in various colors will reflect and highlight one another. Although crisscrossing, they will not obstruct one another. The river banks will be covered with gold dust.

"The streets and roads will be twelve lis wide, all as fresh as a celestial garden sprinkled with water and swept clean. There will be a great dragon-king called Tāraśikhin, who has acquired merit and awesome powers. His lake being near the city, his palace, like a tower made of the seven treasures, will be fully visible from a distance. At each midnight he will assume human form and fill an auspicious bottle with scented water. He will sprinkle this water to drench the dust until the ground looks as moist as if oiled. When pedestrians walk around, there will be no dust.

"Because of the merit of the people, everywhere around the streets and alleys there will be luminous gems mounted on poles, twelve lis in height. Their light, surpassing the sunlight, will reach 80 yojanas in each of the four directions. This pure golden light will shine day and night. In comparison, the light of lamps and candles would be like pooled ink. When fragrant winds blow, the luminous gems on the poles will rain down necklaces of jewels, and people will wear them as naturally as if they were enjoying the bliss in the third dhyāna. Everywhere there will be gold, silver, jewels, precious gems, and so forth, piled high like mountains. These treasure mountains will radiate light to illuminate the entire city. Whenever touched by this light, people will be happy and activate the bodhi mind.

"There will be a great yakṣa called Bhadrapraśāsaka, who protects the city of Ketuma day and night. Followed by the people, he will sprinkle water and sweep the ground clean. The ground will crack open to take in people's waste products and close afterward, and it will grow red lotus flowers to overpower the foul odor.

"When the people of that world grow old and frail, they will voluntarily go to the mountain forest to sit under a tree. As they keep thinking of Buddhas, they will die peacefully and joyfully, without pretense. After death, most of them will be reborn in Great Brahma Heaven or in the presence of Buddhas.

"In that peaceful land, there will be no trouble from bandits or thieves, nor robbing or stealing. The doors in cities and villages will never be closed. Nor will there be any catastrophes of water, fire, weapons, or troops; nor the tribulations of famine or toxins. Taming their faculties, people will live in lovingkindness, respect, and harmony. To one another, they will be like a son loving his father, like a mother loving her son. Taught and guided by Maitreya Buddha with lovingkindness, they will speak humble words. Those who [in this world] have observed the precept of no killing and no eating flesh will be reborn in that world. Their faculties will be serene, and their features will be even and comely, as awe-inspiring as those of celestial youths.

"The city of Ketuma will be situated in the center of 84,000 small cities made of treasures, which serve as its satellites. Men and women, adults and children, living near or far, because of the spiritual power of this Buddha, will be able to see one another without any obstacles.

"Everywhere in that world will be wish-fulfilling jeweled flowers that shine in the night. The sky will rain down flowers made of the seven treasures. Scattered all over the grounds will be flowers of padma, utpala, kumada, puṇḍarīka, māndarāva, mahā-māndarāva, mañjūṣaka, and mahā-mañjūṣaka. Some of them, swept up by winds, will whirl in the air. Near the cities and villages of that land, the bathing ponds, fountains, rivers, and lakes in the gardens and forests will naturally have water with the eight virtues. Singing wonderful melodies will be geese, ducks, mandarin ducks, peacocks, parrots, halcyons, śārīs, melodious cuckoos, jīvajīvas, and the quick-sighted birds. Flying and gathering in trees and ponds will be innumerable birds of diverse species, singing wonderful melodies.

"Blooming day and night, and never wilted, will be golden untainted pure-radiance flowers, carefree pure-wisdom sunlight flowers, bright white seven-day fragrance flowers, and fragrant campaka flowers in six colors, as well as a billion kinds of land and water flowers, unmatched in fragrance and purity. The blue colors will gleam with blue light; yellow colors, yellow light; red colors, red light; white colors, white light. There will be trees bearing wish-fulfilling fruits, with their beautiful aroma permeating the land. Among the treasure mountains in that land will be fragrant trees, which will radiate golden light to illuminate everywhere and emit pleasing scents to suffuse everything.

"There will always be fine fragrance in Jambudvīpa, making it like a mountain of fragrance. Streaming waters will be good and sweet, and able to remove troubles. Rainfalls will be timely and the heavenly fields will ripen aromatic and beautiful crops of grain. Because of the powers of these godlike people, seven harvests will be reaped from one planting. Only a little effort will yield much return. Without weeds or muck, the crops of grains will thrive. As requital for the merit of these sentient beings, grains of one hundred flavors, unmatched in aroma, will melt in their mouths, providing them with strength and vitality.

"In that land will dwell a Wheel-Turning King named Śaṅkha, endowed with the thirty-two major marks. He will have four types of armed forces, but he will not rule the four continents by military power. This king will have 1,000 sons, who are valiant and majestic, and enemies will naturally submit to them. He will have seven precious things: first, the golden wheel, complete with the hub, the rim, and 1,000 spokes; second, the white elephant, white as a snow mountain, a magnificent spectacle as it stands on its seven limbs like a kingly mountain; third, the blue horse, with red mane and tail, hoofs made of the seven treasures, and flowers appearing underneath; fourth, the divine jewel, clearly visible, more than two elbows across, the radiance of which rains down treasures to fulfill sentient beings' wishes; fifth, exquisite maidens, beautiful, wonderful, and limber as if boneless; sixth, the treasure minister, whose mouth spits out jewels, from whose feet spring up jewels, and whose hands manifest jewels; seventh, the military minister, who, by moving his body, can produce from the sky the four types of armed forces, like clouds.

"His 1,000 sons and his people in this kingdom of the seven treasures will regard one another without any malice, but like a mother loving her son. The princes will take precious treasures and construct in front of the main palace a platform of the seven treasures. It will be 13 yojanas in height, with 30 decks. [Equipped with] 1,000 tiller-heads and 1,000 wheels, it will move easily.

"There will be four great treasure stores, each surrounded by four koṭi small treasure stores. The great Elāpattra Treasure Store will be in the kingdom of Gandhāra; the great Pāṇḍuka Treasure Store in the kingdom of Mithilā; the great Piṅgala Treasure Store in the kingdom of Surașṭa; and the great Śaṅkha Treasure Store in the kingdom of Vārāṇasī, near the mountain of ancient ṛṣis. These four great treasure stores, filled with treasures, will be naturally uncovered, each radiating light through a distance of 1,000 yojanas, and each surrounded by four koṭi small treasure stores. There will be four great dragons guarding these four great treasure stores and their respective small treasure stores, which, shaped like lotus flowers, stand above the ground.

"Countless multitudes will go to see these treasures, which will not be guarded by humans. When the multitudes see these treasures, their minds will not covet them. They will leave them on the ground, as they would tiles, stones, grasses, trees, and chunks of dirt. When people see them, they will feel disgusted, saying to one another these words: 'As the Buddha has said, in the past, for the sake of these treasures, sentient beings viciously harmed one another. They stole from and robbed one another, and they lied to and deceived one another, thus multiplying their sin and suffering in saṁsāra. Then they all fell into enormous hells.'

"Nets made with jewels will hover over the city of Ketuma. Jeweled bells, blown by breezes, like bells being struck, will chime harmoniously, expounding taking refuge in the Buddha, taking refuge in the Dharma, and taking refuge in the Saṅgha.

"At that time, in the city there will be a great Brahmin named Brahmāyu. His wife Brahmavatī, gentle in nature, will also be in the Brahmin caste. To them as parents, Maitreya Bodhisattva will be born. His stay in the womb will be like a visit to a celestial palace, and He will radiate great light, unobstructed by dirt and dust.

"[After He has attained Buddhahood] His body will be purple-tinged golden, complete with the thirty-two physical marks of a great man. He will be seated on a jeweled lotus flower, and sentient beings will never tire of beholding him. His radiance will be unsurpassed, something gods and humans have never before seen. His strength will be immeasurable: the strength of each section of His body will surpass that of all the powerful dragons and elephants. The inconceivable radiance from His pores will illuminate across infinite space, unhindered. The light of the sun, the moon, and the stars, as well as the light of water, fire, and gems, will all become inconspicuous like dust. His height will measure eighty elbows of Śākyamuni Buddha. His chest will be twenty-five elbows wide. His face will be twelve and a half elbows long. His nose will be tall and straight, in the center of His face. His appearance will be sublime, complete with the unexcelled marks. Each mark will include 84,000 excellent characteristics, which will adorn Him like a golden statue. Each of His excellent characteristics will emit radiance, illuminating a distance of 1,000 yojanas. His eyes, with distinct blue and white parts, will look clear. The permanent light surrounding His body will be hundreds of yojanas across. Clearly illuminated by this Buddha's light will be the sun, the moon, the stars, precious gems, and jewels, as well as lines of trees made of the seven treasures. All other radiance will be eclipsed. The body of this Buddha will be tall like a golden mountain. Those who see Him will naturally be liberated from the three evil life-journeys.

"Maitreya Bodhisattva will observe carefully the faults of the five desires of the world and pity suffering sentient beings sinking in the long flow of birth and death. Observing suffering, emptiness, and impermanence with the right thoughts, He will not delight in family life, but will consider it as confining as a prison.

"At that time King Śaṅkha, accompanied by the ministers and people of his kingdom, will take that platform made of the seven treasures, together with 1,000 jeweled curtains, 1,000 jeweled carriages, 1,000 koṭi jeweled bells, 1,000 jeweled vessels, and 1,000 jeweled urns, and offer them all to Maitreya Bodhisattva. After accepting them, Maitreya Bodhisattva will give them to the Brahmins. The Brahmins will be surprised to see Maitreya Bodhisattva give such enormous alms. They will then break them into pieces and share them.

"Maitreya Bodhisattva, seeing the evanescence and impermanence of the treasure platform, will know that all saṁskṛta dharmas will perish. Training Himself to remember impermanence, Maitreya Bodhisattva will praise past Buddhas as the cool nectar, with a stanza on impermanence:

> All processes are impermanent,
> Which are the dharma of birth and death.
> Having ended birth and death,
> Nirvāṇa is delight!

"After speaking this stanza, Maitreya Bodhisattva will renounce family life to learn the Way to Buddhahood, and he will sit under the bodhi tree of dragon flowers in the splendid vajra bodhimaṇḍa. This tree will be fifty yojanas tall, with its branches and leaves spreading all about, radiating great bright light. Its branches will be like a jeweled dragon that spits out hundreds of jeweled flowers. Its petals will be in the colors of the seven treasures, and its fruits in various colors will be pleasing to sentient beings. No tree in heavens or the human world will compare with this tree.

"Maitreya Bodhisattva, together with 84,000 Brahmins, will go to this bodhimaṇḍa. To renounce family life and to learn the Way, He will shave off his own hair. He will renounce family life in the morning and, that evening, will subjugate the four kinds of māras and attain anuttara-samyak-saṁbodhi. He will then speak in verse:

> Long thinking of the suffering of sentient beings
> And wanting to rescue them, I was unable to do so.
> Today I have attained bodhi.
> Suddenly, hindrances are no more.
> I have verified the emptiness of sentient beings
> And the true reality of their original nature.
> My sorrow and suffering nevermore,
> My lovingkindness and compassion are unconditional.
>
> For the sake of rescuing you all,
> I have given to innumerable people
> My kingdom, my head, my eyes,
> My hands, my feet, and my wife.
>
> Beginning today are my liberation
> And the unsurpassed great silence and stillness.

I will expound the Dharma to you all
And widely open the Sweet Nectar Way.

Such fruition of the greatest requital
Is born from achieving the six pāramitās,
Such as almsgiving, observing precepts, and developing wisdom,
And is acquired from great lovingkindness and compassion
As well as from untainted merit.

"Having spoken these stanzas, Maitreya Buddha will remain silent. Then, god-kings, dragon-kings, and spirit-kings, without revealing themselves, will rain down flowers as offerings to this Buddha. The Three-Thousand Large Thousandfold World will quake in six different ways. This Buddha's body will emit light, illuminating innumerable lands. Those who can be delivered will see this Buddha.

"At that time, in the Flower Grove Garden, the god-king Śakro-Devānām-Indra, the four god-kings, who protect the world, the great Brahma-kings, and innumerable god-sons will bow their heads down at the feet of this Buddha. Joining their palms, they will ask Him to turn the Dharma wheel. Maitreya Buddha will grant their request in silence. He will tell the Brahma-kings, 'In the long night, I have undergone tremendous suffering and practiced the six pāramitās. Finally, I have today fully revealed the Dharma ocean. To pronounce the Dharma to you all, I will rightfully erect the Dharma banner, beat the Dharma drum, blow the Dharma conch shell, and rain down the Dharma rain. Gods and humans cannot turn the Dharma wheel of the Eightfold Right Path, which can be turned only by Buddhas. This path is impartial, and it leads straight to the unsurpassed silence and stillness of that which is asaṁskṛta. It can enable sentient beings to end their suffering in the long night. This Dharma is so profound that it is hard to obtain, hard to enter, hard to believe, and hard to understand. No one in the world can know it or see it. However, through it, one can cleanse one's mental defilements and accomplish myriads of Brahma actions.'

"As these words are being said, from other worlds, billions of koṭis of god-sons, goddess-daughters, and great Brahma-kings, riding their celestial palaces, will come. Carrying celestial flowers, they will offer them to this Tathāgata and circle Him 100,000 times. They will prostrate themselves on the ground and, joining their palms, they too will implore this Buddha. The celestial music sounding without being played, the Brahma-kings will speak with one voice in verse:

Without a Buddha,
Innumerable, countless years have passed in waste,
And sentient beings have gone down the evil life-paths.
When the eye of the world is gone,
The three evil life-paths will widen and expand,
And the road to heaven will be blocked.

Today a Buddha has appeared in the world.

The three evil life-paths will be annihilated,
And the multitude of gods and humans will increase.
We pray that He will open the Sweet Nectar Door,
Enabling the minds of sentient beings not to cling,
But to attain nirvāṇa quickly.

We, the Brahma-kings, have heard
That a Buddha has appeared in the world.
Because we now have encountered a Buddha,
The supreme Dharma King,
The palaces in Brahma heavens are grander,
And the light of our bodies becomes brighter.

For the sake of all multitudes [in worlds] in the ten directions,
We implore the great guiding teacher,
Praying that He will open the Sweet Nectar [Door]
And turn the unsurpassed Dharma wheel.

"Having spoken these stanzas, they will again bow their heads to the ground. Joining their palms, three times they will implore earnestly, 'We pray only that the World-Honored One will turn the wheel of the profound true Dharma to remove the roots of suffering of sentient beings, enabling them to discard their three poisons and evil karmas, and to break away from the four evil life-paths.'

"Then Maitreya the World-Honored One will smile and emit light in five colors, silently granting the Brahma-kings' request. Having perceived this Buddha's approval, the god-sons and the innumerable multitudes will be so exultant that they feel exuberant all over their bodies. The joy of the multitudes will be like that of filial sons who find their deceased loving father suddenly coming back to life. The multitude of gods will circle the World-Honored One clockwise countless times. With tireless reverence and adoration, they will step back to stand on one side.

"The huge multitude will think: 'Although we can enjoy the pleasures of the five desires for 1,000 koṭi years, we cannot avoid the suffering of the three evil life-paths. Wives and riches cannot save us [from this fate]. The world is impermanent and life will not last for long. We should train purely in the Brahma way in the Buddha Dharma.'

"They will then think: 'Our gratification of the five desires, lasting even as long as the lifespan of gods in No Perception Heaven, which goes on for innumerable koṭis of kalpas, and [our enjoyment of] the fine and smooth tactile sensations, when making merry with beautiful goddesses, will come to an end. Then we will go down the three evil life-paths to undergo immeasurable suffering. The pleasures are small and illusory, not worth mentioning. When we enter into hell, the enormous fire will be horrendously ablaze. It will be hard to be released from the 1,000,000 koṭi kalpas of immeasurable suffering. It will be hard to escape from the tribulations in the long night. Today we have encountered the Buddha, and we should strive to make energetic progress.'

"Then King Śaṅkha will chant aloud in verse:

The pleasures of life in heaven
Will eventually come to an end.
Before long will come a fall into hell,
Which is like a pile of raging fire.
We should take quick action
To renounce family life and learn the Buddha Way.

"Having spoken these words, Śaṅkha the Wheel-Turning King, surrounded reverently by 84,000 great ministers and escorted by the four god-kings, will go to the Flower Grove Garden. Under the dragon flower tree, he will ask Maitreya Buddha for permission to renounce family life, and he will make obeisance to this Buddha. Before he raises his head, his hair and beard will fall off by themselves, and he will be dressed in a monk's robe, becoming a śramaṇa.

"Then Maitreya Buddha, together with King Śaṅkha, surrounded reverently by 84,000 great ministers as well as bhikṣus and innumerable Dharma protectors in the eight classes, such as gods and dragons, will enter into the city of Ketuma. As soon as He steps over the threshold of the gate, the Sahā World will quake in six different ways. The ground of Jambudvīpa will turn golden. The ground in the center of the great city of Ketuma will be made of vajra. From the ground will naturally rise lines of jeweled trees and the jeweled vajra throne, upon which past Buddhas have sat. From the sky, gods will shower enormous jeweled flowers. As an offering to this Buddha, dragon-kings will play music, spit flowers from their mouths, and rain flowers from their pores. This Buddha will be seated on this throne to turn the wheel of the true Dharma. He will pronounce the noble truth of suffering, the noble truth of accumulation of afflictions, the noble truth of cessation of suffering, and the noble truth of the path. He will also expound the Thirty-seven Elements of Bodhi. He will also pronounce the Twelve Links of Dependent Arising: conditioned upon ignorance are karmic actions; conditioned upon karmic actions is [ālaya] consciousness; conditioned upon [ālaya] consciousness are name and form; conditioned upon name and form are the six faculties; conditioned upon the six faculties is contact with sense objects; conditioned upon contact with sense objects is sensory reception; conditioned upon sensory reception is love; conditioned upon love is grasping; conditioned upon grasping is the karmic force for being; conditioned upon the karmic force for being is birth; and conditioned upon birth are old age and death. Thus, one continues [this cycle] with anxiety, sorrow, pain, and distress.

"Then the earth will quake in six different ways. The sound will be heard across the Three-Thousand Large Thousandfold World and even innumerable, boundless worlds, from each Avīci Hell at the bottom to each Akaniṣṭha Heaven at the top. The four god-kings, each leading innumerable ghosts and spirits, will chant loudly, 'When the Buddha sun rises, the Dharma rain will fall. The eye of the world has opened today. Let the eight classes of Dharma protectors of the great earth, who are ready for the Buddha, all hear and know this.'

"The gods in the Thirty-three Heavens, Yāma Heaven, Tuṣita Heaven, Nirmāṇa-rati Heaven, Paranirmita-vaśa-vartin Heaven, and even Great Brahma Heaven will chant loudly in their respective places: 'When the Buddha sun rises, the sweet nectar falls. The eye of the world has opened today. Let all who are ready hear and know this.'

"At that time the eight classes of Dharma protectors, such as gods and dragons, as well as the spirits of mountains, trees, medicinal herbs, water, fire, earth, cities, dwellings, and so forth, joyful and exuberant, will also chant loudly.

"In addition, 84,000 Brahmins, intelligent and wise, following great King Śaṅkha, will renounce family life to learn the Way in the Buddha Dharma. An elder named Sudatta, who is none other than the Elder Sudatta today, together with 84,000 people, will also renounce family life. Two brothers named Ṛṣidatta and Pūraṇa, together with 84,000 people, will also renounce family life. Two great ministers named Brahmadamāli and Sumana, valued by the king, together with 84,000 people, will also renounce family life to learn the Way in the Buddha Dharma. Śāmivatī, the Wheel-Turning King's precious daughter, who is none other than Lady Viśākhā today, together with 84,000 fair ladies, will also renounce family life. Sky Golden Color, King Śaṅkha's crown prince, who is none other than the son of the Elder Devavana today, together with 84,000 people, will also renounce family life. Sumati, the son of a Brahmin related to Maitreya Buddha, who is none other than the son of the bhikṣuṇī Catarabhadra today, together with 84,000 people, will also renounce family life. Only one of the 1,000 sons of King Śaṅkha will be reserved for succeeding to the throne. His other 999 sons, together with 84,000 people, will all renounce family life in order to be in the Buddha Dharma. Countless multitudes such as these, seeing the suffering in the world and the blazing force of the five aggregates, will all renounce family life in order to be in the Dharma of Maitreya Buddha.

"Then, with the mind of great lovingkindness, Maitreya Buddha will speak these words to the multitude: 'You now have come to me, not seeking the pleasures of this life or of the next life in heaven, but the conditions for the eternal bliss of nirvāṇa. You have already planted your roots of goodness in the Buddha Dharma. When Śākyamuni Buddha appeared in the world of the five turbidities, He rebuked you variously, expounded the Dharma to you, and taught you to plant the conditions for the future so that you would see me. I will accept all of you.

"'Among you, there are those who have been reborn in the place where I am, because they have acquired merit, whether by reading and reciting the Tripiṭaka—the Sūtras, the Vinaya, and the Abhidharma—by praising their tenets and expounding them to others, or by, without jealousy, teaching and enabling others to accept and uphold [the Dharma]. Among you, there are those who have been reborn in the place where I am, because they have acquired merit by giving others food and clothing, observing the precepts, and developing wisdom. Among you, there are those who have been reborn in the place where I am, because they have acquired merit by offering Buddhas music, canopies, flowers, incense, and bright lamps. Among you, there are those who have been reborn in the place where I am, because they have acquired merit by offering food regularly to Saṅghas, erecting monks' living quarters, providing monks with the four necessities, or observing the eight precepts regularly for purification and for cultivation of lovingkindness. Among you, there are those who have been reborn in the place where I am, because they have acquired merit by invoking profound compassion for sentient beings in suffering and by personally bearing their suffering to give them happiness. Among you, there are those who have been reborn in the place where I am, because they have acquired merit by observing their precepts, enduring adversities, and developing the pure mind of lovingkindness. Among you, there are those who have been reborn in the place where I am, because they have acquired merit by building temples or offering food to the monks who came from everywhere to attend Dharma assemblies. Among you, there are those who have been reborn in the place where I am, because they have acquired merit by observing their precepts, hearing much [of the Dharma], practicing meditation, and developing affliction-free wisdom. Among you, there are those who have been reborn in the place where I am, because they have acquired merit by erecting pagodas, making offerings to holy relics, or thinking of the dharma body of Buddhas. Among you, there are those who have been reborn in the place where I am, because they have acquired merit by rescuing and liberating people in hardship, poverty, solitude, or bondage to others, people about to be tortured or executed by the law, or people in tremendous suffering because of their tribulation of the eight difficulties. Among you, there are those who have been reborn in the place where I am, because they have acquired merit by skillfully bringing to union and harmony people in tremendous suffering because of love, separation, faction, or dispute.'

"Having spoken these words, Maitreya Buddha will praise [me] Śākyamuni Buddha: 'Very good! Very good! He was able to teach and transform in the world of the five turbidities a billion koṭi evil sentient beings, enabling them to develop their roots of goodness and to be reborn in the place where I am.'

"Maitreya Buddha will repeat three times His praise of Śākyamuni Buddha, then speak in verse:

The great guiding teacher, enduring adversities and boldly valiant,
Was able to teach and transform evil sentient beings, and bring them to maturity
In the evil world of the five turbidities,
Enabling them to train themselves and to see the [next] Buddha.
Enduring enormous suffering in carrying sentient beings,
For them to enter the eternal bliss of that which is asaṁskṛta,
He advised His disciples to come to the place where I would be.

To glorify nirvāṇa, I now will pronounce to you the Four Noble Truths,
As well as the Thirty-seven Elements of Bodhi
And the Twelve Links of Dependent Arising.
You all should observe that which is asaṁskṛta
And enter the state of silent emptiness.

"Having spoken these stanzas, Maitreya Buddha will also praise those who were able to achieve difficult things in the painful evil world. He will say, 'You observed your precepts and did meritorious karmas among people who were greedy, angry, deluded, confused, and short-lived. That is exceptional! During those times sentient beings did not appreciate their parents, nor śramaṇas or Brahmins. Not knowing the Bodhi Way, they harassed and harmed one another, resorting to violence and war. Deeply addicted to the five desires, they were jealous and sycophantic. Deceitful, sinister, and pitiless, they killed, ate flesh, and drank blood. They had no respect for teachers or elders, and they did not know beneficent friends. They did not know such things as requiting kindness. Born into the world of the five turbidities, they had no sense of shame or dishonor. Day and night in the six periods, they continually did evil karmas, such as the five rebellious acts, not knowing when to stop. They gathered evils like densely arranged fish scales, never feeling disgusted. Clans and even nine branches of family could not help one another.

"'Very good! Very good! Śākyamuni Buddha, with great skillfulness and wisdom, out of profound lovingkindness and compassion, was able to speak honest words in a gentle and pleasant manner to suffering sentient beings, announcing that I will deliver all of them. Such a guiding teacher who has illuminating wisdom is a rarity in the world and hard to encounter. Deeply pitying sentient beings in the evil world, He wanted to eradicate their suffering, give them peace and joy, and guide them into the highest meaning of profound dharma nature. In three asaṁkhyeya kalpas, Śākyamuni Buddha, for your sake, trained in difficult ways and ascetic practices, enduring suffering as He gave away His head as alms and cut off His ears, nose, hands, and feet. To benefit you, He took the Eightfold Right Path and achieved total liberation.'

"In this way Maitreya Buddha will guide and comfort innumerable sentient beings, making them happy. They will be imbued with the Dharma. Their minds will be full of the Dharma, and their mouths will always pronounce the Dharma. The population will be composed of those who have merit and wisdom. Even gods will respect, trust, and admire them.

"At that time Maitreya Buddha, the great guiding teacher, will want them to hear about their suffering in the past. He will think: 'The five impure desires are the roots of suffering, but the knowledge that pain and pleasure are both impermanent can remove their anxieties and sorrows.' He will then pronounce to them the five aggregates—form, sensory reception, perception, mental processing, and consciousness—as well as suffering, emptiness, impermanence, and no self. As He speaks these words, 96 koṭi people will no longer embrace dharmas [perceived by the senses]. With no more afflictions to discharge, having liberated their minds, they will attain Arhatship, complete with the Three Clarities, the Six Transcendental Powers, and the Eight Liberations. In all, 36,000 god-sons and 20,000 goddess-daughters will activate the anuttara-samyak-saṁbodhi mind. Among the eight classes of Dharma protectors, such as gods and dragons, some will become Srotāpannas, entering the holy stream, and others will plant the conditions for going the Pratyekabuddha Way. The number of those who will activate the anuttara-samyak-saṁbodhi mind will be beyond reckoning.

"Then Maitreya Buddha, together with 96 koṭi great bhikṣus and King Śaṅkha, who is surrounded by 84,000 great ministers, bhikṣus, and retinues, like the son of the moon-god encircled by stars, will set off from the city of Ketuma and return to the Flower Grove Garden. Elders and lesser kings in the cities and settlements in Jambudvīpa, as well as those in the four castes, will gather under the dragon flower tree in the Flower Grove Garden. [In this second great assembly] Maitreya the World-Honored One will again pronounce the Four Noble Truths and the Twelve Links of Dependent Arising. Then 94 koṭi people will attain Arhatship. Gods from other worlds, the eight classes of Dharma protectors, and others, as numerous as the sands of 64 koṭi Ganges Rivers, will activate the anuttara-samyak-saṁbodhi mind, standing firm at the spiritual level of no regress. In the third great assembly, Maitreya Buddha will again pronounce the Four Noble Truths, turning the profound wonderful Dharma wheel. Then 92 koṭi people will attain Arhatship, and 34 koṭi Dharma protectors in the eight classes, such as gods and dragons, will activate the anuttara-samyak-saṁbodhi mind.

"Having delivered these gods and humans, Maitreya Buddha will lead His voice-hearer disciples and the eight classes of Dharma protectors, such as gods and dragons, together with the multitudes, and enter the city of Ketuma to beg for food. Innumerable gods from pure abode heavens will reverently follow this Buddha into the city. Upon entering the city, this Buddha will demonstrate His spiritual powers with eighteen transformations: water will manifest below His body, like precious gems, then transform into a plateau of light, illuminating worlds in the ten directions. Fire will manifest above His body, radiating purple-tinged golden light as vast as Mount Sumeru. He will appear enormous, filling the sky, then transform into aquamarine. He will appear miniscule, like a mustard seed, then vanish. He will rise in the ten directions then vanish in the ten directions. He will make all humans to have bodies like a Buddha's body. He will perform innumerable manifestations, using various kinds of spiritual powers, and viewers in the right conditions will all be liberated.

"The god-king Śakro-Devānām-Indra, his thirty-two ministers, gods from the desire realm, Brahma-kings and Brahma gods from the form realm, together with god-sons and goddess-daughters, will remove their celestial necklaces and robes, and scatter them over this Buddha, which will change into a canopy of flowers. Celestial music will sound without being played, hymning the merit of this Buddha. As an offering to this Buddha, celestial flowers and various sandalwood scents will rain profusely down from the sky. Banners will be erected on streets and roads. Choice incense will burn, its smoke resembling clouds.

"When Maitreya the World-Honored One enters the city, the god-king from Great Brahma Heaven and the god-king Śakro-Devānām-Indra will reverently join their palms and praise this Buddha in verse:

The Samyak-Saṁbuddha, the Two-Footed Honored One,
In heaven and on earth, no one can compare.
The World-Honored One with the Ten Powers is unique.
He is the unsurpassed supreme fortune field.

Those who make offerings to Him will be reborn in heaven,

And in the future will be liberated and abide in nirvāṇa.
Obeisance to the unsurpassed great attainment!
Obeisance to the great guiding teacher with the mind of lovingkindness!

"The four god-kings—Dhṛtarsaṣtra in the east, Virūḍhaka in the south, Virūpākṣa in the west, and Vaiśravaṇa in the north—together with their retinues, joining their palms reverently, with a pure mind, will praise the World-Honored One in verse:

No one living in the Three Realms can compare
With the one adorned with great compassion,
Who has realized and understood the highest truth.
He has penetrated the nature of sentient beings
And the appearances of all dharmas,
Seeing both abiding in the nature of emptiness.
Standing firm in [His realization of] emptiness,
He diligently makes energetic progress,
Yet nothing made through conditions, no footprints left behind.

I now make obeisance
To the great guiding teacher with the mind of lovingkindness.
When sentient beings do not see a Buddha,
They undergo birth and death in the long night,
Going down the three evil life-paths,
Or assuming female form.

Today a Buddha has appeared in the world,
Who will end suffering and give peace and joy.
The population on the three evil life-paths will decrease,
And women will no longer depend on flattery or deception.
All [evil ways of life] will come to rest.

Having attained the great nirvāṇa,
The one who will relieve suffering with great compassion,
To delight all, has appeared in the world.
When he was a Bodhisattva,
He always gave others all the joy,
Never killing or distressing others,
And His tolerance is like that of the great earth.

I now make obeisance
To the great guiding teacher who has endured all adversities.
I now make obeisance
To the great man who is loving-kind and compassionate.

Having transcended the suffering of birth and death,
He can rescue sentient beings from tribulations.

Like a lotus flower born from fire,
He is unequaled in the world!

"At that time Maitreya the World-Honored One will beg for food from one door to the next. Then he will lead the bhikṣus to the original place, where he will enter deep samādhi, not moving for seven days and seven nights.

"Maitreya Buddha's disciples will be stately in appearance, like the forms of gods, and they will all be tired of birth, aging, illness, and death. They will all hear much [of the Dharma], study and guard the Dharma store, and practice meditative concentration. They will all succeed in abandoning desires, like a bird leaving the eggshell.

"The god-king Śakro-Devānām-Indra, together with god-sons from the desire realm, joyful and exuberant, will speak in verse:

The great guiding teacher, the refuge of the world!
His wisdom-eye clearly sees all [in worlds] in the ten directions.
He surpasses gods in merit and wisdom.
With the right name and meaning, He benefits sentient beings.

May we [beginners] who are like sprouts,
Together with His disciples, go to that mountain
To make offerings to Śākyamuni Buddha's disciple,
Who was foremost in the dhūta way of life?

We should see the Dharma robe worn by the past Buddha
And hear the Dharma He has bequeathed.
For the evil karma in our past lives in the turbid evil kalpa,
We need to repent in order to be purified.

"Then Maitreya Buddha, together with His great disciples and sentient beings that were headstrong in their past lives in the Sahā World, will go to the Gṛdhrakūṭa Mountain. Having arrived at its foot, they will serenely walk up the Wolf Track Mountain. After they have reached the summit, Maitreya Buddha will touch the ground with his big toe. Forthwith, the great earth will move in eighteen different ways. Then Maitreya Buddha will split the cliff with both hands, like a Wheel-Turning King opening the gate of a great city [to find Mahākāśyapa inside].

"Then the Brahma-kings will pour scented oil onto the crown of Mahākāśyapa's head and over his body. Next, they will beat the great Dharma instruments and blow the great Dharma conch shells. Mahākāśyapa will then rise from the Samādhi of Total Halt. He will straighten his robe, bare his right shoulder, kneel on his right knee, and join his palms. Kneeling on both knees, he will hold the Dharma robe worn by Śākyamuni Buddha and offer it to Maitreya Buddha, saying these words: 'The great teacher Śākyamuni, the Tathāgata, Arhat, Samyak-Saṁbuddha, upon His parinirvāṇa, entrusted me with His Dharma robe and commanded me to offer it to the World-Honored One.'

"Meanwhile, everyone in the multitude will ask Maitreya Buddha, 'Why on this mountaintop today is a human-headed worm, puny, ugly, and dressed in the śramaṇa's habit, able to pay homage and make obeisance to the World-Honored One?'

"Then Maitreya Buddha will rebuke His great disciples. He will speak in verse, telling them not to disdain this person:

The peacock has beautiful colors,
But it can be eaten by the eagle.
The white elephant has infinite strength,
But the lion-son, though young,
Can grab and eat it like dirt.
The great dragon has an enormous body,
But it can be snatched by the golden-winged garuḍa.

The tall and large human body,
Plump, white, and handsome,
Is like a vessel made of the seven treasures but filled with feces.
Its filth is unbearable.

This person, though puny,
Has wisdom like refined gold.
Having long ended his afflictions and habits,
With nothing left of the suffering of birth and death,
For protecting the Dharma, he has stayed here.
Most victorious among gods and humans,
He has always carried out the dhūta way of life,
Unequaled in ascetic training.
Śākyamuni, the Two-Footed Honored One,
Has sent him to me.

You all should join your palms with a single mind
And reverently make obeisance to him.

"Having spoken these stanzas, Maitreya Buddha will tell the bhikṣus, 'Śākyamuni the World-Honored One has taught and transformed sentient beings in the world of the five turbidities. Among His 1,250 disciples, there was one with a golden body, who was foremost in the dhūta way of life. To learn the Way, he renounced family life and left his golden wife. Day and night he progressed energetically, as if fighting a fire burning on his head. He was loving-kind and compassionate to sentient beings that were poor and lowly, and always wanted to deliver them. For the sake of the Dharma, he has remained in the world. This person is none other than Mahākāśyapa.'

"Having heard these words, the multitude will all make obeisance to him.

"Then Maitreya Buddha will use Śākyamuni Buddha's Dharma robe to cover his right hand, but it will cover only two of His fingers. Then He will [use it to] cover His left hand, but again it will cover only two of His fingers. The multitude, astonished by the tiny size of the past Buddha, will understand that it was caused by sentient beings' greed and arrogance.

"Maitreya Buddha will tell Mahākāśyapa, 'Now you can demonstrate your spiritual powers and pronounce all the sūtras of the past Buddha.'

"Then Mahākāśyapa will jump up into the sky and display eighteen transformations. He will manifest an enormous body, filling the sky. This huge body will transform into a tiny one, like a grass seed. Water will manifest above his body, and fire will appear under his body. He will walk on the ground as if it were water, then walk on water as if it were ground. He will sit or lie down in the sky, not falling to the ground. He will appear in the east but vanish in the west, then appear in the west but vanish in the east. He will appear in the south but vanish in the north, then appear in the north but vanish in the south. He will appear at the edge but vanish in the center, then appear in the center but vanish at the edge. He will appear above but vanish below, then appear below but vanish above. He will turn into an aquamarine grotto in the sky. By virtue of the spiritual power of this Buddha, he will pronounce with the Brahma tone Śākyamuni Buddha's sūtras in the twelve categories. When the multitude hear [the teachings], they will marvel at them as something that never existed before. Then 80 koṭi people will eradicate their afflictions, becoming Arhats. They will remain in the midst of dharmas [of perceptions] but no longer embrace them. Innumerable gods and humans will activate the bodhi mind.

"Mahākāśyapa will descend from the sky and circle Maitreya Buddha three times. He will make obeisance to this Buddha and state that all saṁskṛta dharmas are impermanent. He will say farewell to Him and return to the place in the Gṛdhrakūṭa Mountain where he has been. Fire will burst from his body, and he will enter parinirvāṇa. Then his relics will be collected, and a pagoda will be erected on the mountaintop to enshrine his relics.

"Maitreya Buddha will again praise him, 'Śākyamuni Buddha, in the midst of the multitude, always praised the bhikṣu Mahākāśyapa, saying that he was foremost in the dhūta way of life and was accomplished in meditation and the Liberation Samādhi. This person, although he had great transcendental powers, was never haughty. Always pitying sentient beings in poverty and squalor, he was able to give them great joy.'

"Maitreya Buddha will extol Mahākāśyapa's relics, saying, 'Very good! Mahākāśyapa, the great disciple of the Śākya lion with great merit, was able to train his mind in that evil world.'

"At that time the relics of Mahākāśyapa will [appear in apparition and] speak in verse:

The dhūta practice is a treasure store.
Observing the precepts is sweet nectar.
One who can carry out the dhūta way of life
Will definitely arrive at the ground of no death.
One who observes one's precepts will be reborn in heaven
And in the bliss of nirvāṇa.

"After speaking this stanza, [the vision of] Mahākāśyapa, like liquid aquamarine, will return into the pagoda.

"The place where Maitreya Buddha will pronounce the Dharma will be 100 yojanas long and 80 yojanas wide. Each person in the multitude, whether sitting or standing, near or far, will see this Buddha pronounce the Dharma to him alone. Maitreya Buddha will remain in the world for 60 koṭi years and, out of sympathy for sentient beings, He will enable them to acquire the dharma-eye. After His parinirvāṇa, gods and humans will cremate His body, and the Wheel-Turning King will collect the relics and enshrine them in 84,000 pagodas on the four continents. The true Dharma will remain in the world for 60,000 years, followed by the Dharma-likeness for another 60,000 years.

"All of you should progress diligently, invoking your pure minds to do good karmas. Then there is no doubt that you will see Maitreya Buddha, the luminous lamp of the world."

After the Buddha finished these words, the venerable Śāriputra and the venerable Ānanda rose from their seats, made obeisance to the Buddha, and knelt on their right knees. Joining their palms, they asked the Buddha, "World-Honored One, what is the name of this sūtra? How should we uphold it?"

The Buddha told Ānanda, "You should remember it well and expound it separately to all gods and humans. Do not be the person who will finally terminate the Dharma. The tenet of this Dharma is that all sentient beings should end the five rebellious acts, annihilate the hindrances caused by afflictions, karmas, and requitals, and cultivate the mind of lovingkindness, in order to walk with Maitreya Buddha. Accept and uphold it as such. This sūtra is also called *All Sentient Beings, by Hearing Maitreya Buddha's Name, Definitely Avoiding the World of the Five Turbidities and Not Going Down the Evil Life-Paths*. Accept and uphold it as such. It is also called *The Certainty of Seeing Maitreya Buddha by Ending One's Evil Voice Karma, with a Mind like the Lotus Flower*. Accept and uphold it as such. It is also called *The Mind of Lovingkindness, No Killing and No Eating Flesh*. Accept and uphold it as such. It is also called *Śākyamuni Buddha's Dharma Robe as the Testament of Trust*. Accept and uphold it as such. It is also called *The Definite Avoidance of the Eight Difficulties by Hearing a Buddha's Name*. Accept and uphold it as such. It is also called *Maitreya Bodhisattva's Attainment of Buddhahood*. Accept and uphold it as such."

The Buddha told Śāriputra, "After my parinirvāṇa, if, among bhikṣus, bhikṣuṇīs, upāsakas, and upāsikās, as well as the eight classes of Dharma protectors, such as gods, dragons, and spirits, there are those who, having heard this sūtra, accept and uphold it, read and recite it, and make obeisance and offerings to it, as well as respect Dharma masters, they will annihilate their three kinds of hindrances: afflictions, karmas, and requitals. They will definitely see Maitreya Buddha and [the rest of] the one thousand Buddhas of this Worthy Kalpa. They will attain one of the three kinds of bodhi according to their wish. They will not be reborn in female form. They will renounce family life with the right views and achieve the great liberation."

Having heard the Buddha's words, the multitude greatly rejoiced. All made obeisance to the Buddha and departed.

7 佛說不增不減經
Buddha Pronounces the Sūtra of Neither Increase Nor Decrease

Translated from Sanskrit into Chinese in the Northern Wei Dynasty
by
The Tripiṭaka Master Bodhiruci from India

Thus I have heard:

At one time the Buddha was staying on the Gṛdhrakūṭa Mountain, near the city of Rājagṛha, together with 1,250 great bhikṣus and an innumerable, countless multitude of Bodhisattva-Mahāsattvas, in numbers beyond reckoning. In the huge multitude, Śāriputra the Wise rose from his seat, came to the Buddha, and bowed down at His feet. He then stepped back to sit on one side. Joining his palms, he said to the Buddha, "World-Honored One, since time without a beginning, sentient beings have been transmigrating, through the four modes of birth, to and fro along the six life-paths in the Three Realms of Existence, suffering endlessly in saṁsāra. World-Honored One, is this mass of sentient beings, or ocean of sentient beings, increasing or decreasing? I am unable to understand this profound meaning. How should I answer if someone asks me about this?"

The World-Honored One told Śāriputra, "Very good! Very good! You are able to ask me about this profound meaning because you want to give peace to all sentient beings, to give happiness to all sentient beings, to sympathize with all sentient beings, to help all sentient beings, and to give comfort and benefits to all sentient beings, such as gods and humans. Śāriputra, if you did not ask the Tathāgata, the Samyak-Saṁbuddha, about this meaning, there would be many faults. Then, in present and future times, gods, humans, and all other sentient beings would long undergo distress and harm, and lose forever [the opportunity for] all benefits, peace, and joy.

"Śāriputra, the enormously wrong view refers to seeing increase or seeing decrease in the realm of sentient beings. Sentient beings that hold this enormously wrong view are born without eyes and walk the evil way in the long night. For this reason, they go down the evil life-paths in their current lives. Śāriputra, the enormous perilous tribulation refers to one's obstinate adherence to the wrong view of increase or decrease in the realm of sentient beings. Śāriputra, those who are obstinate in their wrong adherence willfully walk the evil way in the long night. For this reason, they will go down the evil life-paths in their future lives.

"Śāriputra, foolish ordinary beings do not see the one dharma realm in accord with true reality. Because they do not see the one dharma realm in accord with true reality, they elicit the wrong views in their minds, saying that the realm of sentient beings increases or that the realm of sentient beings decreases. Śāriputra, when the Tathāgata is in the world, my disciples will not take these wrong views. However, over five hundred years after my parinirvāṇa, there will be many sentient beings that are foolish and senseless. Although they will remove their hair and beard, donning the three Dharma robes to appear as a śramaṇa in the Buddha Dharma, they will not have within themselves the virtuous ways of a śramaṇa. Such people are not śramaṇas, but they will claim to be śramaṇas. They are not the disciples of the Buddha though they claim to be, saying, 'I am a śramaṇa, a true disciple of the Buddha.'

"Such people hold the wrong view of increase or decrease. Why? Because these sentient beings follow the Tathāgata's sūtras of provisional meaning. They do not have the wisdom-eye and are far from the view of emptiness, which accords with true reality. They do not know what the Tathāgata has realized since His initial resolve [to attain Buddhahood]; they do not know how to train in and learn, in accord with true reality, the innumerable virtuous ways to realize bodhi; they do not know, in accord with true reality, the innumerable dharmas acquired by the Tathāgata; they do not know, in accord with true reality, the Tathāgata's immeasurable power; they do not know the Tathāgata's immeasurable realm; they do not believe in the Tathāgata's immeasurable action range; they do not know, in accord with true reality, the Tathāgata's inconceivable command of innumerable dharmas; they do not know, in accord with true reality, the Tathāgata's innumerable, inconceivable skillful means; they are unable to differentiate the Tathāgata's immeasurable distinct states; they are incapable of entering into the Tathāgata's inconceivable great compassion; and they do not know, in accord with true reality, the Tathāgata's mahāparinirvāṇa.

"Śāriputra, foolish ordinary beings, because they do not have the wisdom developed from hearing the Dharma, uphold the wrong view of cessation or extinction with respect to the nirvāṇa of a Tathāgata. Because of their perception of cessation or extinction, they claim that the realm of sentient beings does decrease. This is an enormously wrong view and an extremely grave, evil karma.

"Furthermore, Śāriputra, from the wrong view of decrease, these sentient beings elicit three more wrong views. These three views and the view of decrease, never separated from one another, are like a web. What are these three wrong views? The first is the view of cessation, which means the ultimate end. The second is the view of extinction, which is equated to nirvāṇa. The third is the view of void nirvāṇa, which means that nirvāṇa is ultimately nothingness. Śāriputra, so fettering, so gripping, and so contagious are these three wrong views!

"Conditioned upon the force of these three wrong views, successively arise two more wrong views. These two views and those three, never separated from one another, are like a web. What are these two wrong views? One is the view of no motivation, and the other is the view that ultimately there is no nirvāṇa. Derived from the wrong view of no motivation are two more wrong views. These two views and the view of no motivation, never separated from one another, are like a web. What are these two wrong views? One is the view that observing useless precepts will lead to a better rebirth, and the other is the inversion view, such as taking impurity as purity.

"Śāriputra, from the wrong view that ultimately there is no nirvāṇa, six more wrong views arise. These six views and the view of no nirvāṇa, never separated from one another, are like a web. What are these six wrong views? The first is that the world has a beginning; the second is that the world has an end; the third is that sentient beings are created by an illusion; the fourth is that there is no suffering or happiness; the fifth is that there is no such thing as [transmigration of] sentient beings; and the sixth is that there is no holy truth.

"Furthermore, Śāriputra, from the wrong view of increase, these sentient beings elicit two more wrong views. These two views and the view of increase, never separated from one another, are like a web. What are these two wrong views? One is the view that nirvāṇa has birth, and the other is the view that nirvāṇa suddenly comes about without causes or conditions. Śāriputra, these two wrong views cause the minds of sentient beings to have no wish and no drive to progress energetically in good dharmas. Śāriputra, even if seven Buddha-Tathāgatas, the Samyak-Saṁbuddhas, successively appeared in the world to pronounce the Dharma to sentient beings that hold these two wrong views, it would be impossible for them to develop any drive to make energetic progress in good dharmas.

"Śāriputra, these two wrong views are the roots of afflictions arising from ignorance. So wrong are the view that nirvāṇa is formed and the view that it suddenly comes about without causes and conditions!

"Śāriputra, these two wrong views are the dharma of extremely evil, enormous fundamental troubles. Śāriputra, from these two wrong views arise all other wrong views. All other wrong views and these two wrong views, never separated from one another, are like a web. All other wrong views include various kinds of views, such as the view of increase and the view of decrease, whether internal or external, whether coarse, fine, or in between.

"Śāriputra, these two wrong views, however, depend on the one realm, share the one realm, and are included in the one realm. Foolish ordinary beings, because they neither know nor see the one realm in accord with true reality, invoke extremely evil views in their minds, saying that the realm of sentient beings increases or that the realm of sentient beings decreases."

Śāriputra the Wise asked the Buddha, "World-Honored One, what is meant by the one realm? Foolish ordinary beings, because they neither know nor see the one realm in accord with true reality, invoke the extremely evil, enormous wrong views in their minds, saying that the realm of sentient beings increases or that the realm of sentient beings decreases. Very good! World-Honored One, this meaning is too profound for me to understand. I pray only that the Tathāgata will explain to me, to make me understand."

The World-Honored One told Śāriputra the Wise, "This profound meaning is in the realm of Tathāgata wisdom. It is also in the action range of the Tathāgata's mind. Śāriputra, all voice-hearers and Pratyekabuddhas with their wisdom are unable to know, to see, or to observe such profound meaning. Much less can all foolish ordinary beings speculate [about it]. Only Buddha-Tathāgatas with their wisdom are able to observe, to know, and to see this meaning. Śāriputra, all voice-hearers and Pratyekabuddhas with all their wisdom can only believe this meaning out of respect, but they are unable to know, to see, or to observe it in accord with true reality. Śāriputra, this profound meaning is in effect the highest truth, and the highest truth is in effect the realm of sentient beings. The realm of sentient beings is in effect the Tathāgata store, and the Tathāgata store is in effect the dharma body. Śāriputra, the dharma body, as I have explained in the inconceivable Buddha Dharma, is not apart, not removed, not severed, and not different from the merit and wisdom of the Tathāgata, which are more abundant than the sands of the Ganges.

"Śāriputra, taking the ordinary lamp as an analogy, its flame and its brightness are not apart or removed from each other. As another analogy, the form and the luster of a precious jewel are not apart or removed from each other. Likewise is the dharma body, as explained by the Tathāgata in the inconceivable Buddha Dharma. It is not apart, not removed, not severed, and not different from the merit and wisdom of the Tathāgata, which are more abundant than the sands of the Ganges.

"Śāriputra, the dharma body is the dharma of no birth and no death, neither of the past nor of the future, because it is beyond the two opposites. Śāriputra, it is not of the past because it is apart from birth; it is not of the future because it is apart from death. Śāriputra, the dharma body of the Tathāgata is eternal because it is the changeless dharma and the endless dharma. Śāriputra, the dharma body of the Tathāgata is eternal because it is the everlasting refuge and it is equal [in all sentient beings] into the endless future. Śāriputra, the dharma body of the Tathāgata is cool because it is the dharma of non-duality and the dharma of no differentiation. Śāriputra, the dharma body of the Tathāgata never changes because it is the dharma of no formation and no destruction.

"Śāriputra, this dharma body, fettered by endless afflictions more numerous than the sands of the Ganges, has been following along with the world since time without a beginning. When it is drifting to and fro in the ocean waves of birth and death, it is called a sentient being. Śāriputra, when this dharma body, tired of the suffering of repeated birth and death in the world, abandons all desires and quests, practices the six pāramitās and goes through the 84,000 Dharma Doors to train in the Bodhi Way, it is then called a Bodhisattva.

"Furthermore, Śāriputra, it is also this dharma body that, having transcended all suffering in the world and having left behind the bondage of afflictions, will reveal its purity and silence, and will abide in pure dharmas on the opposite shore, arriving on the ground that all sentient beings wish for. One who has achieved the unexcelled, ultimate insight into the realm of dharmas, free from all hindrances and obstructions, and has acquired the power of command in the midst of all dharmas, is called the Tathāgata, the Samyak-Saṁbuddha. Therefore, Śāriputra, not apart from the realm of sentient beings is the dharma body; not apart from the dharma body is the realm of sentient beings. The realm of sentient beings is in effect the dharma body; the dharma body is in effect the realm of sentient beings. Śāriputra, these two dharmas under different names have the same meaning.

"Furthermore, Śāriputra, as I said before, there are three kinds of dharmas in the realm of sentient beings. They all are true suchness, without any distinction or difference. What are these three dharmas? The first is the responsive original body of the Tathāgata store, together with pure dharmas. The second is the unresponsive original body of the Tathāgata store, together with fettering afflictions and impure dharmas. The third is the Tathāgata store, equal and eternal in all dharmas.

"Śāriputra, know that the responsive original body of the Tathāgata store, together with pure dharmas, accords with true reality. It is not false, and is not apart or removed from the inconceivable dharma realm of true suchness and pure wisdom. Since the origin without a beginning, there has always been this dharma body responsive to purity. Śāriputra, pertaining to this pure dharma realm of true suchness, I pronounce to sentient beings this inconceivable dharma, called the inherent pure mind.

"Śāriputra, know that the unresponsive original body of the Tathāgata store, together with fettering afflictions and impure dharmas, since the origin without a beginning, has always been apart from and unresponsive to fettering afflictions and impure dharmas which, however, can be eradicated only by one's bodhi wisdom. Śāriputra, pertaining to this inconceivable dharma realm unresponsive to but fettered by afflictions, I pronounce to sentient beings the inconceivable dharma of the inherent pure mind, though that mind is covered up by afflictions, like dust particles that have become long-term visitors.

"Śāriputra, know that the Tathāgata store, equal and eternal in all dharmas, is the root of all dharmas, complete and replete with all dharmas, and is not apart or removed from the true reality of all worldly dharmas. It underlies all dharmas and encompasses all dharmas. Śāriputra, pertaining to this refuge of the inconceivable pure dharma realm, with neither birth nor death, always cool and never changing, I pronounce that it is called sentient beings. Why? Because sentient beings are in effect the refuge that, with neither birth nor death, is permanent, eternal, cool, and changeless. It is a different name for the inconceivable pure dharma realm. According to this meaning, the pure dharma realm is called sentient beings.

"Śāriputra, all of these three dharmas are true suchness, not distinct, not different. From this neither varying nor changing dharma of true suchness, one never elicits the two extremely evil, wrong views. Why? Because one sees dharmas in accord with true reality. As for the view of increase and the view of decrease, Śāriputra, Buddha-Tathāgatas forever stay far away from these two wrong views. Both views are denounced by Buddha-Tathāgatas.

"Śāriputra, if, among bhikṣus, bhikṣuṇīs, upāsakas, and upāsikās, there are those who hold either or both of these two wrong views, Buddha-Tathāgatas will not be their World-Honored Ones. They are not my disciples. Śāriputra, by holding these two wrong views, these people will go from gloom into gloom, from dark into dark. I say that they are called icchantikas. Therefore, Śāriputra, you all should learn this Dharma to transform sentient beings, enabling them to keep away from these two wrong views and to stay on the right path. Śāriputra, you too should learn this Dharma to keep away from those two wrong views and to stay on the right path."

After the Buddha pronounced this sūtra, Śāriputra the Wise, bhikṣus, bhikṣuṇīs, upāsakas, and upāsikās, as well as Bodhisattva-Mahāsattvas and the eight classes of Dharma protectors—gods, dragons, yakṣas, gandharvas, asuras, garuḍas, kiṁnaras, and mahoragas—together with humans, nonhumans, and others, greatly rejoiced. They all believed in and reverently carried out the teachings.

8 大乘遍照光明藏無字法門經
Mahāyāna Sūtra of the Illuminating Everywhere Radiance-Store Wordless Dharma Door

Translated from Sanskrit into Chinese in the Tang Dynasty
by
The Tripiṭaka Master Divākara from India

Thus I have heard:

At one time the Buddha was dwelling in the city of Rājagṛha, near the Vulture Peak Mountain, together with innumerable hundreds, thousands, koṭis, and nayutas of great Bodhisattvas and bhikṣus.

These Bodhisattvas have all developed great wisdom and skillful means, and they all can penetrate the wordless Dharma store. Delighting in speaking eloquently, they have never contradicted truth or worldly knowledge. Through valiant and energetic progress, they have forever discarded the five coverings and the ten fetters. Having tamed their faculties, they are attached to nothing. They pity every sentient being as they would pity an only son. They prize wisdom-knowledge as they do a great treasure island. Assuming a sense of shame and dishonor as their body, they take meditation and wisdom as their head. Great lovingkindness and compassion being their basic nature, they know dharmas that are good or bad, real or unreal. They stand on the superb Ground, [their wisdom] illuminating the two emptinesses. Having received great names, they remain serene and peaceful. They are resolved to train in the supreme Dharma. Having forever left the base and inferior body born through the womb, they nevertheless have manifested rebirth in order to guard the domain [of the Dharma]. Whatever they have implemented is universally good and worthy. Having left the Three Realms of Existence, they can rescue the Three Realms of Existence. Their pure actions are good for themselves and for others as well.

Among those who have acquired all such merits are Excellent Thinking Bodhisattva, Excellent Journey Bodhisattva, Wonderful Tone Bodhisattva, Beautiful Tone Bodhisattva, Eloquence Fulfilled Bodhisattva, Eloquence Gathered Bodhisattva, Pearl Topknot Bodhisattva, Thousand Spoke Bodhisattva, Dharma Net Bodhisattva, Dharma Echo Bodhisattva, Lotus Face Bodhisattva, Lotus Eye Bodhisattva, Upholding the Earth Bodhisattva, Upholding the World Bodhisattva, and Sound Pervading the Great Earth Bodhisattva.

Bodhisattva-Mahāsattvas such as these, all in the likeness of youths, along with their respective retinues, were at the head of this multitude. Avalokiteśvara Bodhisattva was surrounded by an innumerable, countless multitude of Bodhisattvas who had nectar sprinkled on their heads and their missions assigned. Great Might Arrived Bodhisattva was surrounded by innumerable koṭis of great Brahma gods. Excellent Thinking Bodhisattva was surrounded by innumerable Bodhisattvas and the god-king Śakra. Space Store Bodhisattva was surrounded by innumerable gods led by the four god-kings. Recognized-by-All Bodhisattva was surrounded by innumerable goddess-daughters. Samantabhadra Bodhisattva, Free from Doubt Bodhisattva, Seeing Non-emptiness Bodhisattva, Ending All Coverings Bodhisattva, Immeasurable Skillfulness Medicine King Bodhisattva, and Medicine Superior Bodhisattva were each surrounded by an innumerable multitude of Bodhisattvas.

The Elder Śāriputra, Mahāmaudgalyāyana, Mahākāśyapa, and others were each surrounded by great Arhats. From worlds in the ten directions, which are as numerous as the sands of the Ganges, the sons of the sun-gods and moon-gods, with awesome radiance, each came to the place where the Buddha was. However, because of the spiritual power of the Buddha, their radiance, unable to shine, was dark as pooled ink matched against the gold from the Jambū River. Innumerable Nārāyaṇas, as well as the dragon-king Water Sky Takṣaka, the dragon-king Anavatapta, and others, were each surrounded by their retinues. The gandharva-king Beautiful Tone was also surrounded by an innumerable multitude of gandharvas. The garuḍa-king Turbidity Free was surrounded by a retinue of seven koṭi garuḍas.

From worlds in the ten directions, which are as numerous as the sands of the Ganges, Bodhisattvas, with the permission of their own Buddhas, along with their retinues, all came to this Sahā World. Having presented splendid supra-worldly offerings to the Buddha and Bodhisattvas, they each bowed down at the feet of the Buddha. Then they stepped back to one side, sat down on lotus flower seats, and gazed reverently at the World-Honored One.

Excellent Thinking Bodhisattva-Mahāsattva rose from his seat, bared his right shoulder, and knelt on his right knee. Joining his palms and facing the Buddha, he said, "World-Honored One, for His four groups of disciples, I would like to ask the Tathāgata the meanings of two thoughts. I pray only that the Tathāgata will explain them to me, so as to enable all of us to receive benefits."

The World-Honored One told Excellent Thinking Bodhisattva, "Would the Tathāgata appear in the world for just one sentient being? It is for benefiting innumerable sentient beings that he has appeared in the world. Good man, you now are able to ask me, for the sake of my four groups of disciples, the meanings of two thoughts. I will answer you according to your questions."

Then Excellent Thinking Bodhisattva, with the Buddha's permission, asked the Buddha, "What dharmas should Bodhisattva-Mahāsattvas eradicate or safeguard? Moreover, what dharmas has the Tathāgata perceived and verified? I pray only that the Tathāgata will explain these two meanings to me."

The Buddha praised Excellent Thinking Bodhisattva, saying, "Very good! Very good! Good man, you have acquired immeasurable merit and wisdom. Moreover, by virtue of the awesome spiritual power of the Tathāgata, you are able to ask me these meanings. Hearken! Hearken! Ponder them well. I will explain them separately to you.

"Good man, there is a dharma that Bodhisattva-Mahāsattvas should eradicate. What is this dharma? It is greed. Such a dharma Bodhisattva-Mahāsattvas should eradicate. Good man, there is another dharma that Bodhisattva-Mahāsattvas should eradicate. What is this dharma? It is anger. Such a dharma Bodhisattva-Mahāsattvas should eradicate. Good man, there is another dharma that Bodhisattva-Mahāsattvas should eradicate. What is this dharma? It is delusion. Such a dharma Bodhisattva-Mahāsattvas should eradicate. Good man, there is another dharma that Bodhisattva-Mahāsattvas should eradicate. What is this dharma? It is the wrong view that there is a self in one. Such a dharma Bodhisattva-Mahāsattvas should eradicate. Good man, there is another dharma that Bodhisattva-Mahāsattvas should eradicate. What is this dharma? It is indolence. Such a dharma Bodhisattva-Mahāsattvas should eradicate. Good man, there is another dharma that Bodhisattva-Mahāsattvas should eradicate. What is this dharma? It is torpor. Such a dharma Bodhisattva-Mahāsattvas should eradicate. Good man, there is another dharma that Bodhisattva-Mahāsattvas should eradicate. What is this dharma? It is impure love. Such a dharma Bodhisattva-Mahāsattvas should eradicate. Good man, there is another dharma that Bodhisattva-Mahāsattvas should eradicate. What is this dharma? It is doubt. Such a dharma Bodhisattva-Mahāsattvas should eradicate. Good man, there is another dharma that Bodhisattva-Mahāsattvas should eradicate. What is this dharma? It is ignorance. Such a dharma Bodhisattva-Mahāsattvas should eradicate. Good man, such dharmas as stated before, Bodhisattva-Mahāsattvas should eradicate.

"Good man, you ask me what dharmas Bodhisattva-Mahāsattvas should safeguard. I now tell you. Good man, there is a dharma that Bodhisattva-Mahāsattvas should always safeguard. What is this dharma? Namely, they should not persuade others to do what they themselves do not want to do. Such a dharma Bodhisattva-Mahāsattvas should always safeguard. Why? Because if Bodhisattva-Mahāsattvas safeguard this dharma, they in effect safeguard the entire precept store of Buddha-Tathāgatas. For example, those who love their own lives should not take other sentient beings' lives. Those who love their own possessions should not take things not given. Those who love their own wives should not take liberties [with other women]. Those who love honest words should not deceive others. Those who love harmony should not divide others. Those who love uprightness should not be devious or suggestive. Those who love gentleness should not scold viciously. Those who love contentment should not be greedy. Those who love kind forgiveness should not get angry with others. Those who love the right views should not cause others to elicit the wrong views.

"Good man, when Bodhisattvas such as these earnestly announce 'I now respect and follow the true Dharma of the Tathāgata. I should diligently safeguard this Dharma,' this is what is meant by Bodhisattva-Mahāsattvas safeguarding the one Dharma. Good man, I see Bodhisattvas such as these seek the unsurpassed great bodhi. They all seek bodhi for happiness; no one seeks it for suffering. Good man, that is why I say this: 'Do not persuade others to do what you yourself do not want to do.' Dharmas such as these, Bodhisattva-Mahāsattvas should safeguard."

At that time Excellent Thinking Bodhisattva next asked the Buddha, "World-Honored One, what kind of dharmas has the Tathāgata perceived and verified? I pray only that He will expound its meaning to me."

The Buddha replied, "Good man, there is not a single dharma that the Tathāgata has perceived or verified. Why not? Because the Tathāgata has perceived and verified that there is neither perception nor verification of dharmas. Good man, the Tathāgata has perceived and verified that dharmas have never come into existence. The Tathāgata has perceived and verified that dharmas have never gone into nonexistence. The Tathāgata has perceived and verified that the true nature of all dharmas is apart from such dualities. The Tathāgata has perceived and verified that all dharmas have never had any reality.

"Moreover, good man, all dharmas [in appearance] arise from the forces of karmic causes and conditions. These causes and conditions change from kṣaṇa to kṣaṇa, like a flash of lightning. Such karmic conditions, the Tathāgata has perceived and verified. Therefore, I say that through causes and conditions all dharmas are born and that through causes and conditions all dharmas perish. Without causes and conditions, there would be no karmic requitals. Matters such as these, the Tathāgata has perceived. Good man, the nature of all dharmas perceived as such is called the Illuminating Everywhere Radiance Store. Good man, why is dharma nature called the Store? Because sentient beings' worldly and supra-worldly knowledge relies on and arises from this Store. If one observes dharma nature, one's wisdom-knowledge of true reality will arise from dharma nature. That is why dharma nature is called the Store.

"Furthermore, good man, I also say that all dharmas are like illusions, like mirages, and like the moon in the water. Matters such as these, the Tathāgata has perceived and verified. Moreover, good man, the nature of all dharmas is in the one flavor of liberation. Matters such as these, the Tathāgata has perceived and verified. Good man, dharma nature in the one flavor of liberation is called the Illuminating Everywhere Radiance Store.

"Furthermore, good man, there is another dharma that the Tathāgata has perceived and verified. What is this dharma? Namely, dharmas [in true reality] have neither birth nor death, neither increase nor decrease. They are neither coming nor going, neither causes nor conditions, and are beyond acceptance or rejection. Dharmas such as these, the Tathāgata has perceived and verified.

"Furthermore, good man, the Tathāgata clearly understands that dharmas have no self-essence, and cannot be described by metaphor or explained by words. Dharmas such as these, the Tathāgata has perceived and verified. Good man, these dharmas as stated before, the Tathāgata has perceived and verified."

When the Buddha pronounced this Illuminating Everywhere Radiance-Store Wordless Dharma, Bodhisattvas as numerous as dust particles attained the Tenth Ground, and innumerable Bodhisattvas attained other Grounds. Innumerable Bodhisattvas attained 100,000 great samādhis. Sentient beings as numerous as dust particles activated the anuttara-samyak-saṁbodhi mind. Innumerable, countless sentient beings achieved the fourth voice-hearer fruit, becoming Arhats. Innumerable, countless sentient beings, including hell-dwellers, hungry ghosts, and animals, were liberated from their various kinds of suffering. They were reborn in heaven to enjoy fabulous pleasures. None of those present in the assembly found their attendance a waste. None of them ended up empty-handed.

Then the Buddha said to Rāhula, "Good man, I want you to uphold this Dharma of mine."

When the 99 koṭi Bodhisattva-Mahāsattvas in that assembly heard these words, by virtue of the spiritual power of the Buddha, they said to the Buddha, "World-Honored One, we vow that, at the latter time and latter stage of this Sahā

World, when we see those who are capable of being Dharma vessels, we will pronounce this sūtra to them. We pray only that the World-Honored One will not be worried."

At that time the four god-kings also said to the Buddha, "World-Honored One, if in future times, among good men and good women, there are those who can uphold this sūtra, we will support them and fulfill their wishes. Why? Because these good men and good women who can uphold this sūtra are Dharma vessels."

The World-Honored One, having seen these 99 koṭi Bodhisattvas and the four god-kings make such pledges, spoke these words: "Good men, this Illuminating Everywhere Radiance-Store Wordless Dharma Door I just pronounced is what I have not expounded since I attained Buddhahood. To you all I have expounded it today!

"Good men, if sentient beings in future times are able to hear this rare Dharma Door, know that they have already acquired immeasurable merit and wisdom; that they in effect serve me and make offerings to me; that they in effect carry on the great bodhi of the Buddha; that they will certainly achieve command of eloquence; that they will certainly arrive in pure Buddha Lands; that when their lives come to an end, they will certainly see Amitābha Buddha, surrounded by a multitude of Bodhisattvas; that they will constantly see me on the Vulture Peak Mountain and see a multitude of Bodhisattvas like these here; that they have already acquired the inexhaustible Dharma store; that they will gain past-life knowledge; and that they will never go down the evil life-paths.

"Furthermore, good men, I now have pronounced this Dharma, which was unavailable to you before. Suppose in future times, among good men and good women, there are those who have committed sins, such as the five rebellious sins. If they have heard this Dharma Door, whether they copy this sūtra, read and recite it, or explain it, whether they persuade others to copy it, read and recite it, or explain it, I can see that these individuals will not go down the evil life-paths. Their three kinds of hindrances—afflictions, karmas, and requitals—will all be annihilated. In a future life they will acquire the five eyes. They will have nectar sprinkled on their heads by all Buddhas. These individuals will be protected and remembered by all Buddha-Bhagavāns and Bodhisattvas. Wherever they are reborn in the future, their faculties will definitely be complete, with nothing missing."

After the Buddha pronounced this sūtra, Excellent Thinking Bodhisattva-Mahāsattva and others, as well as the bhikṣus and the eight classes of Dharma protectors, such as gods and dragons, having heard the Buddha's words, greatly rejoiced. They all believed in, accepted, and reverently carried out the teachings.

9 占察善惡業報經卷下
Sūtra of Detecting Good or Evil Karma and Requital

Translated from Sanskrit into Chinese in the Sui Dynasty
by
Master Bodhi Lamp (biography unavailable)

Fascicle 2 (of 2)

At that time Firm Pure Faith Bodhisattva-Mahāsattva asked Earth Store Bodhisattva-Mahāsattva, "Please indicate a viable way for the sake of those who seek the Mahāyāna."

Earth Store Bodhisattva-Mahāsattvas said, "Good man, if there are sentient beings that seek the Mahāyāna, they should first know the initial fundamental karma to do. To know the initial fundamental karma to do means that they need to cultivate faith and understanding by relying on the one true reality. As their faith and understanding grow in strength, they will quickly develop the Bodhisattva character-type. The one true reality refers to the true mind of sentient beings, which, with inherent purity, without hindrances, has neither birth nor death. Like space, it does not differentiate but accommodates all, and it is equal in and universal to all. With the ultimate one appearance, it is perfect everywhere in the ten directions, non-dual and differentiation free, neither changing nor varying, neither increasing nor decreasing. For all sentient beings, voice-hearers, Pratyekabuddhas, Bodhisattvas, and Buddhas, the true mind is the same, which is true suchness, silent and never tainted, with neither birth nor death.

"Why? Because the mind that differentiates is like illusions without any reality. For example, mental functions, such as consciousness, sensory reception, perception, mental processing, memory, deliberation, and cognition, are neither blue nor yellow, neither red nor white, nor of mixed colors. They are neither long nor short, neither square nor round, neither large nor small. One can search for the shape of the mind throughout all worlds in the ten directions, but can never capture it under a classification. However, [the mind of] every sentient being, conditioned by ignorance and delusion, manifests false objects and clings to them through thinking and memory. This mind does not know itself but falsely claims its own existence. Although thoughts of a self and its belongings arise, there is no truth to them because the false mind is not an entity that can be seen. If there is no perception that differentiates, then there cannot be appearances differentiated into objects in space and time, such as the ten directions and the past, present, and future. Dharmas do not have independent existence, and they exist only as differentiations made by the false mind, which thinks of all objects as existent and distinct, identifying this as self and that as others.

"Because dharmas do not exist independently, they have no inherent differences. However, the false mind neither knows nor understands this. Having no substance within, it falsely perceives and recognizes that various dharmas exist outside. It identifies existence and nonexistence, this and that, true and false, good and evil, producing innumerable, boundless perceptions of dharmas. We should know this: All dharmas are born from perception constructed by the false mind. Furthermore, this false mind has no self-essence, and its false existence depends on its objects. Because it can think of and perceive objects, it is called the mind. Although this false mind and its objects depend upon each other and arise simultaneously, the false mind is the originator of objects. Why? Because the false mind does not understand the one appearance of the dharma realm, we say that this is the ignorance of one's mind. Relying on the force of ignorance, it falsely manifests objects. If ignorance ends, then one's attachment to the manifestation of objects will end. We should not say, out of lack of understanding, that objects have ignorance or that they cause ignorance. Evidently, objects do not cause ignorance to arise in Buddhas. The ignorance of one's mind will not end by annihilating objects because objects have no independent existence and their dharma nature has always been in nirvāṇa. For this reason, we say that all dharmas arise from one's mind. Know that dharmas should be called the mind because they in essence are not distinct, but are all encompassed in one's mind. Furthermore, dharmas arise as appearances perceived by one's mind, and manifest as birth and death together with one's perception, never staying. All objects of mind move along with mind, continuing thought after thought. Their seeming stay and existence last temporarily.

"The meaning of mind comprises two aspects. What are these two? One is internal and the other external. The internal aspect of mind is divided into two. What are these two? One is true and other false. The essence of the true mind is changeless, pure, perfect, unobstructed, unimpeded, subtle, invisible, free from places, and eternally indestructible, relying on which all dharmas are constructed and developed [through causes and conditions]. By contrast, the false mind produces thoughts, perceiving, distinguishing, pondering, and recollecting objects. Although it can continuously construct [perception of] various kinds of objects, it is false, not true.

"The external aspect of mind refers to dharmas, or various kinds of objects, which appear according to one's thinking. This is the distinction between the internal and external aspects of mind. Therefore, we should know that the internal false perceptions are the cause and function, and the external false appearances are the results and projections. Considering these meanings, I say that all dharmas are called the mind. Furthermore, the external appearances of one's mind are like objects seen in a dream, which are produced by the thinking mind and are not real external objects. Indeed, all objects perceived are dreams of one's ignorant consciousness, fabricated by one's thinking. Moreover, because the internal false mind does not stay, moving thought after thought, the objects it perceives also do not stay, moving thought after thought. Therefore, various kinds of dharmas arise because the false mind arises, and they cease because the false mind ceases. Such appearances of birth and death cannot be captured because they are in name only. As one's mind does not go to the objects, the objects do not come to one's mind, like reflections in a mirror, neither coming nor going.

"Therefore, the appearance of birth and death of all dharmas cannot be captured because dharmas have no self-essence. They have always been empty, with neither birth nor death. Because dharmas in true reality have neither birth nor death, they have no differentiable appearances as objects. They are in the one flavor of silence and stillness, called true suchness, the highest truth, the inherent pure mind. This inherent pure mind is profound and perfect because it does not distinguish objects. Because it does not distinguish, it is universal. As it is universal, all dharmas rely on it to appear. Furthermore, this mind is called the Tathāgata store, free from afflictions and complete with immeasurable, boundless, inconceivable, pure meritorious karma.

"The dharma body of a Buddha is unobstructed, unhindered, free, and indestructible since the origin without a beginning. Always active, never resting, it manifests various kinds of meritorious karmas everywhere in all worlds, variously transforming and benefiting sentient beings. The dharma body of one Buddha is the dharma bodies of all Buddhas, and the dharma bodies of all Buddhas are the dharma body of one Buddha. The karmas [of all Buddhas] are also undivided, without any distinction between those of one Buddha and those of another Buddha, because they are equal and indistinguishable. Their karmas, based on the one dharma nature, are the same, spontaneously arising as manifestations, without differentiation. As Buddhas' dharma bodies pervade everywhere, perfect and motionless, sentient beings rely on their dharma bodies as they die here then are reborn there. The dharma body is like space, which can accommodate all forms in various shapes and types. For example, the existence of forms in various shapes and types relies on space as they arise, grow, and remain in space. Accommodated in space, they use space as their field. Nothing can be outside the domain of space. We should know that the domain of space containing forms is indestructible. Although space is revealed when forms are destroyed, the domain of space never increases, decreases, moves, or changes. Neither does the dharma body of a sentient being. It can accommodate various kinds of karmic requitals of a sentient being because the existence of such karmic requitals relies on the dharma body. Established and stored in the dharma body, karmic requitals relying on the dharma body as their essence. Nothing can be outside the realm of the dharma body.

"We should know that the dharma body of a sentient being can never be destroyed. When one's afflictions have been eradicated, the dharma body is fully revealed, yet the realm of the dharma body neither increases nor decreases, neither moves nor changes. However, it has been concealed by one's ignorance since time without a beginning. Conditioned by the force of delusion, it manifests false objects through causes and conditions. Further influenced by the false objects, it imagines a self and its belongings through causes and conditions, then does karma to undergo the suffering of birth and death. Those with such a dharma body are called sentient beings. If there are sentient beings that gain strength from the purity of the dharma body, their afflictions will diminish, and they will turn away from the worldly life to seek the Way to nirvāṇa. If they have faith in the one true reality, practice the six pāramitās, and acquire the Thirty-seven Elements of Bodhi, they will be called Bodhisattvas. When these Bodhisattvas have completed all the good dharmas in their training and ultimately discard the dream fabricated by ignorance, their names will be changed to Buddhas. It should be known that sentient beings, Bodhisattvas, and Buddhas are differentiated only by false names and words of the world. Their dharma bodies are ultimately equal, with no distinguishable appearances. Good man, this is a brief explanation of the meaning of the one true reality.

"Those who want to develop their belief in and understanding of the one true reality should learn the approach of two observations. What are these two? One is the observation that all dharmas are only mind and consciousness, and the other is the insight into true suchness. One who wants to learn to know one's mind and consciousness should observe anywhere and at any time that all dharmas are mind, as one does karma with one's body, voice, and mind. One should be aware of all the objects that one's mind dwells on. One should not allow one's mind to pursue objects blindly without being aware. Thought after thought, one should follow each thought and observe its content, enabling one's mind to know that it is producing perceptions and thoughts, not the objects producing thoughts or differentiations. One's mind produces innumerable perceptions, such as long or short, good or evil, right or wrong, gain or loss, advantage or disadvantage, existence or nonexistence, while objects have no differentiating perceptions. As objects never have any perception, they are free from self-images, such as long or short, good or evil, existence or nonexistence. In this way one should observe that all dharmas are produced by one's mind. Apart from one's mind, there is not a single dharma that can perceive distinctions for itself. Never giving up, one should stay with and note one's mind, and know that there are only thoughts and imaginations, no real objects. This is called training in the observation that all dharmas are only mind and consciousness. However, this is not called the observation that all dharmas are mind and consciousness when one's mind is a blank, not knowing what it is thinking, and says there are objects outside itself. One who stays with and notes one's mind should know one's greed, anger, and delusion, as well as wrong views. One should also know one's good, evil, and neutral thoughts, as well as exertions, concerns, and suffering. When one is sitting [in meditation], one should follow the objects of one's mind and know that, thought after thought, only the mind rises and falls. It is like the flow of water and the flame of a lamp, never staying even temporarily. From there one should attain the Samādhi of the Silence of Percepts.

"After one has attained this samādhi, one should next learn to observe one's mind by means of śamatha and vipaśyanā. One who believes in and practices śamatha as a method to observe one's mind should ponder the invisible true mind, which is perfect and free from differentiation, never moving, neither coming nor going, because the mind in its original nature has no birth. One who believes in and practices vipaśyanā should observe that the internal and external objects manifest as birth and death, as the [false] mind rises and falls. Even visualization of a Buddha's physical body occurs in the same way. It follows one's mind in its birth and death, like an illusion, like a conjuration, like the moon in the water, and like the reflection in the mirror. It is not the mind but not apart from the mind, neither coming nor not coming, neither going nor not going, neither born nor not born, neither formed nor not formed. Good man, one who can learn to observe one's mind by these two methods will quickly set off on the Way of the One Vehicle. We should know that the observation that all dharmas are only mind and consciousness is called the supreme door to wisdom. It enables one's mind to be intensely keen, to develop the power of faith and understanding, and to enter quickly into the meaning of emptiness, because one will succeed in activating the unsurpassed great bodhi mind.

"One who wants to develop insight into true suchness should ponder that one's mind in its true nature has neither birth nor death, nor does it abide in perception through faculties, such as seeing, hearing, and knowing. One should ignore the thoughts of differentiation. Then one can gradually pass the four samādhis of the formless realm—Boundless Space, Boundless Consciousness, Nothingness, and Neither with Nor without Perception—and attain the Samādhi of the Likeness of Emptiness. After one has attained the Samādhi of the Likeness of Emptiness, one's coarse differentiation through sensory reception, perception, mental processing, and consciousness will not be active. From then on, one's training and learning will be under the protection and care of beneficent learned friends who have great lovingkindness and compassion. As one trains assiduously, overcoming all obstacles, one can gradually enter the Samādhi of the Silent Mind. Once one has attained this samādhi, one can then enter the Samādhi of the One Action. After one has entered this Samādhi of the One Action, one will see innumerable Buddhas and will take wide-ranging and far-reaching actions, with one's mind set in the Position of Firm Belief.

"Those who firmly believe in and understand these two ways of observation, called śamatha and vipaśyanā, can definitely move in the right direction. They will be able to practice and learn worldly dhyānas and samādhis, without being captivated by them. They will be able to develop all their roots of goodness and train in all the Thirty-seven Elements of Bodhi. They will have no fear of birth and death and have no interest in the Two Vehicles because they can rely on these two ways to observe their minds. These are the most skillful ways because they are the foundation of wisdom-knowledge.

"Furthermore, there are two types of people who can train and learn according to their faith and understanding. What are these two types? One type has high capacity and the other type has low capacity. Those with high capacity already know that the realm of external objects is produced by one's mind and that objects are false and unreal, like dreams and illusions. They definitely have no doubts or concerns in this regard. The driving force of their five aggregates is less obstructive, and their wandering minds are less active. These people should learn to develop insight into true suchness.

"Those with low capacity do not yet know that external objects, false and unreal, are only [projections of] one's own mind. Because it is hard to tame their minds, which are tainted with strong passions and blocked by hindrances, they should first learn to observe that all dharmas are only mind and consciousness. Although they are learning to believe and understand, because their roots of goodness are shallow, they are unable to advance; their evil afflictions cannot be subjugated gradually; and their minds are skeptical and timid. They are fearful of going down the three evil life-paths and of being reborn into the eight difficulties. They are fearful that they may not always encounter Buddhas or Bodhisattvas; that they may not be able to make offerings or hear the true Dharma; and that it would be hard for their faith in bodhi to bring them accomplishment. Those who have such doubts, fears, and various kinds of hindrances should, in all places and at all times, diligently say my name. If they achieve single-mindedness, their roots of goodness will flourish and their motivation will become intensely keen.

"Then they should observe that my dharma body and the dharma bodies of all Buddhas are in essence equal to their own, not different, not distinct. With neither birth nor death, the dharma body is complete with the four virtues: eternity, bliss, true self, and purity, totally worthy of being a refuge. They should also observe the appearances of their own body and mind, which are impermanent, painful, with no self, and impure, like illusions or conjurations, worthy of disgust. If they can learn to observe in this way, they will quickly develop the mind of pure faith, gradually diminishing their hindrances. Why? Because those who have learned to hear my name can also learn to hear the names of Buddhas [in worlds] in the ten directions. Those who have learned to make obeisance and offerings earnestly to me can also learn to make obeisance and offerings earnestly to Buddhas [in worlds] in the ten directions. They are called the ones who learn to hear profound Mahāyāna sūtras. They are called the ones who learn to uphold, copy, revere, and make offerings to profound Mahāyāna sūtras. They are called the ones who learn to accept and uphold, and read and recite, profound Mahāyāna sūtras. They are called the ones who learn to stay far away from the wrong views and not to malign the profound true meanings. They are called the ones who learn to have faith in and understanding of the ultimate, profound highest truth. They are called the ones who can annihilate their hindrances caused by sin. They are called the ones who will accumulate immeasurable merit. These people after death will not go down the evil life-paths or be reborn into the eight difficulties. They will hear the true Dharma again to cultivate faith and to train accordingly. They can also be reborn as they wish in pure Buddha Lands.

"Furthermore, if they wish to be reborn in a Pure Land somewhere, they should remember the name of the Buddha of that world. If they earnestly say His name with a single, undistracted mind, and make observations as described before, they will definitely be reborn in the Pure Land of that Buddha. Their roots of goodness will grow stronger, and they will quickly arrive at the spiritual level of no regress.

"Know that single-minded contemplation of the equality of the dharma bodies of Buddhas, as described before, is the supreme karma for developing one's roots of goodness. Those who practice diligently will gradually head for the Samādhi of the One Action. Attaining this Samādhi of the One Action opens the mind of vast wondrous actions, and is called attaining a likeness of the Endurance in the Realization of the No Birth of Dharmas. Because they can hear my name, they also can hear the names of Buddhas [in worlds] in the ten directions. Because they can earnestly make obeisance and offerings to me, they also can earnestly make obeisance and offerings to Buddhas [in worlds] in the ten directions. Because they can hear profound Mahāyāna sūtras, they also can uphold, copy, revere, and make offerings to these sūtras. Because they can accept and uphold, and read and recite, profound Mahāyāna sūtras, they will not fear the profound, ultimate highest truth, nor will they malign it. [Other reasons] are that they have acquired the right views and are able to believe and understand them; that they will definitely annihilate the hindrances caused by sin; and that they have acquired an accumulation of immeasurable merit. Why? Because as the silent wisdom-knowledge of the differentiation-free bodhi mind arises, viable karmas and various kinds of vows and actions spontaneously manifest. Those who can hear my name will have firm faith and take beneficial actions. Those who can hear my name will even acquire the assurance not to desert the One Vehicle. However, if they recite my name with a muddled and tainted mind, this should not be called hearing my name. Their practice will not produce firm faith or understanding. They will, however, receive worldly good requitals, but not vast, profound, wonderful benefits. With a muddled and tainted mind, they will not be able to gain profound great benefits from all the good karmas they do.

"Good man, know that those who diligently practice dhyāna without appearance, as described before, will receive profound great benefits before long. They will gradually attain Buddhahood. The profound great benefits mean that they will acquire the Position of Firm Faith when they achieve the Endurance in Faith; that they will acquire the Position of Firm Dharma when they achieve the Endurance in Accord; and that they will acquire the Position of Authenticity when they achieve the Endurance in the Realization of the No Birth of Dharmas. Furthermore, they will achieve the Endurance in Faith because they can develop the Tathāgata character-type; they will achieve the Endurance in Conformity because they can understand Tathāgata actions; and they will achieve the Endurance in the Realization of the No Birth of Dharmas because they can engage in Tathāgata work.

"In brief, there are four reasons for one's gradual attainment of Buddhahood. What are these four? First, one attains Buddhahood because one's faith in the Dharma is complete. On the Ground of Character-Type, one definitely believes that dharmas, pure and equal, have neither birth nor death, and that there is nothing to wish for or seek. Second, one attains Buddhahood because one's understanding of the Dharma is complete. On the Training Ground for Excellent Understanding, one has developed profound understanding of dharma nature and knows that Tathāgata work is neither constructed nor formed. One no longer sees the duality between saṁsāra and nirvāṇa because one has no fear. Third, one attains Buddhahood because one's verification of the Dharma is complete. On the Ground of the Pure Mind, one has acquired the differentiation-free, silent dharma knowledge, and acquired inconceivable spontaneous karmas, because one no longer has the intention to seek. Fourth, one attains Buddhahood because one's meritorious actions are complete. On the ultimate Bodhisattva Ground, one can remove all hindrances because the dream fabricated by ignorance has ended.

"Furthermore, we should know that there are three situations in practicing the worldly dhyāna with appearance. What are these three? First, without the power of the right faith and understanding, one can be greedy for the benefits of dhyānas and samādhis and become arrogant. Thus misled, one may fall back to seeking worldly benefits. Second, without the power of the right faith and understanding, one's meditation can trigger biased decisions based on disgust. Out of fear of birth and death, one may fall back to the Two Vehicles. Third, with the power of the right faith and understanding, one can rely on the one true reality to practice intently the two observational ways, śamatha and vipaśyanā. Because one believes and understands that all dharmas are produced by one's mind, like dreams or illusions, one will not be captivated by the benefits gained from worldly dhyānas. Nor will they fall back to seeking the worldly fruits in the Three Realms of Existence. Because they believe and know that saṁsāra in true reality is nirvāṇa, they will not, out of fear, fall back to seeking the Two Vehicles.

"Those who practice and learn dhyānas and samādhis should know that there are ten signs in ascending grade, which fully encompass the progress of meditation. They can help the student to succeed accordingly without mistakes or faults. What are these ten signs? First, the sign of facility in controlling thoughts. Second, the sign of desire to remain in a state. Third, the sign of clarity in a state and in entering or leaving it. Fourth, the sign of firmness in remaining in a state. Fifth, the sign of progress through skillful and intense contemplation. Sixth, the sign of comfort through gradual adjustment, joy, faith, and understanding, which remove doubts. Seventh, the sign of benefits brought by victorious progress in concentration that responds less to distraction. Eighth, the sign of success in remediation because of excellent merit acquired from enhanced clarity and firmness in meditation. Ninth, the sign of no mistakes or faults because one's thoughts can manifest at will as corresponding meritorious karmas. Tenth, the sign of extraordinary command evidenced by adeptly entering and exiting the preceding nine states in sequence and at will. These are the ten successive signs that encompass the progress of meditation."

Firm Faith Bodhisattva asked Earth Store Bodhisattva, "How do you skillfully expound the profound Dharma to help sentient beings discard their timidity and weakness?"

Earth Store Bodhisattva replied, "Good man, those who have just initiated their resolve to seek the Mahāyāna have not yet elicited faith, and are skeptical and timid in regard to the profound Dharma for attaining the unsurpassed bodhi. In that case, I always reveal the true meanings in a suitable way to comfort them, enabling them to discard their timidity and weakness. Therefore, I am called the good speaker of comforting words. How do I comfort them? Sentient beings with low capacity and a small mind, having heard that the unsurpassed Way is most victorious and most wondrous, activate their resolve out of greed for pleasure. Then they are concerned that seeking the unsurpassed bodhi would require them to accumulate immense merit and to carry out difficult actions and ascetic actions for delivering themselves and others. The goal can be achieved only by arduous endeavor through birth and death for a large number of kalpas. For this reason, their minds feel timid and weak.

"I will explain to them the meaning that all dharmas in their original nature are empty. In true reality, there is no self, neither self nor others, neither subject nor object, neither departure nor arrival, neither direction nor place, nor past, present, or future. I will further explain to them the eighteen emptinesses. Whether saṁsāra or nirvāṇa, all dharmas have no definite appearances that one can capture. I will also tell them that dharmas are like illusions or conjurations, like the moon in the water, like reflections in the mirror, like a gandharva city, like echoes in the valley, like mirages, like water bubbles, like dew, like lamplight, like distorted visions, like dreams, like lightning, and like clouds. One's afflictions [that drive one's] birth and death are weak in nature and easy to eradicate because they ultimately have no substance to be captured. They have never been born, and hence can never die. Their true nature being silence and stillness, dharmas are in nirvāṇa. Explanations such as these can shatter all the wrong views and one's attachment to one's body and mind, enabling one to discard one's timidity and weakness.

"Moreover, there are other sentient beings that also feel timid and weak because they are unable to understand the tenets of the Tathāgata's teachings. We should know that the tenets of the Tathāgata's teachings are based on the one true reality that He has seen. They are the Way for one to discard the evils of birth, aging, illness, and death. They are the realization that the dharma body is the accumulation of immeasurable merit, eternally cool and changeless. The Tathāgata sees clearly that, within the bodies of all sentient beings, there are also such true, wondrous, and pure virtues, concealed by the darkness and defilements of ignorance. Consequently, sentient beings undergo immeasurable suffering in the long night of birth, aging, illness, and death. Invoking His mind of great lovingkindness and compassion, the Tathāgata wants to enable all sentient beings to end their suffering and to realize the dharma body, in order to enjoy bliss in the highest truth. The dharma body is apart from thinking and differentiation. It can be realized only if one can transform one's false consciousness so that it no longer clings to illusions through thinking and memory. However, sentient beings delight in differentiating and clinging to dharmas. Because of their delusion, thinking, and imagination, they repeatedly undergo birth and death. Then the Tathāgata, wanting them to discard their thoughts of differentiation and fixation, explains that worldly dharmas do not truly exist and that their essence is ultimate emptiness. Even supra-worldly dharmas do not truly exist and their essence is also ultimate emptiness. An extensive explanation is provided in the eighteen emptinesses. Thus, He reveals to them that all dharmas are not apart from the essence of bodhi, which is neither existence nor extinction, neither nonexistence nor non-extinction, nor both existence and extinction; neither sameness nor difference, neither non-sameness nor non-difference, nor both sameness and difference. Bodhi does not have a single appearance to be captured because it is free from all appearances. Being apart from appearances, it cannot be captured by words. In the dharma of bodhi, there is neither a speaker of words nor a hearer that receives them. Bodhi cannot be known by thinking. In the dharma of bodhi, there is neither a subject that grasps nor an object that is grasped. It is free from the differentiation between the appearances of self and others. Thoughts of differentiation are false, not in accord [with bodhi].

"However, sentient beings with low capacity are unable to comprehend these explanations. They mistakenly believe that the unsurpassed bodhi and the dharma body of the Tathāgata are emptiness only, ultimately nothingness. Their minds, timid and weak, are fearful of ending up with nothing gained. They perceive cessation and extinction and hold the view of increase and decrease. Then they turn around to slander [the Buddha], disdaining themselves and others. I thereupon explain to them that the true nature of the Tathāgata's dharma body is 'not empty' because it in essence is complete with immeasurable pure, meritorious karmas. Since time without a beginning, not by cultivation or formation, it has always been inherently perfect. The dharma body is also complete in the body of every sentient being, neither changing nor varying, neither increasing nor decreasing. Because such explanations will enable them to discard their timidity and weakness, they are called comforting words.

"Then there are foolish and obstinate sentient beings that, having heard such explanations, still remain timid and weak. Reasoning that the dharma body of the Tathāgata is originally perfect, not by cultivation or formation, they too think that there is nothing to gain, and feel timid and weak. Or they may fall into the wrong views, such as naturalism. I then further explain to them that, by doing all the good dharmas, they will develop and perfect the physical body of the Tathāgata, and acquire immeasurable merit, which will bring pure requital. Because such explanations will enable them to discard their timidity and weakness, they are called comforting words.

"The profound meanings I explain are in accord with true reality, without faults, because they are not contradictory. How do you know that they are not contradictory? The dharma body of the Tathāgata is non-verbal, apart from perception, thinking, and appearances, neither empty nor not empty. Although it cannot be revealed by words, according to the worldly truth, it can be reasonably described, through illusory causes and conditions, in relative terms with false names. Because the nature of the dharma body, neither empty nor not empty, is free from differentiation, free from the distinction between self and others, and free from all appearances, one can say that the essence of the dharma body is ultimate emptiness. When one's mind is free from differentiation and thinking, it does not perceive a single appearance, nor does it know itself as something existent. Therefore, this meaning of emptiness is definitely in accord with true reality.

"Furthermore, the meaning of emptiness includes that, when one is free from differentiation and thinking, not a single appearance is there to be considered empty. Because true reality is revealed, it is said to be 'not empty.' Apart from consciousness and perception, without false appearances, true reality is forever neither changing nor varying. There is not a single appearance that can be destroyed or annihilated because true reality is apart from increase and decrease. Free from differentiation, true reality has been complete with the spontaneous karma of immeasurable merit since time without a beginning. Because it is never separated from such meritorious karma, it can be said to be 'not empty.' All sentient beings have such an accumulation of immeasurable merit, but it is concealed and obstructed by the darkness of their ignorance. Because they do not know and see what they have, they cannot acquire these merits and benefits. Then it is no different from not having them. Sentient beings do not have them because they do not know or see their dharma body. Its merits and benefits are not called the belongings of sentient beings because they cannot enjoy them. The only way to realize their dharma body is to carry out all good dharmas to surmount hindrances. Only then will sentient beings acquire its merits and benefits. That is why I say that doing all good dharmas will produce the physical body and the wisdom body of the Tathāgata. Good man, the profound meanings I explain are definitely true, free from contradiction. Know them as such."

When Earth Store Bodhisattva-Mahāsattva was introducing such a superb, viable, profound Dharma Door, 10,000 koṭi sentient beings activated the anuttara-samyak-saṁbodhi mind, standing in the Position of Firm Faith. Moreover, 98,000 Bodhisattva-Mahāsattvas achieved the Endurance in the Realization of the No Birth of Dharmas. [Members of] the huge multitude each offered celestial incense and flowers to the Buddha and Earth Store Bodhisattva-Mahāsattva.

Then the Buddha told the multitudes, "You all should accept and uphold this Dharma Door and circulate it widely in your respective lands. Why? Because such a Dharma Door is hard to encounter, which can bring great benefits. One who has heard Earth Store Bodhisattva-Mahāsattva's name and believes in his words will quickly discard all obstructive matters and attain the unsurpassed bodhi."

Then the multitudes said in unison, "I will accept and uphold it, and circulate it in the world, never to dare forget."

At that time Firm Pure Faith Bodhisattva-Mahāsattva asked the Buddha, "World-Honored One, what is the name of this Dharma Door, which is included in the *Sūtra of the Six Faculties*, pronounced by the Tathāgata? I should accept and uphold the tenets of this Dharma, and enable all in future times to hear them."

The Buddha told Firm Pure Faith Bodhisattva-Mahāsattva, "This Dharma Door is called Detecting Good or Evil Karma and Requital. It is also called Annihilating Hindrances and Developing Pure Faith. It is also called Revealing the Profound Ultimate True Meaning for Facilitating the Progress of Those Who Seek the Mahāyāna. It is also called the Good Comforting Words for Enabling One to Discard Timidity and Weakness, in Order to Enter Quickly the Resolute Dharma Door of Firm Faith. You should accept and uphold these names and meanings."

After the Buddha gave the names of this Dharma Door, all in the assembly rejoiced. They all believed in, accepted, and reverently carried out the teachings.

From the Prajñā Section

10–12 Three Heart Sūtras

Texts 250–55 and 257 (T08n0250–55, 257) are seven Chinese versions of the *Heart Sūtra*, and four of them bear the same name. Text 250 is the earliest translation, done by Kumārajīva (鳩摩羅什, 344–413). Text 256 is a Chinese transliteration of the Sanskrit text, phonetically rendered by the Chinese master Xuanzang (玄奘, 600– or 602–664), which matches his translation in text 251. Text 257 is the latest version, translated by Dānapāla (施護, dates unknown) from Udyāna in northern India, who went to China in 980, during the Northern Song Dynasty. Based on different Sanskrit texts, these seven Chinese translations all include the same key message, starting with the words "form is no different from emptiness," and ending with the mantra.

Sūtras 10–12 are English translations in one-to-one correspondence with texts 250–52, which were translated into Chinese respectively by Kumārajīva, Xuanzang, and Dharmacandra (法月, 653–743). Text 251, translated by Xuanzang, is the popular version that Chinese Buddhists recite from memory. It is the shortest version, a virtual excerpt of text 250, translated by Kumārajīva. Text 252, translated by Dharmacandra, is the longest of the seven versions. It has also adopted many words in the Kumārajīva translation.

There are many English versions of the *Heart Sūtra*, variously translated from Chinese, Sanskrit, and Tibetan texts. Text 251 alone has several English translations online. Also, Buddhist groups have their own in-house translations. It seems no one is satisfied with the available translations.

Each version of the *Heart Sūtra* states, "Dharmas, with empty appearances, have neither birth nor death, neither impurity nor purity, neither increase nor decrease." This is the absolute truth that dharmas are empty and, in true reality, have no birth or death. For example, a dharma, whether each of the five aggregates, each of the twelve fields, each of the eighteen spheres, each of the Twelve Links of Dependent Arising, or each of the Four Noble Truths, is in effect emptiness.

Furthermore, as dharmas in true reality are emptiness, emptiness is vividly manifested as dharmas. This is the Middle Way. Therefore, Bodhisattvas, with the understanding that there is nothing to attain, will still attain the ultimate nirvāṇa, verifying that there is nothing to attain. Such realization is prajñā-pāramitā, the wisdom that can cross one over to the shore of Buddhahood, with no fear or hindrance.

10 摩訶般若波羅蜜大明呪經
Sūtra of the Great Illumination Mantra of Mahā-Prajñā-Pāramitā

Translated from Sanskrit into Chinese in the Later Qin Dynasty
by
The Tripiṭaka Master Kumārajīva from Kucha

As Avalokiteśvara Bodhisattva went deep into prajñā-pāramitā, he saw in his illumination the emptiness of the five aggregates, [the realization of] which delivers one from all suffering and tribulations.

"Śāriputra, because form is empty, it does not have the appearance of decay. Because sensory reception is empty, it does not have the appearance of sensory experience. Because perception is empty, it does not have the appearance of cognition. Because mental processing is empty, it does not have the appearance of formation. Because consciousness is empty, it does not have the appearance of awareness.

"Why? Because, Śāriputra, form is no different from emptiness; emptiness is no different from form. In effect, form is emptiness and emptiness is form. The same is true for sensory reception, perception, mental processing, and consciousness. Śāriputra, dharmas, with empty appearances, have neither birth nor death, neither impurity nor purity, neither increase nor decrease. Emptiness, the true reality, is not of the past, present, or future.

"Therefore, in emptiness there is no form, nor sensory reception, perception, mental processing, or consciousness; no eye, ear, nose, tongue, body, or mental faculty, nor sights, sounds, scents, flavors, tactile sensations, or mental objects; no spheres, from eye sphere to mental consciousness sphere. There is neither ignorance nor ending of ignorance, neither old age and death, nor ending of old age and death. There is no suffering, accumulation [of afflictions], cessation [of suffering], or the path. There is neither wisdom-knowledge nor attainment because there is nothing to attain.

"Bodhisattvas, because they rely on prajñā-pāramitā, have no hindrances in their minds. Without hindrance, they have no fear. Staying far from inverted dreaming and thinking, they will ultimately attain nirvāṇa. Buddhas of the past, present, and future, because they rely on prajñā-pāramitā, all attain anuttara-samyak-saṁbodhi.

"Hence, we know that the Prajñā-Pāramitā [Mantra] is the great illumination mantra, the unsurpassed illumination mantra, the unequaled illumination mantra, which can remove all suffering. It is true, not false. Hence the Prajñā-Pāramitā Mantra is pronounced. Then the mantra goes:

gate gate pāragate pāra-saṁgate bodhi svāhā ||"

11 般若波羅蜜多心經
Sūtra of the Heart of Prajñā-Pāramitā

Translated from Sanskrit into Chinese in the Tang Dynasty
by
The Tripiṭaka Master Xuanzang from China

As Avalokiteśvara Bodhisattva went deep into prajñā-pāramitā, he saw in his illumination the emptiness of the five aggregates, [the realization of] which delivers one from all suffering and tribulations.

"Śāriputra, form is no different from emptiness; emptiness is no different from form. In effect, form is emptiness and emptiness is form. The same is true for sensory reception, perception, mental processing, and consciousness. Śāriputra, dharmas, with empty appearances, have neither birth nor death, neither impurity nor purity, neither increase nor decrease.

"Therefore, in emptiness there is no form, nor sensory reception, perception, mental processing, or consciousness; no eye, ear, nose, tongue, body, or mental faculty, nor sights, sounds, scents, flavors, tactile sensations, or mental objects; no spheres, from eye sphere to mental consciousness sphere. There is neither ignorance nor ending of ignorance, neither old age and death nor ending of old age and death. There is no suffering, accumulation [of afflictions], cessation [of suffering], or the path. There is neither wisdom-knowledge nor attainment because there is nothing to attain.

"Bodhisattvas, because they rely on prajñā-pāramitā, have no hindrances in their minds. Without hindrance, they have no fear. Staying far from inverted dreaming and thinking, they will ultimately attain nirvāṇa. Buddhas of the past, present, and future, because they rely on prajñā-pāramitā, all attain anuttara-samyak-saṁbodhi.

"Hence, we know that the Prajñā-Pāramitā [Mantra] is the great spiritual mantra, the great illumination mantra, the unsurpassed mantra, the unequaled mantra, which can remove all suffering. It is true, not false. Hence the Prajñā-Pāramitā Mantra is pronounced. Then the mantra goes:

gate gate pāragate pāra-saṁgate bodhi svāhā ||"

12 普遍智藏般若波羅蜜多心經
Sūtra of the All-Encompassing Knowledge Store, the Heart of Prajñā-Pāramitā

Translated from Sanskrit into Chinese in the Tang Dynasty
by
The Tripiṭaka Master Dharmacandra from India

Thus I have heard:

At one time the Buddha was staying on the Vulture Peak Mountain near the great city of Rājagṛha, together with 100,000 great bhikṣus and 77,000 Bodhisattva-Mahāsattvas. At their head were Avalokiteśvara Bodhisattva, Mañjuśrī Bodhisattva, Maitreya Bodhisattva, and others. They all had attained the Samādhi of Total Retention, abiding in the inconceivable liberation.

Avalokiteśvara Bodhisattva, seated in the multitude, rose and came to the Buddha. Facing the Buddha, he joined his palms and bent over respectfully. Gazing deferentially at the venerated visage, he said to the Buddha, "World-Honored One, I would like to pronounce in this assembly Bodhisattvas' all-encompassing knowledge store, the heart of prajñā-pāramitā. I pray only that the World-Honored One will permit me to pronounce to the Bodhisattvas the secret tenets of the Dharma."

The World-Honored One replied to Avalokiteśvara Bodhisattva in the Brahma tone: "Very good! Very good! Great Compassionate One, you have my permission to speak and to be the great radiance to sentient beings."

Then Avalokiteśvara Bodhisattva, having received the Buddha's approval and considerate protection, entered the right experience in the Samādhi of Wisdom Light. After he entered this samādhi, with its power, he went deep into prajñā-pāramitā and saw that the self-essence of the five aggregates is all empty. With the understanding that the self-essence of the five aggregates is all empty, he peacefully rose from his samādhi. Forthwith, he told Śāriputra the Wise, "Good man, this Bodhisattva has the heart of prajñā-pāramitā, called the All-Encompassing Knowledge Store. Now hearken and ponder well! I will pronounce it to you."

That having been said, Śāriputra the Wise responded to Avalokiteśvara Bodhisattva, "Yes, Great Pure One, I pray that you will pronounce it. Now is the right time."

Thereupon, he told Śāriputra, "Bodhisattva-Mahāsattvas should learn in this way. The nature of form is emptiness; the nature of emptiness is form. Form is no different from emptiness; emptiness is no different from form. In effect, form is emptiness and emptiness is form. The same is true for sensory reception, perception, mental processing, and consciousness. The nature of consciousness is emptiness; the nature of emptiness is consciousness. Consciousness is no different from emptiness; emptiness is no different from consciousness. In effect, consciousness is emptiness and emptiness is consciousness, Śāriputra, dharmas, with empty appearances, have neither birth nor death, neither impurity nor purity, neither increase nor decrease.

"Therefore, in emptiness there is no form, nor sensory reception, perception, mental processing, or consciousness; no eye, ear, nose, tongue, body, or mental faculty, nor sights, sounds, scents, flavors, tactile sensations, or mental objects; no spheres, from eye sphere to mental consciousness sphere. There is neither ignorance nor ending of ignorance, neither old age and death nor ending of old age and death. There is no suffering, accumulation [of afflictions], cessation [of suffering], or the path. There is neither wisdom-knowledge nor attainment because there is nothing to attain.

"Bodhisattvas, because they rely on prajñā-pāramitā, have no hindrances in their minds. Without hindrance, they have no fear. Staying far from inverted dreaming and thinking, they will ultimately attain nirvāṇa. Buddhas of the past, present, and future, because they rely on prajñā-pāramitā, all attain anuttara-samyak-saṁbodhi.

"Hence, we know that the Prajñā-Pāramitā [Mantra] is the great spiritual mantra, the great illumination mantra, the unsurpassed mantra, the unequaled mantra, which can remove all suffering. It is true, not false. Hence the Prajñā-Pāramitā Mantra is pronounced. Then the mantra goes:

> gate gate pāragate pāra-saṁgate bodhi svāhā ||"

After the Buddha pronounced this sūtra [through Avalokiteśvara Bodhisattva], the multitude of bhikṣus and Bodhisattvas as well as all the gods, humans, asuras, gandharvas, and others in the world, having heard the Buddha's words, greatly rejoiced. They all believed in, accepted, and reverently carried out the teachings.

From the Treasure Pile Section

13 Mahāyāna Sūtra of Consciousness Revealed (in 2 fascicles)

Sūtra 13 is based on text 347 (T12n0347), which was translated from Sanskrit into Chinese in the Tang Dynasty by Divākara (地婆訶羅, 613–87). An earlier Chinese version was translated by Jñānagupta (闍那崛多, 523–600), a monk from northern India, who went to China in 559 or 560. His version is included as the thirty-ninth sūtra in fascicles 109–110 of the *Great Treasure Pile Sūtra* (T11n0310), which is a collection of forty-nine sūtras in 120 fascicles.

The principal interlocutor in Sūtra 13 is Bhadrapāla (Worthy Protector) Bodhisattva, who often appears in Mahāyāna sūtras. Because of his questions, the Buddha gives extensive teachings on ālaya consciousness, the eighth consciousness, though the word *ālaya* is not used in this text. Summarized below are a few features of ālaya consciousness.

As an analogy, a person may cast his reflection in a mirror or in the water. The person is like one's ālaya consciousness, his reflection is like one's karmic body in each life, and a mirror or the water is like the suitable karmic condition for a rebirth.

The life of a sentient being ends because of dissolution of the karmic force, the body, consciousness, and the field of faculties. Ālaya consciousness, carrying the dharma realm of thinking and memory as well as good and evil karmas, goes on to accept the next requital. It is like the wind carrying fragrance and stench to another place. After one's death, the exit of ālaya consciousness is not through one's throat, mouth, or other orifices. Its exit and route are unknown.

In addition, ālaya consciousness means seed, which can sprout a karmic body of any kind as well as perception, thinking, and memory. The way ālaya consciousness forms a body is throughout all parts of the body. Not tainted by afflictions, it permeates the six faculties, six sense objects, and the five aggregates. Through them, the functions of consciousness are evident. Ālaya consciousness is never tainted even if it is in the body of an animal or a hell-dweller.

The Buddha describes how a person with good karma is reborn through miraculous formation to celestial parents in heaven, to live a pleasant celestial life. He also describes how a person with evil karma is reborn through miraculous formation in hell, to undergo dreadful suffering. Transference of ālaya consciousness from one life to the next continues as long as one lingers in saṁsāra, one's cycle of birth and death.

13 大乘顯識經
Mahāyāna Sūtra of Consciousness Revealed

Translated from Sanskrit into Chinese in the Tang Dynasty
by
The Tripiṭaka Master Divākara from India

Fascicle 1 (of 2)

Thus I have heard:

At one time the Bhagavān was in the Karaṇḍa Bamboo Garden of the city of Rājagṛha, together with 1,250 great bhikṣus. All of them were Arhats, who had ended their afflictions and the discharges thereof, and achieved freedom. With their minds completely liberated and their wisdom fully unfolded, like the great dragon, they saw the past, future, and present, hindrance free. Taught by the Buddha, they had completed their undertaking [for Arhatship] and shed the enormous heavy burden. They had acquired benefits for themselves, having ended their suffering in transmigrating through their cycle of birth and death. With the power of true knowledge, they were adept in identifying the proclivities of sentient beings. At the head of the multitude of such great voice-hearers was the Elder Śāriputra. Also in this assembly was an innumerable multitude of Bodhisattva-Mahāsattvas.

In the presence of the World-Honored One, the bhikṣus were tired and drowsy, losing their color and too exhausted to hold up. Then the face of the World-Honored One lit up like a blooming lotus flower. Forthwith the bhikṣus all became alert, each straightening up and thinking: "The Buddha-Bhagavān now looks resplendent, his face glowing with light. What dharma-eye will He open to give us great benefits?"

The youth [Bhadrapāla] Worthy Protector Superior, complete with fine qualities, such as robust good looks, gentleness, and radiance, surrounded by 60,000 merchant lords, together with attendants, with rumbling sounds like an earthquake, came to the Buddha. Seeing the Buddha-Bhagavān silent and peaceful as the store of virtues, and majestic and radiant like a towering golden tree, he pondered as he joined his palms with profound faith and reverence. He thought: "As praised by all, the Buddha, who is all-knowing and all-seeing, is truly the Tathāgata, Arhat, Samyak-Saṁbuddha. It is not false."

He bowed his head down at the feet of the Buddha then gazed at Him. The Buddha saw Worthy Protector and radiated light from His entire body to shine on him. Worthy Protector then acquired fearlessness. He circled the Buddha three times, and again bowed his head down at the Buddha's feet. He said to the Buddha, "I pray only that the World-Honored One will teach me with compassion.

It is only today that I have acquired pure faith here, where the Buddha is. My mind longing for the true Dharma, I would like to ask questions. However, I have long been in my cycle of birth and death, drowning in afflictions and chaotic thoughts. I have no hidden provisions, such as observance of precepts or other good karmas. Anxious as I am, I do not know how to transcend birth and death and be delivered from the web of ignorance, affliction, and doubt. The World-Honored One is all-knowing and all-seeing. The appearance of a Buddha in the world is rare and hard to encounter. As a wish-fulfilling jewel can give happiness to sentient beings, the Buddha is the greatest wish-fulfilling jewel. All sentient beings depend upon the Buddha to acquire great peace and bliss. He is the great parent and sentient beings' root of goodness. Because of the Buddha-parent, one will be able see the right path. I pray only that, out of sympathy, He will remove my doubts and darkness."

The Buddha told Worthy Protector, "You may ask anything about your doubts. I will resolve them separately for you."

Worthy Protector, having received the Buddha's permission, stood on one side to concentrate on his questions. Meanwhile, the Elder Ānanda, seeing the radiance and good features of the youth Worthy Protector, said to the Buddha, "A sight never encountered before! This youth Worthy Protector has great merit, whose radiance and glow outshine the awesome appearances of kings."

The Buddha told Ānanda, "This youth Worthy Protector Superior, because of his meritorious karma, enjoys splendid celestial-life requital while living in the human world. He can frolic and enjoy peace and pleasure totally at will, like the god-king Śakra. No one in Jambudvīpa can compare with him, except for the youth Moon Reality."

Ānanda asked the Buddha, "I pray only that we be told about the youth Worthy Protector, concerning his current resources as karmic requital and the roots of goodness he has planted in the past."

The Buddha told Ānanda, "You should hear the pleasure-requital in the form of enormous resources that Worthy Protector now enjoys and learn the contributing causes from his past. Ānanda, this youth Worthy Protector is attended by 60,000 merchant lords who have an abundance of assets and an accumulation of gold and jewels. They respectfully accept his instructions and follow him at his service. [In his residence there are] 60,000 beds with well-arranged bedding, blankets, fine linens, and pillows, in various colors, beautiful and magnificent. All around are columns, jeweled carvings, colorful silk curtains, and other decorations, as gorgeous as those in a painting. There are 60,000 artistic ladies, dressed in silk in a variety of colors, adorned with golden jewelry and necklaces in dazzling colors, so fine and delicate to the touch that they are like celestial crystal. Their weight can be light or heavy, suiting the wearer's mood. Playing, laughing, talking, singing, these ladies entertain and serve their master with gentleness, prudence, and respect. They withdraw their love and desire for others, lowering their heads with humility or covering their heads for modesty. Their skin is fine, soft, and smooth. The bony joints of their hands, feet, and ankles do not show. Their teeth are white and straight, without gaps, and their black hair curls to the right, like wax shavings portrayed in a painting. They come from families and clans with names known far and wide. Such women are his attendants. Moreover, there are 60,000 women who serve him food, such as rice, bread, and so forth, in various colors. The aromas and flavors are as wonderful as those of celestial food. As requital for his merit, such food cooked without labor arrives at his wish. The water there has the eight virtues, pleasing to one's mind and soothing to one's body, and it cleanses filth and removes diseases.

"His mansions and towers are adorned with 60,000 beautifully arranged jewels, such as precious gems and aquamarine. Bells suspended from ribbons jingle harmoniously in the winds. The ground is like aquamarine, showing myriad reflections, with various flowers scattered around. [The place] is cool and pleasant, inviting leisurely strolls to relax one's mind. There are musical instruments, such as paṇava drums, sitars, pipes, and brass cymbals, playing 60,000 kinds of melodies. The beautiful sounds are harmonious and loud, resonating far and wide. Joy and happiness brought by meritorious karma flow non-stop. Doves and other birds are flying around, their various calls enjoyable to one's mind and pleasant to one's ear. Flowering vines climb up on the towers, adorning them with bright flowers and lush leaves. The tones of bells and musical instruments sound like those in a celestial palace. The halls are spacious like a cavern of Mount Sumeru, where divine medicine flows.

"There are 60,000 cities graced with towers and surrounded by high walls. The streets are well designed with crossroads to reach all directions. Adding to the magnificence are people who come from everywhere, wearing various kinds of clothing, speaking various kinds of languages. They have different facial features and follow diverse customs. Hundreds of thousands of merchants display their extraordinary goods. The raucous sounds of trade shake the entire city.

"In the lush gardens and forests, there are large and small trees, vines, medicinal herbs, and flowers in full bloom. [In their midst are pools] the clear waters of which reflect shimmering light, like a sheet of colorful brocade. Hundreds and thousands of elephants, horses, and carriages move endlessly throughout the city. Ānanda, in these 60,000 cities, the noble and the famous, as well as the wealthy and the merchant lords, praise the youth Worthy Protector every day, broadcasting his merit. They respectfully join their palms and make obeisance to him in reverence.

"Prasenajit, the king of Kauśala, is wealthy because of the power of his merit, but he is poor in comparison with Worthy Protector. The youth Moon Reality is surrounded by 100,000 artistic attendants, serving him respectfully and entertaining him with music and frolics. Even the god-king Śakra is a billion times less fortunate than Moon Reality. Likewise the youth Worthy Protector, with his robust, high-colored good looks, wealth, ease, peace, and pleasures, is also a billion times less fortunate than Moon Reality. Their fortunes, in each case, are not acquired by force, but are a response to their past merits.

"Ānanda, the youth Worthy Protector has a wish-fulfilling carriage inlaid with celestial jewels, radiating bright light like celestial gold or vajra. It is decorated with various kinds of treasures, mixed as beautifully as stars. It moves swiftly, like the wind, like the flight of the golden-winged bird. Riding this jeweled carriage, he arrives at any treasure island on a thought. Then he comes home from his pleasure tour, not tired."

Ānanda bowed down at the feet of the Buddha. He asked the Buddha, "What roots of goodness did the youth Worthy Protector plant and what meritorious karma did he do, now to own enormous assets and to enjoy this great pleasure-requital, living in such magnificent mansions decorated with extraordinary treasures?"

The Buddha told Ānanda, "The youth Worthy Protector, because he planted in the past meritorious karma in the Buddha Dharma, has now received this enormous pleasure-requital. In the past, there was a Buddha called Blissful Light, the Tathāgata, Arhat, Samyak-Saṁbuddha, Knowledge and Conduct Perfected, Sugata, Understanding the World, Unsurpassed One, Tamer of Men, Teacher to Gods and Humans, Buddha the World-Honored One. Worthy Protector renounced family life and became a bhikṣu, called Dharma Topknot, in the Dharma of that Buddha. He was inadequate in observing the precepts for conduct. However, he clearly understood the profound teachings in the Tripiṭaka—the Sūtras, the Vinaya, and the Abhidharma—and he excelled in expounding them. He always pronounced the teachings to sentient beings in solemn, beautiful tones, endlessly giving the Dharma as alms. He was forthright and brilliant in his eloquent exposition, and the hearers delighted in the Dharma they heard. They pondered the teachings and trained themselves accordingly, and those who saved themselves from taking the evil life-journeys were innumerable. Ānanda, the bhikṣu Dharma Topknot, because of his merit of giving the Dharma, enjoyed the celestial-life requital for ninety kalpas. In addition, when Dharma Topknot saw thin and frail bhikṣus who observed their precepts purely, he always gave them food, drink, shoes, and so forth. Because he gave alms courteously and sincerely with a pure mind, he now has received this pleasure-requital in the form of great wealth, magnificent mansions, and extraordinary jeweled carriages. Moreover, Dharma Topknot later encountered Kāśyapa Tathāgata, who gave him teachings and guidance, and told him, 'You will receive a prophecy from the future Buddha Śākyamuni.' Hence he is seeing me now, and I will pronounce the Dharma to him to bring him to maturity."

Ānanda said to the Buddha, "World-Honored One, the youth Worthy Protector Superior has command of such an abundance of riches, gold, and treasures. It is extraordinary that he is gentle and modest, without any pride or arrogance."

The Buddha said, "Ānanda, one with great wisdom does not become arrogant because of wealth, treasures, and sensory pleasures. Worthy Protector has long trained in good works. Supported by good dharmas, he always has fortune fruits to eat."

Worthy Protector, having been praised by the Buddha and Ānanda, joined his palms reverently and bowed down at the feet of the Buddha. He implored the Buddha, "Please pity, accept, and protect all sentient beings. I request permission to ask a few questions."

The Buddha told Worthy Protector, "You have my permission. You may ask me about your doubts. I will explicate them to you."

Worthy Protector said to the Buddha, "World-Honored One, although sentient beings know that there is consciousness, it is like a jewel kept in a box, unrevealed and unknowable. World-Honored One, I do not know the form of this consciousness, nor the reason that it is called consciousness. When a person dies, his hands and feet may convulse, and the look of his eyes changes uncontrollably. As one's faculties perish, the four domains—earth, water, fire, and wind—disperse. Where does one's consciousness go after it has left the current body? What is its essence? What is its form? How does it assume the next body after leaving this body? After this body is abandoned, how does consciousness carry one's faculties in order to accept the next requital, which can be a body of any kind? World-Honored One, how does a sentient being grow new faculties after the expiration of this body? Why does one accumulate meritorious karma in this life, only to receive its requital in the next life: The current body does meritorious karma, and the next body will eat [the karmic fruit]? How does one's consciousness nourish one's body and keep it alive? How do consciousness and faculties develop according to one's body?"

The Buddha said, "Very good! Very good! Worthy Protector, these are good questions. Hearken! Hearken! Ponder this well. I will explain to you."

Worthy Protector said to the Buddha, "World-Honored One, affirmatively I accept Your teachings."

The Buddha told Worthy Protector, "The process and transference of [ālaya] consciousness are like the wind, which is formless, shapeless, and unidentifiable. However, the wind can activate myriad things and display myriad conditions, whether making loud sounds as it shakes the forest or breaks off branches, or causing pleasure or pain as it touches with cold or hot the bodies of sentient beings. The wind does not have hands, feet, face, or shape. Nor does it have various colors, such as black, white, red, or yellow. Worthy Protector, the same is true for the domain of consciousness. It is formless, shapeless, not revealed by light. However, through causes and conditions, it can manifest various kinds of functions. Know that the dharma realms of sensory reception and perception are also formless and shapeless. Through causes and conditions, various functions manifest.

"Worthy Protector, after the death of a sentient being, the dharma realms of sensory reception and perception and the domain of [ālaya] consciousness abandon the body. The way [ālaya] consciousness carries the dharma realms of sensory reception and perception to accept another body is like a gust of wind sweeping across wonderful flowers. The flowers stay put, but their fragrance will flow far. The wind in essence does not grasp the fragrance of the flowers. Fragrance and the wind in essence are both formless and shapeless. However, without the power of the wind, fragrance will not travel far. Worthy Protector, after a person's death, his [ālaya] consciousness carries the dharma realms of sensory reception and perception to the next rebirth, which is conditioned upon his parents entrusted by his [ālaya] consciousness. In this way the dharma realms of sensory reception and perception accompany [ālaya] consciousness. Because of the quality of the flowers, one's nose can detect their scent. Because of one's olfactory power, one smells fragrance, a sense object. The wind touches the flowers because of its power. Because of the power of the wind, fragrance can flow far. Likewise, from consciousness, sensory reception arises; from sensory reception, perception arises; and by perception, mental objects are differentiated. Then one knows good and evil.

"Worthy Protector, by analogy, a painter applies pigments to the wall, and he can paint pictures as neatly and properly as he wishes. The consciousness and intellect of the painter are both formless and shapeless, but they can create various kinds of extraordinary images and shapes. Thus one's consciousness and intellect project the six percepts. The eye sees sights, and the eye consciousness is formless and shapeless; the ear hears sounds, which are formless and shapeless; the nose detects odors, which are formless and shapeless; the tongue tastes flavors, which are formless and shapeless; and the body knows tactile sensations, which are formless and shapeless. As one's faculties and perceptions are formless and shapeless, so too one's consciousness is formless and shapeless.

"Worthy Protector, when [ālaya] consciousness abandons one's current body to accept another life, it is still bound by karma hindrances at the moment of one's death. When one's current requital ends with death, [one's consciousness] is as if in the Samādhi of Total Halt. When an Arhat enters the Samādhi of Total Halt, his sensory reception and perception are suspended. Thus, when [ālaya] consciousness of the dying one abandons the body and its [four] domains, it does so with the power of memory. Upon dying, one's consciousness replays clearly from memory all the karmas one has done in one's entire life. Both body and mind are under stress.

"Worthy Protector, what is the meaning of consciousness? [Ālaya] consciousness means seed, which can sprout a karmic body of any kind. Perception, thinking, and memory are also sprouted from [ālaya] consciousness. It is called consciousness because it knows pleasure, pain, good, and evil, as well as good and evil objects. You ask me how one's [ālaya] consciousness leaves this body to accept the next requital. Worthy Protector, each body sprouted from one's [ālaya] consciousness is like the reflection of a face in a mirror, like the markings in the mud, imprinted by a stamp.

"As an analogy, the light of sunrise removes darkness, which returns after sunset. Darkness has no mass, no shape, neither permanent nor impermanent, but it is always there. The same is true for consciousness. Having no mass and no shape, it is revealed through sensory reception and perception. Consciousness in one's body is like the essence of darkness, which cannot be seen or touched. It is like the fetus inside the mother, who does not know whether it is male or female. Nor does she know whether it looks black, white, or yellow, whether it has complete faculties, whether it has normal hands, feet, ears, and eyes. However, stimulated by hot food and drink [eaten by the mother], the fetus will move, because it feels pain. The presence of consciousness is evident as sentient beings come or go, bend or extend, stare or blink, speak or laugh, carry heavy loads, or do things. However, they do not know the whereabouts of consciousness in their bodies, nor its form. Worthy Protector, the consciousness in essence permeates the sensory fields, but it is not tainted by them. Consciousness permeates the six faculties, the six sense objects, and the five aggregates, but it is not tainted by them. Through them, the functions of consciousness are evident. Worthy Protector, it is like a mechanism which enables a wooden machine to perform various kinds of tasks, whether talking, leaping, jumping, or dancing. What is your opinion? By whose power is this wooden machine enabled to work?"

Worthy Protector replied to the Buddha, "My wisdom and knowledge are too shallow to determine this."

The Buddha told Worthy Protector, "We should know that it is by one's power to do karmas. The power for doing karmas is formless but directed by one's intellect. Thus, a body-machine can do things with the power of consciousness. Whether ṛṣis, gandharvas, dragons, humans, asuras, or sentient beings on other life-journeys, all depend on it to do karmas. [Ālaya] consciousness can form the body as a work machine.

"Consciousness, without any form or mass, can uphold the dharma realm. With complete mental power, it knows even things in one's past lives. By analogy, the pervasive sunlight shines equally on sentient beings with evil karma, corpses, impure things, and stinking things, but it is not tainted by evils. Neither is [ālaya] consciousness. Even when it is in the body of a dog or a pig, which eats impure things, or in the body of anyone taking an evil life-journey, it is never tainted.

"Worthy Protector, [ālaya] consciousness abandons this body and moves away to accept the next requital according to good or evil karma. By analogy, when the wind exits a remote mountain or a steep gorge and sweeps across a forest of fragrant campaka trees, it carries fragrance. When the wind sweeps across a place of feces, corpses, rot, or filth, it carries stench. When it passes through both places, it carries both fragrance and stench. The stronger scent will be manifested first. The wind has no mass, and the scent has no shape. Yet the wind can carry both fragrance and stench far. Likewise, [ālaya] consciousness abandons this body, carrying good and evil karmas, to accept the next requital. It is just like the wind carrying fragrance and stench to another place. It is also like a dreamer who sees myriads of images and does various kinds of karmas in a dream, unaware that he is lying asleep. When a virtuous person dies, the transference of his [ālaya] consciousness is peaceful and unconscious, in the same way as his going somewhere in a dream without any fear. The exit of [ālaya] consciousness is not through one's throat, mouth, or other orifices. Its exit and route are unknown."

The youth Worthy Protector Superior bowed down at the feet of the Buddha. He asked the Buddha, "Where does [ālaya] consciousness enter into the embryo inside the egg of a chicken or goose, the shell of which is impenetrable? If the embryo dies within the egg and if the eggshell has no crack or hole, where does [ālaya] consciousness exit?"

The Buddha replied to Worthy Protector, "By analogy, if black sesame seeds are processed with campaka flowers, the oil will become aromatic and be called campaka oil. It is far superior to ordinary sesame oil. The oil initially does not contain any aroma but becomes aromatic after the seeds have been processed with the flowers. The fragrance does not crack the sesame seeds in order to enter or to exit, nor does it leave any substance in the oil. However, because of the force of causes and conditions, the fragrance is blended into the oil and the oil becomes aromatic. The way [ālaya] consciousness moves into or out of the embryo of a chicken or a goose despite the eggshell is like the infusion of the campaka fragrance into the oil. The transference of [ālaya] consciousness is like the way the sun shines, a jewel sparkles, or wood blazes.

"[Ālaya] consciousness is also like a seed. When a seed is planted and transformed in the ground, its sprouts, stem, branches, and leaves will successively emerge above the ground. Then flowers in a variety of colors, such as white, off-white, and red, will appear; fruits in a variety of flavors will ripen. The same great earth, providing the four domains—earth, water, fire, and wind—grows different things according to their seeds. Similarly, the dharma realm of [ālaya] the one consciousness manifests a sentient being successively reborn with black, white, yellow, or red skin, with different characters, gentle or violent, to undergo birth and death. Worthy Protector, consciousness has neither hands nor feet, neither joints nor speech. In its dharma realm, the power of memory is strong. Upon the death of a sentient being, [ālaya] consciousness abandons the current body and, with the power of memory, it becomes the seed for the next life. Apart from consciousness, there is no dharma realm; apart from dharma realm, there is no consciousness. [Ālaya] consciousness moves away along the [karmic] wind, together with the dharma realm, including the realms of memory and sensory reception."

Worthy Protector further asked the Buddha, "If so, why does World-Honored One say that consciousness is formless?"

The Buddha replied, "Worthy Protector, there are two kinds of form, the internal and the external. Eye consciousness is internal, and eye is external. Similarly, ear consciousness is internal, and ear is external; nose consciousness is internal, and nose is external; tongue consciousness is internal, and tongue is external; body consciousness is internal, and body is external. Worthy Protector, suppose a person born blind dreams of a beautiful woman, and he clearly sees her hands, feet, and beautiful features. He loves the sights as he dreams. When the night's sleep is over and daylight arrives, the blind man describes to a crowd the pleasing things in his dream, saying, 'I saw a beautiful woman whose features were uniquely exquisite, a garden with lush flowers, and hundreds and thousands of well-adorned people, who frolicked merrily. Their skin was lustrous, their shoulders were plump, and their arms were long and rounded like an elephant trunk. I gained great happiness from my dream, and my heart was gladdened.' Worthy Protector, this man was born blind, who has never seen anything with his eyes. Why can he perceive sights in his dream?"

Worthy Protector replied, "I pray that You will indicate the reason."

The Buddha told Worthy Protector, "What one sees in a dream are internal eye objects, differentiated by one's intellect, not through the physical eye. These internal eye objects manifest temporarily in the blind man's dream because of the power of memory. He also recalls the dream with the power of memory. With the right memory at death, one sees internal forms projected by consciousness.

"Furthermore, Worthy Protector, the transference of consciousness upon one's death is like a seed discarded on the ground. With the support of the four domains, it gradually transforms into sprouts, seedling, stem, branches, and leaves. Likewise, one's consciousness is supported by these four dharmas: memory, receptiveness, good, and evil. By analogy, a crystal jewel placed alongside something black or white will appear black or white. Likewise, [ālaya] consciousness supported by good or evil karmas will transfer somewhere to receive corresponding requitals, good or evil."

Worthy Protector next asked the Buddha, "Where does one's body hold consciousness?"

The Buddha replied, "Worthy Protector, consciousness neither accumulates nor gathers, nor does it grow. [The development of consciousness in an embryo] is like the birth of a sprout. The sprout is born neither before the seed is transformed nor after the seed is destroyed. However, when the sprout appears, the seed is spent. Worthy Protector, what is your opinion? Where does the seed stay? In the sprout, the stem, the branches, the leaves, or the top of the tree?"

Worthy Protector replied to the Buddha, "No, World-Honored One, the seed stays nowhere."

[The Buddha continued] "Indeed, Worthy Protector, [ālaya] consciousness does not stay in a particular place in the body, not in the eye, ear, nose, or the tongue. A seed giving birth to a sprout is likened to consciousness becoming dimly aware [in an embryo]. The formation of flower buds is likened to consciousness becoming receptive. The stage from blooming of flowers to bearing of fruits is likened to [ālaya] consciousness forming a body. The way [ālaya] consciousness forms a body is throughout all parts of the body. However, one cannot find where it stays. Without [ālaya] consciousness, the body cannot be formed.

"For example, only a ripe fruit from a tree, not an unripe fruit, is capable of releasing the seed for a new tree to come. Similarly, when one's [current] requital has matured, one dies and the consciousness-seed appears. Because of consciousness, there is sensory reception; because of sensory reception, there is love. Bondage of love produces memory. [Ālaya] consciousness carries memory and moves away like the wind according to good and evil karmas. It also thinks of its parents-to-be and entrusts those who match the causes and conditions. For example, the reflection of one's face does not appear in a mirror if the mirror is not clear. If the mirror is clear, the reflection appears. The image in the mirror has no sensation or thinking, but it follows the person to stretch or bend, to face upward or downward, to open the mouth to speak or joke, to walk or stand, performing various kinds of motion. Worthy Protector, by what force does the reflection appear in a mirror?"

Worthy Protector replied to the Buddha, "It is by the decision of the person. Because of his face, there is its reflection. The form of the reflection is like that of the person's face. Its sense organs, whether complete or incomplete, are like those on his face."

The Buddha said, "The person's face is the cause of the reflection, and the mirror is the condition of the reflection. The reflection appears because of the convergence of causes and conditions. Likewise, [ālaya] consciousness is the cause of one's sensory reception, perception, mental processing, and mental functions, and the parents are the conditions. As the causes and conditions converge, a body appears [like a reflection in the mirror]. As for the person and the mirror, when the person moves away, his mirror reflection is also gone. The person may cast his reflection elsewhere, perhaps in the water. Similarly, carrying good and evil karmas, [ālaya] consciousness abandons this body and moves away to accept the next requital.

"As another analogy, the seed of a banyan tree or a ficus tree is small, but it can grow a huge tree. The tree again bears seeds. The new seed then abandons the old tree to grow a new tree. As the old tree grows weak over time, with its sap exhausted, it will dry out and decay. After [ālaya] consciousness abandons the body of a sentient being, [like a small seed] it will accept a huge body of some kind according to karma. It is also like many kinds of seeds, such as barley, wheat, sesame, mung bean, and legume. Because a seed is planted, sprout, stem, flowers, and fruits will grow and ripen. Similarly, because [ālaya] consciousness has moved into a sentient being of some kind, this being has awareness and sensory reception.

"The way [ālaya] consciousness, holding good and evil karmas, successively accepts a variety of bodies is also like a bee that stops over flowers. With love, pleasure, and attachment, it sucks the flavor of a flower for nourishment. The bee then abandons this flower to seek other flowers at other places. Whether it abandons fragrance for stench or it abandons stench for fragrance, it cannot help loving and coveting the object it stops over. Likewise, [ālaya] consciousness may acquire a celestial body to enjoy the fortune fruit of meritorious karma. It may then abandon the celestial body to enter into hell to accept the misfortune fruit of evil karma. As saṁsāra turns, various kinds of bodies are [successively] formed.

"[Ālaya] consciousness is like the white seed of a red or blue tulip or a puṇḍarīka flower. If one cracks open the seed, one will find no sprout, no flower, and no color. Only if the seed is planted in the ground and watered, will a sprout grow. In time flowers and fruits will thrive and flourish, with the flowers blooming in red or white, or various colors. The sprout and the colorful flowers are not inside the seed, but, without the seed, they cannot come into being. [Ālaya] consciousness abandons a dead body, including its fleshy frame, facial features, faculties, and sensory fields, because it no longer sees the convergence of their causes and conditions. With its special vision, hearing, smelling, tasting, and tactility, as well as its memory, [ālaya] consciousness knows the good and evil karmas one has done, according to which it will accept a requital body.

"As a silkworm constructs a cocoon, binding itself by its own doing, so too does [ālaya] consciousness construct a body to bind itself. It will then abandon that body and transfer into a new body as the next requital. Because of a flower seed, there will be a new plant with colorful and fragrant flowers. Likewise, after [ālaya] consciousness has abandoned a body, wherever it goes, along with it goes the dharma realm, including faculties and sensory reception. Wherever a wish-fulfilling jewel is, it is accompanied by pleasing objects. Wherever the sun is, it is accompanied by bright light. Likewise, wherever consciousness transfers to, it is accompanied by the dharma realm, including sensory reception and perception. After abandoning a body, [ālaya] consciousness, without a body of flesh and bones, takes the cause of form as its body. It has faculties, sensory reception, and subtle thinking, and can grasp good or evil.

"Various kinds of fruits, such as dates, pomegranates, mangoes, and the like, may taste pungent, bitter, sour, sweet, salty, or tart. With a distinct flavor, each fruit serves a different purpose. After the fruit decays, its flavor will be reborn through the transformation of the seed. Thus, as the [ālaya] consciousness-seed transfers, it is accompanied by sensory reception, memory, and good and evil karmas. It is called consciousness because it knows that it has abandoned this body in order to accept the next requital body. It is called consciousness because it knows that it is accompanied by good and evil karmas and that, carrying these karmas, it transfers to accept [the next] requital. It is called consciousness because it knows all about what the body does. By analogy, the wind has no form to grasp and no mass to get hold of but, through causes and conditions, it can do karmas: The wind can carry cold or hot, carry fragrance or stench, shake the woods, or violently devastate anything in its path. Likewise, consciousness has no form or mass, and cannot be detected by sight or hearing. However, through causes and condition, the appearance of consciousness is revealed. Because one's consciousness maintains one's body, the body knows pain or pleasure. Looking radiant and energetic, one's body can walk or stand, speak or laugh, and feel happy or sad. Seeing clearly the karmas done, we should know that there is consciousness."

Fascicle 2 (of 2)

At that time in the assembly, the youth Moon Reality Superior rose from his seat and joined his palms. He asked the Buddha, "World-Honored One, how does one see the cause of form? How does one see the cause of desire? How does one see the cause of perception? How does one see the cause of grasping the precepts?"

The Buddha told Moon Reality, "The wise see objects wisely; the foolish see objects foolishly. When the wise see an attractive body, they understand that it is filth, only an assemblage of flesh bundles, tendons, bones, membranes, pus, secretion, and blood, with large veins, small veins, and hollow and solid organs, such as large intestine, small intestine, bladder, stomach, spleen, gall bladder, liver, brain, heart, kidneys, and lungs, as well as hair and nails. Also wrapped in a thin skin are abominable, disgusting impure discharges, such as bile, phlegm, mucus, saliva, feces, and urine.

"A form is composed of the four domains, and they are the cause of form. Moon Reality, taking the body born from parents as an example, its solidity is in the earth domain; its moisture in the water domain; its warmth in the fire domain; and its motion in the wind domain. Its perception and memory, as well as its sensory fields, such as sounds, scents, flavors, and tactile sensations, are all in the consciousness domain."

The youth Moon Reality next asked the Buddha, "Why does one's consciousness abandon the current body upon its death? How does it transfer into the next body? How does it know when to abandon this body?"

The Buddha told Moon Reality, "A sentient being receives requital according to karma, and the stream of consciousness continuously maintains each requital body. A life ends upon the exhaustion of requital, then [ālaya] consciousness abandons the body. It then moves on to accept [the next body] according to karma. Using watery milk as an example, when it is heated with fire, milk, water, and fat will separate. Thus, Moon Reality, when a sentient being's life ends, because of dissolution of the karmic force, the physical form, consciousness, faculties, and their spheres all separate from one another. As the only reliance, [ālaya] consciousness then carries the dharma realm, including memory and one's good and evil karmas, and goes on to accept the next requital.

"Moon Reality, taking the highly auspicious butter as an example, when [ordinary] butter is cooked with various good medicines, it turns into the highly auspicious butter with medicinal flavors and healing power. Shedding its ordinary quality, the butter now holds the strength of good medicine with six flavors: pungent, bitter, sour, salty, tart, and sweet. With its substance, aromas, and flavors, it can benefit one's body. Similarly, after abandoning the body, [ālaya] consciousness, carrying its dharma realm and good and evil karmas, moves away to accept the next requital. Moon Reality, the substance of the butter is like one's body. Blending medicines with the butter, turning it into the highly auspicious butter is like joining sense objects and faculties to do karma. The medicinal flavors mixed into the butter are like good karma that supports consciousness. If one eats the highly auspicious butter, one will look robust, energetic, radiant, fine, and peaceful, without any trouble. It is like enjoying a pleasure-requital because good karma is stored in one's consciousness. If one eats butter made with the wrong medicine, one's features will turn grim, without healthy colors, chalky like the dead. It is like receiving a pain-requital because evil karma is stored in one's consciousness.

"Moon Reality, the auspicious precious butter does not have hands, feet, or eyes, but it can retain the strength of the substance, aromas, and flavors of good medicines. In the same way, [ālaya] consciousness can retain one's good karma and dharma realm. After abandoning the current body, it will manifest wonderful celestial vision through an interim body. It can see the six desire heavens and the sixteen hells. It can see its [interim] body with shapely hands and feet and fine sense organs. It also can see the abandoned corpse and recognize it as the body of its former life. It also can see tall magnificent celestial palaces with various kinds of adornments, surrounded by flowers, fruits, and trees, and covered with vines so radiant and gorgeous that they are like new gold chains set with jewels. Having seen these things, it will be very joyous. Because of great joy and love, [ālaya] consciousness will entrust itself to this [environment].

"When a person with good karma abandons his body to assume another body, it is peaceful and painless. It is like a horseman abandoning one horse to ride another. It is like a warrior armed with military strategy. When the enemy troops approach, he puts on his sturdy armor and fearlessly rides off on his steed. Likewise, [ālaya] consciousness, supported with one's roots of goodness, abandons the inhalation and exhalation of this body as well as its spheres, and moves away to experience fabulous pleasures by rebirth in heaven, whether a Brahma heaven or even the top heaven in the form realm."

At that time in the assembly, Prince Great Medicine rose from his seat and joined his palms. He asked the Buddha, "What form and image does consciousness assume after it has abandoned the body?"

The Buddha replied, "Very good! Very good! Great Medicine, what you now ask is in the great profound realm of a Buddha. Except for the Tathāgata, no one can understand."

Then the youth Worthy Protector Superior said to the Buddha, "Prince Great Medicine's question is very profound. His wisdom is wonderful, keen, and brilliant."

The Buddha told Worthy Protector, "This prince Great Medicine has planted his roots of goodness under Vipaśyin Buddha. For five hundred lives, he was reborn in non-Buddhist families. When he was a nonbeliever, he often pondered the meaning of consciousness: what consciousness is and why it is consciousness. For five hundred lives, he was unable to solve his problem, unable to find clues as to the coming and going of consciousness. I will today shatter his web of doubts and make him understand."

Then the youth Worthy Protector Superior said to Prince Great Medicine, "Very good! Very good! Your question is wonderful and profound. The meaning of Moon Reality's questions is shallow and narrow, like a child whose mind wanders in the midst of external objects, not knowing his internal realm. It is rare to hear the true Dharma and it is hard to encounter a Buddha, whose vast knowledge and profound wisdom are unfathomable. We should especially request the Buddha to give the utmost wonderful teachings."

Seeing the Buddha's radiant and pleasant features like an autumn lotus flower opening, Prince Great Medicine was exuberant and joyful. He joined his palms single-mindedly and said to the Buddha, "World-Honored One, I love the profound Dharma and I thirst for the profound Dharma. I always have the fear of the Tathāgata entering parinirvāṇa and of my not hearing the true Dharma. Then I would have to be among the sentient beings in the world of the five turbidities, too ignorant to know good versus evil, too ignorant to be aware of the good versus the evil and of maturity versus immaturity [of karma]. I would have to transmigrate in confusion through the painful journeys of birth and death."

The Buddha told Prince Great Medicine, "The true Dharma of the Tathāgata is hard to encounter and hard to acquire. In a past life, for the sake of half a stanza [of teachings], I climbed up a mountain and plunged down, abandoning my life. For the sake of the true Dharma, I underwent innumerable millions of koṭis of various kinds of suffering and tribulations. Great Medicine, you may ask all the questions you wish. I will explicate them to you."

Prince Great Medicine said to the Buddha, "Affirmatively I accept Your teachings. World-Honored One, what is the appearance of consciousness? I pray that You will grant me an explanation."

The Buddha told Great Medicine, "Its appearance is like a person's reflection in the water. Indistinguishable as existent or nonexistent, it cannot be grasped. It is like the shape of a cloud, like an image of [tṛṣṇā] thirsty love."

Prince Great Medicine asked the Buddha, "What is thirsty love?"

The Buddha replied, "When one's eyes follow a pleasing sight, it is called thirsty love. When one holds a mirror, one sees the reflection of one's face. When the face in front of the mirror is gone, so is its reflection. The transference of [ālaya] consciousness is similar, and consciousness and good and evil karmas have no form or shape to see. As a person who is born blind does not know sunrise, sunset, night, day, light, or dark, likewise one cannot see one's consciousness. Nor can one see in one's body thirsty love, sensory reception, perception, or memory. The [four] domains, the [six] faculties, and the [five] aggregates, constituting a sentient being, are all consciousness. The physical eyes, ears, nose, tongue, and body, together with sights, sounds, scents, flavors, and tactile sensations, as well as the nonphysical experience of pain or pleasure, are all consciousness. Great Medicine, for example, one tastes food with one's tongue to detect all six flavors: sweet, bitter, pungent, sour, salty, and tart. The tongue and the food have shapes and forms, but flavors are formless. One detects sensations because of one's body, with its bones, marrows, flesh, and blood. The body has a form, but sensations are without form or shape. Through one's body one can know consciousness as well as the fortune fruit or misfortune fruit it holds."

At that time the youth Worthy Protector Superior bowed down at the feet of the Buddha and asked, "World-Honored One, can one see one's consciousness and know one's fortune or misfortune in store?"

The Buddha replied, "Hearken well! No one can see consciousness without first seeing the truth. Unlike a mango in one's palm, consciousness cannot be seen. Consciousness is not inside one's sense organs, such as the eye. If consciousness were inside any sense organ, such as the eye, one would be able to see it by dissecting the eye. Worthy Protector, as Buddhas as numerous as the sands of the Ganges all see that consciousness is formless, so too I see that consciousness is formless. Consciousness cannot be seen by the ordinary and the foolish. It can be revealed [to them] only by analogy.

"Worthy Protector, to know one's sin or merit stored in consciousness, you now should hearken. Suppose a person is possessed, whether by a deity, such as a gandharva, or by a spirit, such as a skandha. Worthy Protector, what is your opinion? Can one see the possessor, whether a deity or a spirit?"

Worthy Protector replied to the Buddha, "No, World-Honored One, the possessor, a deity or a spirit, has no form or shape. One cannot see it inside or outside that person's body."

[The Buddha continued] "Worthy Protector, if a person is possessed by a great deity with superb merit, he will receive fragrant flowers and choice incense, and will have aromatic fine food and drink, served properly with handsome clean offering paraphernalia. Likewise, because [ālaya] consciousness has a store of merits, one will receive [fortune] fruit in the form of dignity, peace, and happiness, whether as a king among men, a state minister, a dignitary with reputation, a person in command of wealth, an elder, a merchant lord, or a god who enjoys splendid celestial life. One's body receiving pleasure-requital because one's consciousness has a store of merits is like a person possessed by a benign deity. When the deity receives an offering of wonderful flowers, choice incense, and aromatic, fine food and drink, he will be delighted and the possessed patient will be soothed. Therefore, if a person acquires command of rank and wealth in life, we should know that his body enjoys fortune fruit because his consciousness has stored merit.

"Worthy Protector, if a person is possessed by a sordid evil spirit, such as a pūtana, which loves feces, spit, rot, filth, and other impure things, offering these to the spirit's pleasure will suit that person. Because of the power of the spirit, the possessed patient follows its desires and loves impurity, stench, rot, and feces. Likewise, if [ālaya] consciousness is laden with sin, one will be reborn [as a human] in poverty or will take an evil life-journey of some kind, as a hungry ghost or an animal that eats filthy things.

"Worthy Protector, one who is possessed by a superior deity, a formless and shapeless entity, receives various kinds of fragrant and pure offerings. Similarly, one receives pleasure-requital because one's [ālaya] consciousness is stored with meritorious karma. By contrast, one who is possessed by an evil spirit, such as a pūtana, receives impure, filthy, gross food and drink. Similarly, one receives pain-requital because one's [ālaya] consciousness is laden with sinful karma. Worthy Protector, we should know that a body possessed by a deity or a spirit receives fine or gross food and drink is like one who receives pleasure-requital or pain-requital for one's merit or sin stored [in consciousness]."

Prince Great Medicine asked the Buddha, "World-Honored One, how does one see the cause of desire?"

The Buddha replied, "Great Medicine, desire is born from complementary causes, like two pieces of wood rubbed against each other by human effort to produce fire. Thus desire is born from consciousness, together with male and female sights, sounds, scents, flavors, and tactile sensations. As an analogy, fruit is born from flower. However, there is no fruit in a flower. When the fruit is born, the flower has perished. Although consciousness is evident because of the body, it cannot be seen by searching throughout the body. When the [seed for the next] karmic fruit is born in consciousness, the body perishes. Bones, marrow, and impure things will all decompose along with the body.

"For example, carrying the form, aroma, flavor, and feel of the future fruit, a seed leaves the tree to grow. Likewise, [ālaya] consciousness abandons the current body, carrying good and evil karmas, sensory reception, perception, and thinking, to accept the next life as requital. The process is also like a man and a woman who go separate ways after their pleasure meeting of love and desire. Consciousness, joined with karma, engages in love, attachment, play, craving, greed, and stinginess. When the current karmic requital is exhausted, consciousness will accept the next requital according to karma. With the conditions of the parents matched during the intermediate state [after one's death], karmic force will enable [ālaya] consciousness to acquire a body fruit [the karmic fruit]. Love and karma are both without mass or shape. Consciousness and form are the complementary causes for desire to arise. These are the cause of desire.

"Great Medicine, what is the cause for one to grasp the precepts? These precepts—no killing, no stealing, no sexual misconduct, no lying, and no drinking alcohol—are stipulated by a teacher. Grasping these precepts is caused by a [grasping] view that, because of observing these precepts, one will achieve holy fruits, becoming a Srotāpanna, a Sakṛdāgāmin, or an Anāgāmin. However, because of grasping, one will instead gain a good rebirth, assuming human form or celestial form. [Grasping these precepts] is goodness with discharges [of afflictions], not goodness without discharges, because goodness without discharges will not yield such a fruit, a body composed of the five aggregates. Therefore, grasping the precepts means planting an impure seed. Consciousness that holds both good and evil karmas is impure, and it suffers from feverish distress because of afflictions. This is the cause of grasping the precepts."

Great Medicine asked the Buddha, "How does consciousness assume the form of a god or a hell-dweller?"

The Buddha replied, "Great Medicine, [ālaya] consciousness in the intermediate state has extraordinary vision, which does not depend on the physical eye for sight. This special vision, joined with a fortunate condition, sees merrymaking with desire and pleasure in a celestial palace. Consciousness will delight in and be attached to what it sees, and will think: 'I should go there.' Impure love and attachment are the cause of being. When consciousness sees its dead body lying in the place for corpses, it will then think: 'This corpse is my beneficent learned friend. Because it has accumulated good karmas, I now will receive the celestial-life requital.'"

Great Medicine asked the Buddha, "World-Honored One, this consciousness deeply loves the corpse. Why does it not use it?"

The Buddha asked Great Medicine, "Taking the cut hair and beard as an analogy, although they are still black and lustrous, can you plant them on the body to make them grow again?"

Great Medicine replied to the Buddha, "No, World-Honored One, the abandoned hair and beard cannot be planted on the body to make them grow again."

The Buddha said, "Likewise, Great Medicine, the corpse that [ālaya] consciousness has abandoned cannot be reused as the next requital."

Great Medicine further asked the Buddha, "This consciousness is invisible and profound, without any mass or shape to find. How does it maintain the large body of a sentient being, such as an elephant, which is hard, like vajra? How does it enter into and maintain the body of a strong man who can fight off nine elephants?"

The Buddha replied, "Great Medicine, the wind, without mass or shape, stays in a hidden valley or crevice. It can break out with violent force, breaking Mount Sumeru into dust. Great Medicine, what are the form and appearance of the wind that can destroy Mount Sumeru?"

Great Medicine replied to the Buddha, "The wind is intangible, without mass or shape."

The Buddha said, "Great Medicine, as the wind is intangible, without mass or shape, so too is [ālaya] consciousness without mass or shape. However, it can maintain a body, whether large or small, whether of an elephant or of a mosquito. As a bright lamp dispels darkness in a large or small room, likewise consciousness maintains a large or small body according to karma."

Great Medicine asked the Buddha, "World-Honored One, what is the appearance of karma? Through what causes and conditions does it manifest?"

The Buddha replied, "Great Medicine, one's rebirth in a celestial palace to eat wonderful celestial food in peace and happiness is the appearance of a karmic fruit. As an analogy, two thirsty people wander in wilderness. One of them finds cool, good water; the other finds nothing and has to endure thirst and suffering. One of them acquires cool water, not given by anyone; the other in thirst is not obstructed by anyone from finding water. Each person receives pleasure-requital or pain-requital for karmic reasons. Great Medicine, this is the way to see one's good or evil karma, which is white or black, like the two distinct phases of the moon in the sky. It is also like the color of a fruit, which changes as the fruit ripens with the power in its fire domain. Thus, because of abundance of merit, one is reborn into a noble family, with an outstanding physical appearance, plentiful assets, and an overflow of gold and treasures. Or one may be reborn in a celestial palace to enjoy happiness and ease. These fortunate conditions are manifestations of one's good karma.

"As an analogy, a seed is planted in the ground, but fruits appear at the top of the tree. The seed does not go from branch to branch to reach the tree top, nor does anyone place the seed on a branch. One cannot find the seed by cutting open the tree trunk. Even if the tree is chopped down, one still cannot find the seed. The seed cannot be found as the tree is formed and its roots firm. Thus good and evil karmas depend on the body, but cannot be found in the body. As an analogy, the seed is the cause of the flower, but inside the seed there is no flower. The flower is the cause of the fruit, but inside the flower there is no fruit. As the flower and the fruit grow, neither growth shows its cause. Likewise, because of the body there is karma, and because of karma there is the body. When the flower falls at maturity, the fruit with its seed will appear; when the body expires at maturity, the karmic seed will leave it. As the seed is the cause of flowers and fruits, likewise is the body the cause of good and evil karmas. Karma has no shape, no appearance of maturity, like the shadow of one's body, with neither mass nor obstruction. The shadow is not held by or fastened to a person, but it moves along with the person. Never has anyone seen the shadow coming out of his body. Likewise, there are body and karma, but karma cannot be seen as something attached to the body. Yet, without the body, there cannot be karma.

"As an analogy, medicine, which tastes pungent, bitter, or tart, can purge all diseases and make one's body glow with healthy color and radiance, and people will know on sight that [the patient] has taken good medicine. The flavor of medicine can be experienced, but its curative merit is formless, cannot be seen, and cannot be captured. However, it can improve a person's skin tone and glow. Likewise, good karma, which has no mass or shape, can enrich one's body. One who is fortified with good karma is endowed with food, drink, and plentiful internal and external assets. One has good features and shapely, normal hands and feet, lives in a luxurious house piled up with treasures, such as jewels, gold, and silver, and enjoys peace, happiness, and merriment at will. We should know that this is the appearance of good karma.

"By contrast, if one is reborn with repulsive features, stays in a squalid place in a fringe country, in poverty and lowliness, subsists on gross food and drink or has nothing to eat, lacks resources, envying others' enjoyment, we should know that this is the appearance of evil karma. As a clear mirror displays the fineness or grossness of one's face, the reflection in the mirror has no mass and cannot be captured. As [ālaya] consciousness has a store of good and evil karmas, accordingly one is reborn as a god or a human, or is reborn as an animal or a hell-dweller. Great Medicine, this is the way to see karma and [ālaya] consciousness transfer together."

Great Medicine asked, "World-Honored One, how does amazing consciousness acquire a large body and maintain its sense organs?"

The Buddha replied, "Great Medicine, as an analogy, a hunter goes into a mountain forest and shoots an elephant with a poisonous arrow. The poison on the arrow enters into the blood stream of the elephant, disables the body, and destroys its faculties. The poison is lethal and the body turns blue-red like clotted blood. Having killed the elephant, the poison is spent. What is your opinion? How does the quantity of poison compare with the size of the elephant's body? Can they compare?"

Great Medicine replied to the Buddha, "World-Honored One, the poison and the elephant have too wide a disproportion to compare quantity or size. It is like comparing a mustard seed with Mount Sumeru."

"Great Medicine, likewise, [ālaya] consciousness abandons the current body and its spheres and moves on to develop the faculties [of a new body] according to karma."

Great Medicine further asked the Buddha, "Why is the subtle consciousness not fatigued by maintaining a large body?"

The Buddha replied, "Great Medicine, Sumeru, the king of mountains, stands at 84,000 yojanas. The two dragon-kings Nanda and Upananda each circle it three times. They then shake Mount Sumeru with a huge breath, turning the waters of its surrounding sea into poison. These two dragon-kings are gigantic and strong, and the two dragon-kings Vāsuki and Takṣaka are their equals. What is your opinion? Is there any difference in quantity between the consciousness of any of the four dragon-kings and that of a mosquito?"

Great Medicine replied, "World-Honored One, there is no difference between the consciousness of any of the four dragon-kings and that of a mosquito."

"Great Medicine, if a small drop of deadly poison enters the mouth of each of the four dragons, they all will die. What is your opinion? Between a small drop of deadly poison and the venom in the mouth of a dragon, which is stronger?"

Great Medicine replied to the Buddha, "The venom in the dragon's mouth is stronger, and the strength of a small drop of poison is weaker."

"Great Medicine, even for a strong sentient being that can fight off nine elephants, amazing consciousness, with neither form nor shape, not measurable by quantity, maintains its body according to karma. Although the seed of a banyan tree is tiny, after being planted, it can grow into a magnificent huge tree with hundreds and thousands of branches. What is your opinion? Are the seed and the tree of the same size?"

Great Medicine replied, "World-Honored One, the seed and the tree have a vast difference in size, like that between a hole in the lotus root and the domain of space."

"Thus, Great Medicine, the seed cannot be found in the tree. Yet, without the seed, the tree cannot be born. As a tiny banyan seed can grow a huge tree, so too amazing consciousness can grow a huge body. One cannot find consciousness in the body. Yet, without consciousness, the body cannot be."

Great Medicine further asked the Buddha, "Why does consciousness, which is indestructible like an adamantine vajra, stay in a fragile quick-to-decay body?"

The Buddha replied, "Great Medicine, as an analogy, a poor man acquires a wish-fulfilling jewel. By the power of the jewel, spontaneously appear resources and pleasure objects, such as ornately sculpted towers, splendid palatial mansions, lush gardens full of flowers and fruits, elephants and horses, and female attendants. Later, he loses the wish-fulfilling jewel, and all the resources and pleasure objects vanish. Although the wish-fulfilling jewel is so strong and durable that it cannot be destroyed by a thousand vajras, the resources it produces are false and impermanent, which quickly disperse and perish. Likewise, [ālaya] consciousness is strong and indestructible, but the body it produces quickly decays and perishes."

Great Medicine asked, "World-Honored One, how does gentle consciousness penetrate a dense hard form?"

The Buddha said to Great Medicine, "Water is a gentle substance, but its flow can penetrate mountain rocks. What is your opinion? How do you compare the quality of softness and hardness in water and rock?"

Great Medicine replied, "World-Honored One, the quality of a rock is hard, like vajra. The quality of water is soft, pleasant to the touch."

"Great Medicine, Consciousness is like water, most wondrous and most soft, but it can penetrate a strong large body, accepting it as requital."

Great Medicine next asked the Buddha, "World-Honored One, after sentient beings have abandoned their bodies, how are they reborn in heaven, and how are they reborn in hell?"

The Buddha replied to Great Medicine, "Upon the death of a person, if he has stored meritorious karma, he will abandon his original eyesight and acquire the wonderful celestial vision. With the wonderful celestial vision, he will see the six desire heavens, the six life-journeys, and the movement of his body. He will see celestial palaces with all amenities, and joyous gardens where flowers are always in bloom. He will also see beautiful goddess-attendants make merry in the lotus hall, wearing flowers and silk garments, adorned with bangles, bracelets, and other ornaments. Once he sees the goddess-daughters in a heaven, his mind will be filled with happiness and gratification as well as attachment. His features will become relaxed and joyful like a lotus flower. His gaze will not be disoriented, his nose not collapsed, and his breath not foul. His eyes will look bright and clear like green lotus leaves. The joints of his body will not be in pain. His eyes, ears, nose, and mouth will not ooze blood, nor will he lose control of feces or urine. His pores will not enlarge, nor will his hair stand on end. His palms will not be dead yellow, and his nails not blue black. His hands and feet will neither convulse nor contract. As a good sign, he will see a huge hall in the sky, lined with hundreds and thousands of colorful columns with beautiful carvings. The magnificent jeweled hall will be decorated with various kinds of fragrant flowers, and draped with nets, from which hang bells playing beautiful refreshing tones to gentle winds. Frolicking in the hall will be celestial youths adorned with jewels.

"Having seen these things, he will smile contentedly, showing his teeth like flowers in a painting. His eyes will be neither wide open nor closed. His voice will be soft, and his body neither too cold nor too hot. He will not be sad to see family members surrounding him. At sunrise, he will abandon his life. Then he will see light, not dark, with extraordinary fragrances coming from the four directions.

He might even see, with delight and reverence, the honored visage of a Buddha. He will joyfully bid farewell as if to take a short trip. Then he will return to comfort his family and friends, helping them not to mourn the way existence flows, telling them not to have sorrow caused by differentiation, because where there is birth, there must be death. Great Medicine, a person with good karma, before his death, will delight in giving alms, in reciting various stanzas and praises, and in understanding various explanations and teachings of the true Dharma. He will abandon his life peacefully, not in sleep but as if in sleep.

"As the person is about to abandon his life, his celestial parents-to-be will be seated together on one seat. Flowers will naturally appear in the hands of his goddess mother-to-be. Seeing these flowers, she will say to his father-to-be, 'What an auspicious, extraordinary victory fruit! You should know that a time is approaching for joyful celebration for a son.' His goddess mother-to-be will then shake the flowers with her hands. As she plays with the flowers, the person's life will end. His [ālaya] consciousness, formless and invisible, will abandon all faculties and their objects, carrying his karma and other spheres, and it will move away to accept a new requital. It is like a horseman abandoning one horse to ride another. It is like the sun directing its light. It is like wood producing fire. It is like the moon casting its reflection in clear water. His [ālaya] consciousness with a store of good karmas will accept a celestial life as requital. It will be swiftly delivered by [karmic] wind into a flower, and his celestial parents-to-be, seated together on one seat, will both look at the flower. After the wind of desire blows sweet dew on the flower for seven days, a bright clean god-child, adorned with jewels, will appear lively and radiant in the hands of his goddess-mother."

Great Medicine asked the Buddha, "World-Honored One, how does formless consciousness bring a form into being through the power of causes and conditions? Can a form be found inside its causes and conditions?"

The Buddha replied to Great Medicine, "Fire is produced by rubbing two pieces of wood, but fire cannot be found in the wood. Without wood, fire cannot be produced. Fire is born from the convergence of causes and conditions. Without causes and conditions, fire cannot be produced. Examining the wood, one cannot find the appearance of fire. Yet one can see fire rising from the wood. Indeed, Great Medicine, [ālaya] consciousness brings a physical form into being through one's parents as the conditions. Searching through one's body, one cannot find consciousness. Yet, apart from one's body, there is no consciousness. Great Medicine, before the kindling of fire, the appearance of fire is not there. Nor are there such qualities as heat that can be felt. Thus, without a body, Great Medicine, there cannot be consciousness, sensory reception, perception, or mental processing. Great Medicine, when ordinary beings see the bright light of the sun, they do not see the substance of the sun, whether it is black, white, yellow white, or yellow red. They know only that the sun, alternately rising and setting, radiates light and heat. They know the sun through its functions. Consciousness too is known by its functions."

Great Medicine asked the Buddha, "What are the functions of consciousness?"

The Buddha replied to Great Medicine, "Sensory reception, perception, mental processing, thinking, and feeling anxiety, agony, or distress are functions of consciousness. Furthermore, habitual good and evil karmas become seeds stored in consciousness, which manifest as functions."

Great Medicine asked the Buddha, "How does [ālaya] consciousness leave one body and quickly accept another body? If it has abandoned one body but has not yet accepted a new body, what appearance does consciousness assume during this interval?"

The Buddha replied, "Great Medicine, as an analogy, a warrior with long arms, clad in sturdy armor, rides a horse, swift as the wind, into a battle formation and fights bravely with his weapon. Although he falls off his horse in a moment of inattention, he immediately jumps back on because of his good training in martial arts. Likewise, [ālaya] consciousness abandons one body and immediately accepts another body. It is also like a coward who, upon seeing the enemy, out of fear, immediately rides his horse to escape. Likewise, when [ālaya] consciousness with a store of good karmas sees its celestial parents-to-be seated together on the same seat, it quickly entrusts its rebirth to them.

"Great Medicine, you ask what appearance consciousness assumes during the interval after it has abandoned its old body but has not yet accepted a new body. Great Medicine, by analogy, a person's reflection in the water has no mass to grasp. Yet its hands, feet, facial features, and other shapes are no different from the person's. The reflection has no mass, nor does it do karmas. It has neither sense of hot or cold nor sense of touch. Nor does it fatigue or have flesh made with the four domains. Nor does it make sounds of speech, sounds of body, or sounds of pain or pleasure. The same is true for the appearance of [ālaya] consciousness after it has abandoned the old body but has not accepted a new body. Great Medicine, this explains how [ālaya] consciousness with a store of good karmas is reborn in heaven."

Great Medicine asked the Buddha, "How is [ālaya] consciousness reborn in hell?"

The Buddha replied, "Great Medicine, in regard to how those who have done evil karmas enter into hell, you should hearken. Great Medicine, sentient beings that have accumulated roots of evil will have this thought upon dying: 'I now die here with immense anxiety and suffering, abandoning my beloved parents, relatives, and friends.' They will see hells and see themselves doomed to fall into them headfirst. They will see a place covered with blood and will relish its flavor on sight. Conditioned upon their appetite for blood, they will be reborn in hell. The way [ālaya] consciousness deposits itself in the midst of such conditions as putrid evil water and stinking filth is analogous to the birth of maggots through the power of such conditions as feces, filth, spoiled cream, and putrid liquor, in a stinking place. Likewise those who enter into hell are reborn there through foul things."

The youth Worthy Protector Superior joined his palms and asked the Buddha, "What forms and appearances do hell-dwellers assume? What do their bodies look like?"

The Buddha replied, "Great Medicine, those who are reborn in hell because of their love of blood-covered ground will have bodies the color of blood, all radiating bloody light. Those who are reborn in a moat will have bodies like black clouds. Those who are reborn in a milk river will have bodies dotted in various colors, and their bodies will be very delicate, like an infant of nobility. Their bodies will measure more than eight elbows in height, with long head hair and body hair trailing behind. Their hands, feet, and facial features will be crooked and incomplete. People in Jambudvīpa will die if they see them in the distance."

Great Medicine asked the Buddha, "What food do hell-dwellers eat?"

The Buddha replied, "Great Medicine, sentient beings in hell receive no pleasure from eating food. Running about with fear, they will see in the distance red molten copper. Mistaking it for blood, they will rush for it. They will also hear a call saying that the hungry can come quickly to eat. They will then go there and hold their hands as cups before their mouths. The hell warden will pour hot molten copper into their cupped hands and force them to drink it down into their abdomens. Their bones and joints will burst and crack open, their bodies entirely in flames. Great Medicine, the food eaten by sentient beings in hell only augments their suffering, without affording even a little comfort or happiness. Such are the agonies of sentient beings in hell! However, one's [ālaya] consciousness never gives up, nor is it damaged. Even when the body is like a pile of bones, [ālaya] consciousness remains there, not leaving. Until the karmic requital is exhausted, the tormented body will not be abandoned.

"Pressed by the agony of hunger and thirst, they will see a lush green garden with an abundance of thriving trees, flowers, and fruits. Seeing this, they will laugh and say to one another, 'This lush garden is green and the wind is cool.' The multitude will hasten into the garden, seeking a moment of pleasure. However, the tree leaves, flowers, and fruits will all change into knives and swords to hack and slash these sinners. While some of them will be hit and their bodies cut in two, others will scream as they run in the four directions. Wardens will mobilize, holding vajra clubs, iron clubs, iron axes, or iron rods. They will bite their lips in wrath, their bodies bursting flames. Forbidding the sinners to leave the garden, they will slash and batter these sinners, who experience these things because of their own karmas. Chasing after the sinners, the wardens will say to them, 'Where are you going? You can stay here. How can you escape to the east or the west? This garden is adorned with your karmas. Is it possible to leave?'

"Indeed, Great Medicine, sentient beings in hell undergo various kinds of suffering. They die every seven days and are reborn again in hell. Because of the power of karma, they are like worker bees that return to their original place after collecting honey from flowers. Sentient beings with sinful karma are doomed to enter into hell. As they begin to die, they will see death agents arrive, who will lasso their necks and pull them. As if being captured by bandits, they will experience immense suffering in body and mind as they enter vast darkness, wailing these words: 'Oh, oh! Disaster! Agony! I now abandon relatives, friends, and various kinds of loves in Jambudvīpa, to enter into hell. I now do not see the road to heaven but see wretched things. Like a silkworm that produces silk to bind itself to death, I am bound by my own sinful karma. With a noose fastened around my neck, I am dragged and driven into hell.' Worthy Protector, such are the miserable appearances of sentient beings with sinful karma, being reborn in hell!"

Worthy Protector and Prince Great Medicine, having heard these words, were astounded, their hair standing on end. They rose together, joined their palms, and said, "We today take refuge in the Buddha and entreat for His rescue and protection. We pray that, because of the merit of hearing this Dharma, before we are liberated from the stream of existence under the wheel of birth and death, we will not go down the three evil life-paths, never into hell."

Worthy Protector further implored the Buddha, "I pray only that You will grant our wish."

The Buddha said, "You may ask anything you wish."

Worthy Protector asked the Buddha, "What is accumulation? What is gathering? What are the aggregates? What is the meaning of no transference into a body?"

The Buddha replied, "Worthy Protector, the body is composed of four realms: intellect, perception, mental faculty, and ignorance. Including these four realms in one's consciousness is called accumulation. Gathering refers to the six domains, and the six faculties with their six corresponding objects. There are three causes of existence in the Three Realms, and there are two causes for understanding.

"Gathering also means the assemblage of hair, beard, nails, skin, flesh, pus, blood, mucus, saliva, bile, phlegm, secretion, fat, marrow, and fluids, as well as hands, feet, face, and large and small joints. It is called gathering because it is like grain, legume, sesame, and wheat, collected and amassed into large piles. The six domains are earth, water, fire, wind, space, and consciousness. The six faculties are eye, ear, nose, tongue, body, and mental faculty; their corresponding objects are sights, sounds, scents, flavors, tactile sensations, and mental objects.

"The three causes of one's existence in the Three Realms are greed, anger, and delusion, while the three causes [of diseases] are wind, bile, and phlegm. The two causes for understanding are precepts and faith; another two are equability and almsgiving; another two are energetic progress and samādhi; and another two are good and evil.

"Sensory reception, perception, mental processing, and consciousness are called the four formless aggregates. Sensory reception leads to experiencing pain, pleasure, or neither of the two. Perception refers to cognition of pain or pleasure. Mental processing refers to thinking, attention, and sensory contact. Consciousness is the lord of the body, pervading the entire body and directing all of its activities.

"No transference [of one's ālaya consciousness] pertains to attainment of the bodhi fruit because one's body, voice, and mind are purified. After death, one's [ālaya] consciousness abandons the aggregates of existence and moves away joyfully. It no longer undergoes [karmic] existence, transmigrating through life-journeys. No more transference [into a karmic body] is called no transference."

Then Worthy Protector and Prince Great Medicine bowed down at the feet of the Buddha and said, "World-Honored One, this Dharma nugget pronounced by the Buddha, the Omniscient One, will bring great benefits, peace, and joy to sentient beings in the future."

The Buddha said, "The Dharma store of the Tathāgata abides for eternity, never ceasing. The omniscient one knows everything because I have developed wisdom light through immeasurable assiduity and suffering. I now pronounce this sūtra on this true-Dharma day to shine brilliant light on sentient beings and to let virtue and renown flow everywhere from the ocean of omniscience. I pronounce it for the sake of those who are able to control their mind streams. Wherever this sūtra is, wherever it is being recited or explained, gods, spirits, asuras, and mahoragas will all come to make obeisance and to give support. Water, fire, law, and bandits will not be able to do any harm. Bhikṣus, from this day forward, do not pronounce this sūtra to nonbelievers. Nor should you show it to those who intend to find fault with this sūtra. Nor should you pronounce it to non-Buddhists, such as Nirgranthaputra and the Nirgrantha group. Nor should you pronounce it to those who request it with disrespect. Those who disobey my instructions damage Dharma work and in effect damage the Tathāgata. Bhikṣus, if there are those who make obeisance and offerings to this sūtra, you should respect them and honor them with gifts because they uphold the Tathāgata store."

Then the World-Honored One spoke in verse:

> Be brave to transcend the burden of afflictions.
> Train assiduously in the true teachings of the Buddha.
> Annihilate the legions of death,
> Like the elephant trampling on reeds.
>
> Uphold the Dharma, observe the precepts,
> And progress single-mindedly, without negligence or indolence,
> In order to cease the flow of rebirth,
> Reaching the edge of agonizing existence.

After the Buddha pronounced this sūtra, the youth Worthy Protector Superior, Prince Great Medicine, bhikṣus, and Bodhisattva-Mahāsattvas, as well as gods, humans, asuras, gandharvas, and others in the huge assembly, having heard the Buddha's words, rejoiced and reverently carried out the teachings.

From the Dharma Flower Section

14 Sūtra of the Great Dharma Drum (in 2 fascicles)

Sūtra 14 is based on text 270 (T09n0270). This text was translated from Sanskrit into Chinese by Guṇabhadra (求那跋陀羅, 394–468) from central India. In this sūtra, present in the huge assembly of the Buddha is Prasenajit, the king of Kauśala. As an analogy, the king smears his war drum with medicine and suffuses it with the smoke of burning medicine. When those who are shot by arrows hear the sound of the drum, they will have all the arrows pulled out. Likewise, the Buddha beats the Dharma drum to benefit all sentient beings, and they will definitely pull out their three poisonous arrows: greed, anger, and delusion.

The Buddha reveals that the Tathāgata is neither existence nor a sentient being, never born but manifests birth. As a manifested Buddha demonstrates entering parinirvāṇa, the Tathāgata abides eternally. To those who mistakenly believe in a commanding self, the Buddha explains the meaning of no self. To those who, out of misunderstanding of no self, mistakenly hold the view of cessation, the Buddha then explains that nirvāṇa is not extinction but eternal peace and bliss. To be in eternal peace and bliss, there must be a self, the true self.

Using four analogies, the Buddha reveals Buddha nature in all sentient beings. Two of the four analogies are the eye blinded by a disease, and the water in a well to be dug. Like the eye blinded by a disease, sentient beings need treatment to recover their eyesight. To access the underground water, sentient beings must dig a well.

Among the five hundred Bodhisattvas in this assembly is a youth called Entire World Delighted to See, who belongs to the Licchavi clan. After the parinirvāṇa of Śākyamuni Buddha, Mahākāśyapa will uphold His true Dharma for forty years. During the last eighty years of the true Dharma, Entire World Delighted to See will be reborn and become a bhikṣu, who will uphold the Buddha's name and propagate this *Sūtra of the Great Dharma Drum* during his 100-year life. He will demonstrate great spiritual powers then enter parinirvāṇa.

15 Mahāyāna Vaipulya Sūtra of Total Retention

Texts 274–275 (T09n0274–75) are two Chinese versions of this sūtra, each translated from a different Sanskrit text. Text 274 was translated by Dharmarakṣa (竺法護, 3rd century) from Dunhuang (敦煌), who went to China in 265, during the Western Jin Dynasty. Text 275 was translated in the Liu Song Dynasty by Vinītaruci (毘尼多流支, ?–594) from southern India, who went to China in 574. Sūtra 15 is an English translation of text 275, which is slightly shorter than text 274.

The Buddha gives these teachings before His parinirvāṇa, in anticipation of the degeneration of His Dharma. In the Dharma-ending age, there will be those who segregate the Dharma, saying that "Bodhisattvas should not hear, study, or accept the sūtras which the Buddha has pronounced for voice-hearers. . . . Voice-hearers should not hear or accept the Dharmas that Bodhisattvas practice." There will be those who fragment the Dharma, saying that "one can attain bodhi by cultivating prajñā-pāramitā only" and that "only emptiness is the true Dharma while all other Dharmas are not." There will be false teachers who slander true Dharma masters and malign the Dharma. These false teachers will speak contradictory words, and their actions will contradict their words.

The Buddha tells the story of a past life of His when He was a bhikṣu named Dharma. He foolishly slandered another bhikṣu called Pure Life, who upheld the true Dharma. After death, Bhikṣu Dharma fell into hell and underwent suffering for 70 kalpas. He was successively reborn in animal form for over 60 kalpas, then in human form for 60,000 lives, living in sordid conditions. The bhikṣu Pure Life of the past is none other than Amitābha Buddha today, who has attained Buddhahood ten kalpas earlier than Śākyamuni Buddha and now dwells in His Pure Land. Because of these karmic causes and conditions, Śākyamuni Buddha has attained the unsurpassed enlightenment in this world of the five turbidities.

The Buddha states that He has practiced all six pāramitās fully for an immeasurable amount of time. Otherwise, he would not have attained the unsurpassed bodhi. He teaches that the Dharma Doors he has taught should all be retained, because from the time of His attainment of bodhi to the time of His parinirvāṇa, what He has said in this interval is all true, never false. If there are fools who malign the Dharma, they have maligned both the Buddha and the Saṅgha, resulting in severe consequences. Moreover, He advises the slanderers and the slandered to unite in harmony, so that the Dharma can stay in the world for a long time.

16 Sūtra of Immeasurable Meaning

A few months before His parinirvāṇa, the Buddha pronounced this *Sūtra of Immeasurable Meaning* (T09n0276) and, immediately afterward, the *Lotus Sūtra* (T09n0262). Sūtra 16 is an English translation of text 276, which was translated from Sanskrit into Chinese in 481 by Dharmagatayaśas (曇摩伽陀耶舍, 5th–6th centuries) from central India.

This sūtra is divided into three chapters. Chapter 1 describes the virtuous actions of Bodhisattva-Mahāsattvas. Like Buddhas, they skillfully turn the Dharma wheel, benefiting all sentient beings with immeasurable great compassion. Then all in the assembly pay tribute to the Buddha, praising His dharma body, His manifested physical body, and His virtuous actions.

In chapter 2, the Buddha teaches the Dharma Door of Immeasurable Meaning, which is the emptiness of dharmas. Bodhisattvas should observe that just as thoughts, one after another, never stay, all dharmas arise and perish instantly. They should penetrate not only the four appearances of every dharma but also the capacities, natures, and desires of sentient beings. As they pronounce immeasurable meanings of the Dharma to sentient beings, these immeasurable meanings are born from the one dharma of no appearance, which, however, is not apart from appearances.

The Buddha reveals that He has given teachings on emptiness throughout His teaching life, in the beginning, the middle, and the end. However, some hearers become Arhats, some become Pratyekabuddhas, and some become Bodhisattvas, according to their understandings of the same words. The Buddha then praises this *Mahāyāna Sūtra of Immeasurable Meaning* because it comes from the abode of Buddhas, goes to sentient beings for them to activate the bodhi mind, and stays in the action range of Bodhisattvas. This sūtra has immeasurable virtue and inconceivable power, and enables sentient beings to attain anuttara-samyak-saṁbodhi quickly.

In chapter 3, the Buddha describes the ten inconceivable powers of this sūtra for men and women who uphold it. It can cause sentient beings on the ground of ordinary beings to germinate immeasurable bodhi sprouts. It can cause their trees of merit to flourish and expand. Hence this sūtra is also called *The Inconceivable Power of Virtue.*

14 大法鼓經
Sūtra of the Great Dharma Drum

Translated from Sanskrit into Chinese in the Liu Song Dynasty
by
The Tripiṭaka Master Guṇabhadra from India

Fascicle 1 (of 2)

Thus I have heard:

At one time the Buddha was dwelling in the Anāthapiṇḍika Garden of Jetavana Park in the city kingdom of Śrāvastī, together with 500 great bhikṣus, as well as 100,000 Bodhisattva-Mahāsattvas and a multitude of gods, dragons, yakṣas, and gandharvas. Also present were 100,000 upāsakas and upāsikās. In attendance too were the Brahma-kings, rulers of this Sahā World, as well as the god-king Śakra, the four god-kings, and their retinues. From worlds in the ten directions came innumerable bhikṣus, bhikṣuṇīs, upāsakas, and upāsikās, as well as Bodhisattvas.

At that time the Tathāgata pronounced the Dharma to His four groups of disciples, telling them, "With existence, there are pain and pleasure. Without existence, there is neither pain nor pleasure. Therefore, keeping away from pain and pleasure is the foremost bliss of nirvāṇa."

All these 500 voice-hearer bhikṣus were Arhats. They had ended their afflictions and the discharges thereof, and their minds had achieved command and ease. Like the great dragon, with their minds liberated and their wisdom unfolded, they had completed their undertaking [for Arhatship]. Having shed the heavy burden, they had acquired benefits for themselves, ending the bondage of existence. Liberated by true knowledge, they had achieved the foremost pāramitā and total command of their minds.

Of those who were still learning, a countless number had achieved the [voice-hearer] fruits, becoming Srotāpannas, Sakṛdāgāmins, or Anāgāmins. An innumerable multitude of bhikṣus, though still with afflictions, had come to achievement.

Also from worlds in the ten directions came an innumerable multitude of Bodhisattva-Mahāsattvas who had acquired immeasurable asaṁkhyeyas of merits. Their number was beyond calculation or analogy, unknowable to voice-hearers or Pratyekabuddhas. The exceptions were Mañjuśrī Bodhisattva, Great Strength Bodhisattva, Avalokiteśvara Bodhisattva, and Maitreya Bodhisattva-Mahāsattva. Such leading Bodhisattva-Mahāsattvas were in asaṁkhyeya multitudes, as numerous as grasses and trees grown from the earth. Bodhisattvas who came from other directions were countless as well. Also present was the bhikṣuṇī Kṣema, together with a group of bhikṣuṇīs. Present as well were Lady

Viśākhā and Queen Mallikā, together with their innumerable attendants. Also present was the Elder Sudatta, together with innumerable upāsakas.

The World-Honored One, in the midst of this huge multitude, introduced the Dharma Door of Existence and Nonexistence.

Meanwhile, King Prasenajit, rising from his sleep, thought: "I should go to the World-Honored One." Having had this thought, he immediately set off, with drums beating and conch shells blowing, going to the Buddha. The World-Honored One, knowing the reason, still asked, "Ānanda, why is there the sound of drums and conch shells?"

Ānanda replied to the Buddha, "King Prasenajit is coming to the Buddha. Hence the sound of drums and conch shells."

The Buddha told Ānanda, "You should also beat the great Dharma drum because I now will pronounce the *Sūtra of the Great Dharma Drum*."

Ānanda asked the Buddha, "I have never heard of the name of this *Sūtra of the Great Dharma Drum*. Why is it called the *Sūtra of the Great Dharma Drum*?"

The Buddha told Ānanda, "How can you know it? Not even one of the Bodhisattva-Mahāsattvas in this assembly knows this *Sūtra of the Great Dharma Drum*, which has a six-syllable name [in Sanskrit]. Much less have you heard of it."

Ānanda said to the Buddha, "This is unprecedented. The name of this Dharma is truly hard to know."

"Indeed, Ānanda, the fact is not different from your statement. Ānanda, this *Sūtra of the Great Dharma Drum*, like the bloom of the udumbara tree, is rare in the world."

Ānanda asked the Buddha, "Not all Buddhas have this Dharma?"

The Buddha told Ānanda, "Buddhas of the past, present, and future all have this Dharma."

Ānanda asked the Buddha, "If so, why did these Bodhisattvas, the heroes among men, all come to gather here? Why do their Tathāgatas not expound this Dharma in their own lands?"

The Buddha told Ānanda, "For example, an āraṇyaka bhikṣu lives alone in a mountain cave. On his way to the village to beg for food, he sees various human and animal corpses. Having seen them, he feels disgusted and returns without food, thinking: 'Alas, I will definitely be like that.' Then he feels happy, thinking: 'I should go there again to observe corpses to intensify my revulsion.' Again he heads for that village, looking to see corpses in order to strengthen his perception of impurity. Seeing them, he continues to observe them. Then he achieves the holy fruit, becoming an Arhat.

"Buddhas in other worlds do not teach impermanence, suffering, emptiness, or impurity. Why? Because the Dharma in those Buddha Lands should be their way. Those Tathāgatas say to their Bodhisattvas, 'How marvelous! Śākyamuni the World-Honored One, taking the hard way, appears in the land of the five turbidities. For the sake of suffering sentient beings, using various viable approaches, he pronounces the *Sūtra of the Great Dharma Drum*. Therefore, good men, you should learn in that way.' Those Bodhisattvas have come to this assembly because they all want to see me, to pay respects, and to make obeisance. Having come to this assembly, they will attain the First Ground, even up to the Tenth Ground [on the Bodhisattva Way]. Hence the *Sūtra of the Great Dharma Drum* is very hard to encounter. Hence multitudes of great Bodhisattvas from worlds in the ten directions, for the sake of hearing the Dharma, have all gathered here."

Ānanda said to the Buddha, "Very good! Very good! All who attend will benefit. They all will receive the hard-to-acquire Dharma in this sūtra."

The Buddha told Ānanda, "Such a profound sūtra cannot be received by all. Therefore, you should not say that all who attend will benefit."

Ānanda asked the Buddha, "Why will not all who attend benefit?"

The Buddha told Ānanda, "This sūtra is the secret Dharma store of Tathāgatas. It is profound and wondrous, hard to understand and hard to believe. Therefore, Ānanda, you should not say that all who attend will benefit."

Ānanda said to the Buddha, "Then is it not like King Prasenajit beating the huge war drum to launch a battle? When the sound is heard, all [enemy] arrows fall away."

The Buddha told Ānanda, "When King Prasenajit beats the war drum, not all delight in hearing the sound of the drum. The cowardly ones are scared to death, or nearly to death. Indeed, Ānanda, the name of this *Sūtra of the Great Dharma Drum* is the Dharma Door in which riders of the Two Vehicles disbelieve. Therefore, Ānanda, as the huge war drum is beaten only by the king before fighting a battle, so too can this great Dharma drum, the secret of Buddhas, be expounded only by a Buddha who has appeared in the world."

Then the World-Honored One asked Mahākāśyapa, "The bhikṣus here, having left all the scum and chaff, are pure, alike, and truly strong. Are they capable of hearing this *Sūtra of the Great Dharma Drum*?"

Mahākāśyapa replied to the Buddha, "If there are bhikṣus who have breached the precepts or violated the regulations, they are rebuked by Mahāmaudgalyāyana. Even I do not accommodate such bhikṣus, much less would the World-Honored One. The multitude in this assembly is like the sandalwood grove, pure and unvaried."

The Buddha told Mahākāśyapa, "The multitude in this assembly is all pure and homogeneous. However, they do not have good understanding of my veiled statements."

Mahākāśyapa asked the Buddha, "What is meant by veiled statements?"

The Buddha told Mahākāśyapa, "Saying that the Tathāgata enters the ultimate nirvāṇa is making a veiled statement. In truth the Tathāgata abides eternally, never extinct, because parinirvāṇa is not a dharma of destruction. This sūtra leaves the veiled approach and expounds with entirely explicit tones through hundreds of thousands of causes and conditions. Therefore, Mahākāśyapa, you should survey this huge multitude again."

Mahākāśyapa again observed those present and their reason for coming. In the time of a kṣaṇa, sentient beings of weak faith, voice-hearers, Pratyekabuddhas, and novice Bodhisattvas, who considered themselves incapable, had the thought of giving up.

As an analogy, a man named Thousand Strong Men stands up in the midst of a multitude of strong men owned by the royal family. Beating a drum, he chants, "Who is capable of wrestling with me?" The incapable ones remain silent, thinking: "I am incapable of wrestling with him. I might be injured or even lose my life." The one against whom no one in the group dares to fight is the brave, indomitable strong man who can erect the great victory banner.

Thus, inadequate sentient beings, voice-hearers, Pratyekabuddhas, and novice Bodhisattvas each thought: "I am incapable of hearing or accepting this Dharma, which states that the Tathāgata has entered parinirvāṇa and that He is eternally abiding, never extinct."

Having heard in the midst of the multitude what they had never heard before, they left their seats and departed. Why? Because they had cultivated in the long night the view of void with respect to parinirvāṇa. Upon hearing of this pure sūtra, which is free from obscurity, they left their seats and departed. Among the voice-hearers, Pratyekabuddhas, and novice Bodhisattvas, who came from worlds in the ten directions, on the scale of a million koṭi parts, only one part remained.

The Bodhisattva-Mahāsattvas who stayed on believed in the eternal abiding and changelessness of the dharma body. They then could settle in, accept, and uphold all the sūtras about the Tathāgata store. They could also explain to and comfort the world, enabling others to understand all the veiled statements [in these sūtras]. They could well discern sūtras of definitive meaning versus sūtras of non-definitive meaning. They all could subdue sentient beings that violated the prohibitions, and they all could respect and serve the pure, virtuous ones. With great pure faith in the Mahāyāna, they would not consider the Two Vehicles as extraordinary. They would pronounce only mahāvaipulya sūtras, not other sūtras. They would pronounce only that the Tathāgata is eternally abiding and that there is the Tathāgata store, without abandoning emptiness—not only the emptiness of the self-view but also the emptiness of the self-essence of all saṁskṛta dharmas.

The Buddha told Mahākāśyapa, "Ask the huge multitude again whether they want to hear this *Sūtra of the Great Dharma Drum*, the hard-to-believe Mahāyāna sūtra, from the vast One Vehicle. Ask all of them this three times."

Mahākāśyapa said to the Buddha, "Very good, World-Honored One."

Forthwith he rose from his seat, bared his right shoulder, knelt on his right knee, and bowed down at the feet of the Buddha. He then circled the Buddha three times and questioned the huge multitude: "Do you all want to hear this *Sūtra of the Great Dharma Drum*? The Tathāgata now will expound to all of you the One Vehicle, the Mahāyāna, which surpasses the vehicle of voice-hearers and the vehicle of Pratyekabuddhas."

Three times he asked them, and they all replied, "We would be delighted to hear it. Yes, Mahākāśyapa, we all have come here to hear the Dharma. Very good, have sympathy! May the Buddha pronounce to us the *Sūtra of the Great Dharma Drum*!"

Kāśyapa next asked, "Why do you all believe?"

They then replied, "As an analogy, a man 20 years of age has a son 100 years old. If the Buddha says so, we will believe that it is so. Much more will we believe in the true Dharma He is going to pronounce. Why? Because the Tathāgata acts in accordance with His words. The Tathāgata's pure eye shines, perfectly hindrance free. Seeing with His Buddha-eye, He knows our minds."

Kāśyapa praised, "Very good! Very good! You worthy ones are capable of hearing the *Sūtra of the Great Dharma Drum*, to uphold or pronounce it."

The Buddha told Kāśyapa, "As an analogy, a man only 20 years of age has a 100-year-old son. The *Sūtra of the Great Dharma Drum* conveys a similar teaching. Why? Because the Tathāgata enters parinirvāṇa and still abides eternally. Nothing has a self, but the Tathāgata still speaks of a self."

They immediately responded, "Only the Buddha can know. Whatever the World-Honored One says, we will accept and uphold it accordingly."

Kāśyapa asked the Buddha, "I pray only that the World-Honored One will pronounce the *Sūtra of the Great Dharma Drum*, beat the great Dharma drum, and blow the great Dharma conch shell."

The Buddha said, "Very good! Very good! Kāśyapa, you now want to hear me pronounce the *Sūtra of the Great Dharma Drum*?"

Kāśyapa replied to the Buddha, "Affirmatively I accept Your teachings. Why? Because the Tathāgata regards me highly and treats me with respect. What kind of respect? He once said to me, 'Come and sit together with me.' For this reason, I should recognize His kindness."

The Buddha said, "Very good! Kāśyapa, for a good reason, I treat you with respect. For example, King Prasenajit takes good care of his four types of armed forces. When they fight, they beat the huge war drums and blow the huge war conch shells, standing their ground against the enemy. Because of the king's kind caring, they fight, sparing no strength, to defeat the enemy in order to bring peace to the country. Therefore, bhikṣus, after my parinirvāṇa, Mahākāśyapa should protect and uphold this *Sūtra of the Great Dharma Drum*. For this reason, I let him use half of my seat. Accordingly, he should carry on my Way. After my parinirvāṇa, he will be capable of widely expounding the *Sūtra of the Great Dharma Drum*."

Kāśyapa said to the Buddha, "I am the eldest son born from the mouth of the World-Honored One."

The Buddha told the bhikṣus, "As an analogy, King Prasenajit teaches his sons to engage in the [five] studies, so that they will one day be capable of continuing the royal line. Thus, bhikṣus, after my parinirvāṇa, in the same way the bhikṣu Kāśyapa will protect and uphold this sūtra.

"Furthermore, Kāśyapa, for example, King Prasenajit and other kings are enemies, and they battle against one another. During those times, his warriors in the four types of armed forces—elephants, cavalry, chariots, and infantry—upon hearing the sound of the great drum, have no fear, and they hold firm their armor and weapons. The king, out of kindness, regularly bestows on them good food. During a war they are in addition given jewels and even cities. If they have defeated the enemy, they are each crowned with a white silk scarf, decorated as kings. If, among my voice-hearer bhikṣus and bhikṣuṇīs as well as upāsakas and upāsikās, there are those who learn the prātimokṣa precepts and become accomplished in observing these rules of conduct, the Tathāgata will give them the peace and joy of human or celestial life. If there are those who have achieved great merit by subduing the four māras, the Tathāgata will crown their heads with the white silk scarf of liberation, made of the Four Noble Truths. If there are those who, with enhanced faith and understanding, seek the Buddha store, the true self, and the eternally abiding dharma body, the Tathāgata will pour the water of sarvajña [overall wisdom-knowledge] on their heads and crown them with the white silk scarf of the Mahāyāna. Mahākāśyapa, in the same way I now crown your head with the white silk scarf of the Mahāyāna. You should protect and uphold this sūtra in the places where innumerable future Buddhas will be. Kāśyapa, know that, after my parinirvāṇa, you are capable of protecting and upholding this sūtra."

Kāśyapa said to the Buddha, "It will be as You instruct."

He further said to the Buddha, "From today on, and after Your parinirvāṇa, I will always protect, uphold, and widely pronounce this sūtra."

The Buddha told Kāśyapa, "Very good! Very good! I now will pronounce to you the *Sūtra of the Great Dharma Drum*."

Then gods and dragons in the sky praised with one voice, "Very good! Very good! Kāśyapa, today gods rain down celestial flowers, and dragon-kings rain down sweet nectar and finely powdered incense. To comfort and delight all sentient beings, you should be established by the World-Honored One as the eldest son of the Dharma."

Then the multitude of gods and dragons, with one voice, spoke in verse:

> As the king in the city of Śrāvastī
> Beats the war drum and blows the war conch shell,
> The Dharma King in Jetavana Park
> Beats the great Dharma drum.

The Buddha told Kāśyapa, "You should now use questioning as the drumstick to beat the great Dharma drum. The Tathāgata, the Dharma King, will explain to you. The God of Gods will resolve your doubts."

Then the World-Honored One told Mahākāśyapa, "There is a bhikṣu called Faith in the Mahāvaipulya. If, among my four groups of disciples, for those who hear his name, the arrows of their greed, anger, and delusion will all be pulled out. Why? Kāśyapa, King Prasenajit has [a physician called] Superior Medicine, who is the son of Jīva. When King Prasenajit is battling an enemy country, he tells Superior Medicine, 'Quickly bring me the medicine which can pull the arrows out for sentient beings [that are shot].' Then Superior Medicine brings the anti-poison medicine, and the king smears his war drum with the medicine. He beats the drum as he smears it with medicine and suffuses it with the smoke of burning medicine. If sentient beings that have been shot by poisonous arrows hear the sound of the drum, one or two yojanas away, their arrows will all be pulled out.

"Thus, Kāśyapa, if there are those who hear the name of the bhikṣu Faith in the Mahāvaipulya, the arrows of their greed, anger, and delusion will all be pulled out. Why? Because that bhikṣu has propagated the true Dharma through this sūtra and acquired this great fruit as his present achievement. Mahākāśyapa, you should note that even beating a mindless ordinary drum smeared with mindless medicine and suffused with its smoke has such power to benefit sentient beings. Much more, sentient beings that hear the name of a Bodhisattva-Mahāsattva or the name of the bhikṣu Faith in the Mahāvaipulya are enabled to remove their three poisons."

Kāśyapa said to the Buddha, "If hearing the name of a Bodhisattva can remove the three poisonous arrows for sentient beings, it will be more effective if they praise the name and merit of the World-Honored One by saying, 'Namo Śākyamuni.' If praising the name and merit of Śākyamuni can pull the three poisonous arrows out of sentient beings, it will be even more effective if they hear this *Sūtra of the Great Dharma Drum* and expound its verses and stanzas to comfort others. Furthermore, if they expound it widely, it will be impossible for their three poisonous arrows not to be pulled out."

The Buddha told Kāśyapa, "As I just mentioned, bhikṣus who observe their precepts purely can fulfill their wishes at will because of their original vows. All Buddhas have this Dharma, as taught in the *Sūtra of the Great Dharma Drum*, that dharmas, which [in true reality] are not made [through causes and conditions], neither arise nor perish. Therefore, Kāśyapa, in a future life, you will be like me. Why? Because if your four groups of disciples hear your name, their three poisonous arrows will all be pulled out. Therefore, Kāśyapa, you now should request the *Sūtra of the Great Dharma Drum*, and then, after my parinirvāṇa, protect, uphold, and pronounce it for a long time in the world."

Kāśyapa asked the Buddha, "Very good! World-Honored One, please pronounce for my sake the *Sūtra of the Great Dharma Drum*."

The Buddha told Kāśyapa, "You should spare no question about this *Sūtra of the Great Dharma Drum*."

Kāśyapa said to the Buddha, "Very good! World-Honored One, I will ask about my doubts. The World-Honored One says, 'With existence, there are pain and pleasure. Without existence, there is neither pain nor pleasure.' What is meant by that?"

The Buddha told Kāśyapa, "Without existence means the foremost bliss of parinirvāṇa. Therefore, having left pain and pleasure, one acquires the foremost bliss of parinirvāṇa. Pain and pleasure mean that there is existence. Without existence, there is neither pain nor pleasure. Therefore, those who wish to attain parinirvāṇa should seek to cease existing."

Then the World-Honored One, to restate this meaning, spoke in verse:

Existence is impermanent,
Nor is it changeless.
With existence, there are pain and pleasure.
Without existence, there is neither pain nor pleasure.
Not acting [to cause the next rebirth] brings neither pain nor pleasure;
Acting [to cause the next rebirth] brings pain and pleasure.
Do not delight in saṁskṛta dharmas,
Nor be involved with them.

If one acquires pleasure,
One will nevertheless fall into pain.
Before attaining nirvāṇa,
One abides in neither peace nor bliss.

Then Kāśyapa replied in verse:

If sentient beings do not effect their existence,
Nirvāṇa will be their foremost bliss.
That bliss is merely a name
As there is no one experiencing bliss.

Then the World-Honored One again spoke in verse:

The eternal liberation is not just a name,
The wondrous form [of a Buddha] evidently standing.
This is not the state of voice-hearers or Pratyekabuddhas,
Nor that of Bodhisattvas.

Kāśyapa asked the Buddha, "World-Honored One, why do you speak of form then say it is eternally abiding?"

The Buddha told Kāśyapa, "I will give you an analogy. A person comes from Mathurā in the south. Someone asks him, 'Where do you come from?' He answers, 'From Mathurā.' He is next asked, 'Where is Mathurā?' Then this person points to the south. Kāśyapa, will the questioner not believe him? Why? Because this person has seen himself come from the south. Thus, Kāśyapa, because I have seen it, you should believe me."

Then the World-Honored One again spoke in verse:

By analogy, there is a person
Who points his finger to the sky.
I now do the same,
Who pronounce liberation by name.

Analogous to the person
Who comes from the distant south,
I now do the same,
Who come from nirvāṇa.

"However, Kāśyapa, those who see the meaning do not need causes or conditions. If they do not see the meaning, they need causes and conditions. Indeed, Kāśyapa, Buddha-Bhagavāns always indicate liberation through innumerable causes and conditions."

Kāśyapa asked the Buddha, "What is cause?"

The Buddha told Kāśyapa, "Cause is the reason."

Kāśyapa asked the Buddha, "What is condition?"

The Buddha told Kāśyapa, "Condition is a contributing factor."

Kāśyapa asked the Buddha, "I pray that you will further clarify with an analogy."

The Buddha told Kāśyapa, "For example, a child is born from parents. The mother is the cause,[1] and the father is the condition. Thus, a dharma born through causes and conditions is called a formation."

Kāśyapa asked the Buddha, "What is meant by formation?"
The Buddha told Kāśyapa, "Formation refers to a worldly formation."
Kāśyapa asked the Buddha, "What is world?"
The Buddha told Kāśyapa, "It is constructed with an assembly of sentient beings."
Kāśyapa asked the Buddha, "What is a sentient being?"
The Buddha told Kāśyapa, "A sentient being is constructed with an assemblage of dharmas."
Kāśyapa asked the Buddha, "What is dharma?"
The Buddha told Kāśyapa, "Non-dharma is dharma, and dharma is non-dharma. There are two kinds of dharmas. What are these two? Saṁskṛta and asaṁskṛta; form and non-form. There is no third kind."
Kāśyapa asked the Buddha, "What does dharma look like?"
The Buddha told Kāśyapa, "Dharma is non-form."
Kāśyapa asked the Buddha, "What does non-dharma look like?"
The Buddha told Kāśyapa, "Non-dharma is also non-form."
Kāśyapa asked the Buddha, "If both dharma and non-dharma have neither form nor appearance, then what is dharma and what is non-dharma?"
The Buddha told Kāśyapa, "Dharma is nirvāṇa, and non-dharma is saṁsāra."
Kāśyapa asked the Buddha, "If both dharma and non-dharma have neither form nor appearance, how, what, and why can the wise know about their appearances?"
The Buddha told Kāśyapa, "Through their cycle of birth and death, sentient beings that develop various kinds of meritorious, pure roots of goodness are in the right ways. If they carry out these dharmas, pure appearances will arise. Those who perform these dharmas are dharma sentient beings. If they carry out non-dharmas, impure appearances will arise. Those who perform these non-dharmas are non-dharma sentient beings."
Kāśyapa asked the Buddha, "World-Honored One, what is a sentient being?"
The Buddha told Kāśyapa, "A sentient beings is constructed by assembling the four domains—earth, water, fire, and wind—as well as the five faculties, the Twelve Links of Dependent Arising, sensory reception, perception, thinking, mind, mental faculty, and mental consciousness. It is called the sentient-being dharma. Kāśyapa, know that it means all dharmas."
Kāśyapa asked the Buddha, "Which of these component dharmas is a sentient being?"
The Buddha told Kāśyapa, "None of them alone is called a sentient being. Why? Kāśyapa, taking the king Prasenajit's drum as an example, what is a drum?"
Kāśyapa replied to the Buddha, "A so-called drum includes a membrane, wood, and a drumstick. The assemblage of these three dharmas is called a drum."
The Buddha told Kāśyapa, "Likewise a construction with an assemblage of dharmas is called a sentient being."
Kāśyapa asked the Buddha, "Is the sound-producing drum not the drum?"
The Buddha told Kāśyapa, "Besides the sound-producing drum, any drum makes sound to be carried by the wind."
Kāśyapa asked the Buddha, "Is the drum a dharma or a non-dharma?"

The Buddha told Kāśyapa, "The drum is neither a dharma nor a non-dharma."

Kāśyapa asked the Buddha, "What is its name?"

The Buddha told Kāśyapa, "What is neither a dharma nor a non-dharma is called a nonspecific dharma."

Kāśyapa said to the Buddha, "Including the nonspecific dharma, there should be three kinds of dharmas in the world."

The Buddha told Kāśyapa, "An example of a nonspecific appearance would be a person who is neither male nor female. Such a person is called a non-man. The drum is nonspecific in the same way."

Kāśyapa asked the Buddha, "As the World-Honored One says, a child is born from the union of his parents. If they do not have the seeds for forming sentient beings, they are not the parental causes and conditions."

The Buddha told Kāśyapa, "That which does not have the seeds for forming sentient beings is called nirvāṇa. So too is the great eternal non-man. As an analogy, when King Prasenajit battles an enemy country, his warriors who eat men's meals are not called men if they are not bold and fierce. Therefore, those who do not have the seeds of sentient beings are not called parents, and neither is the great eternal non-man."

Kāśyapa asked the Buddha, "World-Honored One, there are good dharmas, bad dharmas, and neutral dharmas. What are good, bad, and neutral dharmas?"

The Buddha told Kāśyapa, "A pleasurable experience is a good dharma. A painful experience is a bad dharma. An experience that is neither pleasurable nor painful is a neutral dharma. Sentient beings are always in contact with these three dharmas. Pleasurable experiences relate to gods or humans gratifying the five desires as requital for their merit. Painful experiences relate to [the life of] hell-dwellers, animals, hungry ghosts, or asuras. Experience in neither pleasure nor pain is like a minor skin disease."

Kāśyapa said to the Buddha, "This is not right."

The Buddha told Kāśyapa, "Pleasure as a cause of pain, and pain as a cause of pain, are also called a neutral experience."

Kāśyapa asked the Buddha, "What would be an analogy?"

The Buddha told Kāśyapa, "For example, one becomes ill because of eating food. Eating food is pleasure, but illness is pain. Like a minor skin disease, this is called a neutral experience."

Kāśyapa said to the Buddha, "If both pleasure and pain can be called a neutral experience, then parents' giving birth to a child is also a neutral experience."

The Buddha told Kāśyapa, "This is not right."

Kāśyapa asked the Buddha, "What would be an analogy?"

The Buddha told Kāśyapa, "Formless gods in Neither with Nor without Perception Heaven, and gods with form in No Perception Heaven, still abide by the law of karma. So does goodness."

Kāśyapa said to the Buddha, "World-Honored One, as the Buddha says, those with sensory reception and perception are sentient beings. Then, formless gods in Neither with Nor without Perception Heaven must not be sentient beings."

The Buddha told Kāśyapa, "They still have mental processing. The dharma of sentient beings that I describe excludes the gods with form in No Perception Heaven."

Kāśyapa asked the Buddha, "Are sentient beings form or non-form?"

The Buddha told Kāśyapa, "Sentient beings are neither form nor non-form.[2] Those who accomplish this dharma are called sentient beings."

Kāśyapa said to the Buddha, "If there are sentient beings formed by a different dharma, formless gods should not be included. Then, there should not be these two realms of existence called the form realm and the formless realm."

The Buddha told Kāśyapa, "Dharmas are non-form, and non-dharmas are also non-form."

Kāśyapa asked the Buddha, "Does it mean that dharmas are attuned to liberation and that non-dharmas are as well? Are formless gods already liberated?"

The Buddha told Kāśyapa, "Not true. There are only saṁskṛta and asaṁskṛta dharmas, and liberation is an asaṁskṛta dharma. Formless gods are in the domain of saṁskṛta dharmas because they still have the disposition to assume form."

Kāśyapa asked the Buddha, "World-Honored One, all saṁskṛta dharmas are form, and asaṁskṛta dharmas are non-form. Seeing the form of formless gods is the state of the Buddha, not our state."

The Buddha told Kāśyapa, "Very good! Very good! It is my state, not yours. Indeed, Buddha-Bhagavāns, having achieved liberation, are free from form but still have form."

The Buddha then asked Kāśyapa, "What are formless gods? Do you know what these gods do? Kāśyapa, can gods with form be considered formless?"

Kāśyapa replied to the Buddha, "This is beyond our state."

The Buddha told Kāśyapa, "Indeed, Buddha-Bhagavāns, who have achieved liberation, all assume form. You should observe them."

Kāśyapa said to the Buddha, "If one achieves liberation in this way, one should still experience pain and pleasure."

The Buddha asked Kāśyapa, "If sick sentient beings take medicine and are cured of their diseases, will they be sick again?"

Kāśyapa replied to the Buddha, "If they have karma, they will still have illnesses."

The Buddha asked Kāśyapa, "Will those who have no karma have illnesses?"

Kāśyapa replied to the Buddha, "No, World-Honored One."

The Buddha told Kāśyapa, "Indeed, leaving pain and pleasure is liberation. Know that pain and pleasure are illness. A great man is one who has attained nirvāṇa."

Kāśyapa asked the Buddha, "If leaving pain and pleasure is liberation, will illness end with the exhaustion of karma?"

The Buddha told Kāśyapa, "Worldly pleasures are in effect pain. One achieves liberation by leaving such pleasures and ending karma."

Kāśyapa asked the Buddha, "Is liberation the final ending?"

The Buddha told Kāśyapa, "One may liken space to the ocean. Is space really like the ocean? As space is beyond analogy, so too is liberation. No one can know that formless gods have form. Nor can one know whether they are like this or like that, whether they stand in this way or frolic in that way. As this [knowledge] is beyond the state of voice-hearers and Pratyekabuddhas, so too is liberation."

Kāśyapa asked the Buddha, "World-Honored One, who forms sentient beings?"

The Buddha told Kāśyapa, "Sentient beings are formed by themselves."

Kāśyapa asked the Buddha, "What does that mean?"

The Buddha told Kāśyapa, "Those who do good are Buddhas. Those who do evil are sentient beings."

Kāśyapa asked the Buddha, "Who made the very first sentient being?"

The Buddha asked Kāśyapa, "Who made the formless gods, such as those in Neither with Nor without Perception Heaven? How do formless gods live and how do they carry themselves?"

Kāśyapa replied to the Buddha, "Although their karmas cannot be known, they are formed by their own karmas. Then who makes sentient beings black in saṁsāra, or white in nirvāṇa?"

The Buddha told Kāśyapa, "It is made by their karmas. Karma gives rise to innumerable dharmas; goodness also gives rise to innumerable dharmas."

Kāśyapa asked the Buddha, "What arises from karma? What arises from goodness?"

The Buddha told Kāśyapa, "Existence arises from karma. Liberation arises from goodness."

Kāśyapa asked the Buddha, "How does goodness arise as a dharma that has no birth?"

The Buddha told Kāśyapa, "These two are not different."

Kāśyapa asked the Buddha, "As goodness arises, how can one realize that it has no birth?"

The Buddha told Kāśyapa, "By doing good karmas."

Kāśyapa asked the Buddha, "Who taught this?"

The Buddha told Kāśyapa, "It has been taught by Buddhas since time without a beginning."

Kāśyapa asked the Buddha, "Who taught and transformed all Buddhas without a beginning in time?"

The Buddha told Kāśyapa, "Time without a beginning is not what voice-hearers or Pratyekabuddhas can know by thinking. If a person who is as wise and well informed as Śāriputra appears in the world, he can think throughout the long night but still cannot know who is the very first of Buddhas, who are without a beginning. Nor can he know His nirvāṇa or the interval in between. Furthermore, Kāśyapa, even Mahāmaudgalyāyana, using his transcendental powers, can never find the very first Buddha World without a beginning. Thus, none of the voice-hearers, Pratyekabuddhas, or Bodhisattvas on the Tenth Ground, such as Maitreya Bodhisattva, can know it. As the origin of Buddhas is hard to know, so too is the origin of sentient beings."

Kāśyapa said to the Buddha, "Therefore, World-Honored One, there is neither a doer [of karma] nor a recipient [of karmic fruit]."

The Buddha told Kāśyapa, "Causation is the doer and the recipient."

Kāśyapa asked the Buddha, "Does the world have an ending, or have no ending?"

The Buddha told Kāśyapa, "The world has not ended. There is nothing to end, nor is there a time of ending."

Then the Buddha asked Kāśyapa, "Suppose you use a hair to draw water from the immense ocean by the drop. Can you deplete the ocean water?"

Kāśyapa replied to the Buddha, "Yes, it can be finished."

The Buddha told Kāśyapa, "Innumerable asaṁkhyeyas of great kalpas ago, a Buddha called Kelava appeared in the world, who widely expounded the Dharma. At that time in the Licchavi clan, there was a youth called Entire World Delighted to See. He was a Wheel-Turning King who ruled with the true Dharma. This king, together with his retinue in the hundreds of thousands, went to that Buddha. He bowed down at the feet of that Buddha and circled Him three times. After presenting his offerings, he asked that Buddha, 'How long will it take me to acquire the Bodhisattva Way?' That Buddha told the great king, 'A Wheel-Turning King is a Bodhisattva. There is no difference. Why? Because no one else can be the god-king Śakra, a Brahma-king, or a Wheel-Turning King. A Bodhisattva is the god-king Śakra, a Brahma-king, or a Wheel-Turning King. First, he is reborn as the god-king Śakra or a Brahma-king many times, then he is reborn as a Wheel-Turning King to rule and deliver people through the true Dharma. You have already been the god-king Śakra or a Brahma-king as many times as the sands of asaṁkhyeya Ganges Rivers. Now you are a Wheel-Turning King.'

"Then the king asked, 'What does the god-king Śakra or a Brahma-king look like?' Kevala Buddha told the great king, 'The god-king Śakra or a Brahma-king looks just like you now, wearing a celestial crown, but their magnificence does not match yours. For example, the form of a Buddha is so sublime and extraordinary that voice-hearers, Pratyekabuddhas, and Bodhisattvas can never compare. As a Buddha is sublime, you in your way are magnificent.'

"Kāśyapa, the noble king next asked Kevala Buddha, 'How long will it take me to attain Buddhahood?' That Buddha replied, 'Great King, attaining Buddhahood requires a vastly long time. Suppose you, Great King, abandon your merit, become an ordinary person, and use a hair to draw water from the immense ocean by the drop. When the ocean water is almost completely gone, and the remaining water is like [puddles in] cow tracks, in the world will appear a Tathāgata called Lamp Light, the Tathāgata, Arhat, Samyak-Saṁbuddha. At that time there will be a king named Earth Sovereign, and Lamp Light Tathāgata will bestow upon him a prophecy that he will be a Buddha. Great King [Entire World Delighted to See], you will be that king's first-born son, upon whom Lamp Light Buddha will also bestow a prophecy. He will say these words: "Great King [Earth Sovereign], your first-born son is born to you, as the water in the immense ocean, diminishing since the past, is near depletion. During this period, he has never been a lesser king, but has been the god-king Śakra, a Brahma-king, or a noble Wheel-Turning King ruling and transforming the world with the true Dharma. This first-born son of yours is boldly valiant and energetically diligent. Great King Earth Sovereign, bodhi is hard to attain. Because of these causes and conditions, I give you an analogy. Earth Sovereign, this first-born son of yours has 60,000 lady attendants. Like goddesses, they are shapely, beautiful, adorned with necklaces of jewels. He will abandon them all like spit. Knowing that desire is impermanent, precarious, and fickle, he will say, 'I will renounce family life.' Having said this, believing that family is not his way of life, he will renounce family life to learn the Way." Therefore, Lamp Light Buddha will bestow a prophecy upon that youth: "In the future, there will be a Buddha called Śākyamuni. His world will be called Endurance. Young man, you will then be reborn in the Licchavi clan and become a youth called Entire World Delighted to See. After the parinirvāṇa of Śākyamuni Buddha, the true Dharma will be perishing. When eighty years still remain, you will be [reborn as] a bhikṣu who upholds this Buddha's name and disseminates this sūtra, not caring even about his own life. After this bhikṣu dies at age one hundred, he will be reborn in the Pure Land of Peace and Bliss and will acquire great spiritual powers, standing on the Eighth Ground. He will manifest one body in Tuṣita Heaven, another body in the Pure Land of Peace and Bliss, and a third body to ask Ajita Buddha questions about this sūtra." Then King Earth Sovereign, having heard the prophecy of his son, will be exultant and exuberant, saying, "Today the Tathāgata has prophesied that my son will be on the Eighth Ground." That youth, having heard the prophecy, will make energetic progress.'"

Kāśyapa said to the Buddha, "Therefore, World-Honored One, drawing water by the drop with a hair can deplete the water in the immense ocean."

The Buddha asked Kāśyapa, "What is meant by that?"

Kāśyapa replied to the Buddha, "World-Honored One, as an analogy, a merchant keeps his gold coins in a container. When his son cries, he gives him a coin. [He knows how] the money in the container decreases day by day. Likewise, Bodhisattva-Mahāsattvas know how the water in the immense ocean decreases drop by drop, as well as how much still remains. Even more, the World-Honored One should know the ending of the infinite mass of sentient beings. However, sentient beings have no ending. All voice-hearers and Pratyekabuddhas are unable to know this. Only Buddha-Bhagavāns can know this."

The Buddha told Kāśyapa, "Very good! Very good! As you say, the infinite mass of sentient beings has no ending."

Kāśyapa asked the Buddha, "Do sentient beings have an ending or not? Does parinirvāṇa mean the end or not?"

The Buddha told Kāśyapa, "Sentient beings have no ending."

Kāśyapa asked the Buddha, "Why do sentient beings not have an ending?"

The Buddha told Kāśyapa, "The ending of sentient beings would mean decrease [in number]. Then this sūtra would be meaningless. Therefore, Kāśyapa, Buddha-Bhagavāns after parinirvāṇa are eternally abiding. Because of this meaning, Buddha-Bhagavāns, having entered parinirvāṇa, are never extinct."

Kāśyapa asked the Buddha, "Why do Buddha-Bhagavāns enter parinirvāṇa, but are not ultimately extinct?"

The Buddha told Kāśyapa, "Indeed! Indeed! When a house is destroyed, space is revealed. Indeed! Indeed! The nirvāṇa of Buddhas is liberation."

Fascicle 2 (of 2)

Then the World-Honored One told Mahākāśyapa, "As an analogy, a king is active in giving alms, and many hidden treasures are uncovered in his kingdom. Why? Because the king widely gives various kinds of relief to unfortunate sentient beings, hidden treasure stores spontaneously turn up. Thus, Kāśyapa, Bodhisattvas who use skillful ways to pronounce the profound Dharma treasure widely will acquire this profound sūtra, which is in accord with [the Three Liberation Doors:] emptiness, no appearance, and no act, and is a sūtra apart from non-dharmas. They will acquire sūtras about the Tathāgata store as well.

"Kāśyapa, on Uttarakuru, the northern continent, food grows naturally, and it never diminishes as the multitudes continue to partake of it. Why? Because the people there, in their entire lives, never have thoughts of belongings, stinginess, or greed. Likewise, Kāśyapa, here on Jambudvīpa, the southern continent, if, among the bhikṣus, bhikṣuṇīs, upāsakas, and upāsikās, there are those who, having acquired this profound sūtra, read and recite it, copy and uphold it, thoroughly penetrate it, and widely pronounce it to others, never maligning it or feeling bored or doubtful, they will always naturally receive, by virtue of Buddhas' spiritual power, offerings to their satisfaction. Until their attainment of bodhi, the offerings will be without any shortage, continuing endlessly, except for those constrained by firm karmic requitals. During their entire lives, as long as bhikṣus observe their precepts without being lax, gods and spirits will serve them and make offerings to them. If they can refrain from thinking even one maligning thought of this profound sūtra, they will gain knowledge of the Tathāgata store and of the eternal abiding of Tathāgatas, and they will often see Buddhas, be close to them, and make offerings to them.

"As the seven treasures always follow the Wheel-Turning King wherever he goes, likewise this sūtra is always where its comforting presenter stays. The seven treasures stay only where the Wheel-Turning King stays, not elsewhere, while lesser treasures stay elsewhere. Likewise, where a comforting presenter stays, this sūtra will come to him from elsewhere, while sūtras in accord with the non-definitive meaning of emptiness will stay elsewhere. When the comforting presenter goes away from his place, this sūtra always accompanies him. Wherever the Wheel-Turning King goes, sentient beings that follow him each thought: 'Where the king stays, I too should be there.' Likewise, wherever the comforting presenter goes, this sūtra always follows him. When a Wheel-Turning King appears in the world, the seven treasures appear. Likewise, when a comforting presenter appears in the world, this sūtra appears. If one of the seven treasures owned by the Wheel-Turning King is lost and the king seeks it, he will definitely arrive in the place where that one treasure is. Likewise, if the comforting presenter, for the sake of hearing this sūtra, seeks everywhere, he will definitely arrive in the place where this sūtra is.

"Furthermore, when a Wheel-Turning King does not appear in the world, the lesser kings, acting like Wheel-Turning Kings, appear in the world along with other kings. However, nowhere does anyone expound this profound sūtra. There are those who pronounce kindred sūtras, primary or secondary. Sentient beings study and follow them. In the course of their study, when they hear of this ultimate profound sūtra about the Tathāgata store and the eternal abiding of the Tathāgata, they elicit doubts in their minds. They bear malice toward the comforting presenter, and dishonor and scorn him. Without any appreciation, they insult and criticize, making such statements as: 'These words are spoken by māras.' Judging this sūtra as destructive to the Dharma, they all reject it and return to their own places. Because they damage the Dharma, breach the precepts, and hold the wrong views, they will never acquire such a sūtra. Why not? Because this sūtra stays only with its comforting presenter.

"There will be many sentient beings that malign Mahāyāna sūtras they see or hear. Do not have fear. Why not? Because as the true Dharma declines during the times of the five turbidities, there will be sentient beings that malign the Mahāyāna. As in a village of seven families, there must be a dhāyini ghost, so too wherever this sūtra is, in a seven-member group, there must be a maligner.

"Kāśyapa, as those who observe the same precepts are delighted to see one another, likewise are those who violate the precepts. When, in the midst of the multitude, they hear this sūtra, they look at one another and scornfully say, 'What is the realm of sentient beings? What is eternal?' Viewing one another's facial expressions, they think: 'These are my companions.' They empathize with one another, keep their ways, and go their ways. As an analogy, an elder in the Brahmin caste has a son who has learned evil ways. After being reproached and admonished by his parents, he neither regrets nor changes his ways. He abandons his family to follow his evil friends, entertaining themselves with bird fights and animal fights. He goes to other lands, banding with his kind and doing non-dharma things together. They are mates. Those who do not appreciate this sūtra do the same. When they see others recite or pronounce this sūtra, they laugh at them. Why? Because most sentient beings will be negligent and indolent. Lax in observing their precepts, they will cause difficulties in preserving the Dharma. Following one another, those mates viciously criticize."

Kāśyapa said to the Buddha, "Alas! Truly that will be an evil time!"

The Buddha told Kāśyapa, "As for the comforting presenters [of this sūtra], what should they do? Kāśyapa, as an analogy, the roadside fields near a city are encroached upon by people, elephants, and horses. The landowner sends a man to guard the fields, but the guard is not vigilant in protecting them. He then increases the number of guards to two, three, four, five, ten, twelve, and even a hundred. The more guards sent, the more trespassers arrive. The last guard thinks: 'Guarding the fields in this way does not really protect them all. There should be a skillful way to keep them from raids.' He then takes the seedlings from the fields and personally hands them out as alms. The recipients are grateful, and the seedlings in the fields are saved. Kāśyapa, likewise those who have skillful means will be able to protect this sūtra after my parinirvāṇa."

Kāśyapa said to the Buddha, "World-Honored One, I can never accommodate those evil ones. I would rather carry Mount Sumeru on my shoulders for 100,000 kalpas than tolerate those evil ones violating the precepts, destroying the Dharma, maligning the Dharma, or defiling the Dharma. Such evils are not the tones of the Dharma. World-Honored One, I would rather be owned by someone as a slave than tolerate those evil ones violating the precepts, countering the

Dharma, abandoning the Dharma, or damaging the Dharma. Such evils are not the tones of the Dharma. World-Honored One, I would rather carry on my head the great earth, mountains, and oceans for 100,000 kalpas than tolerate those evil ones violating the precepts, destroying the Dharma, elevating themselves, or slandering others. Such evils are not the tones of the Dharma. World-Honored One, I would rather be deaf, blind, or mute than tolerate those evil ones damaging and violating the pure precepts, or renouncing family life for benefits, such as others' trust and offerings. Such evils are not the tones of the Dharma. World-Honored One, I would rather quickly abandon my body and enter parinirvāṇa than tolerate those evil ones damaging and violating the pure precepts, committing insidious acts, fawning with their bodies, or telling lies with their mouths. Such evils are not the tones of the Dharma."

The Buddha told Kāśyapa, "Your parinirvāṇa would be that of a voice-hearer, not the ultimate parinirvāṇa."

Kāśyapa asked the Buddha, "If the parinirvāṇa of a voice-hearer or of a Pratyekabuddha is not the ultimate, why does the World-Honored One pronounce the Three Vehicles: the Voice-Hearer Vehicle, the Pratyekabuddha Vehicle, and the Buddha Vehicle? Why does the World-Honored One, having entered parinirvāṇa, enter parinirvāṇa again?"

The Buddha told Kāśyapa, "A voice-hearer enters parinirvāṇa as a voice-hearer, and this parinirvāṇa is not the ultimate. A Pratyekabuddha enters parinirvāṇa as a Pratyekabuddha, and this parinirvāṇa is not the ultimate. If one acquires the merit of all merit, the knowledge of all knowledge, and the Mahāyāna parinirvāṇa, then this is ultimate, or no different from the ultimate."

Kāśyapa asked the Buddha, "World-Honored One, what does this mean?"

The Buddha told Kāśyapa, "For example, cream is produced from milk; fresh butter is produced from cream; melted butter is produced from fresh butter; and ghee is produced from melted butter. Ordinary beings holding the wrong views are like an impure mixture of milk and blood. Those who have taken refuge in the Three Jewels are like pure milk. Those who act according to their faith and newly-resolved Bodhisattvas who stand on the Training Ground for Excellent Understanding are like cream. Voice-hearers in seven ranks who are still learning and Bodhisattvas from the First Ground to the Seventh Ground are like fresh butter. Arhats and Pratyekabuddhas, who can manifest their mind-created bodies, and Bodhisattvas on the Ninth and Tenth Grounds are like melted butter. Tathāgatas, also called Arhats, Samyak-Saṁbuddhas, are like ghee."

Kāśyapa asked the Buddha, "World-Honored One, why does the Tathāgata say that there are the Three Vehicles?"

The Buddha told Kāśyapa, "As an analogy, a valiant, heroic guiding teacher takes his retinue and a huge multitude from their homes to another place. As they pass through wilderness and treacherous, perilous paths, he thinks: 'This group is fatigued, and they might want to turn back.' In order for them to take a rest, he conjures up a great city ahead of them. He points at it in the distance and says to the huge multitude, 'There is a great city ahead, and we should quickly go there.' Those in the multitude, seeing that they are approaching the city, say to one another, 'This is where I can rest.' They all enter into the city to rest and enjoy their stay, unwilling to proceed further. Then the guiding teacher thinks:

'This huge multitude has gained this small pleasure and is satisfied with it. Weak and indolent, they have no intention of advancing further.' Forthwith the guiding teacher dissolves the conjured city. When the huge multitude sees the city vanish, they ask their guiding teacher, 'What was it? An illusion or a dream, or something real?' Hearing this, the guiding teacher tells the huge multitude, 'It was for your respite that I conjured up that great city. We now should go to the next city. We should quickly get there to have peace and joy.' The huge multitude responded, 'Affirmatively we accept your instruction. Why should we enjoy this sordid small place? Together we should go to the great city of peace and joy.' The guiding teacher tells them, 'Very good! We should proceed.' As they advance together, he further tells the huge multitude, 'This great city we go toward is appearing. You should observe that this great city ahead is prosperous and joyous.' As they gradually go forward, they all see the great city. Thereupon the guiding teacher tells the huge multitude, 'Kindly People, know that before you is the great city.' Then all in the huge multitude, seeing the great city in the distance, peaceful, prosperous, and joyous, find delight in their minds. They look at one another with curiosity and ask, 'Is this city real or just another illusion?' The guiding teacher replies, 'This city is real, with all its extraordinary peace, prosperity, and joy.' He tells the multitude to enter this great city, for this is the foremost, ultimate great city. There is no other city beyond this one. After the huge multitude has entered into the city, with wonder and happiness they praise their guiding teacher, 'Very good! Very good! The one with true great wisdom treats us in skillful ways with great compassion!'

"Kāśyapa, know that the conjured city is like the pure knowledge of the Voice-Hearer Vehicle and the Pratyekabuddha Vehicle, the wisdom-knowledge of emptiness, no appearance, and no act. The real great city is like the liberation of a Tathāgata. Therefore, the Tathāgata presents the Three Vehicles and reveals the two nirvāṇas. He then pronounces the One Vehicle."

The Buddha told Kāśyapa, "If there are those who say that this sūtra is nonexistent, they are not my disciples, nor am I their teacher."

Kāśyapa said to the Buddha, "World-Honored One, Mahāyāna sūtras mostly state the meaning of emptiness."

The Buddha told Kāśyapa, "All sūtras about emptiness have unrevealed aspects. Only this sūtra is the unsurpassed pronouncement, without any unrevealed aspect. For example, Kāśyapa, King Prasenajit always sponsors a great assembly of almsgiving in the eleventh month of the year. He first feeds the hungry ghosts, the forlorn ones, and the poor mendicants. He next gives to śramaṇas and Brahmins fine food in various flavors as they wish. In the same way Buddha-Bhagavāns expound various kinds of Dharmas in the sūtras according to sentient beings' desires and preferences.

"There are sentient beings that breach their precepts, are negligent and indolent in training and learning, and reject the wondrous texts concerning the eternal abiding of the Tathāgata store. They prefer to study and learn various sūtras that teach emptiness, whether following the words and phrases, or adding or altering some words and phrases. Why? Because they say these words: 'The Buddha's sūtras all declare that a sentient being has no self.' Nevertheless, they do not know the true meaning of emptiness and no self. Those without wisdom pursue extinction.

"Indeed, emptiness and no self are the Buddha's words. Why? Because immeasurable afflictions, like stored dirt, have always been empty, in nirvāṇa. Indeed, nirvāṇa is the all-encompassing word. It is the word for the great parinirvāṇa attained by Buddhas, eternally in peace and bliss."

Kāśyapa asked the Buddha, "How does one discard [the view of] cessation [and the view of] perpetuity?"

The Buddha told Kāśyapa, "Sentient beings each transmigrate through their cycle of birth and death without a commanding self. Therefore, I explain to them the meaning of no self. However, the great parinirvāṇa attained by Buddhas is eternal peace and bliss. This meaning shatters the two wrong views, cessation and perpetuity."

Kāśyapa said to the Buddha, "Please turn to no self, having talked about self for a while."

The Buddha told Kāśyapa, "I explain the meaning of no self to destroy the worldly view of self. If I did not say so, how could I induce people to accept the Dharma of the great teacher? When the Buddha pronounces no self, sentient beings become curious. To hear what they have never heard before, they come to the Buddha. Then I enable them to enter the Buddha Dharma through hundreds of thousands of causes and conditions. Once they have entered the Buddha Dharma with growing faith, they diligently train and energetically progress in their learning of the Dharma of Emptiness. Then I pronounce to them the eternal peace and bliss, and the liberation that still manifests form. There are worldly doctrines asserting that existence is liberation. To destroy them, I pronounce that liberation leads to nonexistence. If I did not say so, how could I induce people to accept the Dharma of the great teacher? Through hundreds of thousands of causes and conditions, I explain to them liberation, nirvāṇa, and no self. Then I see sentient beings mistake liberation for ultimate extinction. Those without wisdom pursue extinction. Then I pronounce, through hundreds of thousands of causes and conditions, that there still is form after achieving liberation."

Kāśyapa said to the Buddha, "World-Honored One, achieving liberation and command means that sentient beings must be eternal. By analogy, upon seeing smoke, one deduces that there must be fire. If there is a [true] self in one, then there can be liberation. Saying that there is a [true] self means that there is form after achieving liberation. This is not the worldly self-view, nor is it the statement of cessation or perpetuity."

Kāśyapa asked the Buddha, "World-Honored One, why does the Tathāgata, who never enters [extinction through] parinirvāṇa, manifest entering parinirvāṇa? Why does He who is never born manifest birth?"

The Buddha told Kāśyapa, "It is for destroying the idea of perpetuity in sentient beings' calculating minds. The Tathāgata never enters [extinction through] parinirvāṇa but manifests entering parinirvāṇa. He is never born but manifests birth. Why? Because sentient beings would say, 'Even a Buddha has an ending in life and is not in command, not to mention any of us, who has a self and its belongings.' As an analogy, a king is seized by a neighboring nation. In cangue and shackles, he thinks: 'Am I now still the king, the lord? I now am neither the king nor the lord.' Why does he have such tribulations? It is caused by his abandonment of self-restraint. Every sentient being that transmigrates through its cycle of birth and death has no commanding self. The lack of command is the meaning of no self that I have explained.

"As another analogy, a person is pursued by bandits who will harm him with knives. He thinks: 'I now have no strength. How can I avoid death?' With such concerns about the suffering of birth, aging, illness, and death, sentient beings wish to become the god-king Śakra or a Brahma-king. To destroy this kind of mentality, the Tathāgata manifests death. The Tathāgata is the god of gods. If His parinirvāṇa meant extinction, then the world should also go extinct. If it is not extinction, then it means eternal peace and bliss. To be in eternal peace and bliss, there must be a [true] self, as smoke implies fire. If there is no self and one claims to have a self, the world should be filled with selves. [The true] self does not invalidate no self. If there were no [true] self, a [nominal] self could not be established."

Kāśyapa asked the Buddha, "What is existence?"

The Buddha told Kāśyapa, "Existence refers to the twenty-five forms of existence as sentient beings. Nonexistence refers to the state of any no-thinking thing, or any sentient being before its birth or after its death. If thinking beings could be destroyed, sentient beings would eventually be extinct. Because sentient beings [in true reality] have neither birth nor death, they neither increase nor decrease in number."

Kāśyapa asked the Buddha, "World-Honored One, if there is a [true] self in one, why is it covered up by one's afflictions, which are like dirt?"

The Buddha told Kāśyapa, "Very good! Very good! You should ask the Tathāgata this question. As an analogy, a goldsmith perceives the purity of gold. He thinks about why such pure gold is mixed with dirt and seeks the origin of the dirt. Will he find its origin?"

Kāśyapa replied, "No, World-Honored One."

The Buddha told Kāśyapa, "If he spends his entire lifetime thinking about the initial cause of the dirt since time without a beginning, will he find the original state? He will acquire neither gold nor the origin of dirt. However, if he diligently uses skillful means to remove the dirt mixed with the gold, he will acquire the gold."

The Buddha told Kāśyapa, "Thus [one's true] self is covered up by one's afflictions, which are like dirt. If a person who wants to see his [true] self thinks: 'I should search for this self and the origin of afflictions,' will that person find the origin?"

Kāśyapa replied to the Buddha, "No, World-Honored One."

The Buddha told Kāśyapa, "If one diligently uses skillful means to remove one's afflictions, which are like dirt, one will realize one's [true] self. If one, having heard this sūtra, with profound faith and delight, uses skillful means, neither leisurely nor rushed, to do good karmas with one's body, voice, and mind, through these causes and conditions, one will realize one's [true] self."

Kāśyapa asked the Buddha, "If there is true self, why it is not seen?"

The Buddha told Kāśyapa, "I will now give you an analogy. For example, a beginning student is learning the five letters [five sets of five consonants], which are used to compose stanzas of verses. If one wants to know the meanings [of the verses] before learning [the letters], can one know them? One should first learn [the letters], then one will know [the meanings]. Having learned [the letters], one needs to be taught by the teacher, who uses examples to indicate the meanings of verses composed of words. If one can listen to and accept the teacher, one will acquire understanding of the meanings of the verses, and believe and appreciate them. The [true] self is now covered up by the store of afflictions. If someone says, 'Good man, the Tathāgata store is such and such,' then the hearer immediately wants to see it. Is he able to see it?"

Kāśyapa replied, "No, World-Honored One."

The Buddha told Kāśyapa, "For example, the student who does not know the meanings of the verses should follow the teacher on faith. Kāśyapa, know that the Tathāgata is the speaker of truthful words. He truthfully describes the existence of sentient beings. You will know later, like that student who has learned [from his teacher]. I now explain to you the realm of sentient beings by four veiled analogies. These four are the eye blinded by a disease, the moon covered by heavy clouds, the water in a well to be dug, and the flame of a lamp inside a container. Know that these four analogies involve the causes and conditions for realizing one's Buddha nature. All sentient beings have Buddha nature with immeasurable excellent appearance, majesty, and radiance. Because of Buddha nature, all sentient beings can attain parinirvāṇa. For example, the disease of the eye can be cured. Before one has encountered a good physician, one's eye is sightless. Once a good physician appears, one will quickly perceive sights. Indeed, the immeasurable store of afflictions covers and obstructs one's Tathāgata nature. Unless one encounters Buddhas, [holy] voice-hearers, or Pratyekabuddha, one mistakes no self for self, and non-self for belongings of self. After encountering Buddhas, [holy] voice-hearers, or Pratyekabuddhas, one then knows about one's true self. As if cured of a disease, one's eye opens and sees clearly. The eye disease refers to one's afflictions, and the eye refers to one's Tathāgata nature. When the moon is covered by clouds, it is neither bright nor clear. Likewise, when one's Tathāgata nature is covered up by afflictions, it is neither bright nor clear. If one discards one's cloud-like afflictions, one's Tathāgata nature will be bright and clear, like the full moon. When one digs a well, dry dirt indicates that water is still far away. When one gets wet dirt, one knows that water is near. If one gets the water, then it is the ultimate [end]. If one encounters Buddhas, [holy] voice-hearers, or Pratyekabuddhas, and learns to do good karmas and to remove one's afflictions, like dirt, one will realize one's Tathāgata nature, which is like the water. This nature is also like the flame of a lamp inside a container. It is useless to sentient beings when its brilliance is hidden. If the container is removed, then the light of the lamp will shine everywhere. Likewise, one's afflictions are the container that hides one's Tathāgata store, which is useless to sentient beings when its appearance and majesty are neither bright nor clear. If one discards the store of afflictions, eradicating them all forever, then one's Tathāgata nature will fully manifest its excellent appearance and radiance for Buddha work. It is like shattering the container so that sentient beings can enjoy the lamplight. Thus these four analogies illustrate the causes and conditions. As one's [true] self encompasses the realm of sentient beings, the same is true for all sentient beings. The realm of sentient beings is boundless, radiant, and pure."

Kāśyapa asked the Buddha, "World-Honored One, if all sentient beings have the Tathāgata store in one nature and ride the One Vehicle, why does the Tathāgata say there are the Three Vehicles: the Voice-Hearer Vehicle, the Pratyekabuddha Vehicle, and the Buddha Vehicle?"

The Buddha told Kāśyapa, "I should now use an analogy. An elder of great wealth has an only son who, under the care of his wet nurse, was lost in the midst of a crowd. As the elder is near his time, he thinks: 'It has been a long time since I lost my only son. I do not have other sons, nor parents or relatives. Once I die, all my assets will go to the king.' As he is feeling concerned, the lost son, begging on his way, arrives at his original home. He does not recognize his father's house. Why? Because the son has been lost since childhood. His father recognizes him but does not tell him so. Why? Because he is afraid that his son might run away. He gives him some things and says to him, 'I have no offspring, and you can be my son. Do not go elsewhere.' The son answers, 'I cannot bear staying here. Why? Because my staying here would be as painful as if in shackles.' The elder asks, 'What would you like to do?' The son answers, 'I would rather remove filth, tend livestock, or work in the fields.' The elder thinks: 'This child has little fortune, but I should be patient. I will go along with his wish for now.' Then he tells him to remove feces. A long time has passed, and the son has seen the elder gratify the five desires. Delight rising in his heart, he thinks: 'I hope this great elder will, out of pity, accept me as his son and give me riches and treasures.' With this idea in mind, he no longer works diligently. The elder, having seen the change, thinks: 'Before long, he will definitely be my son.' Then the elder finds him and asks, 'Do you now have different ideas which cause you not to work hard?' The son replies, 'My heart wishes to be your son.' The elder says, 'Very good! I am your father, and you are my son. I am really your father though you did not know it. I now give you all that is in my treasure store.' He then makes an announcement in the midst of a huge multitude: 'This is my long-lost son. Unwittingly, he happened to return home. I asked him to be my son, and he refused. Today he willingly asks to be my son.'

"Kāśyapa, that elder tactfully entices his humble-minded son, first telling him to remove feces, next giving him wealth. Then he makes an announcement in the midst of a huge multitude, saying these words: 'He is originally my son who, after having been lost for a long time, has come back by luck and has reckoned that he is my son.' Likewise, Kāśyapa, to those who do not appreciate the One Vehicle, I pronounce the Three Vehicles. Why? Because this is the Tathāgata's skillful approach. All voice-hearers are my sons, just like the feces remover who has come to know his identity only today."

Kāśyapa said to the Buddha, "Alas! Strange! How inferior is the Voice-Hearer Vehicle! [Its riders] are really the sons of the Buddha, but they do not recognize their father."

The Buddha told Kāśyapa, "You should learn [from that elder]. If you cannot bear to rebuke or reprove them, then you should refrain from doing so. When they come to maturity later, you will know it. Furthermore, Kāśyapa, the Voice-Hearer Vehicle and the Mahāyāna often counter each other, like the worldly versus that which is free from afflictions and their discharges, or folly versus wisdom. Moreover, Kāśyapa, you should accommodate those who malign this sūtra. Why? Because the maligners, after death, will fall into boundless darkness. Out of pity for them, you should devise some ways to bring them to maturity through the Dharma of the Mahāyāna. While those who are beyond cure will fall into hell, the faithful ones will believe. As for other sentient beings, you should use the Four Drawing-in Dharmas to help them achieve liberation.

"Moreover, Kāśyapa, if there is a man who has just developed fever, he should not immediately be given medicine or other treatments. Why? Because the time has not come. One should bide the right time to treat the patient. A physician who knows neither the right treatment nor its timing is a failure. Therefore, treatment should be given when the disease has come to a head. If it is not yet ready, one should wait for its time. Likewise, for sentient beings that malign this sūtra, when they come to maturity, they will reprove themselves in remorse, saying, 'Alas! Agony! I now finally realize what I have done.' At that time you should rescue them and draw them in by means of the Four Drawing-in Dharmas."

"Moreover, Kāśyapa, suppose there is a man who, crossing an expanse of wilderness, hears the call of a flock of birds. Dreading that the bird call means there are bandits, he takes another path. He enters an empty marshland and arrives at where tigers and wolves lurk. He is eaten by a tiger. Kāśyapa, likewise, when bhikṣus, bhikṣuṇīs, upāsakas, and upāsikās in future times hear the talk of self as well as the talk of no self, they fear the talk of self. They then enter the vast void, the view of cessation, to study and learn no self. They do not appreciate the profound sūtras that teach the Tathāgata store and the eternal abiding of Buddhas. Furthermore, Kāśyapa, you ask me what I have said to Ānanda: 'With existence, there are pain and pleasure. Without existence, there is neither pain nor pleasure.' Hearken now! Kāśyapa, the Tathāgata is neither existence nor a sentient being, nor does He perish."

Kāśyapa asked the Buddha, "Why not, World-Honored One?"

The Buddha told Kāśyapa, "As an analogy, under the snow mountain, there is a precious jewel radiating pure light. A person who is skilled in identifying precious jewels can recognize one on sight and seize it. It is like the process of refining gold. When the impurities and rubbish are eliminated, pure gold is revealed, which has never been tainted by the filth initially with it. Why? Because it is like the lamp carried by a person walking. Wherever he goes, darkness is dispelled by the bright light of the lamp. As refined pure gold is never tainted by filth, neither is the precious jewel. When moonlight and starlight shine on it, it rains down pure water. When sunlight shines on it, it blazes fire. Kāśyapa, indeed, the Tathāgata, also called Arhat, Samyak-Saṁbuddha, who appears in the world, has forever left birth, aging, illness, and death, and has eradicated all afflictions and habits. He always radiates great light, like a luminous jewel, and He is never tainted, like a pure lotus flower never touched by dirt or water. Furthermore, Kāśyapa, the Tathāgata responsively appears in the world, manifesting an ordinary body with such and such an appearance at such and such a time. He is never tainted by the filth in the birthplace of ordinary beings, nor does He experience the pain or pleasure of the world. The pleasures of the five desires of gods and humans as requital for one's merit in effect are pains. Only liberation is the ultimate eternal bliss."

Kāśyapa said to the Buddha, "Very good! Very good! World-Honored One, I just realize that beginning today I have truly renounced family life, accepted the complete monastic precepts, become a bhikṣu, and attained Arhatship. I should recognize the kindness of the Tathāgata and requite His kindness because the Tathāgata once shared His seat with me. Moreover, today in the midst of His four large groups [of disciples], He poured the Dharma water of the Mahāyāna on the crown of my head."

Among the multitude were those assuming the appearance and deportment of bhikṣus, those assuming the appearance and deportment of upāsakas, and those assuming the appearance and deportment of non-upāsakas. Leaning sideways, bending forward or back, they all were in disguise under the power of the māra. Then Ānanda asked the Buddha, "World-Honored One, this huge multitude, having left the scum, are firm and true like the sandalwood grove. Why do those others stay in this multitude?"

The Buddha advised Ānanda, "Ask Mahākāśyapa."

Ānanda said, "Yes, very good. I should ask him."

He then asked Kāśyapa, "Why do they stay in this multitude?"

Kāśyapa replied, "Those fools are the retinue of the māra, and they have come along with him. That is why, Ānanda, I said earlier that, after the Tathāgata's parinirvāṇa, I would be incapable of protecting the true Dharma by skillful means as if competently guarding the fields. That is why I said earlier, with other details, that I would rather carry the great earth. Thereupon the Tathāgata told me, 'After my parinirvāṇa, you should be capable of protecting and upholding the true Dharma until its end.' I then said to the Buddha, 'I will be capable of protecting and upholding the true Dharma for forty years.' And the Buddha rebuked me, 'Why are you too lazy to protect the Dharma until its end?'"

The Buddha told Kāśyapa, "Identify the māra [in the multitude]. If you can find him, you are capable of protecting the Dharma."

Kāśyapa then searched with his god-eye, but was unable to see the māra. He was like that savage in the city kingdom of Śrāvastī who had lost his son. Searching through a huge multitude, the savage failed to find his son, and he returned tired. Likewise, Kāśyapa searched with his god-eye for the māra in the multitude but could not find him. Forthwith he said to the Buddha, "I am incapable of finding the evil māra."

For the same reason, the 80 great voice-hearers all said that they were incapable. Kāśyapa also ordered the 500 Bodhisattvas, including Worthy Protector Bodhisattva, to find the evil māra. Except for a Bodhisattva called Entire World Delighted to See, all were unable to find him.

Then the World-Honored One told Kāśyapa, "You are incapable of protecting or upholding the Dharma for the last eighty years as the Dharma perishes. A Bodhisattva from the south will be able to protect and uphold it. You will at last find him among the 500 Bodhisattvas, including Worthy Protector Bodhisattva."

Kāśyapa replied, "Very good! I will look for him."

Then he found the youth, called Entire World Delighted to See, who was of the Licchavi clan.

[He said] "World-Honored One, this Licchavi youth called Entire World Delighted to See must be the one."

The Buddha told Kāśyapa, "You should go ask him to find the evil māra."

Then Kāśyapa, together with the 80 great voice-hearers and the 500 Bodhisattvas, including Worthy Protector Bodhisattva, jointly said to the Licchavi youth called Entire World Delighted to See: "Young man, you are designated by the World-Honored One as the one who is capable of finding the evil māra."

This youth in the huge multitude said to Kāśyapa, "I am capable of finding the evil māra. However, there are 80 great voice-hearers and 500 Bodhisattvas, including Worthy Protector, as well as holy Bodhisattvas Mañjuśrī, Avalokiteśvara, Great Might Arrived, Annihilating All Evil Life-Journey, and Maitreya. Why do they not look for him, and why do you make me look for him? It would be appropriate first to have them do it, and next to have me do it."

Kāśyapa asked, "Is subjugating the evil māra not a merit?"

He replied, "Kāśyapa, since you know there is merit, you should do it yourself. I cannot do it for now."

Then Kāśyapa reported the story to the Buddha. The Buddha asked Kāśyapa, "Why did this youth say these words?"

Kāśyapa replied to the Buddha, "This youth said, 'The great virtuous ones have precedence, and I am next in line. I am a worldly person, in a humble caste. These great virtuous ones, such as the 80 great voice-hearers and the 500 leading Bodhisattvas, including Worthy Protector, should go first. I am next.'"

However, these voice-hearers as well as Worthy Protector and others all searched but could not find the māra. Like that savage who had been unable to find his son, they all admitted that they were incapable, and retired to one side.

Then the World-Honored One further told Kāśyapa, "You now have heard this *Sūtra of the Great Dharma Drum*. For forty years after my parinirvāṇa, you should protect and uphold the true Dharma as you do today. You should beat the great Dharma drum, blow the great Dharma conch shell, convene the great Dharma assembly, and erect the great Dharma banner. Then, during the next eighty years, as the true Dharma perishes, the Licchavi youth called Entire World Delighted to See will bind that evil māra and each of his retinue with five strings, like tying up a little rabbit. He will widely pronounce and recite the *Sūtra of the Great Dharma Drum*. He will beat the great Dharma drum, blow the great Dharma conch shell, convene the great Dharma assembly, and erect the great Dharma banner."

Kāśyapa asked the Buddha, "When will this happen?"

The Buddha told Kāśyapa, "During the last eighty years of the true Dharma, as it perishes."

Kāśyapa said to the Buddha, "I would like to see the evil māra."

The Buddha told the youth, "Quickly show the evil māra to the huge multitude."

Then the youth, gazing reverently at the Buddha, said, "Look at this evil māra that has come from elsewhere and is seated among the multitude in the way Bodhisattvas assume the forms of bhikṣus."

The huge multitude all saw him bound by five strings. The māra said, "Young man, I will no longer be a hindrance to this sūtra." Three times he said it.

Then the World-Honored One told the Licchavi youth called Entire World Delighted to See as well as the multitude of Bodhisattvas: "Mahākāśyapa will be able to protect and uphold the true Dharma for forty years after my parinirvāṇa. Who among you all can be the final Dharma protector after I am gone?"

Three times the Buddha asked them, and no one was capable. The Buddha told the multitude, "Do not think less of yourselves. In this multitude I have many disciples who, after my parinirvāṇa, will be able to protect the true Dharma and pronounce this sūtra. The last one among the 500 Bodhisattvas, including Worthy Protector, is the Licchavi youth called Entire World Delighted to See. After my parinirvāṇa, he will beat the great Dharma drum, blow the great Dharma conch shell, convene the great Dharma assembly, and erect the great Dharma banner."

Then the youth released the vile māra. Then the huge multitude said to the youth, "You have received a prophecy from the Buddha."

The Buddha told Mahākāśyapa, "Kāśyapa, like a man guarding the fields without effective skills, you are incapable of protecting or upholding this sūtra. This youth has now heard this sūtra. He will excel in reading and reciting it, will step forward to protect and uphold it, and will expound it to others. He will always assume the form of an ordinary man though he stands on the Seventh Ground. When eighty years still remain for the true Dharma as it perishes, he will be reborn in the south into the Kāyale family, on the bank of the Skillful Means River, in the village of Mahāpari, in the kingdom of Maṇḍala. He will be the bhikṣu who upholds my name as if skillfully guarding and protecting the seedlings in the fields.

"In the midst of an arrogant, negligent, indolent multitude, he will renounce family life, the secular life. He will draw in that multitude by means of the Four Drawing-in Dharmas. After receiving this profound sūtra, he will read, recite, and penetrate it. He will purify the Saṅgha, enabling its members to abandon the impure ways they have accepted. First, he will pronounce to them the *Sūtra of the Great Dharma Drum*. Second, he will pronounce to them Mahāyāna sūtras about emptiness. Third, he will pronounce to them the eternal abiding of the Tathāgata and the realm of sentient beings, according to the *Sūtra of the Great Dharma Drum*. He will beat the great Dharma drum, blow the great Dharma conch shell, convene the great Dharma assembly, and erect the great Dharma banner. In my presence, he will don the armor of great vows. He will pour down the Dharma rain in his entire 100-year lifespan. After living 100 years, he will manifest great spiritual powers and demonstrate parinirvāṇa. He will say these words: 'Śākyamuni Buddha now has come here. All should regard Him reverently, pay respects, and make obeisance. Indeed, the Tathāgata is eternally abiding in peace and bliss. You kindly people should observe that true reality is eternal and blissful as I say.' Thereupon Buddhas from worlds in the ten directions will all appear and say these words, 'Indeed! Indeed! It is just as you say. All should believe in what you have said so well.'"

Kāśyapa asked the Buddha, "World-Honored One, what merits should a Bodhisattva achieve in order to see the eternal, indestructible dharma body of the Tathāgata and, upon dying, to demonstrate great spiritual powers?"

The Buddha told Kāśyapa, "Bodhisattva-Mahāsattvas who have acquired eight merits can presently see the eternal, indestructible dharma body of the Tathāgata. What are these eight merits? First, pronounce this profound sūtra tirelessly. Second, pronounce the teachings of the Three Vehicles also tirelessly. Third, never abandon those who should be delivered. Fourth, bring harmony and unity to disrupted Saṅghas. Fifth, never be intimate with bhikṣuṇīs, women, or eunuchs. Sixth, stay far away from kings or those in power. Seventh, always delight in dhyāna and samādhi. Eighth, ponder and observe impurity and no self. These are the eight merits to acquire.

"There are four more things. What are these four? First, excel in upholding the Dharma. Second, always celebrate the good and joyful things one has done. Third, willingly take refuge [in the Three Jewels] and recognize it as a gain of great benefits. Fourth, resolutely have no doubts about the eternal abiding of the Tathāgata and, day and night, think of the merit of the Tathāgata.

"Through these causes and conditions, before one's death, one will readily see one's eternally abiding dharma body and manifest great spiritual powers. Kāśyapa, wherever such good men and good women stay in cities or villages, I will reveal the dharma body to them and say these words: 'Good men and good women, the Tathāgata is eternally abiding.' From today on, you should accept and uphold this sūtra, and read and recite it. You should explain it to others, saying these words: 'Know that the Tathāgata always abides in peace and bliss. You should wish to see [your dharma body] with an upright mind, neither sycophantic nor deceitful.' You should know that the World-Honored One is indeed eternally abiding. For the pure ones who wish to see me, I will manifest myself to them.

"Mahākāśyapa, you should believe and deliberate. If one does not train in accordance with the Dharma, how can one see me [one's own dharma body]? How can one acquire transcendental powers and demonstrate them? As I have said to the voice-hearers, if a bhikṣu can discard even one [evil] dharma, I assure him that he will achieve a [voice-hearer] fruit, becoming an Anāgāmin. In the same way he will acquire merits. As I said earlier, a bhikṣu who observes his precepts will have gods following and serving him for life. Therefore, you all should never be greedy for benefits or worship. You should cultivate disgust as you meditate on your [physical] body. Furthermore, Kāśyapa, that bhikṣu, who will uphold my name, will bring purity to the Saṅgha."

Kāśyapa asked the Buddha, "Why do you say that?"

The Buddha told Kāśyapa, "That bhikṣu will skillfully guard and protect the Four Drawing-in Dharmas, and will draw in the entire multitude of those who are greedy and corrupt, and those who violate the precepts. Each of the 500 Bodhisattvas, including Worthy Protector, initially considered himself incapable of being the final protector of the Dharma after my parinirvāṇa. They now are still incapable. When that bhikṣu, who will uphold my name, carries out the Drawing-in Dharmas, he will include the bhikṣus who are negligent and indolent and have them learn to make offerings. He will give sūtras to them, diminishing their afflictions and protecting their minds, like a ranger who tames cattle when they are ready. Those who do not reform after inclusion and training should be abandoned. Do not allow poisonous arrows to touch and harm good and pure people. He will have these thoughts: 'Do not allow bhikṣus who are pure in their ways to breach their precepts because of the seamy ones. Nor should they pay respects to those who expound the non-Dharma and carry out the evil ways. Nor should they perform together with the seamy ones the Saṅgha duties, such as Dharma assembly, recitation of precepts, confession, and repentance.' Just as a king subjugates his enemies, he will tame the bhikṣus by skillful means. Having tamed them, for 100 years he will always pour down the Dharma rain, beat the great Dharma drum, blow the great Dharma conch shell, convene the great Dharma assembly, and erect the great Dharma banner. He will demonstrate great spiritual powers and, at death, enter parinirvāṇa. After the appearance of 1,000 Buddhas and 100,000 Pratyekabuddhas, and the parinirvāṇa of 8 Tathāgatas in 62 kalpas, he will then attain Buddhahood. He will be called Knowledge Accumulation Radiance, the Tathāgata, Arhat, Samyak-Saṁbuddha. That bhikṣu, who will uphold my name then ultimately attain Samyak-Saṁbodhi in this land, is now the Licchavi youth called Entire World Delighted to See.

"Kāśyapa, know that it is hard to attain the unsurpassed bodhi. Kāśyapa, is it something an ordinary being can attain?"

Kāśyapa replied to the Buddha, "No, World-Honored One."

The Buddha told Kāśyapa, "As a Buddha does His Buddha work in a one-Buddha world, so too do a second Buddha and a third Buddha [in their respective worlds]. Within a mustard seed, there is a multitude of worlds. Sentient beings are not aware that they move to and fro among worlds, and they do not know who is in command of their comings and goings or who places them somewhere. They cannot help doing things according to what they know. Some know there is [true] self while others do not. In this world, on the Gṛdhrakūṭa Mountain, there is Śākyamuni Buddha, and in the same place, there will be Ajita Buddha. Events may manifest in this world, whether the burning of a kalpa or the pronouncement of the Dharma by a Buddha. Such extraordinary manifestations are rare occurrences.

"What is the foremost extraordinary event? It is the youth Entire World Delighted to See, who has never been reborn into an ordinary family. The families into which he has been reborn are Bodhisattvas. Kāśyapa, know that his supporting family and attendants are all delighted. His loving kin all say these words: 'Such [an extraordinary] person has been born into our family.' These people are all sent by me. Kāśyapa, know that if my four groups of disciples who survive me become the retinue of that Bodhisattva-Mahāsattva, they all will hear him pronounce this *Sūtra of the Great Dharma Drum*. They all will attain the unsurpassed bodhi.

"Kāśyapa, in a life far in the past, I was a Wheel-Turning King called Nandisena, in the city of Vaiśālī. At that time the city of Vaiśālī was like this Sahā World, Jambudvīpa, one of the four continents [of a small world] in this Three-Thousand Large Thousandfold World. My lifespan was inconceivable. As the Wheel-Turning King, I gave generous alms and cultivated virtues in asaṁkhyeya ways. My observance of the precepts was pure, and I trained in good actions, accumulating immeasurable merit. However, if good men and good women, hearing of the *Sūtra of the Great Dharma Drum* of the One Vehicle, go laughing to its presentation or remember it in one thought only, the merit they will acquire surpasses mine as described. It will be beyond reckoning by measurement or calculation, or by analogy. For example, when the mantra-king Blazing Flame recites a mantra, he will be well protected by its power for four months. Kāśyapa, know that the power of even a worldly ordinary mantra can be such. If one reads this *Sūtra of the Great Dharma Drum*, it is impossible that its power will fail to protect one for life. Therefore, if there are sentient beings that can make offerings to this sūtra, they have the definite cause for attaining the unsurpassed bodhi. Until their attainment of the ultimate bodhi, they will not stop pronouncing this sūtra."

Then the huge multitude chanted with one voice, "Very good! Very good! How amazing! World-Honored One, this youth will be [reborn as] the bhikṣu who will uphold the Buddha's name. If this bhikṣu enters parinirvāṇa in the south, the spirits of Jetavana Park here will have nothing to rely on. Instead, have him come from the south to the place where the Buddha was, then enter parinirvāṇa."

The Buddha told the huge multitude, "He will not take the initiative to come here. I will go to him, manifesting myself. I will first have this sūtra sent to him, and then go there. Why? Because if this sūtra is not in his hands, his mind will regress. If he knows sentient beings that should be tamed, I, together with a huge multitude, will stand before him. After he has seen me, he will come here. Having been received here, he will enter parinirvāṇa. He will enter parinirvāṇa in the place where he wishes to deliver sentient beings."

A son of the god-king Śakra called Abhimaṁru had come to this assembly by means of his transcendental powers. Although he was young, he believed and delighted in the Mahāyāna with a truly pure mind. Unique and unmatched, he upheld among the gods this profound Mahāyāna sūtra. Because he explained to them the right cause of liberation, he received a prophecy from the Buddha.

Then the huge multitude, with one voice, spoke in verse:

Amazing!
The youth Entire World Delighted to See
Will be [reborn as] a bhikṣu,
To beat the great Dharma drum
And to protect the Buddha Dharma,
Enabling it to abide for a long time.

After his parinirvāṇa,
The world will be empty like space.
After his parinirvāṇa,
No one can take his place.

Such a bhikṣu,
Rare in the world,
Can pronounce to the world
The ultimate Way.

Kāśyapa, Ānanda, Worthy Protector Bodhisattva, and the innumerable multitude, having heard the Buddha's words, rejoiced and reverently carried out the teachings.

Notes

1. In Buddhist doctrine, usually one's karmic seed is the cause for one's rebirth, and both parents are the conditions (Sūtra 13). In this passage, the Buddha is leading up to the exhaustion of karmic causes and conditions for one's rebirth, as He states later that "those who do not have the seeds of sentient beings are not called parents."

2. The first of the five aggregates that make up a sentient being is form, and the other four are non-form (mental functions). As stated in the *Heart Sūtra* (Sūtras 10–12), form is emptiness. Hence sentient beings are not form. The sūtra then states that emptiness is form. Hence sentient beings are not non-form. It is also possible to interpret at the relative level that sentient beings are not just form because they have mental functions and that they are not just mental functions because they have form.

15 大乘方廣總持經
Mahāyāna Vaipulya Sūtra of Total Retention

Translated from Sanskrit into Chinese in the Sui Dynasty
by
The Tripiṭaka Master Vinītaruci from India

Thus I have heard:

At one time the Buddha was staying on the Gṛdhrakūṭa Mountain, near the city of Rājagṛha, together with 62,000 great bhikṣus, 80 koṭi Bodhisattva-Mahāsattvas, and 60 koṭi 100,000 upāsakas from the kingdom of Magadha.

The summer meditation retreat having ended, nearing the time of His parinirvāṇa, the World-Honored One entered the In-Accord-with-the-Dharma Samādhi. During His samādhi, this Three-Thousand Large Thousandfold World was everywhere adorned with silky banners and canopies. Jeweled incense vases were well placed and fragrances were widely spread. Scattered all about were thousand-petaled lotus flowers. At that time, in this Three-Thousand Large Thousandfold World, multitudes in the hundreds of thousands of koṭis, Brahma-kings, and their retinues in the hundreds of thousands of koṭis came to the Buddha. Upon arrival they bowed their heads down at the feet of the Buddha. With folded palms, facing the Buddha, they stepped back to stand on one side. Also to the Buddha came hundreds of thousands of koṭis of god-sons from pure abode heavens, god-kings Īśvara and Maheśvara, dragon-kings, yakṣa-kings, asura-kings, garuḍa-kings, kiṁnara-kings, mahoraga-kings, together with their respective retinues in the hundreds of thousands of koṭis. Upon arrival they bowed their heads down at the feet of the Buddha. Also to the Buddha, from worlds in the ten directions came Bodhisattva-Mahāsattvas of great awesome virtue, who were as numerous as the sands of the Ganges. Upon arrival they bowed their heads down at the feet of the Buddha. With folded palms, facing the Buddha, they stepped back to stand on one side. Even gods from the top heaven in this Three-Thousand Large Thousandfold World came to join the huge multitude, which filled the space with no room to spare. Also to the assembly came all those others with great awesome power, such as gods, dragons, yakṣas, gandharvas, asuras, garuḍas, kiṁnaras, mahoragas, and others.

The World-Honored One, prompted by the right thought, rose from His samādhi. He looked all over the huge multitude as He stretched His body and opened His mouth. Like a lion-king, three times He stretched. Then the World-Honored One extended from His mouth His wide-ranging, far-reaching tongue, completely covering this Three-Thousand Large Thousandfold World. After the Tathāgata had finished His display of spiritual power, He again looked at the massive crowd. Then all in the huge multitude rose from their seats. They made obeisance with joined palms and stood in silence. Then the Buddha told Maitreya Bodhisattva, "Ajita, before long the Tathāgata will enter parinirvāṇa. If you have doubts regarding the Dharma and would like to ask me, now is the right time, while I am still here. Do not allow yourself to have any distressing regrets after the Buddha is gone."

Then Maitreya Bodhisattva-Mahāsattva said to the Buddha, "Yes, World-Honored One, You best know the right time. The Buddha-Tathāgata has realized the ultimate of all dharmas. I pray only that You will pronounce it, enabling Your dharma-eye to abide in the world for a long time."

In the assembly, the god-king Maheśvara's son and 80 koṭi gods from pure abode heavens, together with their retinues, surrounded the Buddha and bowed their heads down at His feet. Joining their palms reverently, they said to the Buddha, "World-Honored One, the Mahāyāna Vaipulya Total Retention Dharma Door has been taught in the past by innumerable Buddha-Tathāgatas, also called Arhats, Samyak-Saṁbuddhas. We pray only that the Tathāgata now will also expound it to bring benefits, comfort, and delight to innumerable gods and humans, and to enable the Buddha Dharma to abide in the world for a long time."

The Buddha approved in silence. Knowing that the Buddha had granted their request, the god-king Maheśvara's son was joyful and exuberant. Joining his palms, he made obeisance and stepped back to stand on one side. Then the Buddha told Maitreya Bodhisattva-Mahāsattva, "Ajita, this Mahāyāna Vaipulya Total Retention Dharma Door is not taught by me only. Innumerable Buddhas of the past, present, and future, in worlds in the ten directions, have frequently taught it. If there are sentient beings that malign the Dharma and the Saṅgha and say that the Buddha's words are not spoken by the Buddha, these maligners will go down the evil life-paths to undergo suffering in hell."

Then the Buddha told Maitreya Bodhisattva-Mahāsattva, "If, among good men and good women, there are those who have activated the bodhi mind and will accept and uphold, read and recite, and explain to others, this *Mahāyāna Vaipulya Sūtra of Total Retention*, know that these people will not go down the evil life-paths."

Then the World-Honored One asked Maitreya Bodhisattva-Mahāsattva, "Ajita, from the night I attained Buddhahood to the time when I will enter the nirvāṇa without remnant, are there evil karmas arising from oversights in what has been done, spoken, thought of, and pondered by the Buddha's body, voice, and mind?"

Maitreya Bodhisattva-Mahāsattva replied, "No, World-Honored One."

The Buddha said, "Maitreya, as you say, from the time of my attainment of bodhi to the time of my parinirvāṇa, what I have said in this interval is all true, never false. If there are fools who, failing to understand that the Tathāgata's words are skillful tools, judge that 'this Dharma is this way; this Dharma is not this way,' they are maligning the true Dharma as well as Buddhas and Bodhisattvas. I say that they are headed for hell.

"Ajita, after my parinirvāṇa, if, in the world of the five turbidities, among bhikṣus, bhikṣuṇīs, upāsakas, and upāsikās, there are those who are not Bodhisattvas but claim to be Bodhisattvas, they are actually non-Buddhists. Because they in their past lives had made offerings to Buddhas and made their resolve, they have been able to enter the Buddha's Order, renouncing family life.

Wherever they have gone, they have sought fame, benefits, and worship from their kinfolk and friends. They have unscrupulously engaged in impure activities and abandoned their faith. They have not restrained themselves from evil acts. They have not subjugated their greed for benefits and worship. As for all Dharma Doors and what will produce enduring samādhi, they have stayed far away from them and have had no knowledge of them. For the sake of their kinfolk, they have falsely claimed their knowledge and understanding. Standing in flattery and deception, their mouths have spoken contradictory words and their bodies have performed contradictory acts.

"Ajita, in my Bodhi Way all sentient beings are equal and embraced in my great compassion. While using skillful means, I never lose right mindfulness. Abiding peacefully in His unequaled power, the Tathāgata expounds the Dharma, hindrance free. Suppose there are sentient beings that say these words: 'Bodhisattvas should not hear, study, or accept the sūtras the Buddha has pronounced for voice-hearers. These are not the true Dharma, nor the right path. Nor should Bodhisattvas study the Pratyekabuddha Dharma.' Suppose they also say, 'Voice-hearers should not hear or accept the Dharmas that Bodhisattvas practice. Nor should voice-hearers hear or accept the Pratyekabuddha Dharma.' Suppose they also say, 'Whatever Bodhisattvas have to say, voice-hearers and Pratyekabuddhas should not hear or accept.' Their contradictory words and actions are not in accord with the sūtras. They are unable to believe and accept either the true Dharma of Liberation or words that are in accord with true reality. The followers of their ways cannot even be reborn in heaven, much less achieve liberation.

"Ajita, according to their faith, I have expounded the Dharma to and tamed as many [sentient beings] as the sands of the Ganges. Ajita, even now I want to go to worlds in the ten directions to expound the Dharma suitably to sentient beings for their benefit. It is not for those who are not Bodhisattvas but disguised as Bodhisattvas. Nor is it for the evil, deceitful ones who, having heard little of the Dharma, double talk about my Dharma. Suppose the double talker says these words: 'This, Bodhisattvas should learn. This, Bodhisattvas should not learn.' Having maligned the Buddha, the Dharma, and the Saṅgha, the double talker after death will fall into hell and, for hundreds and thousands of kalpas, will not be able to leave there. Suppose he will later be reborn in a poor family and even receive the prophecy of attaining Buddhahood. Then he will eventually attain samyak-saṁbodhi in an evil world of the five turbidities, just like me who has realized Buddha bodhi in this world of the five turbidities. Therefore, you should hearken, believe, and know that such will be the consequences of following the way of evil friends.

"Ajita, as I remember, countless kalpas ago, in the world appeared a Buddha called Untainted Flame Worthy-of-Name King, the Tathāgata, Arhat, Samyak-Saṁbuddha, Knowledge and Action Perfected, Sugata, Understanding the World, Unsurpassed One, Tamer of Men, Teacher to Gods and Humans, Buddha the World-Honored One. During His life of 80,000 nayuta years, that Buddha expounded the Dharma to the multitudes. In the Dharma of Untainted Flame Worthy-of-Name King Tathāgata, there was a bhikṣu called Pure Life. As a great Dharma master, he retained fourteen koṭi sūtras and six million Mahāyāna sūtras. His words were pure and beautiful, his eloquence unhindered. He helped innumerable, countless sentient beings by giving them teachings, benefits, and delight. Untainted Flame Worthy-of-Name King Tathāgata, upon entering parinirvāṇa, told the bhikṣu Pure Life, 'You should protect and uphold my true dharma-eye in future times.' Pure Life, having accepted that Buddha's instruction, for thousands and tens of thousands of years after that Buddha's parinirvāṇa, guarded and circulated the secret store of Buddhas. He accepted and upheld, and read and recited, [texts in] the Vaipulya Total Retention Dharma Door, and had profound understanding of their tenets. He also widely expounded them to all the sentient beings in 80,000 cities in that world according to their wishes and preferences.

"At that time there was a great city called Bhadra. Pure Life went to that city to expound the Dharma to 80 koṭi households according to their preferences. Consequently, 80 koṭi people in that city acquired pure faith, one koṭi people set themselves on the Bodhi Way, and 79 koṭi people accepted the Voice-Hearer Vehicle and were thus trained. Then the Dharma master Pure Life, followed by 10,000 bhikṣus, went to train in the Bodhi Way.

"At that time, in the city of Bhadra, there was a bhikṣu named Dharma. He accepted and upheld 1,000 Mahāyāna vaipulya sūtras and attained the four dhyānas. He was transforming the sentient beings in that city only by means of the Vaipulya Dharma of Emptiness. Unable to speak easily and skillfully, he said these words: 'All dharmas are empty and silent. What I say is truly the words of the Buddha. What the bhikṣu Pure Life says is filthy and impure. This bhikṣu is leading an impure life but calls himself Pure Life. Why? Because this bhikṣu keeps the flowers he has received for his own enjoyment, not for making offerings. He does the same with the solid perfumes and powdered incense. This bhikṣu Pure Life, foolish and senseless, does not know that I have long trained in the Brahma way of life. He is young and has not renounced family life for too long. He is arrogant, faithless, and utterly undisciplined. Those who do not have this knowledge say that Pure Life is a bhikṣu who observes the precepts.'

"Then Dharma who with a vicious mind had slandered the bhikṣu upholding the Dharma, after death, fell into hell. For 70 kalpas, he underwent multitudinous suffering. Upon completion of the 70 kalpas, he was reborn in animal form. After 60 kalpas, he encountered Fragrant Jewel Light Buddha, under whom Dharma activated his bodhi mind. He continued to be reborn in animal form for 90,000 lives. After these 90,000 lives, he was reborn in human form. For 60,000 lives, he did not have a tongue and lived in poverty and sordidness.

"[By contrast] the bhikṣu Pure Life, having gained pure faith in the Dharma, continued to pronounce the Dharma. Subsequently, he encountered 63 nayuta Buddhas. As a Dharma master with the five transcendental powers, he always asked each Buddha to turn the wheel of the true Dharma.

"Ajita, tell me this. Was the bhikṣu Pure Life in the past a different person? Do not view him as someone different. He is none other than Amitābha Buddha today. Ajita, tell me this. Was the bhikṣu Dharma in the past a different person? Do not view him as someone different. He is none other than I today. Because I had slandered Him out of foolishness and senselessness, I underwent such suffering. Through these karmic causes and conditions, I have attained samyak-saṁbodhi in this world of the five turbidities. Therefore, Ajita, if there are

Bodhisattvas who double talk about the Dharma, they will, for these causes and conditions, attain Buddha bodhi in a future world of the five turbidities. When they expound the Dharma, there will be māras in their Buddha Lands, constantly causing hindrances and making trouble."

When the huge assembly heard the Buddha's words, they all wept in grief, tears flowing and noses running. They all said these words: "May we, unlike that bhikṣu, refrain from double talk about the Dharma!"

Then one hundred Bodhisattvas in the assembly rose from their seats, knelt on their right knees, and cried loudly, shedding tears of sorrow. The World-Honored One, knowing the reason, still asked these Bodhisattvas, "Good men, why do you all wail miserably like this?"

These Bodhisattvas replied with one voice to the Buddha: "World-Honored One, we see in ourselves such evil karma hindrances as well."

In confirmation, the World-Honored One spoke these words: "Indeed! Indeed! In the past you renounced family life in the Dharma of Dīpaṅkara Buddha. After the parinirvāṇa of Dīpaṅkara Buddha, there was a bhikṣu called Knowledge Accumulation, and you all slandered this bhikṣu. For this reason, you have since been unable to see Buddhas, unable to activate the bodhi mind, and unable to acquire dhāraṇīs and samādhis. From now on, you all will stay on the Bodhi Way. Good men, under the last Buddha in this Worthy Kalpa, you will achieve the Endurance in the Realization of the No Birth of Dharmas. Afterward, you will walk the Bodhisattva Way for over three asaṁkhyeya kalpas, and then you will attain anuttara-samyak-saṁbodhi.

"Therefore, good men, when Bodhisattvas see other Bodhisattvas, they should not think of self versus others. Instead, they should think that others are like sacred pagodas, like Buddhas. Hence, when Bodhisattvas see other Bodhisattvas, they should not have discriminatory thoughts, considering others as non-Buddhas. Any discriminatory thoughts are self-harming. You should accept and uphold this [instruction]. Without alienating thoughts, you should join others in harmony. If I held the view that newly-resolved Bodhisattvas would be less than a Buddha, I would be deceiving innumerable asaṁkhyeyas of Buddhas of the present, [in worlds] in the ten directions. Therefore, good men, if Bodhisattvas can acquire dhāraṇīs and samādhis in the future, in a world of the five turbidities, it will all be by virtue of the awesome power of Buddhas. Hence, good men, slandering a Dharma master is no different from slandering a Buddha. Good men, after the Buddha's parinirvāṇa, if there is a Dharma master who can well expound the Dharma according to the preferences [of the listeners], and is able to have Bodhisattvas study the Mahāyāna doctrine, and to have the multitude feel as little joy as a hair and even shed one tear, know that it will all be by virtue of the spiritual power of the Buddha.

"Suppose a fool who is not a Bodhisattva but claims to be a Bodhisattva maligns a true Bodhisattva and his actions, even speaking these words: 'What does he know? What does he understand?' Maitreya, I remember in the past, in Jambudvīpa, when I was learning to be a Bodhisattva, I loved and treasured the Dharma. For the sake of a verse or a stanza, I abandoned my head, eyes, wife, and throne, which I cherished. Why? To seek the Dharma. As for the fools who seek only fame, benefits, and worship, confident in their own limited capacity, they do not go to one who imparts the Dharma of the Tathāgata, to hear and receive the true Dharma. Maitreya, if the slanderers and the slandered unite in harmony, they will be able to uphold and circulate my Dharma. If the two groups are in conflict and in dispute, the true Dharma will not prevail. Ajita, you can observe those who malign the Dharma. They have done such enormously sinful karma that they will go down the three evil life-paths, from which it is hard to escape.

"Furthermore, Ajita, in the time since I attained Buddhahood, with true wisdom I have widely expounded the true Dharma to sentient beings. Suppose there are fools who neither believe nor accept the Buddha's words, just like that bhikṣu Dharma. Although he had read and recited 1,000 Mahāyāna sūtras, explained them to others, and attained the four dhyānas, because of his slander of another, he underwent dreadful suffering for 70 kalpas. It is even more severe for those who, foolish and sordid, without any real knowledge [of the Dharma], proclaim these words: 'I am a Dharma master who clearly understands the Mahāyāna and can widely spread it.' They slander the true Dharma master, saying that he has no understanding. For self-elevation, they also malign the Buddha Dharma. If those fools malign even a four-verse stanza in the Buddha's Mahāyāna teachings, know that, for this karma, they will definitely fall into hell. Why? Because they malign the Buddha Dharma and Dharma masters. For these causes and conditions, they will always walk the evil life-paths, never to see Buddhas. Because they have maligned the Buddha, the Dharma, and the Saṅgha, they can also create obstacles for those who have recently activated the bodhi mind, causing them to abandon the right path. Know that those who adorn themselves with enormously sinful karmas will fall into hell to receive horrendous requitals for innumerable kalpas. Fixing an evil eye on one who has activated the bodhi mind will result in the requital of no eyes. Slandering one who has activated the bodhi mind will result in the requital of no tongue. Ajita, I have never seen an evil dharma graver than the sin of sabotaging others' activation of the bodhi mind. Even for this sin, one will go down the evil life-paths. Even graver is [the sin of] slandering Bodhisattvas.

"Bodhisattvas should explain the Dharma truthfully to sentient beings, without holding the wrong views, such as perpetuity or cessation, the definite existence or definite nonexistence of sentient beings, or the existence or nonexistence of dharmas. Ajita, those who are learning to be Bodhisattvas should abide in this way. Abiding in this way is a pure and good karma of Bodhisattvas. They do not cling to what they train in or learn. If sentient beings cling to anything, know that they will be reborn in the world of the five turbidities.

"Furthermore, there are Bodhisattvas who excel in pronouncing the Dharma in various ways to sentient beings according to their natures and desires. Ajita, Bodhisattvas who practice all six pāramitās in this way will be able to attain the unsurpassed bodhi. The fools who believe in what they fixate on may say these words: 'Bodhisattvas should learn prajñā-pāramitā only. Do not learn other pāramitās because prajñā-pāramitā is the supreme one.' This statement is incorrect. Why? Because, Ajita, in the past, when King Kāśaka was training to be a Bodhisattva, he abandoned his head, eyes, bone marrow, and brain, which he cherished. Did this king not have any wisdom?"

Maitreya replied to the Buddha, "World-Honored One, truly as Your Holiness has said, he had wisdom."

The Buddha told Ajita, "I practiced all six pāramitās fully for an immeasurable amount of time. If I had not practiced all six pāramitās fully, I would not have attained the unsurpassed bodhi."

"Indeed, World-Honored One."

The Buddha told Ajita, "As you say, in the past I practiced dāna-pāramitā, śīla-pāramitā, kṣānti-pāramitā, vīrya-pāramitā, dhyāna-pāramitā, and prajñā-pāramitā, each for sixty kalpas. Those fools falsely claim that one can attain bodhi by practicing prajñā-pāramitā only. There is nothing right about their claim. Because they embrace the view of void, they expound the Dharma with such impurity. The body, voice, and mind of those speakers contradict the Dharma. As they explain to others their understanding of emptiness, their do not act according to their words. Without [corresponding] actions, they are far from the [true] meaning of emptiness. Even more than their kinfolk, they harbor jealousy and are attached to benefits and worship. Ajita, when I was a Wheel-Turning King, I abandoned jewels, my head, my eyes, my hands, and my feet, but still could not attain the unsurpassed bodhi. By contrast, those fools, for the sake of food and drink, visit others' homes to make their statement. They only praise the Dharma of Emptiness and claim that what they say is the Bodhi Way and the Bodhisattva action, and that only this Dharma is the true Dharma while all other Dharmas are not. They also say these words: 'My understanding has been realized by and known to innumerable Dharma masters.' For the sake of fame, they praise themselves, saying that they clearly understand hatred and jealousy. Ajita, I see those who set their minds on seeking benefits and worship for a livelihood. Even if they take good actions for one hundred kalpas, they will not develop even a little Endurance in Dharmas, much less attain the unsurpassed bodhi. Ajita, I do not pronounce bodhi to the deceitful ones, who have contradictory mind and mouth. Nor to those who are jealous; nor to those who are arrogant and disrespectful; nor to those who are faithless; nor to those who are untamed; nor to those who engage in sexual misconduct; nor to those who believe that they are right and others wrong. Ajita, those fools, out of arrogance, claim that they have surpassed the Buddha. They malign Mahāyāna sūtras pronounced by the Buddha, alleging that these are actually pronounced by voice-hearers riding the Small Vehicle."

Then the Buddha told the venerable Subhūti, "You should not pronounce prajñā-pāramitā to those who adhere to the view of dualism."

Subhūti said to the Buddha, "No, indeed, World-Honored One, as the Buddha says."

The Buddha said, "Indeed, Subhūti, giving alms without being attached [to the almsgiver, the recipient, or the alms given] is called bodhi."

Subhūti said, "Indeed, World-Honored One."

The Buddha said, "Subhūti, giving without praising oneself and criticizing others is called bodhi."

Subhūti said, "Indeed, World-Honored One."

The Buddha said, "Subhūti, when you see fools who, for the love of their kinfolk, greedy for a living, [wrongly] adhere to the view of self and its belongings, and enjoy accepting offerings from others without any sense of shame or dishonor, you know that they do only evil karma."

"Furthermore, Ajita, Bodhisattvas should have no fear of any dharmas, such as the dharmas of Pratyekabuddhas, voice-hearers, or ordinary beings; afflictions, ending of dharmas, or difficulty in making progress; right or wrong, act or no act, fear or fearlessness, existence or nonexistence, mind or no mind, enlightenment or no enlightenment, karma or no karma, good or bad, peace or no peace, liberation or no liberation, training or not training, dharma or non-dharma, serenity or turmoil, true or false, belief or disbelief, good thoughts or bad thoughts, abiding or not abiding. Thus Bodhisattvas do not have fear of any dharmas.

"Ajita, because I have trained in the past in such fearlessness, I have attained samyak-saṁbodhi. I can know the mental states of all sentient beings without the notion that I am the knower of what I know. I expound what I have realized according to the capacities of Bodhisattvas, enabling those who have heard the Dharma to acquire the Radiant Dhāraṇī Seal. Having acquired this Dharma Seal, they will never regress. If one does not truly know this dharma [of fearlessness] and speaks without eloquence, one will not ultimately attain the unsurpassed bodhi.

"Ajita, when I expound the Dharma to the sentient beings here in this small world comprising four large continents, by virtue of the spiritual power of the Buddha, each of them sees [me] Śākyamuni Tathāgata expound the Dharma only to him. In the same way, from one heaven to the next, up to Akaniṣṭha Heaven, each of the sentient beings there also says that the Tathāgata pronounces the Dharma only to him. It is like this, ranging from a small world comprising four continents to even a Three-Thousand Large Thousandfold world. All sentient beings think: 'Śākyamuni Buddha has come to be born in my country, and He turns the great Dharma wheel only for me.' Ajita, in the morning, using great skill, I observe everywhere sentient beings in innumerable, boundless worlds and expound the Dharma to those that should be transformed. In the midday and in the evening, I observe sentient beings impartially with my dharma-eye and expound the Dharma in their worlds. Such are the states of innumerable Buddhas! All sentient beings that are learning to be Bodhisattvas should train in this way. Those fools who malign the true Dharma pronounced by the Buddha adhere to their wrong understanding as the right understanding. Those who malign the Dharma do not believe in the Buddha. Because of this evil karma, they will fall into hell to undergo multitudinous suffering, never to hear the Dharma. Furthermore, Ajita, you should accept and uphold the secret teachings of the Tathāgata and widely pronounce them to others by skillful means."

Then Bodhisattva-Mahāsattvas, including Mañjuśrī the Youth, Fortune Light Equality Bodhisattva, No Doubt Bodhisattva, Definite Resolve Bodhisattva, Wonder Mind Open Intellect Bodhisattva, Radiance Bodhisattva, Joyful King Bodhisattva, Fearless Bodhisattva, Thoughts Reaching Boundless Buddha Lands Bodhisattva, Avalokiteśvara Bodhisattva, Fragrant Elephant Bodhisattva, Annihilating All Evil Karma Bodhisattva, Abiding in Samādhi Bodhisattva, Hundred Thousand Merits Adorned Bodhisattva, Wonderful Tone Heard Afar Bodhisattva, All Knowledge Unforgotten Bodhisattva, Great Name Shaking

Jeweled Banner Adorned Bodhisattva, Seeking All Dharma Bodhisattva, Abiding in the Buddha State Bodhisattva, Moonlight Adorned Bodhisattva, and Great Multitude in All the World Adorned Bodhisattva, said to the Buddha, "World-Honored One, indeed, indeed, truly as Your Holiness says, when we passed Buddha Lands in the east, which were as numerous as the sands of sixty Ganges Rivers, and reverently made obeisance to the Buddhas there, we saw only Śākyamuni Buddha appearing in every world. We then visited everywhere [in worlds] in the ten directions for seven days and still saw only Śākyamuni Buddha appearing in each world, not other Buddhas. After visiting everywhere, we have returned to this land to hear and accept the true Dharma."

At that time the Buddha told Mañjuśrī the Youth, "Now observe carefully. The wisdom of the Tathāgata is inconceivable, and the state of the Tathāgata is also inconceivable. Such unequaled states are the Tathāgata dharma. Those fools say these words, 'Only prajñā-pāramitā is the Tathāgata action, the Bodhisattva action, and the sweet nectar action.'"

The Buddha told Mañjuśrī, "Their words contradict the Dharma. Why? Because it is very difficult to fully complete the Bodhisattva action. Acting without attachment is the Bodhisattva action; acting without the view of a self and its belongings is the Bodhisattva action; acting with the understanding of emptiness is the Bodhisattva action, and acting with no appearance is the Bodhisattva action. Mañjuśrī, such actions are the Bodhisattva action. Those learning to be Bodhisattvas should accept and uphold it. If those fools embrace the wrong views, you should know that they do not understand my Dharma. Mañjuśrī, you and other Bodhisattvas should all guard and protect your bodies and mouths. Do not allow them to dissipate in bad ways. Fortify your minds and keep them from regressing. As you fully expound the Dharma to sentient beings, you should abide in the Dharma. Since I fully attained the unsurpassed bodhi distant asaṁkhyeya kalpas ago, I have widely and skillfully pronounced the Dharma, enabling sentient beings to stay far away from the evil life-journeys.

"Mañjuśrī, if there are fools who malign the true Dharma, they have maligned both the Buddha and the Saṅgha. Making a statement that this Dharma is correct and that Dharma is incorrect is called maligning the Dharma. Making a statement that this Dharma is pronounced for Bodhisattvas and that Dharma is pronounced for voice-hearers is called maligning the Dharma. Making a statement that these are Bodhisattva studies and those are not Bodhisattva studies is called maligning the Dharma. Making a statement that as the past Buddha is gone, the future Buddha has not yet arrived, and the present Buddha is not staying, only I have acquired the Dhāraṇī Dharma, is called maligning the Dharma. Because of maligning the Dharma, their claim to have acquired the dhāraṇī is an impure dharma. They malign what a true Dharma master is cultivating. They further slander the Dharma master, saying that although he has intellectual understanding, his actions are inconsistent with his words. They further slander the Dharma master, saying that his actions violate the Way. They further slander the Dharma master, saying that his body does not observe the precepts. They further slander the Dharma master, saying that his mind has no wisdom. They further slander the Dharma master, saying that his intellect has no clear understanding. They further slander the Dharma master, saying that his speech is devoid of eloquence. Their minds do not believe or accept the words spoken by the Tathāgata. They also say, 'This sūtra is correct, this sūtra is incorrect; this stanza is correct, this stanza is incorrect; this Dharma is credible, this Dharma is not credible.' They wrongly rebut what is explained correctly. For those who listen to the true Dharma, they create hindrances, making claims, such as 'this is a training, this is not a training; this is an accomplishment, this is not an accomplishment; this is the right time, this is the wrong time.' These statements are all called maligning the Dharma.

"Furthermore, Mañjuśrī, whether voice-hearers pronounce the Dharma, whether Bodhisattvas pronounce the Dharma, know that it is entirely by virtue of the awesome spiritual power of the Tathāgata's protection and consideration, which enables Bodhisattvas and others to say what they say. Mañjuśrī, even now the fools slander the Buddha. After my parinirvāṇa, how can Dharma masters, who accept and uphold my Dharma, not be slandered by them? Why? Because these fools are the retinue of the māras, know that they will go down the evil life-paths. As these fools greedily seek benefits and worship to support their kinfolk, they not only have no faith in the Dharma of the Tathāgata, but also destroy the Dharma taught by the Tathāgata. Their kinfolk, with a clannish mind, go to the houses of Brahmins and elders to praise these fools, claiming that they know and understand the Dharma and its meanings and that they are good at explanations because they know others' capacities and desires. These fools accept others' trust and offerings without any sense of shame or dishonor. Because they malign the Dharma, both they and their retinues will fall into hell.

"Mañjuśrī, I do not pronounce the Bodhisattva action to nonbelievers. Nor do I pronounce the pure Dharma to those who are attached to family life. Nor do I pronounce the Dharma of Liberation to those who adhere to the view of dualism. Nor do I pronounce the supra-worldly Dharma to those who adhere to the view of monism. Nor do I pronounce the pure, true Dharma to those who delight in worldly life.

"Mañjuśrī, with a mind clinging to nothing, I teach to people as many Dharma Doors as the sands of the Ganges. Then with a mind seemingly attached to something, I also teach to sentient beings as many Dharma Doors as the sands of the Ganges. If sentient beings delight in emptiness, I pronounce to them the Dharma of Emptiness. If sentient beings delight in knowledge, I pronounce to them the Dharma of Knowledge. If sentient beings delight in no appearance, I pronounce to them the Dharma of No Appearance. If sentient beings delight in appearance, I pronounce to them the Dharma of Appearance. If sentient beings delight in lovingkindness, I pronounce to them the Dharma of Lovingkindness. If sentient beings delight in causality, I pronounce to them the Dharma of Causality. If sentient beings delight in no causality, I pronounce to them the Dharma of No Causality. [Other Dharmas I have pronounced include] the awe-inspiring deportment and the non-awe-inspiring deportment, emptiness and existence, that which is saṁskṛta and that which is asaṁskṛta, holy beings and ordinary beings, fools, form, ways to draw in sentient beings, the obstructive coverings, that which is bad, and that which is definite."

The Buddha told Mañjuśrī, "Dharmas such as these are the way of prajñā-pāramitā. The words of those fools, which malign the true Dharma of the Buddha, are not in accord with the pure, true teachings of the Tathāgata."

Then Mañjuśrī asked Buddha, "World-Honored One, as You say, such fools, because they are close to evil friends, step forward to voice their slander. Then, World-Honored One, through what causes and conditions, can they avoid this fault?"

The Buddha told Mañjuśrī, "For seven years in the distant past, day and night in the six periods, I repented of the grave sins I had committed with my body, voice, and mind. After being purified, it took me ten kalpas to acquire the Endurance in Dharmas. Mañjuśrī, know that this sūtra is the Bodhisattva Vehicle. It can enable those who have not realized [the truth] to come to realization. If those who, having heard the words of this sūtra, refuse to believe and accept them and even malign them, they will go down the evil life-paths. Bodhisattvas need to understand and accept my Dharma, before they can pronounce it to others. By accepting and upholding [the Dharma] in this way, one can stay far away from the evil life-journeys."

The Buddha told Mañjuśrī, "There are four equality dharmas Bodhisattvas should learn. What are these four? First, Bodhisattvas are impartial to all sentient beings. Second, they are impartial to all dharmas. Third, they are impartial to bodhi. Fourth, they pronounce various Dharmas impartially. These are the four equality dharmas. Bodhisattvas should know these four dharmas and explain them to sentient beings. The believers will stay far away from the evil life-journeys. The nonbelievers will go down the evil life-paths. If, among good men and good women, there are those who abide in these four dharmas, know that they will not have to take the evil life-journeys. There are another four dharmas [for Bodhisattvas to learn]. What are these four? First, their minds do not regress from helping sentient beings. Second, they neither disdain nor slander Dharma masters. Third, they do not slander the wise. Fourth, they always respect everything said by Tathāgatas. If good men and good women can competently train in and learn these four dharmas, they will never go down the evil life-paths.

"Furthermore, Mañjuśrī, Bodhisattvas can take the seven treasures which fill up as many Buddha Lands as the sands of the Ganges, and make offerings every day for as many kalpas as the sands of the Ganges to as many Buddha-Bhagavāns as the sands of the Ganges. If good men and good women can three times read and recite a verse or a stanza in such a wonderful Mahāyāna vaipulya sūtra, the merit they will acquire exceeds that from making those offerings. The merit acquired by those who recite and uphold this sūtra will be twice as much. Suppose there are those who practice almsgiving, observance of precepts, endurance, energetic progress, meditation, and wisdom. The merit they acquire from practicing these six pāramitās also cannot compare [with that of upholding this sūtra]. Mañjuśrī, the name and meaning of such a sūtra are so vast that they are unequaled. You Bodhisattva-Mahāsattvas should study and learn this sūtra, accept and uphold it, read and recite it, and explain it widely to sentient beings."

Then those in the huge multitude and Bodhisattva-Mahāsattvas from the ten directions all said to the Buddha: "World-Honored One, indeed, indeed, we will accept and uphold it as the Buddha instructs."

When the Buddha was pronouncing this Dharma, Bodhisattvas, as numerous as the sands of 30 Ganges Rivers, achieved the Endurance in the Realization of the No Birth of Dharmas. Bodhisattvas as numerous as the sands of 70 Ganges Rivers attained the spiritual level of no regress from the anuttara-samyak-saṁbodhi mind. Furthermore, the massive multitudes in 63 koṭi 100,000 nayuta Three-Thousand Large Thousandfold Worlds, having heard the Buddha's words, heartily rejoiced. They would have to continue flowing in the stream of birth and death for 80 kalpas, and then they too would reach the spiritual level of no regress from the anuttara-samyak-saṁbodhi mind. At the end of another 63 kalpas, they would fully attain the unsurpassed bodhi.

All in the multitude—Bodhisattvas, gods, dragons, yakṣas, gandharvas, asuras, garuḍas, kiṁnaras, and mahoragas, humans, nonhumans, and others—having heard the Buddha's words, greatly rejoiced and made obeisance. Then they reverently carried out the teachings.

16 無量義經
Sūtra of Immeasurable Meaning

Translated from Sanskrit into Chinese in the Xiao Qi Dynasty
by
The Tripiṭaka Master Dharmagatayaśas from India

Chapter 1
The Virtuous Actions

Thus I have heard:

At one time the Buddha was staying on the Gṛdhrakūṭa Mountain, near the city of Rājagṛha, together with 12,000 great bhikṣus and 80,000 Bodhisattva-Mahāsattvas, as well as gods, dragons, yakṣas, gandharvas, asuras, garuḍas, kiṁnaras, and mahoragas. Also present were bhikṣus, bhikṣuṇīs, upāsakas, and upāsikās, as well as great Wheel-Turning Kings and lesser Wheel-Turning Kings, such as gold wheel kings and silver wheel kings, as well as kings, princes, state ministers, citizens, men, women, and elders, surrounded by their retinues in the billions. They all came to the Buddha, bowed their heads down at His feet, and circled Him 100,000 times. They burned incense, scattered flowers, and presented various kinds of offerings. Having made their offerings to the Buddha, they stepped back and sat on one side.

Among the 80,000 Bodhisattva-Mahāsattvas were Mañjuśrī the Dharma Prince, Great Awesome Virtue Store the Dharma Prince, Carefree Store the Dharma Prince, Great Eloquence Store the Dharma Prince, Maitreya Bodhisattva, Guiding Leader Bodhisattva, Medicine King Bodhisattva, Medicine Superior Bodhisattva, Flower Banner Bodhisattva, Flower Radiance Banner Bodhisattva, Dhāraṇī Sovereign King Bodhisattva, Avalokiteśvara Bodhisattva, Great Might Arrived Bodhisattva, Persistent Energetic Progress Bodhisattva, Jewel Seal Hand Bodhisattva, Treasure Pile Bodhisattva, Jewel Staff Bodhisattva, Beyond the Three Realms Bodhisattva, Vimalabhadra Bodhisattva, Fragrant Elephant Bodhisattva, Great Fragrant Elephant Bodhisattva, Lion's Roar King Bodhisattva, Lion Frolic World Bodhisattva, Lion Vigor Bodhisattva, Lion Advance Bodhisattva, Valiant Force Bodhisattva, Lion Fierce Subjugation Bodhisattva, Magnificence Bodhisattva, and Great Magnificence Bodhisattva. All of these Bodhisattva-Mahāsattvas are great ones who have realized their dharma body through perfecting [its five aspects:] precepts, samādhi, wisdom, liberation, and the knowledge and views of liberation. Their minds, silent and meditative, are constantly in samādhi, peaceful, reserved, asaṁskṛta, and free from desire. Inverted thoughts and perceptions no longer arise. Silent, lucid, profound, and vast, their minds can remain still for 100,000 koṭi kalpas, as innumerable Dharma Doors are all present before them. Having unfolded great wisdom and penetrated all dharmas, they understand the true reality of dharmas, which, differentiated by their natures and appearances, clearly manifest as existence or nonexistence, long or short. Moreover, they are adept in identifying the capacities, natures, and desires of sentient beings. Equipped with dhāraṇīs and unimpeded eloquence, they always request Buddhas to turn the Dharma wheel.

Likewise, they are also able to turn it. They first dampen the dust of desire with drizzling drops [of teachings]. As they open the door to nirvāṇa and fan the wind of liberation, they turn the heat of the afflictions of the world into the coolness of the Dharma. They next rain down the profound principle of the Twelve Links of Dependent Arising upon the blazing, glowing sunlight of suffering that runs from ignorance to old age, illness, and death. Then, they cascade a downpour of unexcelled Mahāyāna [teachings] to water the roots of goodness of sentient beings in the Three Realms of Existence. They scatter the seeds of goodness everywhere in merit fields, enabling all to germinate bodhi sprouts. With their wisdom like the sun and the moon, using skillful means and timing, they promote and expand the mission of the Mahāyāna, enabling sentient beings to attain anuttara-samyak-saṁbodhi quickly and to abide in bliss and inconceivable true reality. As these Bodhisattva-Mahāsattvas rescue longsuffering sentient beings with immeasurable great compassion, they are their true beneficent learned friends, their great fortune fields, and their unasked teachers. For sentient beings, they serve as sanctuaries of peace and joy and as places of rescue, protection, and great reliance. In every way they are the great guiding teachers to sentient beings. They can be the eye for those who are born blind and be the ear, nose, and tongue for those who are deaf, unable to smell, and mute. They can complete those who are incomplete in their faculties and can make the deranged think straight. Like the captain, the great captain, of a ship, they carry sentient beings across the river of birth and death to the shore of nirvāṇa. Like the medicine king, the great medicine king, they differentiate the symptoms of diseases, know the properties of medicines, dispense medicines according to the diseases, and make patients enjoy taking them. Like the animal trainer who can train elephants and horses without fail, they, the tamers, the great tamers, always refrain from unrestrained actions. Like the brave fierce lion that subdues all animals, totally undefeatable, they playfully practice the Bodhisattva pāramitās. Unshakably resolved to attain the Tathāgata Ground, they rely on the power of their vows to purify Buddha Lands. Before long, they will attain anuttara-samyak-saṁbodhi. These Bodhisattva-Mahāsattvas all have such inconceivable merits as described.

Among the 12,000 bhikṣus were Śāriputra the Great Wisdom, Maudgalyāyana the Transcendental Power, Subhūti the Wisdom Life, Mahākātyāyana, Pūrṇa (Maitrāyaṇī's son), Ājñātakauṇḍinya, Aniruddha the God-Eye, Upāli the Upholder of the Vinaya, Ānanda (the Buddha's attendant), Rāhula (the Buddha's son), Upananda, Revata, Kapphiṇa, Vakkula, Mahāmaudgalyāyana, Svāgata, Mahākāśyapa the Foremost in Dhūta Training, Uruvilvākāśyapa, Gayākāśyapa, and Nadīkāśyapa. All of them were Arhats, who, having ended their afflictions and the discharges thereof, were free from bondage and truly liberated.

At that time Great Magnificence Bodhisattva-Mahāsattva, seeing the multitude settled calmly, together with the 80,000 Bodhisattva-Mahāsattvas in the assembly, rose from his seat and came to the Buddha. They bowed their heads down at the feet of the Buddha, and circled him 100,000 times. As an offering to the Buddha, celestial incense smoke, flowers, garments, necklaces, and priceless jewels fell spiraling down from the sky and gathered around like clouds. Celestial serving dishes and bowls were filled with delicacies of one hundred celestial flavors, gratifying all with their colors and aromas. Placed everywhere were celestial banners, flags, and canopies, as well as wonderful musical instruments, playing celestial music to entertain the Buddha.

Before the Buddha, they joined their palms and knelt on their right knees. With one mind and one voice, they presented their tribute in verse:

Sublime is the holy lord, the great enlightened one!
With no taint, no defilement, and no attachment,
He is the tamer of gods and men as well as of elephants and horses.
The influence of His Way and the fragrance of His virtue permeate everywhere.
His wisdom is peaceful, His emotions serene, and His cares at rest.
His mental faculty and mental consciousness are still, and His mind silent,
Having forever ceased dreaming, thinking, perception, and rumination.
He no longer takes as real the [six] domains, the [five] aggregates, the [eighteen] spheres, and the [twelve] fields.

Born from neither causes nor conditions, neither self nor others,
His [dharma] body is neither existent nor nonexistent,
Neither square nor round, neither long nor short,
Neither appearing nor disappearing, with neither birth nor death,
Neither constructed nor arisen, neither made nor formed,
Neither sitting nor lying, neither walking nor standing still,
Neither moving nor turning, neither idle nor quiet,
Neither advancing nor retreating, neither safe nor perilous,
Neither right nor wrong, neither gaining nor losing,
Neither this nor that, neither coming nor going,
Neither blue nor yellow, neither red nor white,
Neither scarlet nor purple, nor in a variety of colors.
It is realized through achieving [its five aspects:] precepts, samādhi, wisdom, liberation, and the knowledge and views of liberation.

Accomplished are the Three Clarities, the six transcendental powers, and the [Thirty-seven] Elements of Bodhi.
Arisen are lovingkindness, compassion, the Ten Powers, and the [Four] Fearlessnesses.
In response to the good karmic conditions of sentient beings,
He has appeared in a body ten feet and six inches tall, purple-tinged golden,
Resplendent, radiant, and well proportioned.
The white hair between His eyebrows curls like the new moon, and His halo is like sunlight.
His curling hair is dark blue, and a fleshy mound is on his crown.

His clear eyes are bright, gently looking up and down.
His eyebrows and eyelashes are dark blue, and His mouth and cheeks well formed.
His lips and tongue are red, like a crimson flower.
His forty teeth are white like snow.
His forehead is broad, His nose straight, and His face open.
On His lion chest is the symbol of a svastika.
His palms and soles are soft, marked with a thousand spokes.
His armpits are not hollow, His fingers are webbed,
His arms are long, and His fingers straight and slender.
His skin is fine and soft, with hair curling to the right.
His ankles and knees are not bony, and His male organ is hidden like that of a horse.
Fine muscles wrap His leg bones, like those of the deer-king.

His body is radiant, pure, and fresh,
[Like a lotus flower] untouched by water and untainted by dirt.
His thirty-two physical marks
And eighty excellent characteristics seem to be visible.
In true reality, there is neither form nor appearance
Because appearances before the eye are empty.
As the appearance of no appearance is manifested as His body,
In the same way it is manifested as the bodies of sentient beings.
His appearance enables sentient beings to make obeisance joyfully,
And to pay their respects sincerely and earnestly.
By discarding self-elevation and self-arrogance,
He has acquired such a wonderful body.

All of us together, 80,000 in this multitude,
Make obeisance to and take refuge in the holy one who, with no attachment,
Has skillfully transformed His thinking, perception, mind, mental faculty, and mental consciousness,
As well as tamed elephants and horses.
We bow down to take refuge in the physical form of His dharma body,
A combination of precepts, samādhi, wisdom, liberation, and the knowledge and views of liberation.
We bow down to take refuge in the appearance of the wondrous being.
We bow down to take refuge in the inconceivable one.
His Brahma tone thunders in eight ways,
Wondrous, pure, and far-reaching,
Announcing the Four Noble Truths, the six pāramitās, and the Twelve Links of Dependent Arising,
According to the mind karmas of sentient beings.

None of the hearers will fail to open his mind
And to shatter the bondage of his immeasurable cycle of birth and death.

Some voice-hearers become Srotāpannas,
Sakṛdāgāmins, Anāgāmins, or Arhats.
Some become Pratyekabuddhas, free from afflictions and attachment to saṁskṛta dharmas.
Some realize the no birth and no death of dharmas and ascend to the Bodhisattva Grounds.
Some acquire innumerable dhāraṇīs
And delight in expounding the Dharma with great eloquence.
They pronounce profound, wondrous stanzas,
Playing and bathing in the pure lake of the Dharma.
Some display transcendental powers as they jump up and fly
Or freely go in and out of water or fire.
Such are the manifestations of the Dharma wheel,
Pure, boundless, and inconceivable!

Again we all bow down together to take refuge
In the Dharma wheel that turns at the right time.
We all bow down to take refuge in the Brahma tones.
We all bow down to take refuge in the [principle of] dependent arising, the Four Noble Truths, and the six pāramitās.

For innumerable kalpas in the past,
The World-Honored One arduously trained in virtuous actions.
For Himself, humans, gods, dragons, spirits, kings,
And all other sentient beings,
He was able to abandon all that was hard to abandon,
Such as wife, children, riches, throne, and kingdom.
Never begrudging dharmas, internal or external,
He gave others his head, eyes, bone marrow, and brain.
Observing the pure precepts of Buddhas,
He never caused any harm, even to save His life.
He never became angry when struck by knives or clubs,
Or attacked by insults and abusive words.
For kalpas, He was never tired or indolent in His endeavor.
Day and night, He has kept his mind in meditation.
Having learned all the ways in the Dharma,
He can penetrate the capacities of sentient beings with His wisdom.
Hence, He has now achieved commanding power,
Becoming the Dharma King in command of dharmas.

We all bow down together to take refuge,
So that we can endeavor to do what is hard to do.

Chapter 2
Expounding the Dharma

Great Magnificence Bodhisattva-Mahāsattva and the 80,000 Bodhisattva-Mahāsattvas, having finished the stanza in praise of the Buddha, asked the Buddha, "World-Honored One, all of us 80,000 Bodhisattvas now would like to ask about the Dharma of the Tathāgata. We do not know whether the World-Honored One will grant us permission."

The Buddha told Great Magnificence Bodhisattva and the 80,000 Bodhisattvas: "Very good! Very good! Good men, you best know that this is the right time. You may ask any questions. Before long, the Tathāgata will enter parinirvāṇa, and there should be no doubts remaining after my parinirvāṇa. You may ask me any questions you wish."

Then Great Magnificence Bodhisattva and the 80,000 Bodhisattvas asked the Buddha with one voice, "World-Honored One, if Bodhisattva-Mahāsattvas wish to attain anuttara-samyak-saṁbodhi quickly, through what Dharma Door should they train? What Dharma Door will enable Bodhisattva-Mahāsattvas to attain anuttara-samyak-saṁbodhi quickly?"

The Buddha replied to Great Magnificence Bodhisattva and the 80,000 Bodhisattvas: "Good men, there is one Dharma Door through which Bodhisattvas can attain anuttara-samyak-saṁbodhi quickly. If there are Bodhisattvas who learn this Dharma Door, they can attain anuttara-samyak-saṁbodhi quickly."

"World-Honored One, what is this Dharma Door called? What is its meaning? How should Bodhisattvas train themselves?"

The Buddha replied, "Good men, this one Dharma Door is called Immeasurable Meaning. Bodhisattvas who wish to study and learn the immeasurable meaning should observe that dharmas have always been empty in nature and in appearance. With neither birth nor death, dharmas are neither large nor small, neither moving nor standing still, neither advancing nor retreating. Like space, they are non-dual. However, sentient beings mistakenly calculate this versus that, gain versus loss. They elicit bad thoughts, do evil karmas, and hence transmigrate through the six life-journeys, undergoing dreadful suffering. For innumerable koṭis of kalpas, they are unable to transcend the cycle by themselves. Having observed them carefully in this way and wishing to rescue them, Bodhisattva-Mahāsattvas feel sympathy and exude great lovingkindness and compassion. Moreover, they deeply penetrate all dharmas: with such a dharma appearance, such a dharma is arising; with such a dharma appearance, such a dharma is staying; with such a dharma appearance, such a dharma is changing; with such a dharma appearance, such a dharma is perishing; such a dharma appearance can produce evil dharmas; such a dharma appearance can produce good dharmas. In the same way each dharma stays, changes, and perishes. Having fully observed and understood the ins and outs of the four appearances [of every saṁskṛta dharma], Bodhisattvas next observe intently that all dharmas arise and perish instantly, as thoughts, one after another, never stay. They also observe the instantaneous birth, stay, change, and death of all dharmas. Having made these observations, Bodhisattvas then penetrate the capacities, natures, and desires of sentient beings. Because their capacities, natures, and desires are immeasurable, Bodhisattvas pronounce immeasurable Dharmas. As the Dharmas pronounced are immeasurable, their meanings are also immeasurable. The immeasurable meanings are born from one dharma. This one dharma is no appearance, which is not apart from appearance. The truth that appearance and no appearance are not apart from each other is called true reality. As Bodhisattva-Mahāsattvas abide in this true reality, the lovingkindness and compassion they exude are genuine, not false. They can truly end sentient beings' suffering. Having rescued them from suffering, Bodhisattvas pronounce the Dharma to them, enabling them to experience happiness.

"Good men, if Bodhisattvas can train in this one Dharma Door of Immeasurable Meaning, they will quickly attain anuttara-samyak-saṁbodhi. Good men, this profound, unexcelled *Mahāyāna Sūtra of Immeasurable Meaning* is true in its principle and supreme in its dignity. It is protected by all Buddhas of the past, present, and future. No māras or non-Buddhists can enter it, nor can it be corrupted by the wrong views that perpetuate birth and death. Therefore, good men, Bodhisattva-Mahāsattvas who wish to attain the unsurpassed bodhi should study and learn this profound, unexcelled *Mahāyāna Sūtra of Immeasurable Meaning*."

Great Magnificence Bodhisattva next said to the Buddha, "World-Honored One, the Dharma pronounced by You is inconceivable, the capacities of sentient beings are also inconceivable, and the explanations of the Dharma Doors are inconceivable as well. We no longer have doubts about the Dharma pronounced by the Buddha. However, I need to restate my question because sentient beings have bewildered minds. World-Honored One, since the Tathāgata's attainment of bodhi, for over forty years, You have often expounded to sentient beings that the meaning of the four appearances of every dharma is impermanence, pain, emptiness, and no self. With neither birth nor death, dharmas are neither large nor small, but in the one appearance of no appearance. Dharma nature and dharma appearance have always been empty, neither coming nor going, neither appearing nor disappearing. Of those who have heard these teachings, some have completed [one of the Four Preparatory Trainings:] Warmth, Pinnacle, Endurance, and Foremost in the World; some have become Srotāpannas, Sakṛdāgāmins, Anāgāmins, or Arhats; some have activated the bodhi mind and ascended to the First, Second, Third, or even the Tenth Ground.

"What is the difference in the meaning between the Dharma You have pronounced in the past and what You have stated today, that prompted You to say that Bodhisattvas who train according to this profound, unexcelled *Mahāyāna Sūtra of Immeasurable Meaning* will attain the unsurpassed bodhi quickly? What is the reason? I pray only that the World-Honored One, out of His lovingkindness and compassion for all, will widely explain it to sentient beings, enabling present and future hearers of the Dharma not to have a web of doubts remaining."

Then the Buddha told Great Magnificence Bodhisattva, "Very good! Very good! Man of great goodness, you are able to ask the Tathāgata about such subtle meaning of this profound, unexcelled Mahāyāna. We know that you are able to bring a great many benefits to gods and humans and to rescue suffering sentient beings, giving them all peace and joy. Your great lovingkindness and compassion are true, not false. Because of these causes and conditions, you will definitely attain the unsurpassed bodhi quickly. You will also enable sentient beings in the Three Realms of Existence to attain the unsurpassed bodhi in their present or future lives.

"Good man, after sitting properly for six years under the bodhi tree in my bodhimaṇḍa, I attained anuttara-samyak-saṁbodhi. I then observed all dharmas with my Buddha-eye and decided that some [Dharmas] should not yet be pronounced. Why? Because the natures and desires of sentient beings are varied. Because their natures and desires are varied, my teachings have also been varied. Pronouncing various Dharmas with the power of skillful means for over forty years, I did not reveal the definitive meaning. As a result, there are differences in the bodhi attained by sentient beings, and they are unable to attain the unsurpassed bodhi quickly.

"Good man, the Dharma is like water, which can wash off filth and dirt. Whether water comes from a well, a lake, a stream, a river, a brook, a channel, or an immense ocean, it all can wash off different kinds of dirt. Likewise, the Dharma water can cleanse sentient beings' filthy afflictions.

"Good man, the nature of water is the same, but a stream, a river, a well, a pool, a channel, and an immense ocean are different from one another. Likewise, the nature of the Dharma is the same, and there is no difference in its washing away of filthy afflictions. However, the Three Dharmas, the four [voice-hearer] fruits, and the Two Paths are not the same.

"Good man, although water from any source washes off dirt just the same, a well is not a pool, a pool is neither a stream nor a river, and a brook or a channel is not an immense ocean. The Dharma pronounced by the Tathāgata, the hero in the world, who has command of all dharmas, is like water. Although what is taught at the beginning, in the middle, and at the end all can cleanse sentient beings' afflictions, the beginning is not the middle, nor is the middle the end. The teachings given at the beginning, in the middle, and at the end use the same words but their meanings are different.

"Good man, after I rose from under the bodhi tree, the king of trees, I went to Deer Park in Vārāṇasī and turned the Dharma wheel of the Four Noble Truths for the five people, including Ājñātakauṇḍinya. I pronounced that dharmas have always been empty, changing nonstop, as thoughts arise and perish, thought after thought. During the middle period of my teachings, I expounded everywhere to bhikṣus and Bodhisattvas the Twelve Links of Dependent Arising and the six pāramitās. I also pronounced that dharmas have always been empty, changing nonstop, as thoughts arise and perish, thought after thought. As I now expound this *Mahāyāna Sūtra of Immeasurable Meaning*, I again pronounce that dharmas have always been empty, changing nonstop, as thoughts arise and perish, thought after thought. Therefore, good man, the teachings at the beginning, in the middle, and at the end use the same words, but with different meanings. Because the meanings are different, sentient beings' understandings are different. Because their understandings are different, the Dharma, the fruit, and bodhi they acquire are also different.

"Good man, at the beginning, as I pronounced the Four Noble Truths to those who wanted to be voice-hearers, eight koṭi gods who descended [from their heavens] to hear the Dharma, activated the bodhi mind. In the middle period [of my teaching], as I pronounced everywhere the profound Twelve Links of

Dependent Arising to those who wanted to become Pratyekabuddhas, innumerable sentient beings activated the bodhi mind, while others remained as voice-hearers. I next pronounced sūtras in the twelve categories, including the vaipulya sūtras and the mahāprajñā sūtras, like a splendid ocean of clouds, and I expounded how Bodhisattvas would train themselves for kalpas. However, of the hundreds of thousands of bhikṣus and tens of thousands of koṭis of humans and gods, a countless number became Srotāpannas, Sakṛdāgāmins, Anāgāmins, or Arhats, abiding in the Dharma of Dependent Arising realized by Pratyekabuddhas. Good man, for this reason, know that although the words are the same, their meanings are different. Because the meanings are different, the understandings of sentient beings are different. As their understandings differ, the Dharma, fruit, and bodhi they achieve also differ.

"Good man, after attaining the great bodhi, from the time I started pronouncing the Dharma, to this day on which I expound the *Mahāyāna Sūtra of Immeasurable Meaning*, I have never stopped explaining suffering, emptiness, impermanence, and no self. Nor have I stopped explaining that dharmas, neither real nor unreal, neither large nor small, have never been born, nor do they die. The one appearance of all dharmas is no appearance, as dharma appearance and dharma nature are neither coming nor going. However, sentient beings continue to be driven by the four appearances they perceive [in dharmas].

"Good man, this means that Buddhas, who never speak contradictory words, can respond with one tone universally to all sounds. They each can use one body to manifest as many copies of that body as the sands of innumerable, countless billions of koṭis of nayutas of Ganges Rivers. Each copy can in turn manifest as many kinds of forms as the sands of asaṁkhyeya billions of koṭis of nayutas of Ganges Rivers. Each form can further manifest as many shapes as the sands of asaṁkhyeya billions of koṭis of nayutas of Ganges Rivers. Good man, the inconceivable profound state of Buddhas is unknowable to riders of the Two Vehicles and beyond Bodhisattvas on the Tenth Ground. It is understood only by Buddhas.

"Therefore, good man, I pronounce this wondrous, profound, unexcelled *Mahāyāna Sūtra of Immeasurable Meaning*, which is true in its principle and supreme in its dignity. It is protected by all Buddhas of the past, present, and future. No māras or non-Buddhists can enter it, nor can it be corrupted by the wrong views that perpetuate birth and death. If Bodhisattva-Mahāsattvas wish to attain the unsurpassed bodhi quickly, they should study and learn this profound, unexcelled *Mahāyāna Sūtra of Immeasurable Meaning*."

After the Buddha had finished these words, this Three-Thousand Large Thousandfold World quaked in six different ways. The sky spontaneously rained down various kinds of celestial flowers, such as utpala, padma, kumuda, and puṇḍarīka. As an offering to the Buddha and the huge multitude of Bodhisattvas and voice-hearers, innumerable kinds of celestial incense, garments, necklaces, and priceless jewels fell spiraling down from the sky. Celestial serving dishes and bowls were filled with delicacies of one hundred celestial flavors. Placed everywhere were celestial banners, flags, canopies, and musical instruments. As celestial music and songs were performed to praise the Buddha, the world again quaked in six different ways.

In the east, in Buddha Lands as numerous as the sands of the Ganges, their skies also rained down celestial flowers, incense, garments, necklaces, and priceless jewels. Their celestial serving dishes and bowls too were filled with delicacies of one hundred celestial flavors. Also placed everywhere were celestial banners, flags, canopies, and musical instruments. Celestial music and songs were performed as well, praising their Buddhas and their huge multitude of Bodhisattvas and voice-hearers. Just the same were worlds in the south, west, and north, as well as in the four in-between directions, and toward the zenith and nadir.

Then in the multitude, 32,000 Bodhisattva-Mahāsattvas attained the Samādhi of Immeasurable Meaning, and 24,000 Bodhisattva-Mahāsattvas acquired innumerable, immeasurable Dhāraṇī Doors and were enabled to turn the no-regress Dharma wheel of Buddhas of the past, present, and future. The bhikṣus, bhikṣuṇīs, upāsakas, upāsikās, gods, dragons, yakṣas, gandharvas, asuras, garuḍas, kiṁnaras, and mahoragas, as well as great Wheel-Turning Kings and lesser Wheel-Turning Kings, such as silver wheel kings and iron wheel kings, as well as kings, princes, state ministers, citizens, men, women, and elders, together with their retinues in the hundreds of thousands, having heard the Buddha pronounce this sūtra, all received benefits. Some achieved [one of the Four Preparatory Trainings:] Warmth, Pinnacle, Endurance, and Foremost in the World. Some achieved the [voice-hearer] fruits, becoming Srotāpannas, Sakṛdāgāmins, Anāgāmins, or Arhats. Some became Pratyekabuddhas. Some attained the Bodhisattva Endurance in the Realization of the No Birth of Dharmas. Some acquired one, two, three, four, five, six, seven, eight, nine, or even ten dhāraṇīs; some acquired a billion koṭi dhāraṇīs; some acquired as many dhāraṇīs as the sands of innumerable, countless asaṁkhyeyas of Ganges Rivers. All were enabled to turn the no-regress Dharma wheel. Innumerable sentient beings activated the anuttara-samyak-saṁbodhi mind.

Chapter 3
The Ten Virtues

Great Magnificence Bodhisattva-Mahāsattva next said to the Buddha, "World-Honored One, You have pronounced this wondrous, profound, unexcelled *Mahāyāna Sūtra of Immeasurable Meaning*. Truly it is very profound, very profound, very profound. Why? Because in this multitude of Bodhisattva-Mahāsattvas, Your four groups of disciples, gods, dragons, spirits, kings, state ministers, citizens, and sentient beings, having heard this profound, unexcelled *Mahāyāna Sūtra of Immeasurable Meaning*, no one has failed to acquire the Dhāraṇī Doors, the three dharmas, the four [voice-hearer] fruits, or the bodhi mind. Know that this sūtra is true in its principle and supreme in its dignity. It is protected by all Buddhas of the past, present, and future. No māras or non-Buddhists can enter it, nor can it be corrupted by the wrong views that perpetuate birth and death. Why not? Because by hearing it only once, one is enabled to uphold all Dharmas.

"If there are sentient beings that have heard this sūtra, it is to their great benefit. Why? Because if they train accordingly, they will attain anuttara-samyak-saṁbodhi quickly. If there are sentient beings that are unable to hear this sūtra, know that it is a great loss to them. Even after passing innumerable, limitless, inconceivable asaṁkhyeyas of kalpas, they still will not attain anuttara-samyak-saṁbodhi. Why not? Because not knowing the great Way to bodhi, they take perilous paths which lead to many tribulations.

"World-Honored One, this sūtra is inconceivable! I pray only that the World-Honored One, out of lovingkindness and sympathy, will broadly expound to this huge multitude the profound and inconceivable things about this sūtra. World-Honored One, where does this sūtra come from, where does it go, and where does it stay, to have such immeasurable virtue and inconceivable power, enabling sentient beings to attain anuttara-samyak-saṁbodhi quickly?"

Then the World-Honored One told Great Magnificence Bodhisattva-Mahāsattva, "Very good! Very good! Good man, indeed, indeed, it is just as you say. Good man, I say that truly this sūtra is very profound, very profound, very profound. Why? Because it enables sentient beings to attain anuttara-samyak-saṁbodhi quickly. Hearing it once enables them to uphold all Dharmas. It brings great benefits to sentient beings, and it enables them to walk the great right path without tribulations. Good man, you ask where this sūtra comes from, where it goes, and where it stays. Hearken well! Good man, this sūtra comes from the abode of Buddhas, goes to sentient beings for them to activate the bodhi mind, and stays in the action range of Bodhisattvas. Good man, this sūtra comes in this way, goes in this way, and stays in this way. Indeed, this sūtra has immeasurable virtue and inconceivable power, and can enable sentient beings to attain anuttara-samyak-saṁbodhi quickly. Good man, would you like to hear the ten inconceivable powers of this sūtra's virtue?"

Great Magnificence Bodhisattva replied, "I would be delighted to hear."

The Buddha said: "Good man, first, this sūtra can enable Bodhisattvas who have not activated the bodhi mind to activate the bodhi mind; enable those who have no lovingkindness to invoke the mind of lovingkindness; enable those who enjoy killing to awaken the mind of compassion; enable those who are jealous to open the mind of sympathetic joy; enable those who have love and attachment to cultivate the mind of equability; enable those who are miserly and greedy to unleash the mind of generosity; enable those who are arrogant to observe their precepts; enable those who are easily angered to endure [their own displeasure]; enable those who are negligent and indolent to strive for energetic progress; enable those who are disorderly to develop the meditative mind; enable those who are foolish to unfold the wisdom mind; enable those who are unable to deliver others to have the will to deliver others; enable those who do the ten evil karmas to be motivated to do the ten good karmas; enable those who delight in saṁskṛta dharmas to realize the asaṁskṛta mind; enable those with a regressive mind to invoke the mind that never regresses; enable those who discharge their afflictions to uncover the mind with no affliction to discharge; and enable those who have a great many afflictions to resolve to eradicate them. Good man, these are called the first inconceivable power of this sūtra's virtue.

"Good man, here is the second inconceivable power of this sūtra's virtue. If there are sentient beings that have acquired this sūtra, whether in its entirety or just one stanza or one verse, they will be enabled to penetrate 100,000 koṭi meanings in the Dharma which, for innumerable kalpas, they have upheld but been unable to expound. Why? Because the Dharma in this sūtra has immeasurable meaning. Good man, by analogy, a seed can produce hundreds, thousands, and tens of thousands of seeds. Each seed in turn can produce hundreds, thousands, and tens of thousands of seeds. The seeds successively produced in this way are innumerable. Likewise this sūtra expands. One Dharma gives rise to hundreds and thousands of meanings. Each meaning in turn evokes hundreds, thousands, and tens of thousands of meanings. Expanding in this way, immeasurable, boundless meanings are revealed. Therefore, this sūtra is called Immeasurable Meaning. Good man, these are called the second inconceivable power of this sūtra's virtue.

"Good man, here is the third inconceivable power of this sūtra's virtue. If there are sentient beings that have heard this sūtra, whether in its entirety or just one stanza or one verse, they will be enabled to penetrate a billion koṭi meanings. Although they still have afflictions, they will carry on as if without afflictions. They will go through birth and death without thoughts of fear. They will have sympathy for sentient beings and courage to face all dharmas. As a strong man can carry heavy loads, so too can the upholders of this sūtra shoulder the onerous undertaking to attain the unsurpassed bodhi and to carry sentient beings away from the journey of birth and death. Although they have not delivered themselves, they will be able to deliver others. As an analogy, a severely ill captain of the ship stays on this shore because of his physical disability, but he owns a sturdy ship equipped for transporting people, so he gives it to others to sail away. So too do the upholders of this sūtra. Transmigrating through the five life-paths, with their bodies fettered by 108 grave diseases, they will continue their ignorance, grow old, and die on this shore [of saṁsāra]. However, they have this sturdy *Mahāyāna Sūtra of Immeasurable Meaning* and can deliver others. Sentient beings that train according to its tenets will be delivered from [their cycle of] birth and death. Good man, these are called the third inconceivable power of this sūtra's virtue.

"Good man, here is the fourth inconceivable power of this sūtra's virtue. If there are sentient beings that have heard this sūtra, whether in its entirety or just one stanza or one verse, they will acquire bravery. Although they have not delivered themselves, they will be enabled to deliver others and to have Bodhisattvas as their spiritual family. Buddha-Tathāgatas will often expound the Dharma to them. After hearing it, they will be able to accept and uphold it accordingly, not countering it. They will in turn pronounce it widely to others where appropriate. Good man, they are like the youngest prince born to the king and queen, whether one or two or up to seven days old, whether one or two or up to seven months old, whether one or two or up to seven years old. Although he is unable to administer the affairs of the state, he is already respected by his people. He is in the company of older princes, and the king and queen, with doting love, regularly talk to him. Why? Because he is very young. Good man, fortunate as well are the upholders of this sūtra. Buddhas are the king and this sūtra is the queen. Their union gives birth to Bodhisattva-sons. If these Bodhisattvas have heard this sūtra, whether only one verse or one stanza, whether once or twice, whether ten, one hundred, one thousand, ten thousand times, or even as innumerable times as the sands of tens of thousands of koṭis of

Ganges Rivers, although they are yet unable to realize the ultimate truth, nor can they turn the great Dharma wheel with the thundering Brahma tone to shake the Three-Thousand Large Thousandfold World, they are already respected by [my] four groups of disciples and the eight classes of Dharma protectors, and have great Bodhisattvas as their spiritual family. Penetrating deeply into the secret Dharma of Buddhas, they can expound it without contradictions or faults. Because they are beginning students, they are always protected and remembered by Buddhas and embraced in their lovingkindness. Good man, these are called the fourth inconceivable power of this sūtra's virtue.

"Good man, here is the fifth inconceivable power of this sūtra's virtue. If good men and good women, during the Buddha's life or after His parinirvāṇa, accept and uphold this profound unsurpassed *Mahāyāna Sūtra of Immeasurable Meaning* and recite and copy it, they will be able to indicate the great Bodhi Way, though they are still fettered by afflictions and unable to keep away from the matters of ordinary beings. They will be able to lengthen one day to one hundred kalpas and shorten one hundred kalpas into one day, winning the appreciation and trust of sentient beings. Good man, these good men and good women are like a dragon-son who, only seven days old, already can stir up clouds and pour down rains. Good man, these are called the fifth inconceivable power of this sūtra's virtue.

"Good man, here is the sixth inconceivable power of this sūtra's virtue. If good men and good women, during the Buddha's life or after His parinirvāṇa, accept and uphold this sūtra and read and recite it, though still with afflictions, they will pronounce the Dharma to sentient beings, enabling them to stay far away from afflictions and saṁsāra and to end all suffering. Having heard it from them, sentient beings that train accordingly will acquire the Dharma, [holy] fruits, and bodhi, just as if taught by Buddha-Tathāgatas, without any difference. As an analogy, although the prince is still very young, if the king is traveling or ill, he appoints the prince to administer the affairs of the state. The prince, following the great king's order, properly commands his retinues and one hundred state ministers to proclaim the true Dharma. His kingdom and people will live in peace, just as if ruled by the great king, without any difference. The good men and good women who uphold this sūtra can do the same. Whether during the Buddha's life or after his parinirvāṇa, although they have not ascended to the First Bodhisattva Ground called Joy, they will be able to expound the teachings by relying on the Buddha's spoken words. Having heard [the teachings] from them, sentient beings that train single-mindedly will be able to eradicate their afflictions and acquire the Dharma, [holy] fruits, and even bodhi. Good man, these are called the sixth inconceivable power of this sūtra's virtue.

"Good man, here is the seventh inconceivable power of this sūtra's virtue. If good men and good women, during the Buddha's life or after His parinirvāṇa, have heard this sūtra, with joy and faith they appreciate its precious rarity. Moreover, they accept and uphold it, read and recite it, and copy and explain it; they train in accordance with the Dharma and activate the bodhi mind; and they develop their roots of goodness and invoke the mind of great compassion, resolved to deliver all suffering sentient beings. Although they have not practiced the six pāramitās, the six pāramitās will spontaneously be present before them. Then they will achieve in their present lives the Endurance in the

Realization of the No Birth of Dharmas. They will eradicate at once the afflictions of birth and death and ascend to the Seventh Ground, each assuming the position of a great Bodhisattva. By analogy, a strong man vanquishes the enemy for the king. With the enemy eliminated, the king in his delight bestows half of his kingdom upon him. Men and women who uphold this sūtra can do the same. These spiritual trainees are truly courageous and vigorous. The six pāramitās, the Dharma treasure, will come to them without their quest, the enemy—birth and death—will perish spontaneously, and they will achieve the Endurance in the Realization of the No Birth of Dharmas. They will be awarded the treasure, half of a Buddha Land, to live in peace and bliss. Good man, these are called the seventh power of this sūtra's virtue.

"Good man, here is the eighth power of this sūtra's virtue. Suppose good men and good women, during the Buddha's life or after His parinirvāṇa, having acquired this sūtra, revere and believe it, regarding it as the Buddha's body, without any difference. Delighting in this sūtra, they accept and uphold it, read and recite it, copy it, and respectfully train in accordance with the Dharma. They fortify their observance of precepts and their endurance as they practice almsgiving. Exuding profound lovingkindness and compassion, they widely pronounce to others this unexcelled *Mahāyāna Sūtra of Immeasurable Meaning*. If the hearers initially do not believe that sin and merit exist, they will show the hearers this sūtra and devise various skillful, persuasive ways to help them believe. By virtue of the awesome power of this sūtra, the minds [of nonbelievers] will be turned around. Once their faith is kindled, they will courageously make energetic progress. Because of the power and virtue of this sūtra, they will acquire the Way and achieve [holy] fruits. Moreover, these good men and good women, because of their merit of transforming others, will in their present lives achieve the Endurance in the Realization of the No Birth of Dharmas and ascend to the next higher Ground [Eighth Ground], and they will have Bodhisattvas as their spiritual family. They will enable sentient beings quickly to come to [spiritual] achievement, and they will purify Buddha Lands. Before long, they will attain the unsurpassed bodhi. Good men, these are called the eighth inconceivable power of this sūtra's virtue.

"Good man, here is the ninth inconceivable power of this sūtra's virtue. If good men and good women, during the Buddha's life or after His parinirvāṇa, have acquired this sūtra, with joy and exuberance they appreciate it as something that never existed before. If they accept and uphold it, read and recite it, copy it, make offerings to it, and explain its meaning to others, their past karmas, remaining sins, and severe hindrances will all be expunged at once. They will acquire purity and great eloquence, achieve the pāramitās one after another, and attain samādhis. Through the Śūraṅgama Samādhi, they will enter the great Door of Total Retention. Having gained the power of energetic progress, they will quickly ascend to the next higher Ground [Ninth Ground]. They will be adept in manifesting copies of their bodies everywhere in worlds in the ten directions. They will be able to rescue sentient beings in extreme suffering in the twenty-five forms of existence, enabling them to achieve liberation. Indeed, this sūtra has such powers. Good man, these are called the ninth inconceivable power of this sūtra's virtue.

"Good man, here is the tenth inconceivable power of this sūtra's virtue. Suppose good men and good women, during the Buddha's life or after His parinirvāṇa, having received this sūtra, express great joy in appreciation of its precious rarity. They not only accept and uphold it, read and recite it, copy it, make offerings to it, and train accordingly, but also convince lay and monastic people to accept and uphold it, read and recite it, copy and explain it, make offerings to it, and train in accordance with the Dharma. Those people will acquire the Way and achieve the [holy] fruit because of their training and the power of this sūtra. Their achievement is credited to the mind of lovingkindness and the power of persuasion of these good men and good women. For this reason, these good men and good women will in their present lives acquire innumerable Dhāraṇī Doors. Though still standing on the ground of ordinary beings, they will spontaneously be able to make innumerable asaṁkhyeyas of great vows to rescue with great compassion all sentient beings in suffering. They will bulk up their roots of goodness as they benefit all. Like channeling water to parched land, they will expound the Dharma as if giving Dharma medicine to sentient beings, and they will give peace and joy to all. They will gradually ascend to the Dharma Cloud Ground [Tenth Ground]. Hereupon, their charity will be universal and their lovingkindness all-encompassing, drawing suffering sentient beings to the right path. Therefore, before long, these good men and good women will attain anuttara-samyak-saṁbodhi. Good man, these are called the tenth inconceivable power of this sūtra's virtue.

"Good man, this unexcelled *Mahāyāna Sūtra of Immeasurable Meaning* has great awesome spiritual power. Supreme in its dignity, it can enable ordinary beings to achieve the holy fruit, forever free from their cycle of birth and death. Therefore, this sūtra is called Immeasurable Meaning. It can cause sentient beings on the ground of ordinary beings to germinate immeasurable Bodhisattva bodhi sprouts. It can cause their trees of merit to flourish and expand. Hence this sūtra is called *The Inconceivable Power of Virtue*."

Then Great Magnificence Bodhisattva-Mahāsattva and the 80,000 Bodhisattva-Mahāsattvas said to the Buddha with one voice: "World-Honored One, this wondrous, profound, unexcelled *Mahāyāna Sūtra of Immeasurable Meaning* pronounced by the Buddha is true in its principle and supreme in its dignity. It is protected by Buddhas of the past, present, and future. No māras or non-Buddhists can enter it, nor can it be corrupted by the wrong views that perpetuate birth and death. Hence this sūtra has these ten inconceivable powers of virtue, to give immeasurable great benefits to all sentient beings. It can enable Bodhisattva-Mahāsattvas each to attain the Samādhi of Immeasurable Meaning. Some will acquire 100,000 Dhāraṇī Doors; some will achieve endurance on the Bodhisattva Grounds; some will become Pratyekabuddhas or achieve the four [voice-hearer] fruits. World-Honored One, out of lovingkindness and sympathy, You have directly pronounced to us such teachings, giving us great Dharma benefits. This is so extraordinary, so unprecedented. The kindness and grace of the World-Honored One are truly hard to requite."

That having been said, the Three-Thousand Thousandfold World quaked in six different ways. The sky rained down various kinds of celestial flowers—utpala, padma, kumuda, and puṇḍarīka. As an offering to the Buddha and the huge multitude of Bodhisattvas and voice-hearers, various kinds of celestial incense, garments, necklaces, and priceless jewels fell spiraling down from the sky. Celestial serving dishes and bowls were filled with delicacies of one hundred celestial flavors, which gratified all with their colors and aromas. Placed everywhere were celestial banners, flags, and canopies, as well as wonderful musical instruments. As celestial music and songs were performed to praise the Buddha, the world again quaked in six different ways.

In the east, in Buddha Lands as numerous as the sands of the Ganges, their skies also rained down celestial flowers, incense, garments, necklaces, and priceless jewels. Their celestial serving dishes and bowls too were filled with delicacies of one hundred celestial flavors, which gratified all with their colors and aromas. Placed everywhere as well were celestial banners, flags, and canopies. Their wonderful celestial musical instruments also played celestial music, praising their Buddhas and their huge multitudes of Bodhisattvas and voice-hearers. Just the same were the worlds in the south, west, north, as well as in the four in-between directions, and toward the zenith and nadir.

Then the Buddha told Great Magnificence Bodhisattva-Mahāsattvas and the 80,000 Bodhisattva-Mahāsattvas: "You all should invoke the reverent mind for this sūtra and train in accordance with the Dharma. You should widely circulate this sūtra and transform all people. Day and night you should diligently protect this sūtra and enable sentient beings to receive Dharma benefits. You all truly have great lovingkindness and great compassion! Use your transcendental powers and the power of your vows to protect this sūtra. Do not allow it to be subject to doubts or blockages. Circulate it widely in Jambudvīpa far into the future and enable all sentient beings to see and hear it, read and recite it, copy it, and make offerings to it. Because of your effort, you all will be able to attain anuttara-samyak-saṁbodhi quickly."

Great Magnificence Bodhisattva and the 80,000 Bodhisattva-Mahāsattvas rose from their seats, came forward to the Buddha, and bowed their heads down at His feet. They circled the Buddha 100,000 times. Then they knelt on their right knees and said to the Buddha with one voice, "World-Honored One, we are so fortunate that the World-Honored One has bestowed His loving sympathy on us and has pronounced to us this wondrous, profound, unexcelled *Mahāyāna Sūtra of Immeasurable Meaning*. We respectfully accept the Buddha's command. After the parinirvāṇa of the Tathāgata, we will widely circulate this sūtra, enabling all to accept and uphold it, read and recite it, copy it, and make offerings to it. We pray only that the World-Honored One will not be worried. We will use the power of our vows to enable all sentient beings to acquire the awesome spiritual power of this sūtra."

The Buddha praised, "Very good! Very good! Good men, you now are truly the sons of the Buddha and are able to rescue, with great lovingkindness and great compassion, those who are in suffering and tribulations. As you widely give Dharma benefits to all, you are the good fortune field for all sentient beings, the competent guide for all sentient beings, the great refuge for all sentient beings, and the noble benefactor for all sentient beings."

All in the huge assembly greatly rejoiced. They made obeisance to the Buddha, accepted and upheld the teachings, and departed.

PART II

Ancient Translators
Prayers
Mantras

Ancient Translators

Kumārajīva

Kumārajīva (鳩摩羅什, 344–413) means youth life. He is one of the four great sūtra translators in China. He lived during the turbulent period of the Sixteen Kingdoms (304–439), which posed a threat to the Eastern Jin Dynasty (317–420). His father, Kumārāyana, was from a noble family in India, who went to Kucha (龜茲, or 庫車, in present-day Aksu Prefecture, Xinjiang, China) and married the king's sister, Princess Jīva. From their union, Kumārajīva was born.

Jīva renounced family life when Kumārajīva was seven. Mother and son traveled in India, studying under renowned Buddhist masters. Even at such a young age, Kumārajīva had already committed to memory many sūtras and texts, and his name was heard throughout the five kingdoms of India. At twelve, he traveled with his mother to Turfan (吐魯番, an oasis city in Xinjiang, China), but the king of Kucha went to Turfan to ask him to return to Kucha. So he returned to his homeland and stayed there until his destiny called.

Fujian (苻堅), ruler of the Former Qin Kingdom (前秦) in China, had heard of the marvelous Kumārajīva and wanted to bring him to China. In 382, he sent his general Luguang (呂光) to conquer Kucha. Kucha fell the next year, and Luguang captured Kumārajīva. On their way to China, Luguang got the news that Fujian had been defeated at the Battle of the Fei River. Luguang then settled in Liangzhou (涼州), in present-day Gansu Province, and founded a state called Later Liang (後涼). For seventeen years, Kumārajīva was detained there. Finally, Yaoxing (姚興), ruler of Later Qin (後秦, 384–417), conquered Later Liang and took Kumārajīva to China.

In 401, Kumārajīva arrived in Chang-an (長安), China's capital, and Yaoxing honored him as the Imperial Teacher and forced him to marry ten women for the purpose of producing descendants of his caliber. He stayed at the Xiaoyao Garden (逍遙園) and began his great translation work with a team of assistants. During the rest of his life, he translated, from Sanskrit into Chinese, seventy-four texts in 384 fascicles, including the *Amitābha Sūtra* (T12n0366), *Mahā-prajñā-pāramitā Sūtra* (T08n0223), the *Diamond Sūtra* (T08n0235), the *Heart Sūtra* (T08n0250), the *Lotus Sūtra* (T09n0262), the *Vimalakīrti-nirdeśa Sūtra* (T14n0475), and the *Brahma Net Sūtra* (T24n1484), as well as treatises, such as the *Mahā-prajñā-pāramitā-śāstra* (T25n1509), the *Mūlamadhyamaka-kārikā* (T30n1564), and the *Dvādaśanikāya-śāstra* (T30n1568), authored by Ācārya Nāgārjuna (龍樹菩薩, circa 150–250).

Kumārajīva's fluid and elegant translations greatly contributed to the propagation of the Dharma in China. Before his death, he said that if his translations were truthful, his tongue would not be destroyed by fire. After cremation of his body, indeed, his tongue was found intact.

Guṇabhadra

Guṇabhadra (求那跋陀羅, 394–468) means merit worthy (功德賢). He was from central India. Being in the Brahmin caste, he started the five studies as a child, and learned astrology, literature, medicine, and mantra practices. After studying the *Heart Treatise on the Abhidharma*, he turned to the teachings of the Buddha, renounced family life, and became a fully ordained monk.

Guṇabhadra first studied the Tripiṭaka of the Small Vehicle, then Mahāyāna teachings. With profound understanding of the *Mahā-Prajñā-Pāramitā Sūtra* and the *Mahāvaipulya Sūtra of Buddha Adornment*, he began to teach. He even converted his father to Buddhism.

In 435, the twelfth year of the Yuanjia (元嘉) years of the Liu Song Dynasty (劉宋, 420–79), Guṇabhadra went to China by sea. Emperor Wen (文帝) sent an emissary to welcome and take him to the Qihuan Temple (祇洹寺) in Jiankang (建康), present-day Nanjing. With the help of Huiyan (慧嚴), Huiguan (慧觀), and student monks, he translated the Saṁyukta Āgama (T02n0099) in 50 fascicles.

Guṇabhadra's life in China spanned the reigns of three emperors—Wen, Xiaowu, and Ming (文帝、孝武帝、明帝)—and he was highly revered by all of them. Because of his contribution to the Mahāyāna teachings, people called him Mahāyāna. Altogether, he translated, from Sanskrit into Chinese, fifty-two sūtras in 134 fascicles, including the *Sūtra of the Great Dharma Drum* (T09n0270), the *Śrīmālādevi Sūtra* (T12n0353), the 4-fascicle version of the *Laṅkāvatāra Sūtra* (T16n0670), and the mantra for rebirth in Amitābha Buddha's Pure Land (Mantra 5). Guṇabhadra died in 468, at the age of seventy-five. On the day he died, he saw celestial flowers and the holy images of Amitābha Buddha and His retinue.

Dharmagatayaśas

Dharmagatayaśas (曇摩伽陀耶舍, 5th–6th centuries) means Dharma come to renown (法生稱). He was a Buddhist monk from central India, who could write Chinese. In 481, the third year of the Jianyuan (建元) years of the Xiao Qi Dynasty (蕭齊, 479–501, second of the four successive Southern Dynasties), at the Chaoting Temple (朝亭寺) in Guangzhou (廣州), Guangdong Province, he translated, from Sanskrit into Chinese, the *Sūtra of Immeasurable Meaning* (T09n0276). Nothing more is known about him.

Bodhiruci

Bodhiruci (菩提留支, 5th–6th centuries) means bodhi splendor. A Buddhist master from northern India, he was versed in mantra practices and the Tripiṭaka. Aspiring to propagate the Dharma, in 502, the first year of the Yongping (永平) years of the Northern Wei Dynasty (386–534), he arrived in Luoyang (洛陽), China's capital. Emperor Xuanwu (魏宣武帝) valued him highly and commanded him to stay in the Yongning Temple (永寧寺) to translate Sanskrit texts into Chinese. He translated thirty-nine texts in 127 fascicles, including the *Diamond*

Sūtra (T08n0236), the *Buddha Name Sūtra* (T14n0440), the 10-fascicle version of the *Laṅkāvatāra Sūtra* (T16n0671), the *Sūtra of the Profound Secret Liberation* (T16n0675), the *Sūtra of Neither Increase Nor Decrease* (T16n0668), and the *Dharma Collection Sūtra* (T17n0761), as well as treatises, such as the *Treatise on the Ten Grounds Sūtra* (T26n1522), the *Treatise on the Great Treasure Pile Sūtra* (T26n1523), and the *Upadeśa on the Sūtra of Amitāyus Buddha* (T26n1524). After 537, Bodhiruci was not seen again.

Bodhiruci expressed his unique view on the Buddha's teachings. Based on the *Mahāparinirvāṇa Sūtra* (T12n0374), he said that, for the first twelve years, the Buddha gave only half-worded teachings, followed afterward by fully-worded teachings. Bodhiruci also proposed the one tone theory, saying that the Buddha pronounces teachings in one tone, and sentient beings come to a variety of understandings according to their capacities. Furthermore, based on the *Laṅkāvatāra Sūtra,* he proposed the distinction between immediate and gradual enlightenment.

Vinītaruci

Vinītaruci (毘尼多流支, ?–594) means subdued pleasure (滅喜). He was born in the sixth century, in southern India. In 574, the sixth year of the Taijian (太建) years of the Chen Dynasty (557–89, the last of the four Southern Dynasties), he went to Chang-an (長安), China, in search of the Dharma. He met Sengcan (僧璨, dates unknown), the third patriarch of the Chan School, in Ye County (鄴縣), Hunan Province, who imparted to him the Mind Seal and commanded him to go to southern China to deliver the multitudes.

He then went down south to Guangdong Province and became the abbot of the Zhizhie Temple (制止寺) in the city of Guangzhou (廣州). There he translated, from Sanskrit into Chinese, the *Mahāyāna Vaipulya Sūtra of Total Retention* (T09n0275) and the *Buddha Pronounces the Sūtra of the Elephant Head Ashram* (T14n0466).

In 580, the twelfth year of the Taijian years, Vinītaruci went to northern Vietnam and became the abbot of the Fayun Temple (法雲寺). He started his Vinītaruci Chan School and propagated the Dharma in Vietnam for over ten years until his death in 594, during the Sui Dynasty (581–619). His teachings included that true suchness and Buddha nature are never born and never die and that all sentient beings have the same nature of true suchness. The Vinītaruci Chan School prospered in Vietnam for over six hundred years. His disciple Faxian (法賢, ?–626) was the first patriarch, who successively passed the lineage down to Yishan (依山, ?–1216). Then this Chan School declined into obscurity.

Xuanzang

Xuanzang (玄奘, 600– or 602–64) was a Tripiṭaka master in the Tang Dynasty (618–907). He is well known and revered in China for his overland trip to India and his translating into Chinese the voluminous Sanskrit texts he brought back from India. Xuanzang was a native of Henan Province, China. His secular name was Chen Hui (陳褘). He lived for five years with his elder brother, who was a monk at the Jingtu Monastery (淨土寺) in Luoyang (洛陽), China's capital in the Sui Dynasty (581–618). Xuanzang studied both Theravāda and Mahāyāna texts and became a novice monk at the age of thirteen. During the chaos in the transition from the Sui Dynasty to the Tang Dynasty, the two brothers traveled widely in China, and then they studied the Abhidharma under Buddhist masters Daoji, Baoqian, and Zhenfa (道基、寶遷、震法). In 622, Xuanzang was fully ordained as a monk.

Dissatisfied with the discrepancies and contradictions in available texts, Xuanzang vowed to bring more texts from India. He began his pilgrimage in 627 or 629, traveling alone to the west by way of the so-called Silk Roads, encountering many Buddhist monasteries and holy sites. He arrived in the Indian kingdom of Magadha in 631 or 633. He studied under Master Śīlabhadra (戒賢) at the Nālandā Monastery for five years, learning logic, the *Yogācārya-bhūmi-śāstra* [Treatise on the yoga teacher ground], the *Mūlamadhyamaka-kārikā* [Middle treatise], and other texts. Xuanzang then traveled widely in India, visiting renowned masters and collecting scriptural texts.

When Xuanzang returned to the monastery, Master Śīlabhadra ordered him to expound the *Mahāyāna-Saṁparigraha-śāstra* [Treatise on accepting the Mahāyāna], authored by Asaṅga, and other treatises. He then composed thousands of verses, which refuted the views of two Indian masters who opposed to the Yogācāra and the Mahāyāna, and his name spread throughout the five kingdoms of India. The king Śīlāditya (戒日王) sponsored an assembly of debate in the city of Kānyakubja (曲女城) and appointed Xuanzang the master presiding over the forum. This renowned assembly was attended by the eighteen kings of the five kingdoms of India as well as Brahmins and about seven thousand Buddhist monks of both the Theravāda and the Mahāyāna Schools. Xuanzang posted outside the gate his essay entitled "The True Measure of Consciousness-Only." For eighteen days, no one was able to debate his statement. After the assembly ended, the eighteen kings respectfully took refuge under Xuanzang. As a farewell event in honor of Xuanzang, the king Śīlāditya invited the eighteen kings to launch the quinquennial Unreserved Assembly for Almsgiving (無遮布施大會). For seventy-five days, whether monastic or secular, all participants were given alms in the form of the Dharma and of life-supporting goods.

Xuanzang departed India in 643 and arrived in 645 in Chang-an (長安), China's capital in the Tang Dynasty. His round trip to India took seventeen years, covering 50,000 lis (about 25,000 kilometers). He brought back many Buddha statues and 150 Buddha relics, and 657 Sanskrit texts. He was revered by Emperor Taizong (唐太宗), who honored him as the Tripiṭaka Dharma Master. For the following nineteen years, Xuanzang translated, from Sanskrit into Chinese, seventy-five sūtras and treatises, in 1,335 fascicles, including the *Mahā-prajnā-sūtra* (T05n0220) in 600 fascicles, the *Yogācārya-bhūmi-śāstra* (T30n1579) in 100 fascicles, the *Mahā-bhūmi-vibhāṣā-śāstra* (T27n1545) in 200 fascicles, and more. His book *Datang xiyuji* 大唐西域記 (T51n2087), which means journey to the West in the great Tang Dynasty, has great historical value as a major source for the study of the culture and geography of medieval India and central Asia.

Xuanzang died in the second month of 664. Emperor Kaozong (唐高宗) was so grieved that he did not go to court for three days. He ordered a memorial pagoda to be erected to enshrine Xuanzang's relics, which later were moved to another pagoda in Nanjing. This pagoda was destroyed during the Rebellion of Great Peace (太平天國, 1859–64). Finally, during the Sino-Japanese War (1937–45), the Japanese troops occupying Nanjing found the relics when they dug the ground to repair the road. They took the relics to Japan and later returned to China a part of the skull, which is now enshrined in the Xuanzang Temple in Taiwan.

Xuanzang's study and translation of texts on Yogācāra (瑜伽行派), or the consciousness-only doctrine (唯識), led to the founding of the Faxiang (dharma appearance) School (法相宗), and his foremost disciple, Kuiji (窺基), is recognized as the first patriarch. Although this school soon declined in China, its tenets have had far-reaching influence in the development of Mahāyāna Buddhism in East Asia.

Divākara

Divākara (地婆訶羅, 613–87), or Rizhao (日照) in Chinese, was born in central India in the Brahmin caste. He became a monk when he was just a child, and he spent many years at the Mahābodhi Temple and the Nālandā Monastery. He was an accomplished Tripiṭaka master, excelled in the five studies and especially in mantra practices.

Already in his sixties, Divākara went to Chang-an (長安), China, in 676, the first year of the Yifeng (儀鳳) years of the Tang Dynasty (618–907). Emperor Gaozong (唐高宗) treated him as respectfully as he had treated the illustrious Tripiṭaka master Xuanzang. In 680, the first year of the Yonglong (永隆) years, the emperor commanded ten learned monks to assist Divākara in translating sūtras from Sanskrit into Chinese. In six years Divākara translated eighteen sūtras, including the *Sūtra of the Buddha-Crown Superb Victory Dhāraṇī* (T19n0970), the *Sūtra of the Great Cundī Dhāraṇī* (T20n1077), and the *Mahāyāna Sūtra of Consciousness Revealed* (T12n0347). Longing to see his mother again, he petitioned for permission to go home. Unfortunately, although permission was granted, he fell ill and died in the twelfth month of 687, the third year of the Chuigong (垂拱) years, at the age of seventy-five. Empress Wu (武后則天) had him buried properly at the Xiangshan Monastery (香山寺) in Luoyang (洛陽).

Dharmacandra

Dharmacandra (法月, 653–743) is known to be from either eastern India or the kingdom of Magadha in central India. He traveled widely in central India and was accomplished in medical arts and the Tripiṭaka. Then he went to the kingdom of Kucha (龜茲, or 庫車, in present-day Aksu Prefecture, Xinjiang, China), where he taught his disciple Zhenyue (真月) and others.

At the written recommendation of Lu Xiulin (呂休林), the governor appointed to keep peace with the western region (安西節度使), in 732, the twentieth year of the Kaiyuan (開元) years of Emperor Xuanzong (唐玄宗) of the Tang Dynasty (618–907), Dharmacandra arrived in Chang-an (長安), China. As an offering to the Emperor, he presented Sanskrit texts on alchemy and herbal remedies, as well as the *Sūtra of the Mighty Vidya King Ucchuṣma* (T21n1227), translated by Ajitasena, who was from northern India. With the help of his disciple Liyan (利言), Dharmacandra translated into Chinese the Sanskrit text of herbal remedies as well as of the *Sūtra of the All-Encompassing Knowledge Store, the Heart of Prajñā-Pāramitā* (T08n0252).

During an uprising in China, Dharmacandra moved to the kingdom of Yutian (于闐), or Khotan, present-day Hetian (和田), in Xinjiang, China. He stayed at the Golden Wheel Temple (金輪寺), teaching people attracted to him, until his death in 743, at the age of ninety-one.

Amoghavajra

Amoghavajra (不空金剛, 705–74) is referred to as Not Empty Vajra in China. He is the sixth patriarch in the Buddhist esoteric lineage. Born in the Lion Kingdom, present-day Sri Lanka, in southern India, he traveled in his youth with his uncle. Later he renounced family life and studied under Vajrabodhi (金剛智), who took him to Luoyang (洛陽) in 720, the eighth year of the Kaiyuan (開元) years of Emperor Xuanzong (唐玄宗) of the Tang Dynasty (618–907). Amoghavajra was then sixteen. Another version of the story goes that he was the son of a Brahmin in northern India. Orphaned as a child, he went to China with his uncle and then studied under Vajrabodhi.

At twenty, Amoghavajra was fully ordained at the Guangfu Temple (廣福寺) in Luoyang (洛陽). Exceptionally intelligent, he was well regarded by his teacher Vajrabodhi, who imparted to him all five divisions of the teachings on the three secrets: body, voice, and mind. After Vajrabodhi died, Amoghavajra, honoring his teacher's instruction, set out for India in search of the esoteric Dharma. Together with Hanguang (含光), Huibian (慧辯), and others, he traveled by sea. He first visited Sri Lanka and received from Nāgabodhi (龍智) the Vajra Summit Yoga, which had been initially imparted in eighteen assemblies, and the Mahāvairocana Great Compassion Store, as well as the Five-Division Empowerment, the *Secret Book of Mantras*, and some five hundred sūtras and treatises. He also received teachings on the secret mudrās of the deities. After traveling extensively across the five regions of India, Amoghavajra returned to Chang-an (長安), China's capital, in 746, the fifth year of the Tianbao (天寶) years. There he gave an esoteric empowerment to Emperor Xuanzong (唐玄宗). Later on, the emperor named him Knowledge Store and bestowed upon him the purple robe because his practice successfully brought rainfall.

In 771, the sixth year of the Dali (大曆) years of Emperor Daizong (唐代宗), Amoghavajra presented his Chinese translations of seventy-seven Sanskrit texts in 101 fascicles with a table of contents, and requested to have them included in the Tripiṭaka. Then the emperor conferred upon him a title, Great Vast Knowledge Tripiṭaka Master. In the sixth month of 774, sensing that his time was due, Amoghavajra wrote the emperor a farewell letter and offered his ritual objects, a bell and a five-spoke vajra. Lying on his side, he died at the age of seventy. A memorial pagoda was erected at the Daxingshan Temple (大興善寺), for keeping his relics.

Kumārajīva (鳩摩羅什, 344–413), Paramārtha (真諦, 499–569), Xuanzang (玄奘, 600– or 602–64), and Amoghavajra (不空金剛, 705–74) are honored in China as the four great translators, who contributed greatly to establishing the correspondence between Sanskrit and Chinese in sounds and rhythms. Subhakara-Siṁha (善無畏, 637–735), Vajrabodhi (金剛智, 671?–741), and Amoghavajra are called the Three Great Ones during the Kaiyuan (開元) years. Amoghavajra's Chinese disciple Huiguo (惠果, 746–805) received full impartation of the Dharma from him and became the seventh patriarch, the last one in China. During their days, the Esoteric School of Buddhism flourished in China. Then the esoteric lineage was carried on by Huiguo's Japanese disciple Konghai (空海, 774–835), who became the first patriarch of the True Word School (Mantra School) in Japan, which has thrived to this day.

Fatian

Born in central India, Fatian (法天, ?–1001), or Dharmadeva, had been a monk in the Nālandā Monastery in the kingdom of Magadha. In 973, the sixth year of the Kaibao (開寶) years of the Northern Song Dynasty (960–1127), he went to China and stayed in Pujin (蒲津), in Lu County (漉州). He translated, from Sanskrit into Chinese, the *Sūtra of the Dhāraṇī of Infinite-Life Resolute Radiance King Tathāgata* (T19n0937), the *Stanzas in Praise of the Seven Buddhas* (T32n1682), and other texts. His translations were recorded and edited by Fajin (法進), an Indian monk of the Kaiyuan Temple (開元寺) in Hezhongfu (河中府).

In 980, the fifth year of the Taiping-Xinguo (太平興國) years, the county official presented a written recommendation of Fatian to Emperor Taizong (宋太宗). Very pleased with what he read in the report, the emperor summoned Fatian to the capital city and bestowed upon him the purple robe. Furthermore, he decreed the building of an institute for sūtra translation. In 982, at the command of the emperor, Fatian, Tianxizai (天息災), Shihu (施護), and others moved into the institute, starting to translate into Chinese the Sanskrit texts each had brought. In the seventh month, Fatian completed his translation of the *Mahāyāna Sūtra of the Holy Auspicious Upholding-the-World Dhāranī* (T20n1164). Then the emperor named him Great Master of the Teachings. Between 982 and 1000, he translated forty-six sūtras. Fatian died in 1001, the fourth year of the Xianping (咸平) years, his age unknown. The emperor conferred upon him a posthumous title, Great Master of Profound Enlightenment.

Prayers

1 Opening the Sūtra 開經偈

The unsurpassed, profound true Dharma
無上甚深微妙法
Is hard to encounter in billions of kalpas.
百千萬劫難遭遇
This I now have seen and heard, and can accept and uphold,
我今見聞得受持
Hoping to understand the true meaning of the Tathāgatas.
願解如來真實義

2 Transferring Merit 回向偈

May the merit of my practice
願以此功德
Adorn Buddhas' Pure Lands,
莊嚴佛淨土
Requite the fourfold kindness from above,
上報四重恩
And relieve the suffering of the three life-journeys below.
下濟三途苦
Universally wishing sentient beings,
普願諸眾生
Friends, foes, and karmic creditors,
冤親諸債主
All to activate the bodhi mind,
悉發菩提心
And all to be reborn in the Land of Ultimate Bliss.
同生極樂國

3 The Four Vast Vows 四弘誓願

Sentient beings are countless; I vow to deliver them all.
眾生無邊誓願度
Afflictions are endless; I vow to eradicate them all.
煩惱無盡誓願斷
Dharma Doors are measureless; I vow to learn them all.
法門無量誓願學
Buddha bodhi is unsurpassed; I vow to attain it.
佛道無上誓願成

4 The Universally Worthy Vow of the Ten Great Actions
普賢十大行願

First, make obeisance to Buddhas.
一者禮敬諸佛
Second, praise Tathāgatas.
二者稱讚如來
Third, make expansive offerings.
三者廣修供養
Fourth, repent of karma, the cause of hindrances.
四者懺悔業障
Fifth, express sympathetic joy over others' merits.
五者隨喜功德
Sixth, request Buddhas to turn the Dharma wheel.
六者請轉法輪
Seventh, beseech Buddhas to abide in the world.
七者請佛住世
Eighth, always follow Buddhas to learn.
八者常隨佛學
Ninth, forever support sentient beings.
九者恒順衆生
Tenth, universally transfer all merits to others.
十者普皆迴向

5 Always Walking the Bodhisattva Way 常行菩薩道

May the three kinds of hindrances and all afflictions be annihilated.
願消三障諸煩惱
May I gain wisdom and true understanding.
願得智慧真明了
May all hindrances caused by sin be removed.
普願罪障悉消除
May I always walk the Bodhisattva Way, life after life.
世世常行菩薩道

6 Repenting of All Sins 懺悔偈

The evil karmas I have done with my body, voice, and mind are caused by greed, anger, and delusion, which are without a beginning in time. Before Buddhas I now supplicate for my repentance.
往昔所造諸惡業，皆由無始貪瞋癡，從身語意之所生。今對佛前求懺悔。
The evil karmas I have done with my body, voice, and mind are caused by greed, anger, and delusion, which are without a beginning in time. I repent of all sins, the cause of hindrances.
往昔所造諸惡業，皆由無始貪瞋癡，從身語意之所生。一切罪障皆懺悔。

The evil karmas I have done with my body, voice, and mind are caused by greed, anger, and delusion, which are without a beginning in time. I repent of all the roots of sin.
往昔所造諸惡業，皆由無始貪瞋癡，從身語意之所生。一切罪根皆懺悔。

7 Wishing to Be Reborn in the Pure Land 願生淨土

I wish to be reborn in the Western Pure Land.
願生西方淨土中
I wish to have as my parents a lotus flower in nine grades.
九品蓮花爲父母
When the flower opens, I will see that Buddha and realize that dharmas have no birth,
花開見佛悟無生
And I will have as my companions the Bodhisattvas who never regress.
不退菩薩爲伴侶

8 Supplicating to Be Reborn in the Pure Land 求生淨土

I single-mindedly take refuge in Amitābha Buddha in the World of Ultimate Bliss. Illuminate me with Your pure light and draw me in with Your loving, kind vows. Thinking only of You, I now call the name of the Tathāgata. For the sake of the Bodhi Way, I supplicate to be reborn in Your Pure Land.
一心皈命極樂世界阿彌陀佛。願以淨光照我、慈誓攝我。我今正念稱如來名，爲菩提道求生淨土。
Before this Buddha attained Buddhahood in the past, he made a vow: "Suppose there are sentient beings that, with earnest faith and delight, wish to be reborn in my land, even if by only thinking ten thoughts. If they should fail to be reborn there, I would not attain the perfect enlightenment."
佛昔本誓：若有眾生欲生我國，志心信樂乃至十念，若不生者不取正覺。
My thinking of this Buddha is why I have gained entrance into the Tathāgata's ocean of great vows. By the power of this Buddha's lovingkindness, my sins will be expunged and my roots of goodness will grow stronger. At the end of my life, I will know the coming of my time. My body will have no illness or suffering. My heart will have no greed or attachments. My mind will not be demented but will be peaceful as if in meditative concentration. This Buddha, holding a golden lotus-borne platform in His hands, together with a holy multitude, will come to receive me. In the instant of a thought, I will be reborn in the Land of Ultimate Bliss. When the lotus flower opens, I will see this Buddha and hear the Buddha Vehicle, and my Buddha wisdom will immediately unfold. I will widely deliver sentient beings, fulfilling my bodhi vow.
以此念佛因緣，得入如來大誓海中。承佛慈力，眾罪消滅、善根增長。若臨命終，自知時至。身無病苦、心不貪戀、意不顛倒，如入禪定。佛及聖眾手執金臺來迎接我。於一念頃，生極樂國。華開見佛，即聞佛乘、頓開佛慧、廣度眾生滿菩提願。

Homage to all Buddhas of the past, present, and future, in worlds in the ten directions!
Homage to all Bodhisattva-Mahāsattvas!
Homage to mahā-prajñā-pāramitā!
十方三世一切佛。一切菩薩摩訶薩。摩訶般若波羅蜜。

9 Ascending the Golden Steps 上金階

In the ocean-like lotus pond assembly, seated on lotus-borne platforms are Amitābha Tathāgata and Bodhisattvas Avalokiteśvara and Great Might Arrived, who welcome me to ascend the golden steps. I majestically declare my great vows, wishing to leave all afflictions behind.
蓮池海會，彌陀如來觀音勢至坐蓮臺，接引上金階。大誓弘開，普願離塵埃。

Homage to Buddhas and Bodhisattvas in the ocean-like lotus pond assembly! (Repeat three times.)
蓮池海會佛菩薩 (三稱)

10 Praising Amitābha Buddha 讚阿彌陀佛

Amitābha Buddha in a golden body is
阿彌陀佛身金色
Unsurpassed in His excellent appearance and radiance.
相好光明無等倫
The curling white hair between His eyebrows is like five Sumeru Mountains.
白毫宛轉五須彌
His blue eyes are as clear as four great oceans.
紺目澄清四大海
Present in His radiance are innumerable koṭis of magically manifested Buddhas
光中化佛無數億
And countless magically manifested Bodhisattvas.
化菩薩眾亦無邊
He has made forty-eight vows to deliver sentient beings,
四十八願度眾生
Enabling them to arrive in nine grades at the opposite shore.
九品咸令登彼岸

Namo Amitābha Buddha of great lovingkindness and great compassion, in the Western Land of Ultimate Bliss!
Namo Amitābha Buddha! (Say these words or "namo amituo fo" as many times as one wishes.)
南無西方極樂世界。大慈大悲阿彌陀佛。
南無阿彌陀佛 (多稱)

Mantras

At that time the great Brahma-king rose from his seat and arranged his attire. Joining his palms respectfully, he said to Avalokiteśvara Bodhisattva, "Very good! Great One, I have attended innumerable assemblies of the Buddha and have heard various kinds of Dharmas and various kinds of dhāraṇīs. Never have I heard such wonderful phrases as in this Hindrance-Free Great Compassion-Mind Dhāraṇī. Great One, please tell us the features and characteristics of this dhāraṇī. This large assembly and I would be delighted to hear them."

Avalokiteśvara Bodhisattva said to the Brahma-king, "For the convenience and benefit of all sentient beings, you ask me this question. Now hearken well! I will briefly tell you all a few of them."

Avalokiteśvara Bodhisattva said, "They are the great loving-kind, compassionate mind, the equality mind, the asaṁskṛta mind, the no-attachment mind, the emptiness-seeing mind, the reverent mind, the humble mind, the unflustered mind, the not-taking-wrong-views mind, and the unsurpassed bodhi mind. You should know that such minds are the features of this dhāraṇī. Accordingly you should cultivate yourselves."

—Sūtra of the Vast, Perfect, Hindrance-Free Great Compassion-Mind Dhāraṇī of the Thousand-Hand Thousand-Eye Avalokiteśvara Bodhisattva
Translated from the Chinese Canon (T20n1060, 0108a4–15)

How to Recite a Mantra

The features of the Great Compassion-Mind Dhāraṇī are true for all the mantras pronounced by Buddhas and Bodhisattvas. One would be wise to cultivate these features whether one recites a mantra, studies a sūtra, or carries on one's daily life.

Those who have contact with Tibetan Tantrism may have some concern about receiving "transmission" of a mantra from a "highly realized" lama, vested with the authority of a certain lineage. This has never been a problem in the Mahāyāna tradition. First, the Buddha has always instructed us to do our best to disseminate the mantras which He has imparted in His teachings. Second, the aspiration to recite a mantra arises from one's own Buddha mind, one's root lama. Can one find a lama higher than the Buddha or one's own Buddha mind? Given the mantra texts, one can feel authorized to enjoy mantra recitation with a peaceful and grateful mind, in addition to those minds taught by Avalokiteśvara Bodhisattva.

The mantras on the following pages contain compound words. A compound word in Sanskrit can be overwhelmingly long. To show the components of a compound word, whether created by the rule of pronunciation or other rules, hyphens are used to connect the components. For example, tathāgatāya-arhate actually should be written and pronounced as tathāgatāyārhate, bodhimaṇḍa-alaṁkāra-alaṁkṛte as bodhimaṇḍālaṁkārālaṁkṛte, sama-āśvāsa-adhiṣṭhite as samāśvāsādhiṣṭhite, and yogi-īśvarāya as yogīśvarāya. By comparing a compound word with its components, one can see that two vowels, short or long, connected by a hyphen are merged into one long vowel. One should pronounce a compound word as one word, but it is possible to steal a breath, if needed, after a long syllable.

A mantra has boundless meanings if the meanings of the words are not known. However, some of the mantra words are well known to Buddhist students, and this knowledge by no means diminishes the power of the mantra. Sanskrit students interested in the meanings of mantra words can consult the Monier-Williams Sanskrit Dictionary.

Introduction to the Eleven Mantras

Dhāraṇī, often in the form of a long mantra, means total retention, the power to unite all dharmas and hold all meanings. Mantras 2, 4, 5, and 7 are included in the ten short mantras that Chinese Buddhists recite in their morning recitation practice.

Mantras 1–4 are dhāraṇīs in one-to-one correspondence with those in Sūtras 1–4, in which the Buddha has explained in detail their use and power.

Mantras 5 and 6 are the mantras for rebirth in Amitābha Buddha's Pure Land, and they are referred to as the Rebirth Mantras. The Chinese version of Mantra 5 is in text 368 (T12n0368, 0351c8–12), which was translated into Chinese by Guṇabhadra (求那跋陀羅, 394–468) from central India. In group practice, Chinese Buddhists usually recite this mantra three times immediately after their recitation of the *Heart Sūtra* or the *Amitābha Sūtra*. Not well known to them is Mantra 6, the longer of the two Rebirth Mantras. The Chinese version of this mantra is in text 930 (T19n0930, 0071b5–18), which was translated into Chinese by Amoghavajra (不空金剛, 705–774) from present-day Sri Lanka.

Mantra 7 is based on the *Sūtra of the Original Vows of the Seven Medicine Buddhas*, in text 451 (T14n0451, 0414b29–c3). This mantra is imparted by the seventh Medicine Buddha called Vaiḍūrya Light King Tathāgata, after He has pronounced His twelve great vows. The popular Tibetan version differs in its last phrase, which is given below for comparison.

tad-yathā oṁ bhaiṣajye bhaiṣajye mahā-bhaiṣajye rāja samudgate svāhā ||

Tibetan Buddhists and Chinese Buddhists have been reciting their respective versions of this mantra for centuries. Their testimonies provide evidence for the healing power of this mantra in both versions.

Mantra 8 is the heart mantra of the complete dhāraṇī in text 944A (T19n0944A, 0102c12–15). Another version is found in the *Śūraṅgama Sūtra* (T19n0945), which was translated into Chinese by Pramiti (般剌蜜帝, 7th–8th centuries) from central India. Although the full name of this dhāraṇī is Tathāgata-Crown White Umbrella Unsurpassed Subjugation Dhāraṇī, Chinese

Buddhists just call it the Śūraṅgama Mantra because it is in the *Śūraṅgama Sūtra*. The Buddha describes in this sūtra the inconceivable power of this dhāraṇī to annihilate hindrances, eradicate one's afflictions, and facilitate one's attainment of Buddhahood. Many Chinese Buddhists are able to recite from memory the complete dhāraṇī in their morning recitation practice. The good news is that its heart mantra, the last few phrases of the complete dhāraṇī, is just as powerful and efficacious as the full version. It is recommended that one recite it twenty-one times a day.

Mantra 9 is copied from chapter 26 of the 27-chapter *Lotus Sūtra* on the website of the Digital Sanskrit Buddhist Canon. Its corresponding Chinese version is in the 28-chapter *Lotus Sūtra* (T09n0262, 0061b19–27), fascicle 7, chapter 28. Samantabhadra Bodhisattva pledges to the Buddha that he will safeguard the *Lotus Sūtra*, and protect and comfort those who recite and uphold this sūtra. Those who have heard his mantra will know the awesome spiritual power of Samantabhadra Bodhisattva and be able to carry out his worthy actions as well.

Mantra 10 is copied from Answers.com, and differs from the popular Chinese version in the *Sūtra of the Vast, Perfect, Hindrance-Free Great Compassion-Mind Dhāraṇī of the Thousand-Hand Thousand-Eye Avalokiteśvara Bodhisattva* (T20n1060, 0107b25–c25). Well known for its healing power, this Great Compassion Mantra is most popular among Chinese Buddhists, as Guanyin (Avalokiteśvara) is their favorite Bodhisattva.

Different Chinese versions of this mantra are in texts 1061–64, 1111, 1113A, and 1113B. Texts 1061 and 1113B each include a Siddham version of this mantra. However, these texts are too corrupt to transliterate into Sanskrit. There exists an English version of this mantra, phonetically translated from the version in text 1060. As intended, it sounds like Chinese.

In this sūtra, Avalokiteśvara Bodhisattva teaches us to make a vow to attain the ultimate enlightenment and rescue other sentient beings with great compassion. One should chant his name and Amitābha Buddha's name, then recite this mantra. Upon completion of only five repetitions of this mantra, one's grave sins, which would entail 100,000 koṭi kalpas of birth and death, will all be expunged. If one recites this spiritual mantra as one's regular practice, upon one's death, Buddhas will come from worlds in the ten directions to extend their helping hands, and one will be reborn in a Buddha Land according to one's wish. Recitation of this mantra will be the distant cause for one's ultimate attainment of bodhi. On the worldly plane, those who recite this mantra will not die an evil death, and they will live a good life with fifteen benefits. Not only can they ward off evil forces by reciting this mantra, but Avalokiteśvara Bodhisattva will dispatch guards to protect them from such forces.

Mantra 11 is the Prajñā-Pāramitā Mantra included in any version of the *Heart Sūtra*. The Sanskrit word *pāramita* means gone across to the opposite shore. This mantra affirms the crossing—from "gate gate" (gone, gone) to "pāragate" (gone across to the opposite shore), then to "pāra-saṁgate" (completely gone across to the opposite shore)—and ends with "bodhi svāhā" (enlightenment hail). This crossing is achieved through one's prajñā (wisdom) in the true reality of all dharmas.

Corrections of typographical or grammatical errors in the source texts of these mantras are bolded and italicized.

The Eleven Mantras

1 Buddha-Crown Superb Victory Dhāraṇī (Uṣnīṣa vijaya dhāraṇī) 佛頂尊勝陀羅尼

namo bhagavate trai-lokya prativiśiṣṭāya buddhāya bhagavate | tad-yathā oṁ viśodhaya viśodhaya | asamasama samanta-avabhāsa spharaṇa gati gahana svabhāva viśuddhe | abhiṣiñcatu māṁ | sugata vara vacana | amṛta-abhi***ṣeke*** mahāmantra ***pāne*** | āhara āhara āyuḥ sandhāraṇi | śodhaya śodhaya gagana viśuddhe | uṣṇīṣa vijaya viśuddhe | sahasra-raśmi saṁcodite | sarva tathāgata-avaloka***na*** ṣaṭ-pāramitā paripūraṇi | sarva tathāgata hṛdaya-adhiṣṭhāna-adhiṣṭhita mahāmudre | vajra-kāya saṁha***ra***ṇa viśuddhe | sarva-āvaraṇa-apāya-durgati pari-viśuddhe | prati-nivartaya-āyuḥ śuddhe | samaya-adhiṣṭhite maṇi maṇi mahāmaṇi | ta***thātā*** bhūta koṭi pariśuddhe | visphuṭa buddhi śuddhe | jaya jaya vijaya vijaya smara smara | sarva buddha-adhiṣṭhita śuddhe | vajre vajra-garbhe vajraṁ bhavatu mama śarīraṁ | sarva sattvānāṁ ca kāya pari-viśuddhe | sarva gati pariśuddhe | sarva tathāgatāśca me sama-āśvāsayantu | sarva tathāgata sama-āśvāsa-adhiṣṭhite | budhya budhya vibudhya vibudhya | bodhaya bodhaya vibodhaya vibodhaya | samanta pariśuddhe | sarva tathāgata hṛdaya-adhiṣṭhāna-adhiṣṭhita mahāmudre svāhā ||

The Heart Mantra
oṁ amṛta tejovati svāhā ||

2 Great Cundī Dhāraṇī 准提神咒

namaḥ saptānāṁ samyak-saṁbuddha koṭīnā***ṁ*** | tad-yathā oṁ cale cule cundi svāhā ||

3 Whole-Body Relic Treasure Chest Seal Dhāraṇī 全身舍利寶篋印陀羅尼

namas tryadhvikānāṁ sarva tathāgatānāṁ | oṁ bhuvi-bhavana-vare vacana-vacati | suru suru dhara dhara | sarva tathāgata dhātu dhare padmaṁ bhavati | jaya vare mudre | smara tathāgata dharma-cakra pravartana vajre bodhimaṇḍa-alaṁkāra-alaṁkṛte | sarva tathāgata-adhiṣṭhite | bodhaya bodhaya bodhi bodhi budhya budhya | saṁbodhani saṁbodhaya | cala cala calantu sarva-āvaraṇāni | sarva pāpa vigate | huru huru sarva śoka vigate | sarva tathāgata hṛdaya vajriṇi | saṁbhāra saṁbhāra | sarva tathāgata guhya dhāraṇī mudre | bhūte subhūte | sarva tathāgata-adhiṣṭhita dhātu garbhe svāhā | samaya-adhiṣṭhite svāhā | sarva tathāgata hṛdaya dhātu mudre svāhā | supratiṣṭhita stūpe tathāgata-adhiṣṭhite huru huru hūṁ hūṁ svāhā | oṁ sarva tathāgatoṣṇīṣa dhātu mudrāṇi sarva tathāgata sadhātu vibhūṣita-adhiṣṭhite hūṁ hūṁ svāhā ||

4 Dhāraṇī of Infinite-Life Resolute Radiance King Tathāgata
聖無量壽決定光明王如來陀羅尼

namo bhagavate aparimita-āyur-jñāna-suviniścita-tejorājāya | tathāgatāya-arhate samyak-saṁbuddhāya | tad-yathā [oṁ puṇya mahā-puṇya | aparimita-puṇya | aparimita-āyuḥ-puṇya-jñāna-saṁbhāropacite |] oṁ sarva saṁskāra pariśuddha dharmate gagana samudgate | svabhāva viśuddhe mahānaya parivāre svāhā ||

5 Dhāraṇī for Rebirth in the Pure Land
拔一切業障根本得生淨土陀羅尼

namo amitābhāya tathāgatāya | tad-yathā oṁ amṛtod bhave | amṛta siddhaṁ bhave | amṛta vikrānte | amṛta vikrānta-gāmini | gagana-kīrti-kare svāhā ||

6 Root Dhāraṇī of Infinite-Life Tathāgata
無量壽如來根本陀羅尼

namo ratna trayāya | nama ārya-amitābhāya tathāgatāya-arhate samyak-saṁbuddhāya | tad-yathā oṁ amṛte amṛtod bhave | amṛta saṁbhave | amṛta garbhe | amṛta siddhe | amṛta teje | amṛta vikrānte | amṛta vikrānta-gāmini | amṛta gagana kīrti-kare | amṛta dundubhi svare | sarvārtha sādhane | sarva karma kleśa kṣayaṁkare svāhā ||

The Heart Mantra
oṁ amṛta teje hara hūṁ ||

7 Mantra of Medicine Master Tathāgata 藥師灌頂真言

namo bhagavate bhaiṣajya-guru-vaiḍūrya-prabhā-rājāya | tathāgatāya-arhate samyak-saṁbuddhāya | tad-yathā oṁ bhaiṣajye bhaiṣajye bhaiṣajya samudgate svāhā ||

8 The Tathāgata-Crown White Umbrella Unsurpassed Subjugation Dhāraṇī (Tathāgatoṣṇīṣāṁ sitāta patraṁ aparājitaṁ pratyuṅgiraṁ dhāraṇī) 大佛頂首楞嚴神咒

The Heart Mantra 楞嚴咒心
tad-yathā oṁ anale anale viśada viśada bandha bandha bandhani bandhani vaira-vajrapāṇi phaṭ hūṁ bhrūṁ phaṭ svāhā ||

9 Samantabhadra Bodhisattva's Mantra 普賢菩薩所說咒

adaṇḍe daṇḍapati daṇḍa-āvartani daṇḍa-kuśale daṇḍa-sudhāri | sudhārapati buddhapaśyane sarvadhāraṇi | āvartani saṁvartani saṁgha-parīkṣite saṁgha-nirghātani | dharma-parīkṣite sarva-sattva ruta kauśalya-anugate | siṁha-vikrīḍite anuvarte vartani vartāli svāhā ||

10 Great Compassion-Mind Dhāraṇī (Nīlakaṇṭha dhāraṇī) 大悲咒

namo ratna-trayāya | nama ārya-avalokiteśvarāya bodhisattvāya mahāsattvāya mahākāruṇikāya | oṁ sarva-bhaya-śodhanāya tasya namaskṛtvā | ***idam***_ārya-avalokiteśvara tava namo nīlakaṇṭha | hṛdayaṁ vartayiṣyāmi sarvārtha-sādhanaṁ śubham_ajeyaṁ sarva-bhūtānāṁ bhava-mārga-viśodhakaṁ | tad-yathā oṁ āloka-adhipati loka-atikrānta | ehi mahā-bodhisattva sarpa sarpa smara smara hṛdayaṁ | kuru kuru karma | dhuru dhuru vijayate mahā-vijayate | dhara dhara dhāraṇī-rāja | cala cala mama vimala-amūrtte | ehi ehi ***cīrṇa cīrṇa ārṣaṁ*** pracali | vaśa***ṁ*** vaśaṁ pranāśaya | hur***u*** hur***u*** smara | huru huru sara sara siri siri suru suru | ***budhya budhya*** bodhaya bodhaya | maitreya nīlakaṇṭha [dehi me] darśanaṁ | praharāyamānāya svāhā | siddhāya svāhā | mahā-siddhāya svāhā | siddha-yogi-īśvarāya svāhā | nīlakaṇṭhāya svāhā | varāha-mukhāya svāhā | nara-siṁha-mukhāya svāhā | gadā-hastāya svāhā | cakra-hastāya svāhā | padma-hastāya svāhā | nīlakaṇṭha-pāndarāya svāhā | mahāta***la***-śaṁkarāya svāhā | namo ratna-trayāya | nama ārya-avalokiteśvarāya bodhisattvāya svāhā | oṁ siddhyantu mantra-padā***ni*** svāhā (This concluding phrase appears in another text.) ||

The Heart Mantra
oṁ vajra dharma hrīḥ ||

11 The Prajñā-Pāramitā Mantra 般若波羅蜜多咒

gate gate pāragate pāra-saṁgate bodhi svāhā ||

Appendix

Table A. The Sanskrit Alphabet

	33 Consonants							13 Vowels			
	Unvoiced			Voiced				Voiced			
								Simple		Diphthong	
	Un aspirate	Aspirate	Sibilant (aspirate)	Un aspirate	Aspirate	Nasal	Semi-vowel	Short	Long	Long	
1 Velar	ka	kha	ha	ga	gha	ṅa		a	ā	a+i	ā+i
2 Palatal	ca	cha	śa	ja	jha	ña	ya	i	ī	=e	=ai
3 Cerebral	ṭa	ṭha	ṣa	ḍa	ḍha	ṇa	ra	ṛ	ṝ		
4 Dental	ta	tha	sa	da	dha	na	la	ḷ		a+u	ā+u
5 Labial	pa	pha		ba	bha	ma	va	u	ū	=o	=au
Anusvāra						ṁ					
Visarga			ḥ								

Note:

1. The sounds of the twenty-five consonants are formed by *complete* contact of the tongue with the palate.
2. The four semi-vowels are voiced and unaspirated, and their sounds are formed by *slight* contact.
3. Three of the four sibilants (excepting *ha*) are unvoiced and aspirated, and their sounds are formed by *half* contact. Note that *ha* is a voiced velar sound but classified as a sibilant.
4. Voiced consonants are low and soft; unvoiced consonants are crisp and sharp. To feel the difference between a voiced and an unvoiced sound, hold the front of your throat with your hand and pronounce a syllable. It is a voiced sound if your hand detects a vibration in your throat, an unvoiced sound if no vibration. To know the difference between an aspirated and an unaspirated sound, place your palm in front of your mouth and pronounce a syllable. It is an aspirated sound if your breath hits your palm, an unaspirated sound if there is no hit. Native English speakers may find it difficult to pronounce the five unvoiced, unaspirated syllables in column one. This difficulty can be overcome once you understand the difference.
5. In Table A, each consonant is followed by the short vowel *a* to facilitate pronunciation. To learn the Sanskrit alphabet, follow the pronunciation guideline in Table B and Table C. Recite the thirteen vowels in Table B row by row. Recite the thirty-three consonants in the first column of Table C, also adding the short vowel *a* to each. Unlike the consonants, the sounds of anusvāra and visarga in the last two rows of Table A or Table C depend on the vowel preceding them. Textbooks include them with the vowels.

Table B. Pronunciation of the 13 Vowels

5 short vowels (Each lasts one count)		8 long vowels (Each lasts two counts)	
a	atra (here), like *a*bout or *a*like	ā	mahā (great), like f*a*ther
i	iva (as if, like), like *ea*sy but not like *i* t or *i* s	ī	kīrti (fame), like *ease*
u	guru (heavy), like p*u*ll	ū	bhūta (reality, being), like p*oo*l
ṛ	amṛta (nectar for immortality), like p*re*tty but not like p*ri*ck	ṝ	pitṝn (fathers, accusative case), like p*re*tty lengthened
ḷ	kḷpta (arranged), like app*le* or kett*le*		
		e = a+i	ehi (come near!), like s*a*fe
		ai = ā+i	maitreya (benevolent), like *ai*sle
		o = a+u	namo (homage), like *o*cean without bunching the lips as if to pronounce the word *woe*
		au = ā+u	kauśalya (skillfulness), like l*ou*d

Table C. Pronunciation of the 33 Consonants

1. Velar or guttural sounds are produced by touching the rear of the tongue to the soft palate near the throat.	
k	kāya (body), like s*k*ill or s*k*in
kh	sukha (happiness), like *k*ill or *k*in
g	gagana (sky), like *g*azelle or *g*o
gh	gharma (heat), like do*gh*ouse
ṅ	gaṅgā (the Ganges), like mi*n*gle or hu*n*ger
2. Palatal sounds are produced by touching the blade of the tongue to the front palate.	
c	cakra (wheel), like *ch*uck or *ch*oke, but without aspiration
ch	chāya (shadow), like *ch*uck or *ch*oke
j	jaya (victory), like *j*ug or *j*oke
jh	nirjhara (waterfall), like *j-h*ug or fu*dge-h*ome
ñ	jñāna (wisdom), like ca*ny*on. Some people change the sound of *j* and pronounce this word like g*ny*āna, or like d*ny*āna.
3. Cerebral sounds are produced by retroflexing the tongue to touch the hard palate.	
ṭ	koṭi (ten million, the edge), like s*t*ar or s*t*ow, with the tongue retroflexed
ṭh	adhiṣṭhāna (rule over), like *t*ar or *t*ow, with the tongue retroflexed
ḍ	vaiḍūrya (aquamarine), like *d*ouse or *d*ead, with the tongue retroflexed
ḍh	mūḍha (perplexed), like ma*dh*ouse or re*dh*ead, with the tongue retroflexed
ṇ	maṇi (jewel), like *n*ativity or *n*ote, with the tongue retroflexed
4. Dental sounds are produced by touching the tip of the tongue to the back of the front teeth near their roots.	
t	tad (he, she, or it), like s*t*ar or s*t*ow
th	tathāgata (the thus-come one), like *t*ar or *t*ow
da	dāna (the act of giving), like *d*ouse or *d*ead
dh	dhāranī (retention), like ma*dh*ouse or re*dh*ead
n	nāga (dragon), like *n*ativity or *n*ote
5. Labial sounds are produced by closing and opening the lips.	
p	padma (red lotus), like s*p*in or s*p*oke
ph	phala (fruit), like *p*in or *p*oke
b	bodhi (enlightenment), like *b*ore or *b*out
bh	bhagavān (the world-honored one), like a*bh*or or ho*bh*ouse
m	mudrā (seal), like *m*agenta or *m*ode

Table C Continued

6. Four semi-vowels, the sounds of which are formed by slight contact	
y	hṛdaya (heart, mind), like *y*east or *y*oga
r	ratna (jewel), like ***r***ite or ***r***ote, with the tongue slightly tapping the front palate. Avoid bunching the lips for the implicit *w* before the r-syllable as in English, which causes ***r***ite to be pronounced as write, ***r***ote as wrote.
l	loka (world), like *l*agoon or *l*otus
v	If not preceded by a consonant, it is pronounced as *v;* e.g., avidyā (ignorance). If preceded by a constant, it may be pronounced as *w*. Thus, sattva (being, creature) may be pronounced as sa-ttwa, sarva (all) as sar-wa, adhvan (time) as a-dhwan, and svāhā (hail) as swā-hā.
7. Four sibilants, the sounds of which are formed by half contact	
ś	śuddha (pure), like ***sh***ip or ***sh***ow
ṣ	uṣṇīṣa (crown of the head), like ***sh***ip or ***sh***ow, with the tongue retroflexed
s	sama (equal), like ***s***alute or ***s***olo
h	sahasra (thousand), like ***h***abituate or ***h***oly
8. Other sounds	
Anusvāra (ṁ)	The preceding verb is nasalized; e.g., saṁskāṛa (formation) is pronounced as sa***ng***-skā-ra, and hūṁ (a mantra syllable) as hū***ng***.
Visarga (ḥ)	The preceding verb is faintly echoed; e.g., namaḥ (homage) is pronounced as nama***ha***, narayoḥ (of the two men) as narayo***ho***, naraiḥ (with the men) as narai***hi***, and duḥkha (sorrow) as du***hu***kha.

Note:

1. A vowel as the first letter of a word, or a consonant followed by a vowel, forms a syllable, which is short or long, depending upon the vowel. All consonants are pronounced. For example, tadyathā is pronounced as tad-ya-thā, ratna as rat-na, and sattva as satt-va or sa-ttwa.
2. The stressed syllable, or guru syllable, in a multi-syllable word is the penultimate syllable if (1) it has a long vowel, or (2) it has a short vowel followed by two or more consonants. For example, the stressed syllable in bālābhyām (with, for, or from the two boys) is *lā* because it meets the first condition, and in saṁyukta (complex) is *yu* because it meets the second condition. If the penultimate syllable meets neither condition, then check the anti-penultimate syllable, and so on. For example, the stressed syllable in udbhavakara (productive) is *u*, the fifth syllable from the last.
3. The nasal sound of anusvāra (ṁ) may extend a count or two. For example, the mantra syllable hūṁ or oṁ can last two to four counts.

Glossary

affliction (kleśa, 煩惱). Something that agitates one's mind, resulting in evil karmas done with one's body and/or voice. The three root afflictions, called the three poisons, are (1) greed, (2) anger, and (3) delusion. Derived from these three are (4) arrogance, (5) doubt, and (6) wrong views. The list can be extended to ten by distinguishing five kinds of wrong views: (6) the self-view that an embodied self exists in a person composed of the five aggregates and that this self owns the five aggregates and things considered as external; (7) the diametric view of perpetuity or cessation; (8) the evil view of no causality; (9) the preceding three wrong views, plus certain inferior views; (10) observance of useless precepts, such as staying naked, covering oneself with ashes, imitating cows or dogs, and self-harm, futilely hoping to achieve a better rebirth. These ten afflictions drive sentient beings. The first five are called the chronic drivers (鈍使), which can be removed gradually; they are also called thinking confusions (思惑) because they arise from one's thinking of self, others, or both. The last five are called the acute drivers (利使), which can be removed quickly; they are also called view confusions (見惑). Ignorance of the truth is the root of all afflictions.

agalloch (沉水). The fragrant, resinous wood of an East Indian tree, aquilaria agallocha, also called agarwood, used as incense in the Orient. It is called in China the sink-in-water fragrant wood.

Akaniṣṭha Heaven (阿迦尼吒天), or Ultimate Form Heaven (色究竟天). It is the top heaven (有頂天) of the eighteen heavens in the form realm (see Three Realms of Existence).

ālaya-vijñāna (阿賴耶識). The store consciousness (藏識), also known as the eighth consciousness, which stores the pure, impure, and neutral seeds of one's experience since time without a beginning. These seeds manifest as causes and conditions that lead to karmic events in one's life, which in turn become seeds. Maintaining the physical and mental life of a sentient being, ālaya is neither different from nor the same as the physical body. As the base of the other seven consciousnesses (see eighteen spheres), ālaya is the root consciousness (mūla-vijñāna). After one's death, ālaya may either immediately manifest a rebirth according to karmic forces and conditions or first produce an ethereal interim body, which can last up to forty-nine days, pending the right karmic conditions for a rebirth. Ālaya is also identified with the thus-come store (tathāgata-garbha) as well as Buddha nature (see true suchness). The seeds in a Buddha's mind are all pure seeds which no longer change, and the name ālaya-vijñāna is then changed to amala-vijñāna, the stainless consciousness.

Anāthapiṇḍika (給孤獨). Provider for the Deprived, a name given to the Elder Sudatta for his generosity to the poor and forlorn. He bought a garden from Prince Jeta as an offering to the Buddha.

anuttara-samyak-saṁbodhi (阿耨多羅三藐三菩提). The unsurpassed, equally perfect enlightenment (無上正等正覺). *Anuttara* means unsurpassed; *samyak* is derived from the stem *samyañc*, which means same or identical; *saṁbodhi* means perfect enlightenment. *Equally* means that the perfect enlightenment of all Buddhas is the same. The third epithet of a Buddha is Samyak-Saṁbuddha, the Equally, Perfectly Enlightened One.

anuttara-samyak-saṁbodhi mind (阿耨多羅三藐三菩提心). The resolve to attain the unsurpassed, equally perfect enlightenment, to benefit self and others.

apasamāra (阿波悉魔羅). A ghost that scares children.

araṇya (阿蘭若). A forest, or a quiet remote place for spiritual training. One who stays in such a place is called an āraṇyaka (阿蘭若迦). Such a way of life is called the araṇya way, which is one of the twelve dhūta practices. A temple in an area away from urban noise is also called an araṇya.

Arhat (阿羅漢). A voice-hearer who has attained the fourth and highest fruit on the Liberation Way (see voice-hearer fruits) by shattering his fixation on having an autonomous self and eradicating all his afflictions. A Buddha is also an Arhat, but not vice versa (see bodhi). As the second of a Buddha's ten epithets, Arhat means worthy of offerings.

arrogance (慢). Arrogance has seven types: (1) arrogance (慢) is vaunting one's superiority over inferiors; (2) over-arrogance (過慢) is asserting one's superiority over equals; (3) arrogant over-arrogance (慢過慢) is alleging one's superiority over superiors; (4) self-arrogance (我慢) is the root of all other arrogances, considering oneself by definition to be superior to others; (5) exceeding arrogance (增上慢) is alleging realization of truth one has not realized; (6) humility-camouflaged arrogance (卑慢) is admitting slight inferiority to those who are much superior; and (7) evil arrogance (邪慢) is boasting of virtues one does not have.

asaṁkhyeya (阿僧祇). Innumerable, or an exceedingly large number.

asaṁskṛta (無爲). Not formed or made through causes and conditions. Although *asaṁskṛta* is an antonym of *saṁskṛta* (有爲), the asaṁskṛta dharma is the true reality of saṁskṛta dharmas, not their opposite.

asura (阿修羅). A sub-god or non-god. An asura may assume the form of god, human, animal, or hungry ghost. Given to anger and jealousy, an asura is considered more an evil life-journey than a good one.

attuning thought (一念相應). Actually not a thought. In a flash of attunement, one enters a non-dual state, realizing one's true mind and/or seeing one's Buddha nature. In Chan Buddhism, experiencing an attuning thought means breaking through the first or the second gateless gate.

Avīci Hell (阿鼻地獄). The last of the eight hot hells. It is a hell of uninterrupted suffering for those who have committed grave sins, such as the five rebellious sins.

avinivartanīya (阿鞞跋致). The spiritual level from which a Bodhisattva will never regress (不退). Bodhisattvas with the first six or more of the ten faithful minds will never regress from faith; Bodhisattvas at the seventh level of abiding or above will never abandon the Mahāyāna; Bodhisattvas on the First Ground or above will never lose their spiritual realization; Bodhisattvas on the Eighth Ground or above will never lose their mindfulness, and their progress will be effortless (see stages of the Bodhisattva Way).

Bhagavān (薄伽梵). The tenth epithet of a Buddha is Buddha-Bhagavān, or Buddha the World-Honored One.

bhikṣu (比丘). A fully ordained monk in the Buddha's Order, who observes, in the Mahāyāna tradition, 250 monastic precepts.

bhikṣuṇī (比丘尼). A fully ordained nun in the Buddha's Order, who observes, in the Mahāyāna tradition, 500 monastic precepts.

birth-death (jāti-maraṇa, 生死). See saṁsāra.

bodhi (菩提). Enlightenment or unsurpassed wisdom. There are three kinds of bodhi, corresponding to the enlightenment of the holy beings of the Three Vehicles: (1) the bodhi of a voice-hearer who has attained Arhatship; (2) the greater bodhi of a Pratyekabuddha; (3) the greatest bodhi of a Buddha. In old translations, bodhi is translated into Chinese as the Way (道), which should be distinguished from the path (mārga).

bodhi mind (bodhi-citta, 菩提心). See anuttara-samyak-saṁbodhi mind.

bodhimaṇḍa (道場). The bodhi place, which refers to the vajra seat of a Buddha sitting under the bodhi tree where He attains Buddhahood. In a general sense, it is a place for spiritual learning and practice, such as a temple or one's home. In a profound sense, since the Way to Buddhahood is one's mind, all sentient beings are bodhi places.

Bodhisattva (菩薩). A bodhi being who rides the Mahāyāna and delivers sentient beings along the Way. He will eventually attain Buddhahood, to benefit himself and others.

Bodhisattva-Mahāsattva (菩薩摩訶薩). A holy Bodhisattva who is a mahāsattva (great being) because of his great vows, great actions, and the great number of sentient beings he delivers.

Bodhisattva precepts (菩薩戒). Precepts for both lay and monastic Buddhists who ride the Mahāyāna. They are called the three clusters of pure precepts (三聚淨戒), consisting of (1) restraining precepts, (2) precepts for doing good dharmas, and (3) precepts for benefiting sentient beings. The first cluster is to prevent negative actions, and the other two are to cultivate the positive qualities essential to the development of a Bodhisattva. Bodhisattva precepts vary with their sources. In the *Brahma Net Sūtra* (T24n1484), there are ten major and forty-eight minor precepts; in the *Sūtra of the Upāsaka Precepts* (T24n1488), there are six major and twenty-eight minor precepts. Chinese monastic Buddhists observe the former set of Bodhisattva precepts. Lay Buddhists may choose to accept either set of Bodhisattva precepts.

Brahmā (梵). Purity, or freedom from desire. It is deified in Hinduism as the Creator. The Brahma way of life in the desire realm is celibacy.

Brahma gods (梵天). Gods, who have only pure desires, reside in the Brahma World (brahma-loka), i.e., the first of the four dhyāna heavens in the form realm. The first dhyāna heaven comprises three heavens: Brahma Multitude (Brahma-pāriṣadya), Brahma Minister (Brahma-purohita), and Great Brahmā (Mahābrahmā). The Brahma-king Śikhin, assisted by his ministers, rules all Brahma gods in these three heavens (see Three Realms of Existence).

Brahmin (婆羅門). A member of the highest of the four Indian castes. As a priest, a Brahmin officiates at religious rites and teaches Vedic literature.

Buddha (佛). The Enlightened One. According to the Mahāyāna tradition, Śākyamuni Buddha (circa 563–483 BCE) is the present one in a line of past and future Buddhas. Each Buddha has a particular name, such as Śākyamuni, to suit the needs of sentient beings of His time. The ten epithets common to all Buddhas are (1) Tathāgata (Thus-Come One or Thus-Gone One), (2) Arhat (Worthy of Offerings), (3) Samyak-Saṁbuddha (Equally, Perfectly Enlightened One), (4) Vidyācaraṇa-Sampanna (Knowledge and Conduct Perfected), (5) Sugata (Well-Arrived One or Well-Gone One), (6) Lokavid (Understanding the World), (7) Anuttara (Unsurpassed One), (8) Puruṣa-Damya-Sārathi (Tamer of Men), (9) Śāstā Deva-Manuṣyāṇām (Teacher to Gods and Humans), and (10) Buddha-Bhagavān (Buddha the World-Honored One).

Buddha-crown (buddhoṣṇīṣa, 佛頂), or Tathāgata-crown (tathāgatoṣṇīṣa). A fleshy mound on the crown of a Buddha's head, which is one of the thirty-two physical marks of a Buddha, a sign resulting from countless lives of doing good dharmas and teaching others to do so. The same term also refers to the invisible top of a Buddha's head, which is one of the eighty excellent characteristics of a Buddha, a sign resulting from countless lives of venerating, praising, and making obeisance to innumerable holy beings, teachers, and parents. The invisible Buddha-crown signifies one's true mind, which is free from causes and conditions.

Buddha Vehicle (Buddha-yāna, 佛乘). The destination of the Great Vehicle (Mahāyāna) is Buddhahood, so it is also called the Buddha Vehicle. In the *Lotus Sūtra* (T09n0262), the Buddha introduces the One Vehicle (eka-yāna, 一乘), declaring that not only riders of the Two Vehicles but all sentient beings will eventually attain Buddhahood.

bhūta (部多). A living being or the ghost of a deceased person.

Cause Ground (因地). It means the training ground of a Bodhisattva before attaining Buddhahood, the Fruit (Result) Ground, or the Buddha Ground. It may also refer to the training ground of a Bodhisattva before ascending to the First Ground (see stages of the Bodhisattva Way).

chamber of great compassion (大悲精室). One's own mind of great compassion. In the Lotus Sūtra (T09n0262), chapter 10, it is called the Tathāgata's chamber.

character-type (gotra, 種性). The Sanskrit word *gotra* means family. According to the *Garland Sūtra* (T24n1485), Bodhisattvas are classified into five character-types, corresponding to the middle five of the seven stages of the Bodhisattva Way: (1) the learning character-type (習種性) is developed through the ten levels of abiding; (2) The nature character-type (性種性) is developed through the ten levels of action; (3) the bodhi character-type (道種性) is developed through the ten levels of transference of merit; (4) the holy character-type (聖種性) is developed through the Ten Grounds; (5) the virtually perfect enlightenment nature (等覺性) is developed when a Bodhisattva attains enlightenment nearly equal to that of a Buddha. At the seventh stage, a Bodhisattva becomes a Buddha, whose perfect enlightenment nature (妙覺性) is fully revealed. Besides, those with affinity for the Voice-Hearer Vehicle are called the voice-hearer character-type; those with affinity for the Pratyekabuddha Vehicle are called the Pratyekabuddha character-type (see Two Vehicles).

Command of the Eight Great Displays (八大自在). According to the *Mahāparinirvāṇa Sūtra* (T12n0375), fascicle 23, the true self of a Buddha has total command of the eight great displays: (1) one physical body can manifest many copies; (2) one physical body can fill a Large Thousandfold World; (3) this vast body can lift off and travel far; (4) it can remain in one land and manifest innumerable varieties of forms in response to sentient beings; (5) the functions of its five faculties can be interchangeable; (6) He can attain all dharmas with no attachment to any attainment; (7) He can expound the meaning of one stanza for innumerable kalpas; (8) His body can pervade everywhere, like space.

cow dung (gomaya, 瞿摩夷). It is considered a pure substance.

Cundī Bodhisattva (准提菩薩). One of the six special forms of Avalokiteśvara Bodhisattva (Guanyin in Chinese), who is forever active in delivering sentient beings that transmigrate through the six life-journeys. Hailed as mother of seven koṭi Buddhas, Cundī is portrayed in female form with three eyes and eighteen arms, adorned with a white conch shell on her wrist. In text 1076 (T20n1076), the Buddha states that *cun* means the unsurpassed enlightenment; *di* means that all phenomena are illusions, irrelevant to being accepted or rejected; *Cundī* means the inherent purity of the nature of one's true mind.

deliverance (度). Liberation achieved by crossing over to that shore of nirvāṇa from this shore of saṁsāra. Those who have achieved deliverance are Arhats, Pratyekabuddhas, and Buddhas. The first two have achieved the liberation fruit and the bodhi fruit for themselves. Buddhas have achieved not only the liberation fruit for themselves but also the great bodhi fruit of omniscience, for delivering sentient beings.

dhāraṇī (陀羅尼). Usually in the form of a long mantra, it means total retention (總持). With excellent memory, samādhi, and wisdom, A Bodhisattva has the inconceivable power to unite all dharmas and hold all meanings. He can not only retain all good dharmas but also stop the rise of evil dharmas.

dharma (法). (1) The teachings of a Buddha (the word dharma in this meaning is capitalized in English); (2) law; (3) anything (mental, physical, event); (4) a mental object of consciousness, such as a thought.

dharma-eye (法眼). The spiritual eye that not only penetrates the true reality of all things but also discriminates all things. Bodhisattvas who have realized the no birth of dharmas ascend to the First Ground and acquire the pure dharma-eye, with which they continue to help sentient beings according to their natures and preferences (see five eyes).

Dharma Seal (dharma-mudrā, 法印). Buddhist teachings are summarized in Dharma Seals, against which other doctrines should be measured. The Four Dharma Seals are as follows: (1) processes are impermanent; (2) experiences boil down to suffering; (3) dharmas have no selves; (4) nirvāṇa is silence and stillness. Because suffering is the consequence of the impermanence of everything in the life of a sentient being, including itself, the second Dharma Seal can be omitted from the list to make the Three Dharma Seals. Five Dharma Seals can be established by adding a fifth Dharma Seal: (5) dharmas are empty. In the Mahāyāna doctrine, all these seals are integrated into one, the one true reality.

Dharma vessel (法器). (1) A person capable of accepting and learning the Buddha Dharma. (2) A Buddhist ritual object, such a drum, a bell, or a wooden fish.

dhūta (頭陀). Shaken off. To shake off one's desire for creature comfort in food, clothing, and shelter, one follows these twelve rules as a way of life: (1) beg for food; (2) beg for food from one door to the next without discrimination; (3) eat only one meal a day, at noon; (4) eat with moderation in quantity; (5) do not drink liquids after lunch; (6) wear clothes made of cast-away rags; (7) keep only three garments; (8) live in a quiet remote area; (9) live among graves; (10) live under a tree; (11) sit on open ground under the open sky; (12) sit, without reclining.

dhyāna (禪). Meditation. Meditation above the desire-realm level is generally classified into four levels, called the four dhyānas (四禪) of the form realm. In the first dhyāna, one's mind is undisturbed by the pleasures of the desire realm, but it has coarse and subtle perception. In the second dhyāna, there is bliss in meditation. In the third dhyāna, there is subtle joy after abandoning the bliss of the second dhyāna. In the fourth dhyāna, one's mind is in pure meditation, free from any subtle feelings or movements. Each level of dhyāna is also called the Root Samādhi, from which will grow virtues, such as the Four Immeasurable Minds and the eight liberations (see the four samādhis of the formless realm).

dhyāna with appearance (有相禪). Meditation supported by the appearance of a mental object. One can focus one's attention on a point of the body, count the breaths, recite mantra syllables silently, gaze at an object, or visualize an object.

dhyāna without appearance (無相禪). Meditation unsupported by the appearance of any mental object. One can ponder true suchness without thoughts or think of a Buddha without saying His name or visualizing His body.

discharge (āsrava, 漏). Outflow of afflictions, characteristic of sentient beings engaged in their cycle of birth and death. For example, anger is an affliction in one's mind, which is discharged through one's body and voice. Any discharge is a display of one's affliction, and it does not decrease affliction.

dragon (nāga, 龍). (1) A serpent-like sea creature, which can take a little water and pour down rains. (2) A symbol of one's true mind in the statement that the great nāga is always in samādhi, never moving. An Arhat is likened to the great dragon.

eight classes of Dharma protectors (八部護法). The nonhuman protectors of the Dharma are gods, dragons, gandharvas, asuras, yakṣas, garuḍas, kiṁnaras, and mahoragas.

eight difficulties (八難). One has either no opportunity or no motivation to see a Buddha or hear His Dharma, while in any of the eight difficulties: (1) as a hell-dweller; (2) as a hungry ghost; (3) as an animal; (4) as an inhabitant of

Uttarakuru, the northern continent, where life is too pleasant; (5) in deep meditation in a formless heaven; (6) being blind, deaf, or mute; (7) as a worldly eloquent intellectual; (8) in the period between the presence of one Buddha and the next.

eight holy ranks (八聖). See voice-hearer fruits.

eight liberations (aṣṭa-vimokṣa, 八解脫, 八背捨). Through samādhi power, one successively achieves eight liberations from one's greed for rebirth in the form and formless realms: (1) liberation from perceptible desires for form by visualizing the impurity of external objects; (2) liberation from imperceptible desires for form by visualizing the impurity of external objects; (3) liberation from all desires for form by visualizing the purity of external objects; (4) liberation from visualization of the purity of external objects through the mental state of boundless space; (5) liberation from the state of boundless space through the mental state of boundless consciousness; (6) liberation from the state of boundless consciousness through the mental state of nothingness; (7) liberation from the state of nothingness through the mental state of neither with nor without perception; and (8) liberation from the state of neither with nor without perception through the mental state of total suspension of sensory reception and perception. Liberations 1–2 correspond to the first two dhyānas, and liberation 3 corresponds to the fourth dhyāna. The third dhyāna is not used because one's mind is not vigilant in a subtle joyful state. Liberations 4–7 correspond to the four samādhis in the formless realm (see samādhi), and liberation 8 is the liberation samādhi attained by an Arhat.

eight precepts (aṣṭa-śīla, 八關齋戒). Besides the five precepts, which are observed for life at all times, lay Buddhists may accept the eight precepts. They should observe them regularly each lunar month on the six purification days. The eight precepts are (1) no killing; (2) no stealing; (3) no sex; (4) no lying; (5) no drinking alcohol; (6) no wearing perfumes or adornments, and no singing, dancing, or watching song-dance entertainments; (7) no sleeping on a luxurious bed; and (8) no eating after lunch, until morning. Note that the third of the eight precepts is no sex whereas the third of the five precepts is no sexual misconduct. Observing these eight prohibitions (關) for 24 hours at a time, one abstains (齋) not only from sins prohibited by the five precepts but also from sensory gratification.

eight tones (八音). The Tathāgata's Brahma tone has eight qualities: (1) fine, (2) gentle, (3) harmonious, (4) awe-inspiring, (5) manly, (6) error-free, (7) far-reaching, and (8) carrying inexhaustible meaning.

eighteen emptinesses (十八空). Given in the *Mahā-prajñā-pāramitā Sūtra* (T08n0223, 0218c17) is the emptiness of (1) the insides of the body; (2) anything outside of the body; (3) the appearance of inside or outside; (4) the preceding three emptinesses; (5) the four domains; (6) the highest truth [nirvāṇa]; (7) that which is saṁskṛta; (8) that which is asaṁskṛta; (9) the preceding eight emptinesses; (10) sentient beings without a beginning; (11) a composite thing disassembled; (12) self-essence of anything; (13) general and particular appearances of anything; (14) dharmas that make up a sentient being, such as the five aggregates, the twelve fields, and the eighteen spheres; (15) dharmas, which can never be captured; (16) existence; (17) nonexistence; and (18) the appearance of existence or nonexistence.

Eighteen Exclusive Dharmas (aṣṭādaśa-āveṇika-dharma, 十八不共法). Only Buddhas have these eighteen attainments, which Arhats, Pratyekabuddhas, and Bodhisattvas do not have. They include (1–3) perfection in conduct, speech, and mindfulness; (4) impartiality to all; (5) constant serenity; (6) equability toward sensory experiences; (7) unceasing desire to deliver sentient beings; (8) inexhaustible energy for helping sentient beings; (9) unfailing memory of the Buddha Dharma; (10) perfect wisdom in everything; (11) total liberation from afflictions and habits; (12) perfect knowledge and views of liberation; (13–15) perfect body karmas, voice karmas, and mind karmas, led by wisdom; (16–18) perfect knowledge of the past, present, and future. Another set of eighteen includes the Ten Powers, the Four Fearlessnesses, the Threefold Mindfulness of Equality, and the Great Compassion. The Threefold Mindfulness of Equality means that a Buddha's mind abides in equality toward (1) those who listen to the Dharma reverently, (2) those who listen to the Dharma irreverently, and (3) these two groups.

eighteen spheres (aṣṭādaśa-dhātu, 十八界). A sentient being is composed of the eighteen spheres: the six faculties (eye, ear, nose, tongue, body, and mental faculty [manas]), the six sense objects (sights, sounds, scents, flavors, tactile sensations, and mental objects), and the six consciousnesses (eye consciousness, ear consciousness, nose consciousness, tongue consciousness, body consciousness, and mental consciousness). Mental consciousness, the sixth consciousness, functions by itself as well as together with the first five consciousnesses. As the eye is the physical base from which eye consciousness arises, likewise manas (mental faculty) is the mental base from which mental consciousness arises. In the Mahāyāna doctrine, manas is also designated as the seventh consciousness, which has four inborn defilements: (1) self-delusion (我癡), (2) self-love (我愛), (3) self-view (我見), and (4) self-arrogance (我慢). Ālaya, the eighth consciousness, though not explicitly included in the eighteen spheres, is the root of them all.

Eightfold Right Path (八正道). The right path to one's liberation from one's cycle of birth and death includes (1) right views, (2) right thinking, (3) right speech, (4) right action, (5) right livelihood, (6) right effort, (7) right mindfulness, and (8) right meditative absorption (samādhi). Paths 1–2 educate one with understanding, paths 3–5 establish one on the ground of morality, paths 7–8 develop one's mental power and wisdom through meditation, and path 6 is applied to the other seven paths of training.

emptiness (śūnyatā, 空). The lack of self-essence (independent inherent existence) of any dharma that arises and perishes through causes and conditions. Emptiness is not nothingness because it does not deny the illusory existence of all things. The non-duality of emptiness and manifestations, and of nirvāṇa and saṁsāra, is the Middle View of the Mahāyāna doctrine (see two emptinesses).

Endurance in Dharmas (法忍). It includes not only endurance of persecution or suffering but also continued acceptance of the truth that dharmas are never born.

Endurance in the Realization of the No Birth of Dharmas (無生法忍). The lasting realization of the truth that dharmas have neither birth nor death as they appear and disappear through causes and conditions (see Three Endurances in the Dharma).

Five Āgamas (五阿含). An āgama is a collection of early Buddhist scriptures. The Five Āgamas in the Chinese Canon are the Dīrgha Āgama (long discourses), the Madhyama Āgama (middle-length discourses), the Saṁyukta Āgama (connected discourses), the Ekottarika Āgama (discourses ordered by the number of dharmas in each discourse), and the Kṣudraka Āgama (minor discourses). They are parallel but not identical to the Five Nikāyas in the Pāli Canon, which are the Dīgha Nikāya, the Majjhima Nikāya, the Saṁyutta Nikāya, the Aṅguttara Nikāya, and the Khuddaka Nikāya.

five aggregates (pañca-skandha, 五蘊, 五陰). A sentient being is composed of the five aggregates: rūpa (form), vedanā (sensory reception), saṁjñā (perception), saṁskāra (mental processing), and vijñāna (consciousness). The first one is material and the other four are mental. Since these four are non-form (非色), thus present in name only, the five aggregates are summarized as name and form (名色). *Skandha* (蘊) in Sanskrit also means that which covers or conceals (陰), and the regular working of the five skandhas conceals true reality from a sentient being.

five coverings (pañca-āvaraṇa, 五蓋). One's true mind is covered up by (1) greed, (2) anger, (3) torpor, (4) restlessness, and (5) doubt.

five desires (五欲). One's desires for pleasures in the five sense objects are (1) sights, (2) sounds, (3) scents, (4) flavors, and (5) tactile sensations. One also has the desire for pleasure in (6) mental objects, verbal or nonverbal, coarse or subtle. Humans are driven especially by their desires for (1) riches, (2) sex, (3) reputation, (4) food and drink, and (5) sleep. These are impure desires in the desire realm, and there are pure desires in the form and formless realms.

five eyes (pañca-cakṣu, 五眼). These are (1) the physical-eye that a sentient being is born with; (2) the god-eye that can see anything anywhere; (3) the wisdom-eye that can see the emptiness of dharmas; (4) the dharma-eye that can discriminate all dharmas; and (5) the Buddha-eye of omniscience, which includes the preceding four at the highest level (see three wisdom-knowledges).

five faculties (pañca-indrya, 五根). The first five of the six faculties.

Five Powers. See Thirty-seven Elements of Bodhi.

five precepts (pañca-śīla, 五戒). For lay Buddhists, the five precepts are (1) no killing, (2) no stealing, (3) no sexual misconduct, (4) no lying, and (5) no drinking alcohol.

five rebellious acts or sins (五逆). These are (1) patricide, (2) matricide, (3) killing an Arhat, (4) shedding the blood of a Buddha (including maligning His Dharma), and (5) destroying the harmony of a Saṅgha. They are also called the karma of the five no interruptions because any of them drives one into Avīci Hell, the hell of the five no interruptions.

Five Roots. See Thirty-seven Elements of Bodhi.

five studies (pañca-vidyā, 五明). These are (1) language and composition, (2) science and technology, (3) medical arts, (4) logic, and (5) inner knowledge in a certain discipline.

five sūtras and one treatise (五經一論). The Pure Land School follows (1) the *Sūtra of Amitāyus Buddha* (T12n0360); (2) the *Sūtra of Amitābha Buddha* (T12n0366); (3) the *Sūtra of Visualization of Amitāyus Buddha* (T12n0365); (4) "Great Might Arrived Bodhisattva's Thinking-of-Buddhas as the Perfect Passage" (a subsection in fascicle 5 of the *Śūraṅgama Sūtra* [T19n0945]); (5) "The Universally Worthy Action Vow" (fascicle 40 of the 40-fascicle version of the *Mahāvaipulya Sūtra of Buddha Adornment* [T10n0293]); and (6) the *Upadeśa on the Sūtra of Amitāyus Buddha* (T26n1524).

five transcendental powers (五通). Through meditation, one can develop these powers: (1) the god-eye to see anything anywhere; (2) the god-ear to hear any sound anywhere; (3) the ability to know the past lives of self and others; (4) the ability to know the thoughts of others; (5) the ability to transform one's body and to travel instantly to any place.

five turbidities (pañca-kaṣāya, 五濁). The five kinds of degeneracy which begin, in a decreasing kalpa, when human lifespan has decreased from 80,000 years to 20,000 years, and become more severe as human lifespan decreases to 10 years. They are (1) the turbidity of a kalpa in decay, which is characterized by the next four turbidities; (2) the turbidity of views, such as the five wrong views; (3) the turbidity of afflictions, including greed, anger, delusion, arrogance, and doubt; (4) the turbidity of sentient beings that live a wicked life and are in increasing suffering; (5) the turbidity of human lifespan as it decreases to 10 years. The wrong views in (2) and the afflictions in (3) are turbidity itself, which leads to the results in (4) and (5).

Flowers mentioned in the sūtras are listed below. A question mark next to the Chinese name of a plant indicates the failure to find its corresponding Sanskrit name. Then a Sanskrit name is constructed phonetically from Chinese.

utpala (優波羅)—blue lotus
padma (波頭摩)—red lotus
kumuda (拘物頭)—white lotus
puṇḍarīka (分陀利華)—large white lotus
atimuktaka (阿提目多花)—an herbaceous plant which has fragrant red or white blooms
cāka (遮迦花?)
campaka (瞻蔔)—the champaka (玉蘭) tree which has fragrant golden or white flowers
caṇa (栴那花)—the chickpea plant
canuttara (栴奴多羅花?)
kiṁśuka (甄叔迦)—the tree butea frondosa, or its bright orange-red flowers
locana (盧遮那花)—a certain plant
māndarāva (曼陀羅花)—the red blooms of the coral tree, considered as celestial flowers

mañjūṣaka (曼殊沙花)—the white blooms of an herbaceous plant, considered as celestial flowers
palāśa (波樓沙花)—the flaming orange blooms of a tree called butea monosperma, native to India and Southeast Asia
pāṭali (波羅羅花)—a tree which has fragrant purple flowers
raṇi (羅尼花?)
gauraṇi (瞿羅尼花?)
suloci (蘇樓至?)
sumana (須曼那華)—the jasmine plant, which has fragrant white, yellow, or red blooms
tāla (他邏)—the fan palm tree
udumbara (烏曇跋羅)—the ficus glomerata, a tree that produces fruit with hidden flowers. Hence the appearance of its bloom is likened to the rare appearance of a Buddha.

four appearances (四相).

A. The four appearances of any saṁskṛta dharma are the four stages of a process: (1) arising, (2) staying, (3) changing, and (4) perishing. In the case of a sentient being, these four are (1) birth, (2) aging, (3) illness, and (4) death (see ten appearances). In the case of a world, these four are (1) formation, (2) staying, (3) destruction, and (4) void.

B. The four appearances in the *Diamond Sūtra* (T08n0235) are the self-images of a sentient being: (1) an autonomous self, which relates to everything conceived or perceived as non-self; (2) a human being with something in common with or different from other human beings; (3) a sentient being with something in common with or different from other sentient beings; and (4) a living being that has a lifespan to terminate, preserve, or prolong. The latter three are derived from the first. These are also called the four views (四見).

four continents (catur-dvīpa, 四洲). In the center of a small world in the Three Realms of Existence is Mount Sumeru. It is encircled by eight concentric mountain ranges, and these nine mountains are separated by eight oceans. Rising above the salty ocean between the outermost mountain range and the seventh inner mountain range are four large continents aligned with the four sides of Mount Sumeru. In the east is Pūrvavideha; in the south is Jambudvīpa; in the west is Aparagodānīya; in the north is Uttarakuru, where life is too pleasant for its inhabitants to seek the Dharma. Between every two large continents are two medium-sized continents and five hundred uninhabited small continents.

Four Dharmas to Rely Upon (四依法). In the *Mahāparinirvāṇa Sūtra* (T12n0375 [different from the *Mahāparinibbāna Sutta* in the Pāli Canon]), fascicle 6, the Buddha teaches us to rely upon (1) the Dharma, not an individual; (2) sūtras of definitive meaning, not those of provisional meaning; (3) the true meaning, not just the words; (4) one's wisdom-knowledge, not consciousness. In summary, dharma means dharma nature; definitive meaning refers to Mahāyāna sūtras; true meaning refers to the eternal abiding and changelessness of the Tathāgata; wisdom-knowledge means the understanding that all sentient beings have Buddha nature.

four domains (catur-dhātu, 四界). According to ancient Indian philosophy, matter is made of the four domains—earth, water, fire, and wind—which have four corresponding appearances: solid, liquid, heat, and mobility. Hence they are also called the great seeds (mahābhūta, 大種) with the four appearances as their self-essence, or changeless qualities. In fact, these appearances are the states of matter under prevailing conditions (see six domains).

Four Drawing-in Dharmas (四攝法). To draw sentient beings into the Dharma, one should use these four skillful ways: (1) almsgiving, (2) loving words, (3) beneficial actions, and (4) collaborative work.

Four Fearlessnesses (四無畏). Only a Buddha has (1) fearlessness because knowledge of all knowledge has been acquired; (2) fearlessness because all afflictions have been eradicated; (3) fearlessness in explaining hindrances that obstruct one's realization of bodhi; and (4) fearlessness in explaining the right path to end one's suffering.

Four Foundations of Mindfulness (四念住).

A. According to the Pāli Canon of the Theravāda School, one practices (1) mindfulness of one's body in stillness and in motion; (2) mindfulness of one's sensory experience as pleasant, unpleasant, or neutral; (3) mindfulness of one's mental afflictions: greed, anger, and delusion; and (4) mindfulness of one's mental objects, including the teachings of the Buddha. Through vigilant mindfulness, one realizes that all dharmas are impermanent and that there is no self in command.

B. According to the Mahāyāna doctrine, one needs to observe these: (1) the body is impure; (2) all experiences boil down to suffering; (3) the mind is constantly changing; and (4) all dharmas have no selves (see right mindfulness).

four god-kings (四天王). They reside halfway up Mount Sumeru, in the first of the six desire heavens. As protectors of the world, they ward off the attacks of asuras. On the east side is Dhṛtarsaṣtra, the god-king Upholding the Kingdom; on the south side is Virūḍhaka, the god-king Increase and Growth; on the west side is Virūpākṣa, the god-king Broad Eye; and on the north side is Vaiśravaṇa, the god-king Hearing Much.

four grave prohibitions (四重禁). These are the prohibitions against committing the four grave root sins: (1) killing, (2) stealing, (3) sexual misconduct, and (4) lying, especially alleging spiritual attainment one does not have. The third root sin for monastic Buddhists is having sex.

four groups of disciples (四眾). See Saṅgha.

Four Immeasurable Minds (四無量心). These are (1) lovingkindness, (2) compassion, (3) sympathetic joy, and (4) equability.

four Indian castes (四姓). These are (1) Brahmin (priest), (2) kṣatriya (royalty and warrior), (3) vaiśya (farmer and merchant), and (4) śūdra (serf). The Buddha ruled that all from the four castes would be allowed to become Buddhist śramaṇas as the fifth caste, the highest of all castes.

four modes of birth (四生). Sentient beings are born through (1) the womb, such as humans and other mammals; (2) the egg, such as birds and reptiles; (3)

moisture, such as fishes and insects; (4) miraculous formation, such as gods, ghosts, and hell-dwellers.

four necessities (四事供養). Offerings to a monk, usually including (1) food and drink, (2) clothing, (3) bedding, and (4) medicine.

Four Noble Truths (四聖諦). In His first turning of the Dharma wheel, the Buddha taught the Four Noble Truths: (1) suffering (duḥkha), (2) accumulation (samudaya), (3) cessation (nirodha), and (4) the path (mārga). Suffering is the essence of repeated birth and death through the six life-journeys; accumulation of afflictions, especially thirsty love (tṛṣṇā), is the cause of suffering; cessation of suffering reveals nirvāṇa; and the Eightfold Right Path is the path to nirvāṇa. As a condensed version of the Twelve Links of Dependent Arising, the first two truths reveal that, for continuing the flow of saṁsāra, the cause is the accumulation of afflictions and the effect is suffering. The last two truths reveal that, for terminating the flow of saṁsāra, the cause is taking the Eightfold Right Path and the effect is cessation of suffering, realizing nirvāṇa.

Four Preparatory Trainings (四加行), or Four Roots of Goodness (四善根位). According to the Consciousness-Only School, after the stage of Gathering Provisions is completed, one embarks upon the stage of Preparatory Trainings by investigating the four aspects of dharmas: name, meaning, self-essence, and differentiation, to successively develop the four roots of goodness: (1) Warmth—one realizes in the Illumination Samādhi that objects are empty; (2) Pinnacle—one affirms the same realization through the Enhanced Illumination Samādhi; (3) Endurance—one realizes in the Sealing-in-Accord Samādhi that consciousness as the agent of differentiation is empty; (4) Foremost in the World—one ascertains in the Uninterrupted Samādhi that both the object perceived and the agent that perceives are empty. With this realization, one ascends to the First Bodhisattva Ground (see stages of the Bodhisattva Way), beginning the holy stage toward Buddhahood.

four types of armed forces (四種兵). These are (1) cavalry, (2) elephants, (3) chariots, and (4) infantry.

fourfold kindness (四重恩). Kindness comes from (1) parents and teachers, (2) the Three Jewels, (3) country, and (4) sentient beings.

gandharva (乾闥婆). A fragrance eater who is also a celestial musician playing in the court of gods.

garuḍa (迦樓羅). A large bird-like being that eats dragons.

god (deva, 天). The highest life form in the Three Realms of Existence. According to their merits and mental states, gods reside in six desire heavens, eighteen form heavens, and four formless heavens.

Gṛdhrakūṭa Mountain (耆闍崛山). The Vulture Peak Mountain (靈鷲山), northeast of the city of Rājagṛha. There the Buddha pronounced the *Lotus Sūtra* (T09n0262) and many other sūtras.

Hīnayāna (小乘). The Small Vehicle (see Two Vehicles).

icchantika (一闡提迦). One who has cut off one's roots of goodness and has no desire for Buddhahood. However, Buddhas do not abandon any sentient being and, through their spiritual power, an icchantika may replant his roots of goodness through causes and conditions in a future life and eventually attain Buddhahood. A Bodhisattva who has made a vow not to become a Buddha until all sentient beings have been delivered is called an icchantika of great compassion.

inversion (顛倒). The seven inversions are (1) taking the impermanence of dharmas as permanence; (2) taking misery as happiness; (3) taking impurity as purity; (4) taking no self as self; (5) inverted perceptions, which refer to the inverted differentiations in the first four inversions; (6) inverted views, which refer to the establishment of, attachment to, and delight in the first four inversions; and (7) inverted mind, which refers to afflictions arising from the first four inversions. According to the *Mahāparinirvāṇa Sūtra* (T12n0375), fascicle 7, the first four inversions also include (1) taking the eternity of the Tathāgata as impermanence, (2) taking the bliss of the Tathāgata as suffering, (3) taking the purity of the Tathāgata as impurity, and (4) taking the true self as no self.

Jambudvīpa (贍部洲). One of the four continents surrounding Mount Sumeru in a small world. Located south of Mount Sumeru and identified by the huge jambu tree, Jambudvīpa, the southern continent, is where humans and animals reside.

Jetavana (祇樹園). The Jeta Grove, a garden near Śrāvastī, presented to the Buddha by the Elder Sudatta, who purchased it from Prince Jeta with gold covering its ground. In honor of the two benefactors, the estate was henceforth known as the Garden of Jeta and Anāthapiṇḍika (祇樹給孤獨園). The Buddha spent nineteen rainy seasons with His 1,250 monks in the monastery built on the land. There he gave many of His teachings.

jīvajīva (耆婆耆婆). A legendary two-headed bird (命命鳥) with a beautiful call.

kalaviṅka (迦陵頻伽). A bird with a melodious voice, found in the Himalayas. It has beautiful black plumage and a red beak. It starts singing in the eggshell before it is hatched. Its beautiful voice surpasses that of humans, gods, kiṁnaras, and other birds, and is likened to the wondrous tones of Buddhas and holy Bodhisattvas.

kalpa (劫). An eon. A large kalpa is the long period of formation, staying, destruction, and void of a world. It is divided into eighty small kalpas, each lasting 16,800,000 years.

karma (業).

A. An action, a work, or a deed done with one's body, voice, or mind. Good and evil karmas bring corresponding requitals in one's present and/or future lives. Neutral karmas (無記業) are actions that cannot be accounted as good or evil.

B. Karma (羯磨) is also the work in a ceremony for imparting Buddhist precepts or for repentance. It includes four requirements: (1) the dharma, i.e., the procedure; (2) the purpose; (3) people meeting the quorum; (4) the designated place.

kaṭa-pūtana (迦吒富單那). A stinking hungry ghost that stays at cremation grounds.

Kauśala (憍薩羅國), or Kośala. Situated in central India, it is one of the sixteen ancient kingdoms of India.

kiṁnara (緊那羅). A celestial musician that resembles human, but with horns on his head.

koṭi (俱胝). The edge, the highest point. As a numeral, koṭi means one hundred thousand, one million, or ten million.

kṣaṇa (剎那). The smallest unit of time, something like a nanosecond. According to Buddhist doctrine, a thought lasts 60 kṣaṇas. In each kṣaṇa 900 sets of arising and ceasing of mental processing take place.

kumbhāṇḍa (鳩槃荼). A ghost, shaped like a pot, which feeds on the vitality of humans.

Kuśinagara (拘尸那竭). A city named after the sacred kuśa grass, the capital city of the ancient kingdom of Malla. It was the place where Śākyamuni Buddha entered parinirvāṇa. It is identified by Professor Vogel with Kasia, 180 miles northwest of Patna.

Laṅkā (楞迦). Present-day Sri Lanka or the name of a mountain of gemstones in Sri Lanka.

li (里). A traditional Chinese unit of distance, a Chinese mile. A li now has a standardized length of 500 meters, or half a kilometer.

Licchavi (離車). An Indian clan in the kṣatriya caste, which was a ruling dynasty of the ancient kingdom of Vaiśālī in central India. After the Buddha's parinirvāṇa, the Licchavi people received one eighth of His relics.

life-journey (gati, 趣), or life-path (道). The life experience of a life form in its cycle of birth and death. According to past karmas, a sentient being continues to transmigrate through the six life-journeys in corresponding life forms: god, asura, human, animal, hungry ghost, and hell-dweller. The first three life-journeys are considered the good (fortunate) ones; the last three, the evil (unfortunate) ones. Given to anger and jealousy, asuras may be considered the fourth evil life-journey. Sometimes, only five life-journeys are mentioned in the sūtras because asuras may assume any of the first four life forms and live among sentient beings in these forms. In comparison with life in the Pure Land of Ultimate Bliss, all life-journeys in this world are evil.

ludicrous statement (戲論). All wrong views are ludicrous statements. Furthermore, a statement is composed of words, which are empty names and appearances employed to make differentiations. It is ludicrous because in true reality it is empty.

Magadha (摩竭陀). A kingdom in central India, the headquarters of Buddhism up to year 400.

mahāvaipulya sūtras (大方廣經). Extensive Mahāyāna sūtras that are great in explaining the right principles and great in their vast scope.

Mahāyāna (大乘). The Great Vehicle that can carry many people to Buddhahood. It is also called the Bodhisattva Vehicle because its riders are Bodhisattvas, who are resolved to attain Buddhahood, to benefit themselves and others (see Buddha Vehicle). The Mahāyāna doctrine, widely followed in Northeast Asia (China, Korea, and Japan), refers to the Theravāda School in Southeast Asia (Sri Lanka, Burma, Thailand, Laos, and Cambodia) as the Small Vehicle (Hīnayāna, 小乘), which can be either or both of the Two Vehicles (二乘).

mahoraga (摩呼洛迦). A serpent or land dragon.

mantra (咒). An esoteric incantation. Buddhist mantras are imparted by Buddhas, sometimes through holy Bodhisattvas or Dharma protectors.

māra (魔). Killer, destroyer, evil one, or devil. The four kinds of māras are (1) the celestial māra, a god named Pāpīyān, residing with legions of subordinates in Paranirmita-vaśa-vartin Heaven, the sixth desire heaven; (2) māra of the five aggregates, which conceals one's Buddha mind; (3) māra of afflictions, which drives one to do evil karma; and (4) māra of death, which ends one's life.

mudrā (印). A seal, symbolized by positions of the hands and intertwinings of the fingers, used in ritual practices. A seal possesses secret meanings and magical efficacy (see Dharma Seal).

namo (南無). Reverential homage, salutation, adoration, or obeisance. Based on the Sanskrit rule of pronunciation, this word may be spelled as namo, nama, namaḥ, namas, or namaś, according to the initial letter of the next word.

Nārāyaṇa (那羅延天). A Hindu god who has great strength. He is identified as Viṣṇu in the desire realm, and is included in the trinity of Brahmā, Nārāyaṇa, and Maheśvara (Śiva, in Hinduism).

nayuta (那由他), or niyuta. A numeral, meaning one hundred thousand, one million, or ten million.

Nirgranthaputra (尼乾子). One of the six non-Buddhist groups in ancient India. Nirgrantha means untied, which is the former name of the devotees of Jainism, who wander naked, untied to possessions. Nirgrantha-Jñātaputra (尼乾陀若提子), named after his mother, Jñātī, was the 24th and last patriarch of the Jain School, and he is now revered as the Mahāvīra (great hero). Their doctrine is fatalistic, stating that no spiritual practice can change one's good or evil karma and that all sentient beings would be automatically liberated after 80,000 kalpas of birth and death.

nirvāṇa (涅槃). By taking the Eightfold Right Path, one eradicates one's afflictions and realizes nirvāṇa, liberating oneself from one's cycle of birth and death. The four nirvāṇas are (1) the inherent nirvāṇa (自性涅槃), which means true reality, the no birth and no death of all dharmas; (2) the nirvāṇa with remnant (有餘依涅槃), which means the enlightenment of an Arhat or a Pratyekabuddha who is still living; (3) the nirvāṇa without remnant (無餘依涅槃), which means the death of an Arhat or a Pratyekabuddha, who has abandoned his body, the remnant of his karmic existence; and (4) the nirvāṇa that abides nowhere (無住處涅槃), which means the supreme enlightenment of a Buddha. The great nirvāṇa of a Buddha includes the realization of the eternity, bliss, true self, and purity of the Tathāgata, and the attainment of powers unavailable to an Arhat or a Pratyekabuddha. Beyond the duality of existence and nonexistence, saṁsāra and nirvāṇa, a Buddha continues to manifest in most suitable ways in response to the needs of sentient beings, thus abiding nowhere.

no regress. See avinivartanīya.

nourishment (食). Provided by (1) ingestion of food; (2) contact with enjoyable sense objects, such as sights, sounds, scents, flavors, and tactile sensations; (3) formation of mental food, such as ideas, expectations, and recollections; and (4) ālaya consciousness that maintains one's physiological and mental processes as well as carries karmic seeds, which will lead to future rebirths.

An ordinary being in the desire realm requires these four kinds of nourishment to survive.

one appearance (eka-lakṣaṇa, 一相). All dharmas are in the one appearance of true suchness, which is beyond differentiation of appearances and beyond differentiation between appearance and no appearance. However, the one appearance is often referred to as the one appearance of no appearance.

one flavor (eka-rasa, 一味). (1) All dharmas are in the one flavor of true suchness. (2) The Buddha's teachings of the Three Vehicles are all in the one flavor of the One Vehicle. As the one appearance of dharmas is likened to the earth, the one flavor of the Buddha's teachings is likened to the rain nourishing all the plants on earth.

parinirvāṇa (般涅槃). It means beyond nirvāṇa, the death of an Arhat or a Buddha by entering profound samādhi. Whether or not He has abandoned His body in demonstrating parinirvāṇa, a Buddha is in the nirvāṇa that abides nowhere, beyond the duality of existence and nonexistence. A Buddha's parinirvāṇa is called mahāparinirvāṇa.

past seven Buddhas (過去七佛). The last 3 of the 1,000 Buddhas of the preceding Majestic Kalpa are Vipaśyin, Śikhin, and Viśvabhū; the first 4 of the 1,000 Buddhas of the present Worthy Kalpa are Krakucchanda, Kanakamuni, Kāśyapa, and Śākyamuni.

perfect passage (圓通). A Dharma Door, the perfect practice of meditation, through which one can pass from ignorance to significant realizations. In the *Śūraṅgama Sūtra* (T19n0945), at the Buddha's command, twenty-five Arhats and holy Bodhisattvas reveal their perfect passages.

piśāca (畢舍遮). A demonic ghost that eats human flesh and sucks human vitality.

pippala (畢鉢羅). The fig (ficus religiosa) tree, a species of banyan fig, native to India. This sacred tree is renamed the bodhi tree because Śākyamuni Buddha was enlightened sitting under it.

prātimokṣa (波羅提木叉). The Sanskrit word *prati* means toward or severally, and *mokṣa* means liberation. The term *prātimokṣa* is translated into Chinese as "liberation achieved severally" (別解脫). It is also referred to as prātimokṣa-saṁvara, where *saṁvara* means restraint (律儀), or more commonly as prātimokṣa-śīla, where *śīla* means precept (戒), because observance of different precepts leads to liberation severally from corresponding evils of one's body, voice, and mind. Moreover, prātimokṣa precepts instituted by the Buddha for His seven groups of disciples in the desire realm are separate from precepts naturally arising in one's mind from one's meditation at the form-realm level (定共戒), and from precepts naturally arising in one's mind from one's realization of bodhi (道共戒).

Pratyekabuddha (緣覺佛). One who is enlightened through contemplating the Twelve Links of Dependent Arising. He is also called a solitary Buddha (獨覺佛) because, living in solitude, he has realized the truth without receiving teachings from a Buddha.

pure abode heavens (淨居天). The top five of the nine heavens that constitute the fourth dhyāna heaven in the form realm (see Three Realms of Existence).

pūtana (富單那). A stinking hungry ghost that is shaped like a hog and scares children.

Rājagṛha (王舍城). The capital city of Magadha in central India, near the Vulture Peak Mountain.

rakṣasa (羅剎). A demonic ghost that eats human flesh. Rakṣasas are said to be the original inhabitants of Sri Lanka.

right mindfulness (samyak-smṛti, 正念). The seventh in the Eightfold Right Path. A few examples of right mindfulness include (1) practice of the Four Foundations of Mindfulness; (2) remembrance of the Dharma, such as the no birth of all dharmas; (3) remembrance of a Buddha; and (4) the inconceivable mindfulness of a Buddha.

roots of goodness (kuśala-mūla, 善根). These are (1) no greed, (2) no anger, and (3) no delusion. The five roots in Thirty-seven Elements of Bodhi are goodness in themselves and can grow other good dharmas (also see Four Preparatory Trainings).

ṛṣi (仙人). An ascetic hermit considered to be an immortal or a godlike human. Śākyamuni Buddha is also revered as the Great Ṛṣi. In the *Śūraṅgama Sūtra* (T19n0945), the Buddha describes ten kinds of ṛṣis, who live thousands or tens of thousands of years, with the five transcendental powers, such as walking on land, traveling across sky, changing themselves into any form, etc.

Sahā World (sahā-lokadhātu, 娑婆世界). The endurance world. It refers to Jambudvīpa or the Three-Thousand Large Thousandfold World, where its inhabitants are able to endure their suffering and may even find their lives enjoyable.

Śakro-Devānām-Indra (釋提桓因). The title of the god-king of Trayastriṁśa Heaven, often abbreviated as Śakra or Indra. The Buddha calls the incumbent Śakra by his family name, Kauśika.

samādhi (定). A state of mental absorption in meditation. Above the level of the desire realm, there are eight levels of worldly samādhi (八定). The first four levels are the four dhyānas (四禪) of the form realm. The next four levels are the four samādhis of the formless realm (四空定): Boundless Space (空無邊), Boundless Consciousness (識無邊), Nothingness (無所有), and Neither with Nor without Perception (非有想非無想). A Buddhist or non-Buddhist who has attained any of the eight levels of meditation can be reborn in a corresponding heaven in the form or formless realm. Only an Arhat can attain the ninth level called the Samādhi of Total Halt (滅盡定), also more appropriately called the Samādhi of Total Suspension of Sensory Reception and Perception (滅受想定). To enter the Samādhi Door of Buddhas is to attain innumerable samādhis.

śamatha (奢摩他). It means stillness, a mental state in which one's mind is in single-minded concentration (see vipaśyanā).

saṁsāra (輪迴), or jāti-maraṇa (生死). The cycle of birth and death, in which every sentient being transmigrates through the six life-journeys in the Three Realms of Existence. This endless cycle is called the hard-to-cross ocean, also called the ocean of suffering (see two types of birth and death).

saṁskṛta (有爲). Formed or made through causes and conditions. Each saṁskṛta dharma is a process with the four appearances. Sentient beings and all the things they perceive or conceive are saṁskṛta dharmas (see asaṁskṛta).

samyak-saṁbodhi (等正覺). See anuttara-samyak-saṁbodhi.

Saṅgha (僧伽). A community comprising a Buddha's four groups of disciples (四眾): monks (bhikṣu), nuns (bhikṣuṇī), laymen (upāsaka), and laywomen (upāsikā).

śārī (舍利). A mynah bird. Śārikā was the name of Śāriputra's mother because her eyes were bright and clever like those of a mynah.

sarvajña. See three wisdom-knowledges.

self-essence (svabhāva, 自性). An inherent state of being, self-made, self-determined, and changeless. This is a false reality that sentient beings attach to their perceptions. In truth, nothing has self-essence because everything is constantly changing through causes and conditions. That all dharmas are without self-essence is the true reality defined as emptiness.

Seven Bodhi Factors (七覺分). These are (1) critical examination of theories, (2) energetic progress, (3) joyful mentality, (4) lightness and peacefulness in body and mind, (5) mindfulness in all activities and remembrance of the true Dharma, (6) samādhi, and (7) equability under favorable or unfavorable circumstances.

seven noble treasures (七聖財). These are (1) faith, (2) wisdom, (3) observing the precepts, (4) hearing teachings, (5) having a sense of shame, (6) having a sense of dishonor, and (7) discarding afflictions.

seven treasures (七寶). These are (1) suvarṇa (金, gold); (2) rūpya (銀, silver); (3) vaiḍūrya (琉璃, aquamarine); (4) sphaṭika (頗梨, crystal); (5) musāragalva (硨磲, conch shell or white coral); (6) lohita-muktikā (赤珠, ruby); and (7) aśmagarbha (瑪瑙, emerald). Sometimes coral and amber are included in place of crystal and ruby. F. Max Müller cites a reference in *Buddhist Mahāyāna Texts* (Cowell et al. [1894] 1969, part 2, 92), in which vaiḍūrya is matched with lapis lazuli, and aśmagarbha with diamond. While lapis lazuli is an opaque intense blue stone, indications in the sūtras are that vaiḍūrya should be a transparent blue beryl, such as aquamarine. According to the *Monier-Williams Online Dictionary*, aśmagarbha is emerald; vajra (伐折羅) is diamond, an adamantine mineral (金剛).

siddhi (悉地). Achievement through spiritual training using one's body, voice, and mind. The ultimate siddhi is Buddhahood.

six desire heavens (六欲天). (1) Heaven of the Four God-Kings (Cātur-mahārāja-kāyika-deva, 四天王天); (2) Trayastriṁśa Heaven (忉利天), or Thirty-three Heavens (三十三天), ruled by Śakra-Devānām-Indra; (3) Yāma Heaven (夜摩天), ruled by Suyāma-devarāja; (4) Tuṣita Heaven (兜率天), ruled by Saṁtuṣita-devarāja; (5) Nirmāṇa-rati Heaven (化自在天), ruled by Sunirmita-devarāja; (6) Paranirmita-vaśa-vartin Heaven (他化自在天), ruled by Vaśavartti-devarāja. The first two heavens are earth-abode heavens; all other heavens are sky-abode heavens.

six domains (ṣad-dhātu, 六界, 六大). A sentient being is made of the six domains—earth, water, fire, wind, space, and consciousness—and appears to have these features: solid substance, fluid, heat, motion, space within the body, and consciousness. A non-sentient thing (plant or nonliving thing) is made of the first five domains (see four domains).

six faculties (ṣaḍ-indriya, 六根, 六入). These are eye, ear, nose, tongue, body, and mental faculty (manas). The first five are sense organs, which function as sensory entrances (see twelve fields).

six pāramitās (六度, 六波羅蜜). The Sanskrit word *pāramita* means gone across to the opposite shore. To succeed in crossing over to that shore of nirvāṇa, opposite this shore of saṁsāra, a Bodhisattva needs to achieve the six pāramitās: (1) dāna (almsgiving), (2) śīla (observance of precepts), (3) kṣānti (endurance of adversity), (4) vīrya (energetic progress), (5) dhyāna (meditation), and (6) prajñā (development of wisdom). See ten pāramitās.

six periods (六時). The day is divided into morning (6–10 a.m.), midday (10 a.m. – 2 p.m.), and afternoon (2–6 p.m.); the night into evening (6–10 p.m.), midnight (10 p.m.–2 a.m.), and post-midnight (2–6 a.m.). Each period has four hours.

six transcendental powers (六通). With no more afflictions to discharge, an Arhat has liberated himself from his cycle of birth and death. Hence, eradication of afflictions, which ends their discharges (漏盡通), is called the sixth transcendental power of an Arhat, which is unavailable to those who have not attained Arhatship. It also makes his achievement in the first five transcendental powers superior to that of those others.

sixty-two views (六十二見). The wrong views held by ancient Indian philosophers. One set of 62 views argues about each of the five aggregates of a sentient being: in the past it is permanent, impermanent, both, or neither; in the present it is with boundary, without boundary, both, or neither; in the future it is going, not going, both, or neither. To these 60 views, two polar opposites, perpetuity and cessation of existence, are added to make a total of 62. Another set of 62 views includes 56 views of self and 6 views of existence. They hold that each of the five aggregates of a sentient being in the desire realm and the form realm and each of the four aggregates of a god in the formless realm is self, not self, both, or neither, totaling 56 views. In addition, perpetuity and cessation of existence in the Three Realms comes to 6 views.

śramaṇa (沙門). An ascetic or a monk, one who has renounced family life and lives a life of purity, poverty, and diligent training, seeking the truth.

Śrāvastī (舍衛國). The capital city of the ancient kingdom of Kauśala.

stages of the Bodhisattva Way (菩薩階位). The spiritual levels of a Bodhisattva on the Way to Buddhahood. According to the 80-fascicle version of the *Mahāvaipulya Sūtra of Buddha Adornment* (T10n0279), a Bodhisattva advances through fifty-two levels, which are grouped into seven stages: (1) ten faithful minds, (2) ten levels of abiding, (3) ten levels of action, (4) ten levels of transference of merit, (5) Ten Grounds, (6) virtually perfect enlightenment, and (7) perfect enlightenment. A Bodhisattva will continue to be an ordinary being as he cultivates the ten faithful minds; he will be a sage as he practices the ten pāramitās, progressing through the ten levels of abiding, ten levels of action, and ten levels of transference of merit; and he will be a holy being as he progresses through the Ten Grounds. A Bodhisattva will ascend to the

First Ground when he realizes that all dharmas have no birth. As he progresses from the First Ground to the Tenth Ground, he will achieve the ten pāramitās one after another, in one-to-one correspondence with the Ten Grounds. At the fifty-first level, his enlightenment being virtually perfect, he will be in the holy position of waiting to become a Buddha in his next life. At the fifty-second level, he attains the perfect enlightenment, achieving the ultimate fruit of the aspiration and training of a Bodhisattva.

store (藏). A paraphrase of the Sanskrit word *garbha*, which means the womb or the child in the womb. Then the thus-come store (tathāgata-garbha) is one's true mind, also called the vajra (indestructible) store. One's true mind is likened to the space store in its vastness, and to the earth store in its supportiveness and hidden treasures. The realm of all dharmas is the dharma store. The aggregate of all Dharmas (Buddhas' teachings) is the Dharma store; the collection of all precepts is the precept store.

stūpa (窣堵婆). A memorial pagoda for the remains of a holy being, whether relics of bones or scriptures.

suffering (duḥkha, 苦). The first of the Four Noble Truths.

A. The eight kinds of suffering are (1) birth, (2) old age, (3) illness, (4) death, (5) inability to get what one wants, (6) loss of what one loves, (7) encounter with what one hates, and (8) the driving force of the five aggregates. Driven by the five aggregates, one experiences impermanence, pain, and sorrow in the preceding seven situations.

B. The three kinds of suffering are (1) pain brought by a cause (苦苦), (2) deterioration of pleasure (壞苦), and (3) continuous change in all processes (行苦).

sūtras in the twelve categories (十二部經). The teachings of the Buddha are classified by content and form into the twelve categories: (1) sūtra, discourses in prose; (2) geya, songs that repeat the teachings; (3) vyākaraṇa, prophecies; (4) gāthā, stanzas; (5) udāna, self-initiated utterances; (6) nidāna, causes for the discourses; (7) avadāna, parables; (8) itivṛttaka, sūtras that begin with "so it has been said"; (9) jātaka, past lives of the Buddha; (10) vaipulya, extensive teachings; (11) adbhuta-dharma, marvelous events; and (12) upadeśa, pointing-out instructions.

svastika (萬). The auspicious symbol on the chest of a Buddha, one of His thirty-two major marks. This symbol (卍) initially describes His hair turning to the right, like an ocean of clouds, bringing joy to viewers. The flip side (卐) of this symbol is also used in different editions of the Chinese Buddhist Canon. However, it was adopted by Nazi Germany in the twentieth century and became stigmatized.

Tathāgata (如來). The Thus-Come One, the first of the ten epithets of a Buddha, which signifies true suchness. Although the Tathāgata never moves, a Buddha appears to have come and gone in the same way as have past Buddhas.

ten appearances (十相). As stated in the *Mahāparinirvāṇa Sūtra* (T12n0375), the appearances of a sentient being are (1) sights, (2) sounds, (3) scents, (4) flavors, (5) tactile sensations, (6) birth, (7) staying, (8) death, (9) male, and (10) female (see four appearances).

ten directions (十方). The spatial directions of east, southeast, south, southwest, west, northwest, north, northeast, the nadir, and the zenith.

ten evil karmas (十惡). These are (1) killing, (2) stealing, (3) sexual misconduct, (4) false speech, (5) divisive speech, (6) abusive speech, (7) suggestive speech, (8) greed, (9) anger, and (10) the wrong views.

ten fetters (十纏). These are (1) no sense of shame, (2) no sense of dishonor, (3) jealousy, (4) stinginess, (5) remorse, (6) torpor, (7) restlessness, (8) stupor, (9) rage, and (10) concealing one's wrongdoings.

ten good karmas (十善). The opposites of the ten evil karmas are (1) no killing, (2) no stealing, (3) no sexual misconduct, (4) no false speech, (5) no divisive speech, (6) no abusive speech, (7) no suggestive speech, (8) no greed, (9) no anger, and (10) no wrong views.

ten pāramitās (十度, 十波羅蜜). In parallel with the Ten Grounds for Bodhisattva development (see stages of the Bodhisattva Way), added to the list of six pāramitās are four more pāramitās: (7) upāya (skillful means), (8) praṇidhāna (earnest wish), (9) bala (power), and (10) jñāna (wisdom-knowledge).

Ten Powers (daśa-bala, 十力). Only a Buddha has perfect knowledge of (1) the right or wrong in every situation and its corresponding karmic consequences; (2) the karmic requitals of every sentient being in the past, present, and future; (3) all stages of dhyāna and samādhi; (4) the capacity and future attainment of every sentient being; (5) the desires and inclinations of every sentient being; (6) the nature and condition of every sentient being; (7) the consequences of all actions with or without afflictions; (8) all past lives of every sentient being and their karmic reasons; (9) all future rebirths of every sentient being and their karmic reasons; and (10) the permanent termination of all afflictions and habits upon attainment of Buddhahood.

ten precepts (daśa-śīla, 十戒). Observed by novice monks and nuns, the ten precepts include the eight precepts, but precepts 7 and 8 are renumbered 8 and 9, because precept 6 is divided into two: (6) no wearing perfumes or adornments, and (7) no singing, dancing, or watching song-dance entertainments. A tenth precept is added: (10) no touching or hoarding money or treasures.

Thirty-seven Elements of Bodhi (三十七道品). Trainings for attaining bodhi include

A. Four Foundations of Mindfulness;
B. Four Right Endeavors [(1) end forever the existing evil, (2) do not allow new evil to arise, (3) cause new goodness to arise, and (4) expand existing goodness];
C. Four Works to Attain Samādhi [(1) aspiration, (2) energetic progress, (3) focus, and (4) contemplation];
D. Five Roots [(1) faith, (2) energetic progress, (3) remembrance of the true Dharma, (4) samādhi, and (5) wisdom];
E. Five Powers [(1) power in faith, (2) power in energetic progress, (3) power in remembrance of the true Dharma, (4) power in samādhi, and (5) power in wisdom];
F. Seven Bodhi Factors;
G. Eightfold Right Path.

three ages of the Dharma (正像末期). The Dharma of Śākyamuni Buddha will end after these three ages: (1) The true Dharma age (正法) lasted 500 to 1,000 years after His passing. During this period, there were teachings, carrying out of the teachings, and attaining of fruits. (2) The Dharma-likeness age (像法) lasted 500 to 1,000 years. During this period, there were teachings and carrying out of the teachings, but no attaining of fruits. (3) The Dharma-ending age (末法) will last 10,000 years. During this period, the teachings will gradually vanish, and there will be neither carrying out of the teachings nor attaining of fruits. Because people will no longer be receptive, the Dharma will be gone for a long time until the advent of the next Buddha. In the *Bodhisattva in the Womb Sūtra* (T12n384, 1025c15–19), fascicle 2, the Buddha prophesies that, after 56 koṭi and 70 million years, which means 630 million years (if a koṭi is 10 million), Maitreya Bodhisattva will descend from Tuṣita Heaven and become the next Buddha, bringing the Dharma to a renewed world.

three bodies of a Buddha (三身). These are (1) dharmakāya (the dharma body or truth body), which is emptiness, the true reality of all dharmas; (2) saṁbhogakāya (the reward body or enjoyment body) in a sublime ethereal form, which represents the immeasurable merit of a Buddha; and (3) nirmāṇakāya (a response body through birth or a miraculously manifested body), which is the manifestation of a Buddha in response to sentient beings that are ready to accept the Dharma. The reward body and the response body are the appearances of the dharma body, and these three bodies are inseparable. According to the Tiantai School of China, of the latest Buddha, Vairocana is the dharmakāya, Rocana is the saṁbhogakāya, and Śākyamuni is the nirmāṇakāya.

three Buddha natures (三佛性). These are (1) Buddha nature inherent in all sentient beings but unknown to them, (2) Buddha nature gradually revealed through one's spiritual training, and (3) Buddha nature evident in a Buddha.

Three Clarities (三明). An Arhat has achieved (1) clear knowledge of the past lives of himself and others and their causes and conditions, (2) clarity of his god-eye that sees others' future lives and their causes and conditions, and (3) clear knowledge that his afflictions have ceased and will never arise again. The Three Clarities of a Buddha are supreme and are called the Three Thorough Clarities (三達).

three dharmas (三法). Teachings, practices, and realization of holy fruit.

Three Endurances in the Dharma (三法忍). According to the *Sūtra of Amitāyus Buddha* (T12n0360), these are (1) Endurance in Hearing the Sounds (音響忍), which means acceptance of the Dharma through hearing it; (2) Endurance in Accord (柔順忍), which means agreement with the Dharma through pondering in accord with the truth; and (3) Endurance in the Realization of the No Birth of Dharmas (無生法忍), which is the lasting realization of the truth that dharmas have neither birth nor death.

three fortune fields (三福田). These are (1) the reverence field (敬田), which means the Three Jewels; (2) the kindness field (恩田), which means one's parents and teachers; and (3) the compassion field (悲田), which means the poor, the sick, and animals. By making offerings to any of these three fortune fields, one plants seeds which will yield harvests of fortune in one's present and future lives.

Three Jewels (三寶). These are (1) the Buddha, the unsurpassed perfectly enlightened teacher; (2) the Dharma, His teachings; and (3) the Saṅgha, the Buddhist community.

three kinds of hindrances (三障). Hindrances to realization of one's true mind are (1) afflictions, such as greed, anger, and delusion, which agitate one's mind and lead to negative karmas; (2) karmas, done with one's body, voice, and mind, which lead to requitals; and (3) requitals, such as an unfortunate rebirth in human form with incomplete faculties, or in the form of animal, hungry ghost, or hell-dweller.

Three Liberation Doors (trīṇi vimokṣa-mokha, 三解脫門), or Three Samādhis. These are (1) emptiness, (2) no appearance, and (3) no wish or no act. Through samādhi, one realizes emptiness, penetrating the no birth of all dharmas. One also realizes that the illusory appearances of dharmas conceived or perceived are no appearance. One makes no wish and does nothing for future rebirths in the Three Realms of Existence.

Three Realms of Existence (trayo-dhātu, 三界, 三有). The world of illusory existence, in which sentient beings transmigrate, comprises (1) the desire realm (欲界), where reside sentient beings with the full range of afflictions, such as hell-dwellers, ghosts, animals, humans, asuras, and some gods; (2) the form realm (色界), where Brahma gods, who have only pure desires, reside in eighteen form heavens classified into the four dhyāna heavens (四禪天), or four levels of meditation; and (3) the formless realm (無色界), where formless gods are in mental existence in four formless heavens, or at four levels of long, deep meditative absorption (see samādhi).

Three Refuges (三皈依). One becomes a Buddhist by taking refuge, for protection and guidance, in the Three Jewels: the Buddha, the Dharma, and the Saṅgha. In the *Sūtra of the Upāsaka Precepts* (T24n1488), the Buddha teaches the Four Refuges, and the fourth one is the Precepts.

Three Samādhis (三三昧). See Three Liberation Doors.

Three Vehicles (三乘). The Great Vehicle (Mahāyāna) and the Two Vehicles.

three white foods (三白食). Milk, cream or curd, and white rice.

three wisdom-knowledges (三智). These are (1) the overall wisdom-knowledge (sarvajña, 一切智), which is the emptiness of everything, realized by an Arhat, a Pratyekabuddha, and a holy Bodhisattva; (2) discriminatory wisdom-knowledge (道種智), which is developed in a holy Bodhisattva, who differentiates all displays of illusory existence in order to deliver sentient beings; and (3) knowledge of all knowledge (sarvajña-jñāna, 一切種智), or omniscience (sarvajñatā), which is a Buddha's perfect wisdom-knowledge of all beings and all things in their general and particular aspects, and of the non-duality of emptiness and myriad displays.

Three-Thousand Large Thousandfold World (三千大千世界). A galaxy, the educational district of a Buddha. It consists of a billion small worlds, each including a Mount Sumeru surrounded by four continents and interlaying circles of eight oceans and eight mountain ranges. One thousand such small worlds constitute a Small Thousandfold World. One thousand Small

Thousandfold Worlds constitute a Medium Thousandfold World. Finally, one thousand Medium Thousandfold Worlds constitute a Large Thousandfold World. Therefore, *Three-Thousand* does not mean 3,000, but 1,000 raised to the power of 3, as described above. It can also mean that there are three kinds of Thousandfold World: small, medium, and large.

total retention (總持). See dhāraṇī.

Trayastriṁśa Heaven (忉利天). The second of the six desire heavens. It is on the top of Mount Sumeru, and the first desire heaven is halfway up Mount Sumeru, while all other heavens are up in the sky. Trayastriṁśa Heaven means Thirty-three Heavens, all ruled by the god-king Śakro-Devānām-Indra, who is commonly called Śakra or Indra.

Tripiṭaka (三藏). The three collections of texts of the Buddhist canon: (1) the Sūtra-piṭaka, discourses of the Buddha; (2) the Vinaya-piṭaka, rules of conduct; and (3) the Abhidharma-piṭaka, treatises on the Dharma. A Tripiṭaka master is accomplished in all three areas.

true suchness (bhūta-tathatā, 真如). The changeless true reality of all dharmas, the absolute truth that dharmas have neither birth nor death. It has other names, including emptiness, true emptiness, ultimate emptiness, one appearance, one flavor, true reality, ultimate reality (bhūta-koṭi), primal state, Buddha mind, true mind, inherent pure mind, the Thus-Come One (Tathāgata), the thus-come store (Tathāgata-garbha), vajra store, dharma-kāya, Buddha nature, dharma nature, dharma realm, the one true dharma realm, the highest truth (paramārtha), the great seal, and the great perfection. One's body and mental states, and objects perceived as external, are all manifestations of one's true mind, projected through causes and conditions from the pure, impure, and neutral seeds stored in ālaya consciousness.

twelve fields (dvādaśa-āyatana, 十二處, 十二入). A sentient being is composed of the twelve fields: the six faculties (eye, ear, nose, tongue, body, and mental faculty [manas]) and their six objects (sights, sounds, scents, flavors, tactile sensations, and mental objects). The six faculties are also called the six internal fields, and their objects are called the six external fields. The Consciousness-only School calls the latter "projected appearances" (影像相分). And modern neurologists recognize that percepts are "brain representations" (see eighteen spheres).

Twelve Links of Dependent Arising (十二因緣法). The principle that explains why and how a sentient being continues to be reborn according to karma. Each link is the main condition for the next one to arise. These twelve links are (1) ignorance, (2) karmic actions, (3) consciousness, (4) name and form, (5) six faculties, (6) contact with sense objects, (7) sensory reception, (8) love, (9) grasping, (10) karmic force for being, (11) birth, and (12) old age and death. Links 1–2 refer to the afflictions and karmic seeds from previous lives, links 3–7 refer to the karmic fruit in the present life, links 8–10 refer to karmas in the present life, and links 11–12 refer to the karmic fruit in the next life. In this sequence, the twelve links connect one's lives from the past to the present, continuing to the future. With ignorance, one goes from affliction to karma to suffering, continuing the endless spiral of birth and death. By ending ignorance one will disengage the remaining eleven links and end one's cycle of birth and death.

twenty-five forms of existence (二十五有). There are fourteen in the desire realm (欲界), seven in the form realm (色界), and four in the formless realm (無色界).

two emptinesses (二空). (1) The emptiness of a sentient being (人空) composed of dharmas, such as the five aggregates, and dependent on causes and conditions; (2) the emptiness of a dharma (法空) dependent on causes and conditions (see eighteen emptinesses).

Two Paths (二道).

A. (1) The Path with Discharges (有漏道) is the worldly path taken by those with afflictions, as they follow the first two of the Four Noble Truths and transmigrate in the Three Realms of Existence; (2) the Path without Discharges (無漏道) is the holy path taken by those who follow the last two of the Four Noble Truths, in order to eradicate their afflictions and transcend the Three Realms (see discharge).

B. (1) The Difficult Path (難行道) to Buddhahood is through repeated birth and death in the Three Realms of Existence; (2) the Easy Path (易行道) to Buddhahood is through rebirth in a Pure Buddha Land to train there.

two types of birth and death (二種生死). (1) An ordinary being, whose lifespan and life form are governed by the law of karma, repeatedly undergoes karmic birth and death (分段生死). (2) A holy Bodhisattva on any of the Ten Grounds, whose lifespan and mind-created body (意生身) are changeable at will, undergoes changeable birth and death (變易生死). Only a Buddha has ended both types of birth and death.

Two Vehicles (二乘). The Voice-Hearer Vehicle that leads to Arhatship and the Pratyekabuddha Vehicle that leads to Pratyekabuddhahood, for one's own liberation only. The Mahāyāna doctrine refers to the Theravāda School in Southeast Asia (Sri Lanka, Burma, Thailand, Laos, and Cambodia) as the Small Vehicle (Hīnayāna), which can be either or both of these Two Vehicles.

Two-Footed Honored One (dvipadottama, 兩足尊). A Buddha is the most honored one among sentient beings standing on two feet, i.e., gods and humans. Moreover, the two feet of a Buddha are compared to meditation and moral conduct, merit and wisdom, knowledge in the relative and absolute truth, knowledge and action, or vow and action. A Buddha has perfected both.

unimpeded eloquence (無礙辯). This includes (1) unimpeded understanding of dharmas, (2) unimpeded interpretation of their meanings, (3) unimpeded forms of expression, and (4) unimpeded delight in articulation according to the capacity of the listeners.

upadeśa (優波提舍). A pointing-out instruction, usually interpreted as a treatise (see sūtras in the twelve categories).

upaniṣad (優波尼薩曇). Sitting down at the feet of another to listen to his words. It suggests secret knowledge given in this manner. It may be an esoteric unit of measure.

upāsaka (優婆塞). A Buddhist layman (see Saṅgha).

upāsikā (優婆夷). A Buddhist laywoman. (see Saṅgha).

Vairocana (毘盧遮那). The name of the dharmakāya or saṁbhogakāya of a Buddha (see three bodies of a Buddha). Vairocana means pervasive radiance, and signifies the universal equality of everything in true suchness as well as the all-encompassing wisdom of a Buddha. According to the *Mahāvaipulya Sūtra of Buddha Adornment* (T09n278) in 60 fascicles, Vairocana is the name for a Buddha's dharmakāya. According to the *Brahma Net Sūtra* (T24n1484), Rocana is the name for a Buddha's saṁbhogakāya. Śākyamuni Buddha, in his nirmāṇakāya, is sometimes referred to as Vairocana Buddha or Rocana Buddha.

Vaiśālī (毘舍離). The domicile of the Licchavi clan, one of the sixteen great city kingdoms of ancient India. One hundred years after the Buddha's parinirvāṇa, in this city, 700 sages gathered in the second assembly for the compilation and revision of the Buddhist Canon.

vajra (伐折羅, 金剛). (1) Adamantine and indestructible, a description of the true suchness of all dharmas. (2) Diamond, considered to be as hard as the thunderbolt. (3) A ritual object, as a symbol of skillful means for delivering oneself and others from the cycle of birth and death.

Vārāṇasī (波羅奈國). An ancient city state on the Ganges, the present-day city of Benares. Nearby is Deer Park, where the Buddha gave His first teachings to five monks.

Veda (吠陀). Sacred knowledge, the general name of the Hindu canonical sacred texts. The four Vedas are the Ṛg-veda, Sāma-veda, Yajur-veda, and Athara-veda. They include mantras, prayers, hymns, and rituals. The Ṛg-veda is the only original work of the first three Vedas. Its texts are assigned to a period between 1400 and 1000 BCE. The fourth Veda, Athara-veda, emerged later.

vessel world (器世間). The living environment of a sentient being, e.g., a birdcage holding a bird. For this sentient being, assuming the life form of a bird is the main requital (正報), and living in a birdcage, its vessel world, is the reliance requital (依報). Although the main requital does not change during the life of a sentient being, its reliance requital may change, e.g., the bird may be released from its cage.

view of void (空見). The wrong view that the emptiness of dharmas means nothingness and that therefore causality can be ignored.

vipaśyanā (毗婆舍那). Correct observation or clear seeing, which leads to insight. Śamatha-vipaśyanā has been translated as stillness and observation (止觀), or as silent illumination (默照). When śamatha and vipaśyanā are balanced in power, one may realize the non-dual state of one's mind.

voice-hearer (śrāvaka, 聲聞). One who has received oral teachings from a Buddha. The four groups of disciples of Śākyamuni Buddha were all voice-hearers. In the *Lotus Sūtra* (T09n0262), the Buddha bestows upon 1,200 Arhats and 2,000 voice-hearers the prophecy of attaining Buddhahood. Listed below are a few disciples of the Buddha:

Ājñātakauṇḍinya (阿若憍陳如) was one of the first five disciples of the Buddha. He is well regarded as an Elder.

Ānanda (阿難) was the younger brother of Devadatta. As the Buddha's attendant, he is noted for hearing and remembering all the teachings of the Buddha. Ānanda became an Arhat after the Buddha's parinirvāṇa. In the first assembly of Arhats, he recited from memory all the teachings for the compilation of the sūtras. Succeeding Mahākāśyapa, he is reckoned as the second patriarch of the Buddhist lineage.

Aniruddha (阿那律) became a disciple soon after the Buddha's enlightenment. He used to fall asleep when the Buddha was teaching and was reproved by the Buddha. Ashamed, he practiced day and night without sleep and lost his eyesight. However, he was able to see with his god-eye.

Cullapatka (周梨槃陀迦), also called Śuddhipanthaka, and his twin brother, Patka (Panthaka), were born on a roadside while their parents were traveling. He was forgetful of the Buddha's teachings. Then the Buddha told him to remember the short phrase "remove the dust and filth" as he did cleaning work in his daily life. He then attained Arhatship and transcendental powers.

Devadatta (提婆達多) was a cousin of the Buddha, with whom he had competed since childhood. He became a disciple after the Buddha had attained perfect enlightenment. He trained hard for twelve years but did not attain Arhatship. Disgusted, he studied magic and formed his own group. Devadatta beat a nun to death and made several attempts to murder the Buddha and destroy the Saṅgha. He fell into hell after his death. However, in a previous life he had given the Buddha Mahāyāna teachings. Despite the wicked deeds in his life, the Buddha prophesies in the *Lotus Sūtra* (T09n0262) that Devadatta will become a Buddha called Devarāja.

Kapphiṇa (劫賓那) was born under the constellation Scorpio. He is said to have understood astronomy, been the king of Southern Kauśala, and then become a disciple of the Buddha, receiving his monastic name Mahākapphiṇa. In the *Lotus Sūtra* (T09n0262), the Buddha prophesies that Kapphiṇa will become a Buddha called Samanta-prabhāsa.

Kāśyapa brothers (三迦葉) were Uruvilvākāśyapa (優樓頻螺迦葉), Nadīkāśyapa (那提迦葉), and Gayākāśyapa (伽耶迦葉). Initially fire-worshippers, they joined the Buddha's Order together with their 1,000 followers.

Mahāculla (摩訶周那), also called Patka, Panthaka, or Mahāpanthaka, was the elder twin brother of Cullapatka. More intelligent than his twin, he soon attained Arhatship after joining the Buddha's Order.

Mahākāśyapa (摩訶迦葉) was initially a Brahmin in Magadha. He became a disciple three years after the Buddha had attained enlightenment. In eight days, Mahākāśyapa attained Arhatship. He is considered foremost in ascetic practices. When the Buddha held up a flower, only Mahākāśyapa in the huge assembly understood the meaning and responded with a smile (X01n0027, 0442c16–21). Then the Buddha entrusted him with the continuation of the lineage, and he became the first patriarch after the Buddha's parinirvāṇa. After entrusting the lineage to Ānanda, Mahākāśyapa went to the Vulture Peak (Gṛdhrakūṭa) Mountain. There he has remained in samādhi. He will enter parinirvāṇa after the advent the next Buddha, Maitreya.

Mahākātyāyana (摩訶迦旃延) was born into the Brahmin caste in the kingdom of Avanti in western India. He studied the Vedas under his uncle Asita, a ṛṣi, who foresaw that Prince Siddhārtha would attain Buddhahood. Mahākātyāyana then followed the Buddha in honor of Asita's death wish. Through diligent training under the Buddha, Mahākātyāyana attained Arhatship. After the parinirvāṇa of the Buddha, he often debated with non-Buddhists, and is considered foremost in polemic.

Mahāmaudgalyāyana (大目揵連), together with his own disciples, following his good friend Śāriputra, became a disciple of the Buddha and attained Arhatship in a month. Śāriputra is portrayed as standing on the Buddha's right, with Maudgalyāyana on His left. Maudgalyāyana was stoned to death by Brahmins shortly before the Buddha's parinirvāṇa. He is considered foremost in transcendental powers.

Patka (半託迦), also called Panthaka or Mahāpanthaka, was the elder twin brother of Cullapatka. More intelligent than his twin, he was accomplished in the five studies. He attained Arhatship soon after joining the Buddha's Order.

Pūrṇa (富樓那) is also called Pūrṇa-Maitrāyaṇīputra, under his mother's family name Maitrāyaṇī. He was the son of a minister of King Śuddhodana of the kingdom of Kapilavastu. He was very intelligent, and studied the Vedas at a young age. On the night Prince Siddhārtha left the palace to seek the truth, he too left with thirty friends to practice asceticism in the snow mountain. He attained the four dhyānas and the five transcendental powers. After Siddhārtha attained Buddhahood and did the first turning of the Dharma wheel in Deer Park, he became a monk in the Buddha's Order and soon attained Arhatship. He is considered foremost in expounding the Dharma because some 99,000 people were delivered through his teachings.

Rāhula (羅睺羅) was the only son of Śākyamuni Buddha and Yaśodharā. He had been in gestation for six years and was born on the lunar eclipse after the Buddha had attained perfect enlightenment. Rāhula was six years old when the Buddha returned to the city kingdom of Kapilavastu, and he became a novice monk at the command of the Buddha. Foremost in secret training, he is to be reborn as the eldest son of every future Buddha.

Revata (離婆多) is the younger brother of Śāriputra. In his meditation at a temple, he saw two ghosts fighting to eat a corpse. Realizing the illusoriness of the body, he renounced family life and became a disciple of the Buddha. Traveling barefoot in a snow country, his feet were frostbitten. The Buddha praised him for his contentment with few material things and allowed him to wear shoes.

Śāriputra (舍利弗), together with his own disciples, joined the Buddha's Order soon after the Buddha's enlightenment. After being a principal disciple for forty-four years, to avoid his grief over the Buddha's parinirvāṇa, he requested and received the Buddha's permission to enter parinirvāṇa sooner than the Buddha. He is considered foremost in wisdom among the disciples.

Subhūti (須菩提) is foremost among the disciples in understanding the meaning of emptiness. He is the principal interlocutor in the *Prajñā-Pāramitā Sūtra*.

Svāgata (莎伽陀). In the *Buddha Pronounces the Sūtra of the Bhikṣu Svāgata's Merit* (T14n0501), this bhikṣu named Svāgata lay drunk under a tree. The Buddha praised his merit for subjugating a vengeful dragon and explained that Svāgata was not really drunk but pretended drunkenness for a purpose.

Upāli (優波離) had been a barber in the royal court. He became a disciple, together with Ānanda, six years after the Buddha had attained perfect enlightenment. Foremost in observing the precepts, he contributed to the compilation of the Vinaya in the first assembly of the Arhats after the Buddha's parinirvāṇa.

Upananda (跋難陀) and his brother Nanda (難陀) often caused disciplinary problems. Because of their misconduct, the Buddha had to add a few more precepts to the collection. Upananda rejoiced over the Buddha's parinirvāṇa because in his opinion it freed the disciples from restraint.

Vakkula (薄拘羅), or Vakula, was a disciple who lived to age 160 without a moment's illness or pain.

voice-hearer fruits (聲聞果).

A. The four holy fruits achieved by voice-hearers on the Liberation Way are (1) Srotāpanna, the Stream Enterer, who will attain Arhatship after at most seven times being reborn as a god then a human; (2) Sakṛdāgāmin, the Once Returner, who will be reborn as a human only once more before attaining Arhatship; (3) Anāgāmin, the Never Returner, who will not be reborn as a human but will attain Arhatship in a pure abode heaven in the form realm; and (4) Arhat, the Foe Destroyer, who has realized the nirvāṇa with remnant by annihilating his fixation on having an autonomous self and eradicating all his afflictions.

B. These four holy fruits and the corresponding nearness to them are called the eight holy ranks (八聖). Actually, one who is in the first rank, nearing the first holy fruit, is only a sage, and those in the higher seven ranks are holy beings. Those who are still learning (śaikṣa, 有學) are in the first seven ranks. Only Arhats, in the eight rank, are those who have nothing more to learn (aśaikṣa, 無學).

Vulture Peak Mountain. See Gṛdhrakūṭa Mountain.

water with the eight virtues (八功德水). According to the *Praising the Pure Land Sūtra* (T12n0367), these eight virtues are (1) purity and clarity, (2) coolness, (3) sweetness, (4) lightness and softness, (5) soothing, (6) peace and harmony, (7) quenching of thirst, and (8) nourishing and vitalizing.

Way (道). The Way in the Mahāyāna doctrine is to find the ultimate truth within one's own mind. Those who see objects as existing outside their minds are considered not on the Way. The word *Way* (Dao or Tao) in Chinese Daoism means the natural order of things in the world, contrary to its meaning in Buddhist doctrine.

Wheel-Turning King (cakra-vartī-rāja, 轉輪王). A ruler, the wheels of whose chariot roll everywhere unimpeded. The wheel (cakra), one of the seven precious things he owns, comes in four ranks: iron, copper, silver, and gold. The iron wheel king rules over one continent, the south; the copper wheel king, over two, east and south; the silver wheel king, over three, east, west, and south; the gold wheel king, over all four continents. A Buddha, the universal Dharma King, turns the Dharma wheel, giving teachings to sentient beings.

Wolf Track Mountain (狼跡山). Identified with the Cock's Foot Mountain (Kukkuṭapāda), northeast of Buddhagayā, in central India. It has three spires, like the upturned foot of a cock. Mahākāśyapa is now in samādhi in this mountain, waiting for the advent of Maitreya Bodhisattva.

yakṣa (夜叉). A demonic ghost that eats human flesh.

Yama (夜摩). The king of the underworld and superintendent of the karmic punishment of hell-dwellers.

yojana (由旬). The distance covered by one day's march of an army or by one day's walk of a yoked bull. One yojana may equal 4 or 8 krośas, each krośa being the distance at which a bull's bellow can be heard. The estimated distance of a yojana varies from 8 to 19 kilometers.

Reference

In English

Chang, Garma C. C., ed. 1985. *A Treasury of Mahāyāna Sūtras.* University Park and London: Pennsylvania State University Press.

Cowell, E. B., and Others, eds. 1969. *Buddhist Mahāyāna Texts.* New York: Dover Publications. (An unabridged and unaltered republication of Volume XLIX of *The Sacred Books of the East*. Oxford: Clarendon Press, 1894.)

Edelman, Gerald M. 2004. *Wider Than the Sky.* New Haven and London: Yale University Press.

Kato, Bunno, Yohiro Tamura, and Kojiro Miyasaka, trans. 1975. *The Threefold Lotus Sutra.* Tokyo: Kosei Publishing Company.

Keown, Damien. 2003. *Oxford Dictionary of Buddhism.* New York: Oxford University Press.

LeDoux, Joseph. 2002. *Synaptic Self.* Harmondswort, Middlesex, England: Viking Penguin, a member of Penguin Putnam Inc.

Marcus, Gary. 2004. *The Birth of the Mind.* New York: Basic Books.

Olivelle, Patrick, trans. 2008. *Upaniṣads.* New York: Oxford University Press. (Orig. pub. 1996.)

In Chinese

Chinese Electronic Tripiṭaka Collection 電子佛典集成. DVD-ROM, 2008 version. Containing the Taishō Tripiṭaka 大正藏, vols. 1–55, 85, and the Shinsan Zokuzōkyō 卍續藏, vols. 1–88. Taipei, Taiwan: Chinese Buddhist Electronic Text Association. Also available online at http://cbeta.org/

Foguang dacidian 佛光大辭典 [Buddha's light dictionary]. 1988. Kaoshiung, Taiwan: Buddha's Light Publishing. Also available online at http://www.fgs.org.tw/fgs_book/fgs_drser.aspx

Soothill, W. E., and Lewis Hodous, comps. 1962. *A Dictionary of Chinese Buddhist Terms* 中英佛學辭典. Kaoshiung, Taiwan: Buddhist Culture Service. Also available online at http://ybh.chibs.edu.tw/2L_data_ybh/dict/dict-s/soothill-hodous.htm

Zhencang fanwen zhouben 珍藏梵文咒本 [Precious collection of Sanskrit mantras]. 2003. Taipei, Taiwan: Mahayana Vihara Press.

On the Internet

Chart Comparing Pali, Chinese, and Tibetan Canons. http://www.zhaxizhuoma.net/DHARMA/Tripitaka/CanonCompare.htm/

Reference

Online Buddhist Dictionary 在線佛學辭典.
http://www.baus-ebs.org/fodict%5Fonline/

Online Buddhist Sutras. http://www.fodian.net/world/

Pang Huey Yong 彭偉洋. http://www.siddham-sanskrit.com/

Rulu 如露. http://www.sutrasmantras.info/

Sanskrit, Tamil and Pahlavi Dictionaries. http://webapps.uni-koeln.de/tamil/

University of the West. Digital Sanskrit Buddhist Canon.
http://www.uwest.edu/sanskritcanon/dp/

WIKIPEDIA: the Free Encyclopedia. http://en.wikipedia.org/

21432703R00169

Made in the USA
Lexington, KY
12 March 2013